Cross-Cultural Management

D0139440

All cultures appear to share the belief that they do things 'correctly', while others, until proven otherwise, are assumed to be ignorant or barbaric. When people from different cultures work together and cannot take shared meanings for granted, managers face serious challenges. An individual's parsing of an experience and its meaning may vary according to several cultural scales – national, professional, industrial and local. Awareness of cultural differences and the willingness to view them as a positive are therefore crucial assets.

This edited textbook sets itself apart from existing cross-cultural management texts by emphasizing to the reader the need to avoid both ethnocentrism and the belief in the universality of his or her own values and ways of thinking: the success of international negotiations and intercultural management depends on such openness and acceptance of real differences. It encourages the development of 'nomadic intelligence' and the creative use of a culture's resources, according to a symbolic anthropology perspective. Through the essays and case studies in the chapters, readers will become aware of the intercultural dimension of business activities and better understand how they affect work.

Cross-Cultural Management will help interested parties – students of business management, international relations and other disciplines, and business managers and other professionals – develop their ability to interact, take action and give direction in an intercultural context.

Jean-François Chanlat is Professor of Management at the University of Paris–Dauphine, France.

Eduardo Davel is Professor of Management at the University of Quebec at Montreal, Canada.

Jean-Pierre Dupuis is Professor of Management at HEC Montréal, Canada.

Cross-Cultural Management

Culture and management across the world

**Edited by
Jean-François Chanlat, Eduardo Davel and
Jean-Pierre Dupuis**

Routledge
Taylor & Francis Group

LONDON AND NEW YORK

English language edition first published 2013
by Routledge
2 Park Square, Milton Park, Abingdon, Oxon OX14 4RN

Simultaneously published in the USA and Canada
by Routledge
711 Third Avenue, New York, NY 10017

Routledge is an imprint of the Taylor & Francis Group, an informa business

Originally published under the title *Gestion en context intercultural: Approches, problématiques, pratiques et plongées*, edited by Eduardo Davel, Jean-Pierre Dupuis and Jean-François Chanlat © Les Presses de l'Université Laval, 2009

British Library Cataloguing in Publication Data
A catalogue record for this book is available from the British Library

Library of Congress Cataloging in Publication Data
Cross-cultural management : culture and management across the world / edited by Jean-François Chanlat, Eduardo Davel and Jean-Pierre Dupuis.
    p. cm.
Includes bibliographical references and index.
1. Management–Cross-cultural studies. 2. International business enterprises– Personnel management. 3. Intercultural communication. I. Chanlat, Jean-François, 1950- II. Davel, Eduardo. III. Dupuis, Jean-Pierre.
HD31.C748 2013
658.30089–dc23   2012032023

ISBN: 978-0-415-68816-1 (hbk)
ISBN: 978-0-415-68818-5 (pbk)
ISBN: 978-0-203-06680-5 (ebk)

Typeset in Times New Roman
by Cenveo Publisher Services

Printed and bound by CPI Group (UK) Ltd, Croydon, CR0 4YY

Contents

vi *Contents*

Figures

Tables

Boxes

Contributors

Fabien Blanchot has a Ph.D. in Management Sciences from the University of Burgundy, France, and teaches as an Associate Professor at the University of Paris–Dauphine. His research covers alliances, mergers and acquisitions. He has authored many academic journal articles and book contributions.

Jean-François Chanlat is Professor of Management at the University of Paris–Dauphine, France, after having been Professor at HEC Montréal for 20 years. His main domains of teaching and research are organization theory, organizational behaviour, anthropology of organizations, and sociology of business firms, cultures and organizations. He has published several books and numerous articles in French, English, Spanish, Portuguese and Arabic, and he is currently Associate Editor of *Management International*. Between 1994 and 2006 he was Research Committee President elect of the 'Sociology of Organizations' of the International Sociological Association, and from 1992 to 2008 he was co-chairman of the Business and Society Committee of the International Association of the French speaking Sociologists.

Sylvie Chevrier has a Ph.D. in business administration from the University of Quebec, Montreal. She is a Professor at the University of Marne La Vallée, near Paris, France. Her research interests cover the management of intercultural teams. She is the author of several academic articles and books, such as *Le Management des équipes interculturelles* (Presses Universitaires de France 2000) and *Le Management interculturel* (Presses Universitaires de France 2003). This chapter draws on a series of works done with the Management and Society research team.

Eduardo Davel is Professor of Management Studies at Télé-université, the distance learning university within the University of Quebec, Montreal. He obtained his Ph.D. in management from Montreal's École des Hautes Études Commerciales. On the strength of his extensive experience with symbol- and emotion-intensive organizations, he studies management through the lens of sociocultural and socio-practice issues. He highlights several major challenges for contemporary management practice: human potential and the need for building high-quality relationships prior to achieving employee creativity, collaboration, commitment, and learning. His research draws heavily on empirical studies of companies located in Brazil and Quebec. He is also Associate Editor of the RAE journal *Revista da Administraçao das Empresas*, and associate researcher with the Interdisciplinary Center for Social Development and Managing at the School of Management of the Federal University of Bahia, Brazil. He also works as a reviewer for various academic journals and associations and has published several books in French and Portuguese on the topics described above.

Jean-Pierre Dupuis is a Full Professor at the Department of management of HEC Montréal. He is a leading sociologist and anthropologist in the francophone field. His main research interests are: organizational anthropology, the sociology of labour organizations, culture and organization, and the revival of family farm businesses. He has published several books and numerous articles in French on the experience of Quebec managers in Quebec and abroad, and of the experience of foreign managers in Quebec, notably the French. He also sits on the editorial boards of various French speaking journals, and has contributed to the *Sage International Encyclopedia of Organization Studies*.

Djahanchah Philip Ghadiri is Assistant Professor of Management at HEC Montréal, Canada. He has a Ph.D. in Management Studies from the Judge Business School (University of Cambridge, UK). His research interests are related to identity issues within organizations.

Philippe d'Iribarne has advanced degrees from France's École Polytechnique, MINES ParisTech (École des Mines) and Sciences Po (Institut d'Études Politiques). He is a research director at France's National Centre for Scientific Research (Centre National de la Recherche Scientifique, or CNRS) and founded and directs a research team, Management and Society. Its work aims to show the many ways of living and working together in the world. He is the author of numerous academic articles and books in French, including two that have been translated into English: *Managing Corporate Values in Diverse National Cultures: The Challenge of Differences*, published by Routledge in 2012; and *Successful Companies in the Developing World: Managing in Synergy with Cultures*, published by the Agence Française de Développement (French Development Agency) in 2007 in their collection, *Notes et Documents n° 36*.

Olivier Irrmann is Senior Researcher at Aalto University, Finland, and Affiliate Professor in Management at HEC Montréal, Canada. He holds a Ph.D. in International Business from the Helsinki School of Economics (now Aalto University). His research focuses on the impact of culture and communication on international management and development processes, particularly in the context of cross-border mergers and acquisitions, international cooperation and the co-creation of knowledge in inter-organizational networks.

Philippe Pierre holds a Ph.D. in Sociology from the Institut d'Études Politiques de Paris (Sciences Po) and teaches at a number of international institutions. He is the co-director of MCM (Master in Cross-Cultural Management) at the University of Paris–Dauphine (www.management-interculturel.dauphine.fr) along with Jean-François Chanlat. He was the training director for the hairstylist division of L'Oréal, as well as a researcher at the Interdisciplinary Laboratory for Economic Sociology (LISE-CNRS). His research interests concern the management of human resources, international mobility and intercultural management. He is the author of over forty books and academic articles, including, *Des usages de l'ethnicité dans l'entreprise mondialisée* (Sides, 2003) and *Les Métamorphoses du monde: Sociologie de la mondialisation* (Le Seuil, 2003, in collaboration with D. Martin and J. L. Metzger).

Jean-Claude Usunier is a Professor at the University of Lausanne (Faculty of Business and Economics, HEC), Switzerland. He is a well recognized researcher in international marketing and intercultural management. He is a member of the Academy of International

Business and sits on the editorial boards of the following academic journals: *International Journal of Cross-Cultural Management, Management International Review, Journal of Business Research, International Marketing Review, Journal of World Business, Journal of Teaching in International Business*, and *International Business Review*. He is the author with Pervez N. Ghauri of *International Business Negotiations* (2nd edition, Pergamon/Elsevier, 2003). He defends a plural vision of the world and sees cultural diversity has a key asset for increasing the range of solutions to complex problems.

Acknowledgements

Like all intellectual production, this book is the result of a particular history and a series of meetings all its own. In fact, the present text began its journey in Montreal nearly 20 years ago when two of its editors, Jean-François Chanlat and Jean-Pierre Dupuis, discussed the role and importance of national and regional culture within the dynamics of organizations and management. At the time, both of these individuals had already been inspired by Philippe d'Iribarne's 1989 text, *La logique de l'honneur*, which both called into question the universality of management practices and took a new approach to culture that differed from the work of Geert Hofstede, whose 1980 text was at the time already widely known and utilized in management and in organizational studies.

It would only be after this conference and other international meetings – in France, Quebec and Latin America – that we would become convinced of the relevance of synthesizing this subject and providing a complementary alternative to the texts already offered by the most renowned authors on the English-speaking intellectual landscape, mainly Hall, Hofstede and Trompenaars.

Such an opportunity first arose when in 2007, when our friend and colleague Eduardo Davel proposed that we prepare a book for a course on management in an intercultural context at the Télé-Université du Québec (Quebec Open University). It was from this project that the present book was born. In the years that followed, we elaborated a series of research projects and teaching models that would ultimately signal the necessity of a project that could synthesize such developments. This work[1] had from its very beginnings adopted a perspective that sought to resituate the human being at the center of organizational life and management, a perspective stemming from the knowledge that we have of living humanity and of the symbolic university in which it inscribes itself.

This work has benefitted from numerous contributions and means of support that we wish to recognize here. First off, we would like to warmly thank all of the colleagues that accepted our invitation to contribute a chapter to this book. We chose these individuals because in our linguistic universe, they are essential references in the field of intercultural management, particularly Philippe d'Iribarne, who is seen as the field's pioneer. We would also like to wholeheartedly thank the colleagues that have contributed chapters on over thirty countries, all of which will be available online via Routledge's companion website to this volume. We also wish to express our gratitude both to our French-language publisher – les Presses de l'Université Laval – and notably its publisher Denis Dion and reviewers, who did an outstanding editing job on the project – and to the Télé-Université du Québec for having done such a professional job in creating the DVD that contains the chapters on the countries not included herein.

For the English edition that the reader will discover in the pages that follow, we would also like to genuinely thank Terry Clague of Routledge for having agreed to publish the book in this language, Alexander Krause for having followed the manuscript with such great attention, and Andy Soutter and Peter Lloyd for having taken care of the final revisions. We would also like to express our deepest gratitude to the Chair of Management and Diversity and to the GFR of Management and Organization at the University of Paris–Dauphine for providing the financial support for the translation of the majority of these chapters. Similarly, we wish to warmly thank our translators: Suzan Nolan and Leila Whittmore (Chapters 1, 4, 6, 7 and 9), who has always sought to move beyond the idea of language, and Nancy Dunham (Chapter 2). In other words, without the work of these translators and the cordial welcome and professionalism of Routledge, this book would simply not exist in English.

In the age of globalization, we are happy to affirm that Routledge did not hesitate in breathing life for English-speaking readers into a reflection rooted in the French language, which we view as being important in both francophone and Latin countries. In essence, this book's very existence illustrates what its chapters defend – intercultural dialogue, which as Umberto Eco has rightly pointed out, relies largely on translation.

Finally, the reflections that make up the content of this book have also benefitted from countless conversations that we have had over the years with numerous other individuals, colleagues and friends from North America, Latin America, Europe, Africa and the Asia-Pacific. While the individuals with whom these conversations have taken place are far too numerous to cite individually, we are sure that they will recognize themselves in these pages with little difficulty. We would also like to highlight the institutions and organizations that have made these meetings and dialogues possible: our respective institutions, HEC Montréal, the University of Paris–Dauphine, Téluq, the Administration Department at the Federal University of Bahia; the seminars and international conferences regularly organized by the International Sociology Association, the Association Internationale des Sociologues de Langue Française (the International Association of French-Speaking Sociologists), the Association Internationale de Management Stratégique (AIMS), the Association Francophone de Management International (Francophone Association of International Management, AFMI), EGOS, EURAM, APROS, ANPAD and ENEO (Brazil), ACACIA (Mexico); and our journals, notably *Management International*.

As a final word, we wish to thank our future English-speaking readers, and hope that this book will be of as much interest to them as it has been for readers in French, all while allowing them to access an anthropological approach to human behavior in an organized context, an approach that follows in the footsteps of a largely European and French intellectual tradition, but that has also been influenced by work done in the English language.

Jean-François Chanlat
Eduardo Davel
Jean-Pierre Dupuis

Note

1   See Philippe d'Iribarne (1994) 'The honour principle', in the *Bureaucratic Phenomenon*, January, vol. 15, no. 1: 81–97; Jean-François Chanlat (1994) 'Towards an anthropology of organizations', chapter 7 in John Hassard and Martin Parker (eds) *Towards a New Theory of Organizations*, London: Routledge, pp. 155–189; J.-F. Chanlat (1994) 'Francophone organizational analysis: an overview (1950–1990)', *Organization Studies*, January, vol. 15, no. 1: 47–79; Jean-François Chanlat (2008) 'Organizational literature, francophone', in James Bayley and Stewart Clegg (eds) *International Encyclopedia of Organization Studies*, Thousand Oaks, CA: Sage, vol. III, p. 1116; Jean Pierre Dupuis (2008) 'Organizational culture', in James Bayley and Stewart Clegg (eds) *International Encyclopedia of Organization Studies*, Thousand Oaks, CA: Sage, vol. III, pp. 1035–1038.

Introduction

Jean-François Chanlat, Eduardo Davel and
Jean-Pierre Dupuis

The Chinese always use two hands to present business cards. So when an arriving American consultant started a meeting by offering his own one-handed – as if dealing playing cards – none of his Chinese interlocutors would accept one. In such a transaction, such observed behaviors might lead the Chinese to think of Americans as uncivilized – barbarians – even though the Americans are doing everything 'right' according to their own social and cultural references. Incidents like these, trivial as they might seem, go to the heart of what this volume proposes to explore. Managers in international enterprises confront cultural differences constantly, in ways that affect cooperation, collaboration, effectiveness and efficiency.

A book on intercultural management issues necessarily starts with the importance of addressing one's own – and others' – cultural stereotypes and prejudices. All cultures appear to share the belief that they do things 'correctly', while others, until proven otherwise, are assumed to be ignorant or downright barbaric. When people from different cultures work together and cannot take shared meanings for granted, managers face serious challenges. An individual's parsing of an experience and its meaning may vary according to several cultural scales – national, professional, industrial and local. Awareness of cultural differences and the willingness to view them as positives are therefore crucial assets. Throughout this volume, the reader will see the need to avoid both ethnocentrism and the belief in the universality of his or her own values and ways of thinking. The success of international negotiations and intercultural management depends on such openness and acceptance of real differences.

This multimedia volume aims to help interested parties – students of business management, international relations and other disciplines, and business managers and other professionals – to develop their ability to interact, take action and give direction in an intercultural context. It encourages the development of 'nomadic intelligence' as Fernandez (2002) calls it, and the creative use of a culture's resources, as proposed and explained by Iribarne and his colleagues (1998). The essays and case studies in the chapters orchestrate an intercultural apprenticeship: readers will become aware of the intercultural dimension of business activities, and better understand how they affect work. The apprenticeship will be very multi-disciplinary: the field of intercultural management is a colorful universe that draws from anthropology, sociology, psychology, communications, history and other fields. (Bosche 1993; Gudykunst and Ting-Toomey 1988; Chanlat 1990, 2012). Of course, reading and thinking alone cannot take the place of practical experience (Gherardi 2006; Gherardi, Nicolini and Odella 1998; Wenger 1998), which is why we present experts and professionals discussing their case studies in the accompanying companion website.

Three ways of viewing the intercultural experience

If sense and meaning are the basic units of a cultural *order* (Sahlins 1976; Geertz 1973), we postulate that management is a cultural *activity* dependent on both its originating culture and the one in which it operates. Such an approach challenges the model that dominated twentieth-century managerial thought: that of universal 'best practices', applicable everywhere and in all cases. The implicit question has been whether there is one preferred mode of international management, or whether a multiple-focus approach would succeed better. Since the first attempts to bring national or regional culture into management practice, notably with the well-known Hofstede study of the early 1980s (Hofstede 1980) research in this field has grown enormously (Chanlat 2007, 2012; Gannon and Newman 2001; Schneider and Barsoux 2002; Trompenaars and Hampden-Turner 2004; Smith et al. 2008). But most of this work depends upon the assumptions of the seminal Hofstedian study (Hofstede 2001; Hofstede et al. 2010).

The present volume comes from a different background and proposes a different approach. Based on Clifford Geertz's concept of cultures as a universe of meanings (Geertz 1973), and the seminal work in the Latin countries done by Philippe d'Iribarne (1989, 1998, 2003, 2006, 2008 and 2009), this book synthesizes a 'symbolic' approach to cultures in management. A symbolic approach seeks to understand the cultural meaning and sense of actions, as well as words, to discern the culture's 'grammar' of effective behavior. Such a vision not only illuminates managerial practices in a more and more internationalized world, but also demonstrates why many mergers and acquisitions processes and managerial tools stand or fall according to the participants' degree of intercultural understanding. In other words, this book defends the idea that culture matters in managerial performance. If management thinking has tended historically to identify the 'best practices' and seek unitary solutions, real-life analysis shows us that social contexts frame and determine those managerial practices. Within this social context, national and regional cultures play critical roles.

Currently, three approaches or 'lenses' dominate discussions of the intercultural experience: convergence, hybridization and divergence. The convergence lens views globalization as the construction of a global culture that gradually neutralizes the effects of national culture (Dunphy 1987; Strange 1996). While differences between cultures remain, researchers who adopt the convergence point of view believe those differences decline in influence as a global business culture rallies decision-makers to move in the same direction. We cannot deny the rise and influence of American-style capitalistic business culture on a global scale. The entry of Russia, China and India into the global capitalist economy provides convincing examples. Conversely, nothing indicates that the Russians, Chinese or Indians conceive of a business and its management in exactly the same way as Americans do. The development of capitalism in communist China is clearly proof that things do not happen in the same way in China as in the West. It is possible to speak about a worldwide convergence toward a capitalist model and private enterprise, but this convergence may be primarily technological and structural, while national culture still influences ways of seeing and doing things within an enterprise (Child 1981; Iribarne 1989, 2009; Chanlat 1990, 1994; Smith et al. 2008).

The hybridization lens emphasizes how several forms of colonization have promoted cultural encounters, collisions and exchanges (Bhabha 1994), which in turn lead to new blended (hybrid) cultures (Faist and Ozveren 2004). Transnational spaces represent social and symbolic ties maintained by people, organizations and networks whose activities transcend the borders of nation-states. They serve as cultural pathways for actors, symbols and practices: migrations and diasporas are emblematic examples, as are the stable and homogeneous environments created by multinational companies, business groups and transnational scientific groups across the globe (Veltz 2010).

The divergence lens recurs most often in intercultural management analyses. It emphasizes the importance of cultural differences and their still considerable repercussions on management practices. Divergence analyses assume that management practices are specific to their location rather than universal. This multimedia volume provides convincing evidence for the divergence lens, although we recognize that globalization still affects national cultures, and hybridization's impact should not be underestimated.

The word 'globalization' signifies a historic process through which individual human activities and political structures grow more mutually dependent, while material as well as virtual exchanges increase over large distances on a global scale. Globalization implies increasing interdependence of national economies, promoting expanded human interaction and trade. The genesis of this process is most often seen as economic globalization, the growth of trade in goods and services, hastened at the end of the 1980s by the creation of global financial markets. However, globalization acquires a cultural dimension when a large part of the world's population can access the cultural capital of distant peoples, and when developed countries as a whole become aware of the diversity of the world's cultures and become more diverse themselves (Ozbilgin and Tatli 2008). Globalization therefore comes to combine an objective aspect – the progressive increase of interconnectivity – with cultural and subjective issues (Robertson 1992) that show culturally bounded effects and temporalities[1] specific to each person (Bauman 2004).

Several anthropologists, such as Appadurai (2001) and Inda and Rosaldo (2002), acknowledge globalization's effects on local, regional and national cultures, but point out several nuances or refinements to the dominant view of convergence theorists. One is that the actual effects differ from the expected ones, which assume that local reference points vanish with the adoption of Western or transnational practices. Cultures around the world interpret and use these new practices and models in many different ways, always within local categories and meanings (Inda and Rosaldo 2002; Smith et al. 2008). The original meaning of a model or practice often changes entirely once it reaches a new locale. Cultures can integrate elements of modernity as well as tradition, as Canclini maintains (1992).

A second refinement of the convergence model argues that the direction of cultural exchanges runs from not only North America and Europe toward the developing world, but from the rest of the world to the West. Rich Western countries integrate cultural elements from around the world, as seen in the spreading of 'world' music (Jamaican reggae, Algerian rai, Brazilian samba, Senegalese mbalax, Korean music) and cuisines (Indian, Japanese, Chinese, Mexican), which are extremely popular today outside their countries of origin. A third nuance observes that *all* national cultures are currently in a state of transformation and hybridization (Pieterse 1994). This does not imply that they will all resemble one another in the future. Hybridization is less a recent phenomenon than a permanent, intrinsic process of cultural change. That means that while globalization will change cultures, each will integrate various 'global' elements in its own way. The results will necessarily vary because each culture will adapt these elements based on its own history, its current realities and cultural categories. In any event, cultures are always under construction, synthesizing movements and influences. That will hold for the future as well; 'national' cultures may decline in importance, but at present they still play the primary role in assimilating globalization's effects. In addition, we can see an increasing hybridization of management practices as national cultures encounter globalized markets (Ralston et al. 1997; Iribarne 2003, 2009). Ralston and his colleagues (1997) demonstrated this in a case study of the United States,

Russia, Japan and China: the national culture of each country had as strong an operant effect as the economic ideology dominating their global context.

Contrasts between management cultures can create multiple misunderstandings, as when European and North American managers started working in newly acquired Russian companies or Russian subsidiaries (Michailova 2000, 2002). The Russian employees resisted their foreign managers' employee 'empowerment' strategies because they genuinely did not want more autonomy. For decades, the Russians had been accustomed to the presence of a strong leader, and they preferred to take orders rather than participate in discussions. They perceived the empowerment efforts either as an abdication of responsibility on the part of management – possibly due to a lack of professionalism – or as extra work that the managers were requiring them to assume. The foreign managers and their Russian employees simply did not share a common notion of 'they way we are supposed to work', and without comprehending cultural differences – or even anticipating their existence – the Russians tended to negatively interpret actions intended as positive.

To summarize, the three lenses we describe each have their merits and adherents in intercultural management theory and practice. The cultural *convergence* lens often dominates the views of economists and business people. The second lens sees cultural *divergence* in these same management practices, and has defenders among social science specialists and organizations; and the last focuses on cultural *hybridization* of management practices, an emerging theory in the social sciences. We suspect that hybridization offers the most promising lens in the current global context; but understanding the hybridization of practices calls for the study of what they blend, and for that, national cultures offer the best vantage point. Despite their continued transformation, nation-states have persisted as the dominant cultural formation of the last 200 years. Their globalized transformation has yet to eliminate cultural matrices, which is why we propose studying them through this multimedia volume.

Aims of *Cross-Cultural Management*

This multimedia set (book and chapters available at the Routledge website) goes beyond simply describing cross-cultural differences; it provides an apprenticeship in management practices for intercultural contexts, i.e. where people of different cultures must communicate with each other in business settings. The content focuses on four aspects of the intercultural experience: (1) various approaches to intercultural analysis; (2) intercultural issues raised by international business; (3) the types of management practices that evolve in these contexts; and (4) intercultural immersions in selected national cultures presented by the different chapters on the website. Each aspect allows the reader to acquire certain skills: a solid grounding in theory, recognition of key problems and their possible solutions, and detection of some subtler managerial requirements in targeted cultural contexts.

A different expert has written each chapter, so the works demonstrate a disciplinary and conceptual openness to intercultural knowledge, rather than conforming to a single type of analysis or school of thought. This runs the risk of some lexical ambiguity, whereby the same term may have diverse meanings depending on its theory of origin. However, this risk should benefit the reader in the long term, by offering exposure to diverse concepts and a critical basis for evaluating different theories. Furthermore, the reader will be able to see intercultural management not as a single truth, but instead will acquire multiple tools for analyzing complex intercultural situations.

Carlos Ghosn is one such expert featuring in this volume. A French business executive of Lebanese origin, he is currently CEO of the French automobile company Renault and the

Japanese company Nissan (which he is widely credited with having turned around). He describes how managers need to see beyond a single perspective:

> Imagine a French executive arriving in Japan. He might say to himself, 'My, they are very slow to make any decisions!' There he criticizes the difference. He could also say, 'The execution is perfect. We could learn something.' Here he capitalizes on the difference. It is the same thing for the Japanese executive. He goes to France and says, 'They talk a lot but don't do much.' Or he could find a conceptual richness, where he can learn strategic thinking and decision-making. The entire art is in looking at the positive side and asking yourself, 'What can I learn from Japan, or from France?' One of our key concepts is to look at the bottle as being half full rather than half empty!
>
> (Ghosn 2007: p. 9)

An intercultural management apprenticeship poses many challenges. It draws attention to the requirements of more detailed and individualized management practices, and complex and uncertain situations (Tjosvold and Leung 2003; Baldwin 2006). Mass training of the least-qualified people alongside more qualified candidates may have its uses, but is no longer a solution. For example, managers who must confront complex situations of expatriation and intercultural negotiation should have personalized career management assistance. The internationalization of businesses leads to an increasing number of managers who must use new practices and skills, in addition to their traditional managerial and other expertise. As their business moves them beyond purely national territories, they need language skills, the ability to work with people from other cultures, and the current wherewithal to follow new career paths within a company (Chevrier 2012).

How to use *Cross-Cultural Management*

The chapters in this book present a range of resources for apprenticeship – theoretical, intellectual and practical. Chapter readings, combined with a selection of companion website chapters, expose the 'apprentice' to expert explanations and intercultural experiences as lived by international managers; together, these provide an immersion in the culture and management style of a society. Each chapter proceeds with a more or less original theoretical and conceptual approach, which enriches and enlarges our understanding of intercultural analysis by showing diverse ways of 'doing it right'.

Evaluating conceptual approaches and theories

Part I addresses the variety of existing approaches to intercultural analysis. All of the chapters in Part I highlight the strengths and weaknesses of certain approaches, while illustrating the way each theory may be applied. Chapter 1, 'Intercultural analysis and the social sciences' by Jean-François Chanlat, raises fundamental issues in intercultural analysis, such as otherness, misunderstandings, language, space–time, history, and the textual, co-textual and contextual elements of communication. These issues are at the heart of the social sciences' concerns. Chapter 2, 'Intercultural analysis in management: decompartmentalizing the classical approaches' by Jean-Pierre Dupuis, presents some seminal perspectives, such as those of Geert Hofstede and Philippe d'Iribarne, and suggests a larger and more enveloping model to overcome their limits. Chapter 3, 'An interactionist approach to intercultural management analysis' by Olivier Irrmann, continues the discussion, focusing on communication and interpersonal interaction.

Understanding the challenges and problematics

Part II highlights the key challenges and problematics, or difficulties inherent in situations or planning, when businesses become more international. Each chapter unveils fundamental challenges facing those who must resolve intercultural issues – in organization, personnel management, business strategy, negotiations and business ethics. Chapter 4, 'The international manager' by Philippe Pierre, examines international mobility and its repercussions on personal and national identification, focusing on strategies that expatriated managers use to reclaim their (national) identity. Chapter 5, 'International negotiations' by Jean-Claude Usunier, presents national influences in international negotiations, highlighting steps, procedures, aspects, strategies and tactics linked to the process. Chapter 6, 'The effect of culture on business ethics' by Philippe d'Iribarne, compares business ethics in France to those of the United States, addressing corruption and the ethics of interpersonal relationships in each society's context.

Drawing inspiration from practices and tools

The goal of Part III is to spark thinking about management practices and tools in an intercultural context. It addresses management practices in three contexts: multicultural teams, multicultural personnel and international alliances between businesses. The practices described do not claim to be miraculous management recipes or ready-to-wear solutions. Rather, they aim to inspire and to encourage use of the theories and concepts presented in Part I. Chapter 7, 'Managing multicultural teams' by Sylvie Chevrier, proposes a typology and characterization of working teams in a multicultural context. It also presents practices for managing multicultural teams, while stressing the influence of cultural differences on the way teams function. Chapter 8, 'Managing multiculturalism in the workplace' by Eduardo Davel and Djahanchah Philip Ghadiri, examines multicultural personnel management practices; it emphasizes diversity management based on apprenticeship, with training and conflicts as key components. Chapter 9, 'Managing international alliances' by Fabien Blanchot, examines the influence of cultural differences on the success of international alliances, looking at length at the Renault and Nissan case.

Analyzing cultural complexity based on real-life examples

Case studies – or what we call 'intercultural immersions', diving deep into a specific culture – figure largely in this multimedia work. The accompanying material which will be accessible via the Routledge website covers four large continental regions: North and South America; Europe; Africa and the Middle East; and Asia, Australia and the Pacific Islands. Each of these four chapters includes several immersions that look at a country's or society's culture, inviting the viewer to discover the details and uniqueness of each and, consequently, of their management practices. National cultures and their influence on management practices and local organization are analyzed and described in depth.

There are several ways to conduct an apprenticeship in contemporary intercultural management practices. On-the-job training is one: business trips to other countries and regions, working in multicultural teams, executing a corporate merger or acquisition, and so on. However, acquiring key concepts, ideas and theories also plays its part. This multimedia volume aims to provide both: a study of management in an intercultural context, enriched by the real-life experiences of managers and experts in the field, providing the reader with a useful synthesis of theory and practice.

Given the importance of effective cooperation and coordination in today's business world, research on intercultural management proliferates as rapidly as globalized value chains do. Meanwhile, worldwide management practices continue to evolve through the sometimes confused, often contested and even contradictory interactions of diverse global, supranational, national and local economic and cultural forces. We hope this book, together with the chapters available on the companion website, will inspire readers to join in the effort to 'look at the glass as being half-full' – deciphering ever-evolving meanings more accurately and with greater ease, leading to greater understanding and achievements. By using the theories and tools herein, we hope that readers will improve their skills in intercultural communication, strengthening their perspective on other cultures and their colleagues, clients and competitors.

Note

1 For the French philosopher Jean Baudrillard, 'temporality' connotes living one's life in a certain pattern or rhythm.

References

Appadurai, A. (2001) *Après le colonialisme: les conséquences culturelles de la globalization*. Paris: Payot.

Baldwin, R. (2006) *Globalisation: the great unbundling(s)*. Geneva: Graduate Institute of International Studies.

Bauman, Z. (2004) *Le Coût humain de la mondialisation*. Paris: Gallimard, Pluriel.

Bhabha, H. K. (1994) *The location of culture*. London: Routledge.

Bosche, M. (1993) *Le Management intercultural*. Paris: Nathan.

Canclini, G. N. (1992) *Culturas hibridas: estrategias para entrar y salir de la modernidad*. Buenos Aires: Editorial Sudamericana.

Chanlat, J. F. (ed.) (1990) *L'Individu et l'organisation: les dimensions oubliées*. Sainte-Foy: Les Presses de l'Université Laval. Paris: Eska.

——— (1994) 'Towards an anthropology of organizations', chapter 7 in John Hassard and Martin Parker (eds) *Towards a new theory of organizations*, London: Routledge, pp. 155–89.

——— (2007) 'Organizational anthropology', in James Bayley and Stewart Clegg (eds), *International encyclopedia of organization studies*, Thousand Oaks, CA: Sage, vol. III, pp. 1012–14.

——— (2012) 'Anthropologie des organisations', in José Allouche (ed.), *Encyclopédie des ressources humaines*, Paris: Vuibert, pp. 34–40.

Chevrier, S. (2012) *Gérer des equipes internationales: tirer parti de la rencontre des cultures dans les organisations*. Sainte-Foy: Les Presses de L'Université Laval.

Child, J. D. (1981) 'Culture, contingency and capitalism in the cross-national study of organizations', in L. L. Cummings and B. W. Straw (eds), *Research in organizational behavior*, Greenwich, CT: JAI Publishers, vol. 3, pp. 303–56.

Demorgon, J. (2000) *L'Interculturation du monde*. Paris: Anthropos.

Dunphy, D. (1987) 'Convergence/divergence: a temporal review of the Japanese enterprise and its management'. *Academy of Management Review* 12 (3), 445–59.

Faist, T. and Ozveren, E. (eds) (2004) *Transnational social spaces: agents, networks and institutions*. Burlington, VT: Ashgate.

Fernandez, B. (2002) *Identité nomade: de l'expérience d'Occidentaux en Asie*. Paris: Anthropos.

Gannon, M. J. and Newman, K. (2001) *Handbook of cross-cultural management*. Oxford: Blackwell.

Geertz, C. (1973) *The interpretation of cultures*. New York: Basic Books.

Gherardi, S. (2006) *Organizational knowledge: the texture of workplace learning*. Oxford: Blackwell.

Gherardi, S., Nicolini, D. and Odella, F. (1998) 'Toward a social understanding of how people learn in organizations: a notion of situated curriculum'. *Management Learning* 29 (3), 273–97.

Ghosn, C. (2007) 'Intercultural management'. Speech on 29 May at the Maison de la Culture du Japon. www.cefj.org/fr/archives/CR/Ghosn.pdf, 9. Paris: MCJP.

Gudykunst, W. B. and Ting-Toomey, S. (1988) *Culture and interpersonal communication*. Newbury Park, CA: Sage.

Hofstede, G. (1980) *Culture's consequences: international differences in work-related values*. Beverly Hills, CA: Sage.

—— (2001) *Culture's consequences: comparing values, behaviors, institutions and organizations across nations*, 2nd edn. Thousand Oaks, CA: Sage.

Hofstede, G., Hofstede, J. and Minkov, M. (2010) *Cultures and organizations: software of the mind*. Revised and expanded 3rd edn. New York: McGraw-Hill USA.

Inda, J. X. and Rosaldo, R. (eds) (2002) *The anthropology of globalization*. Malden, MA: Blackwell.

Iribarne, P. d' (2009) *L'épreuve des différences: l'expérience d'une entreprise mondiale*. Paris: Seuil.

—— (2008) *Penser la diversité du monde*. Paris: Seuil.

—— (2006) *L'étrangeté française*. Paris: Seuil.

—— (2003) *Le tiers-monde qui réussit. Nouveaux modèles*. Paris: Éditions Jacob.

—— (1998) *Cultures et mondialisation: gérer par-delà les frontières*. Paris: Seuil.

—— (1989) *La logique de l'honneur*. Paris: Seuil.

Michailova, S. (2002) 'When common sense becomes uncommon: participation and empowerment in Russian companies with Western participation'. *Journal of World Business* 37 (3), 180–87.

—— (2000) 'Contrasts in culture: Russian and Western perspectives on organizational change'. *Academy of Management Executive* 14 (4), 99–112.

Ozbilgin, M. and Tatli, A. (2008) *Global diversity management: an evidence-based approach*. London: Palgrave Macmillan.

Pieterse, J. N. (1994) 'Globalisation as hybridization'. *International Sociology* 9 (2), 161–84.

Ralston, D. A., Holt, D. A., Terpstra, R. H. and Yu, K. C. (1997) 'The impact of national culture and economic ideology on managerial work values: a study of the United States, Russia, Japan, and China'. *Journal of International Business Studies* 28 (1), 177–207.

Robertson, R. (1992) *Globalization: social theory and global culture*. London: Sage.

Sahlins, M. (1976) *Culture and practical reason*. Chicago: University of Chicago Press.

Schneider, S. and Barsoux, J.-L. (2002) *Managing across cultures*. London: FT/Prentice Hall.

Smith, P. B., Peterson, M. F. and Thomas, D. C. (2008) *The handbook of cross-cultural research*. London: Sage.

Strange, S. (1996) 'L'avenir du capitalisme mondial. La diversité peut-elle persister indéfiniment?' In C. Crouch and W. Streeck (eds), *Les capitalismes en Europe*, Paris: La Découverte, pp. 247–60.

Thiesse, A.-M. (2000) 'La fabrication culturelle des nations européennes'. *Sciences Humaines* 110, 38–42.

Tjosvold, D. and Leung, K. (2003) *Cross-cultural management: foundations and future*. London: Ashgate.

Trompenaars, F. and Hampden-Turner, C. (2004) *Managing people across cultures*. Chichester: Capstone.

Veltz, P. (2010) 'Globalization: an urban opportunity?' (S. Nolan, trans.). In P. Jacquet, R. Pauchauri and L. Tubaina (eds), *A planet for life*, New Delhi: Teri Press, ch. 3, pp. 25–35.

Wenger, E. (1998) *Communities of practice: learning, meaning and identity*. Cambridge: Cambridge University Press.

Part I
Approaches

1 Intercultural analysis and the social sciences

Jean-François Chanlat

Translated from the French by
Suzan Nolan and Leila Whittemore

Introduction

Cultural differences have emerged as a popular subject in the world of business management during the past two decades or so. Companies and nations have been strongly affected by a combination of expanded international trade and increased economic regionalization – witness NAFTA, the Southern Common Market, Asia-Pacific Economic Cooperation, the European Union, communist countries' transition to capitalism after the fall of the Berlin Wall, and China's and India's rise in power. Foreign direct investment has increased, and national and international mergers and acquisitions have multiplied in many sectors, including pharmaceuticals, financial services, automobile manufacture and steel production. Strategic alliances have also expanded, such as those between automobile companies (e.g. Renault–Nissan) and the airline networks, while privatization of large publicly-owned enterprises has created giant international corporations.

In tandem with these economic movements, massive migrations have transformed national demographics almost globally, especially in North America and Europe. These movements have deeply affected the West's social and economic fabric (Martin et al. 2003), instigating new social configurations and stresses in intercultural relations. Varied attitudes to 'otherness' affect how people behave and interact with one another, influencing intercultural relations.

During the last two decades, a number of researchers, teachers and management consultants have worked to improve understanding of the relationship between management and culture, particularly 'national' culture (Desjeux and Taponier 1994; Hofstede 2002; Trompenaars and Hampden-Turner 2004; Dupriez and Simons 2002; Iribarne 1998, 2003; Kamdem 2002; Pesqueux 2004; *Management International* 2004). These efforts have inspired a new managerial field: intercultural management (Schneider and Barsoux 2003; Chevrier 2003). However, these works have not addressed many aspects of intercultural comparison and confrontation.

In this chapter, we will review a few of the key elements of relations with 'the other' – the fears, attractions, prejudices, misunderstandings, conflicts and racist behaviors they provoke – and the role of history in understanding confrontations seen today. We will attempt to answer three main questions: what happens when two people from different cultures encounter one another? What are the main types of intercultural misunderstanding? How can the history of relations between different peoples illuminate the attitudes and behaviors we observe today?

Inevitably, such analyses must be colored by the cultural assumptions of the writer – a fact worth acknowledging in a work initially written for a French-speaking audience and now addressed to an international anglophone one. As the discussion here will suggest, this is in itself no insignificant cultural divide; there is always a risk that the very cultural differences this chapter examines may also interfere with its reception among English-speaking readers. But this, too, opens a space for the kind of dialogue that this volume aims to provide. There is no true Archimedean point from which to analyze these phenomena, still less our inquiry into their origins and effects. While the research discussed here is international in authorship and scope, the present writer's perspective remains unavoidably – and unapologetically – a French one.

Intercultural encounters and otherness

Everyone shapes themself in relation to others. As the British psychoanalyst Donald Winnicott so adroitly put it, 'It is a joy to be hidden but a disaster not to be found' (Winnicott 1965). This is because awareness of oneself is inseparable from awareness of the other. This relation to the other constitutes the basis of individual identity at a personal level (Tap 1986a, 1986b; Dubar 2000), and of social identity at the collective one (Tap 1986a, 1986b; Dubar 2000). As Freud reminds us, the other is at one and the same time a model, an object of investment, a support, an adversary, and even a scapegoat.

The other's presence also plays a role in the genesis of social and cultural identity; each group of humans differentiates itself upon contact with another. This double relation – individual and collective – to otherness penetrates all levels of social life. Individuals and communities see their relation to themselves and others modified when international relations intensify, when global upheavals result in major migrations, when Western societies see their social fabric diversify, as is happening today. Newspapers daily remind us of discrimination in hiring, xenophobic attacks, inter-ethnic fighting, racist slogans at football games and racially-motivated crimes.

Ethnic-based conflict, xenophobia and violence – especially arising from demographic shifts, such as when a newly-arrived minority clashes with the dominant culture – have marked not only conflicts in developing countries but, increasingly, in the West. Such conflicts have a long history. Since its beginning, the United States has known racism against Native Americans and African-Americans, and has experienced strains within its communities following each wave of immigration. In Canada – *the* country of multiculturalism, if there is one – discrimination occurs daily. In Europe, Great Britain has seen inter-ethnic clashes and has questioned some of its discriminatory policing practices. Bombing attacks in London in July 2005, conducted by some young British Muslims, have been answered with firebombs by some non-Muslims; these violent outbursts have shocked the country. The Netherlands, long thought to be a haven of tolerance, has also discovered racial tension among some of its Dutch and Arab and/or Muslim immigrants. Italians see racist slurs and gestures on the rise in football stadiums across their country. France must deal with riots brought on by discrimination-related problems that immigrants of North African origin experience daily. Spaniards see similar tensions increasing in the southern part of their country. Germans note a rise in anti-Turkish racism in recent years. Elsewhere in the world, similar behaviors occur: some Hindus and some Muslims in India have poor relations, Russians treat Africans badly, Asians show racism toward non-Asians.

What makes individuals and groups react in such ways? We can explain it in terms of *insights* provided by psychology (specifically psychoanalysis) and the *analysis* of social and historical contexts.

The individual discovers otherness

According to psychoanalysts, at the beginning of its life a baby lives in fusion with its mother in a state of non-differentiation. At 8 months, it begins to discern its mother's environment. Her absence becomes a source of anguish; the young child tends to project its angry impulses onto strangers. Over time, it learns to tolerate differences between its mother and the stranger. As the Franco-Belgian psychoanalyst Lydia Flem (1985) notes:

> Human development seems to never end completely and can always revert or remain infiltrated by ancient mechanisms. A natural process – a feeling of torment – can occur throughout one's lifetime, every time worrisome circumstances – internal or external – exceed one's capacity to react to problems, inciting an intense intolerance for frustration and the destructive feelings it awakens.
>
> (pp. 22–23)

In other words, a human being begins as one self, and over time discovers a copy of itself – the other. In the same way, 'the relation with otherness is born. It causes outrage, and sets up a disaster: the presence of someone different to oneself constitutes a threat – a threat to one's integrity, to one's identity' (Vincent 1990, p. 385). As we can see, psychology places the fear of the other, and all that follows from it, at the foundation of an individual's developmental history. This suggests that the psyche is – practically by definition – all too apt to assign negative associations to individuals and groups. That sums up the psychological point of view; however, the relation to others also has a historically-situated social connection.

The group discovers otherness

Cultural differences have occupied thought for as long as there have been books, if not before, particularly in the West. The Ancient Greeks established a line separating themselves from others, whom they called 'barbarians', meaning 'people who speak Greek poorly'. In subsequent Western civilizations, images of 'savages' and 'primitives' colored views of people encountered through imperialist, colonialist and mercantilist processes in various geographic locales.

We recall the famous Las Casas–Sepúlveda controversy (1550–51), where a Spanish friar, Bartolomé Las Casas, shocked by his Dominican brothers' abuses of power in Spanish America, Mexico and the Antilles, argued the humanity of New World natives with Juan Ginés de Sepúlveda, a prominent humanist and Greek scholar, in a theological debate at Valladolid, Spain. Following this public discussion, the Spaniards allowed that the natives had a soul and thus belonged to the same species as the Spanish and Christians generally. However, this recognition was not given to blacks. It was not until the nineteenth century that all Western countries would abolish black slavery. The dialectic of 'the same' and 'the other' arises in the context of each period's social views.

Even though we can easily situate Western discourse about 'otherness', we must remember that anthropological works have shown that the concept appears among non-Westerners as well. All peoples, even the smallest groups, create representations of the other, of any group different from themselves. According to Claude Lévi-Strauss (1961), people also have a tendency to define humanity according to their own selves, drawing its frontier at their own tribe's border. Thus, in Inuktitut the word 'Inuit' signifies 'man' while many other Inuktitut words define all other human groups (Lévi-Strauss 1961). Lévi-Strauss postulates that such acts constitute a human characteristic we all share; in our very attempt to establish ways of discriminating between cultures and customs, we identify with those whose existence we are trying to deny. By rejecting the humanity of people who appear more 'savage' or 'barbarian' than ourselves, we simply borrow one of their typical attitudes: 'The barbarian is, first and foremost, a man who believes in barbarism' (Lévi-Strauss 1961, p. 5).

Thus, these categories of defining the other demonstrate how each culture tends to see itself as the center of the world, and to see those outside its social circle as different beings. This allows the group in question to constitute an identity; it is by differentiating ourselves from others that we define ourselves – Westerner vs. Asian, African vs. European, American vs. Canadian, Canadian vs. Quebecer, Mexican vs. American, Brazilian vs. Argentinean, Dutch vs. Belgian, British vs. French, Chinese vs. Japanese, and so forth. Nevertheless, since intercultural relations can also enrich – as history constantly reminds us – we may investigate the human compulsion to find others threatening.

Theories on the origins of racism and xenophobia abound and vary considerably according to discipline and method. Some authors explain that natural human cruelty causes this sense of threat (Memmi 1982; Delacampagne 1983; Langaney 1981). As a species, humans developed into predators; to survive, they had to fight other species and rival groups. Apparently humans have no innate mechanism to inhibit aggressive behaviors, unlike other species (Eibl-Eibesfeldt 2002). Only culture and morality serve this function; when one's space feels threatened, one human may destroy another without much restraint.

Other authors research the fears, stereotypes and prejudices that can lead to racism. Such studies abound in the social sciences, helping us understand what is at work in intercultural relations. Albert Memmi (1982), who spent his entire life trying to understand attitudes to differences in various contexts (and to shed light on racism in particular), started with the first observable reaction when two people meet. The meeting may have a negative cast, known as heterophobia, from the Greek *phobos* (fear) and *heteros* (different), characterized by a fear of differences and of foreigners. Or it may have a positive cast, known as xenophilia, from the Greek *philia* (love) and *xenos* (stranger), and characterized by an attraction to differences and all that is foreign (Memmi 1982). A community may encourage one or the other type of reaction depending on the moment in its social history, with consequences for everyday intercultural relations, as history has shown. Western history alone abounds with the rhetoric of these differences – witness speeches about foreigners invading 'us', immigrants who take 'our' jobs, the 'Arab terrorist', the 'Jewish plot', the 'Yellow peril'.

Human evolutionary history explains a first level of behavior, the fearful reaction; Langaney (1981) describes it as altruism, as in the case of an animal that makes a warning cry, exposing itself by revealing its location to a predator, but benefitting others of its kind. This level of behavior draws on a primal racism that is related to an individual's or a group's defensive reaction when confronted by the unknown. But what leads us to have a positive or negative image of the other? Why will some traits, such as skin color, clothing, eating manners or type of housing, dominate others? From what moment does the other group distinguish itself from one's own?

Some social scientists start with the fact that humans are visual animals, discovering others by looking at them; consequently, the other's body, clothing, stance, gestures, attitudes and expressions give rise to instant perceptions (Langaney 1981). Others emphasize the human mind's tendency to classify things (Mauss 1968; Lévi-Strauss 1961; Flem 1985), a vital skill for orienting oneself in nature and society. However, as Saussure (1978) taught, the linguistic sign is itself arbitrary: its ability to classify is purely associative and contextual.

Therefore, all classification results from our senses' acuity, our technical ability and our subjective connection with the object in question, and from social and historical contexts.

Perhaps it is because we are visual beings that we give great importance to skin color, clothing and behaviors. However, other senses can also participate in the classification process. It can take place through the sense of smell, actual or ascribed; and the sense of hearing can play a part, according to the type of sound, i.e. cacophonous versus 'civilized' music. Taste, too – sweet or salty, raw or cooked, spicy or bland – can trigger reactions that differentiate one type of person from another.

This first, cognitive level of classification seems unproblematic; classifying things is completely natural. However, problems appear at the second cognitive level, when the other is disdained and situated in a hierarchy, one that very often constitutes the classification's very framework. In Western tradition, the ancient Greeks were the first to make such distinctions. They defined their social universe as harmonious and their geographic location as temperate. Others lived under monarchical or even tyrannical regimes rather than democratic ones, and in places either too hot or too cold. The Greeks thought of themselves as the center of the world and, because of this, established a social order where they came first. They were victims of their ethnocentrism – a very common attitude within human groups. One sees it in ancient and modern maps of the world, where the country of origin is often in the center; an ethnocentric view arranges space around it.

This spatial ethnocentrism readily carries over into notions of social hierarchy, where relative status and position also rest on self/other oppositions – from 'civilized' vs. 'barbarian', one may move to other moral and physical qualities. Eighteenth- and nineteenth-century ideas about progress and evolution reinforced a Western conception of hierarchy; Westerners situated themselves at the top, with each Western country ranking itself the highest. Langaney (1981) calls this ranking phenomenon 'secondary racism'. It is a rationalization of primal racism (here meaning heterophobia) positioned within economic or political rivalries between groups of humans, in competition between neighboring communities that differ in culture or daily habits, or in feelings of hostility arising from one community's past abuses of another (Langaney 1981, pp. 97–98). However, this xenophobia, said to arise from diverse sources – biological, social, cultural – can also transform into its positive counterpart, as we have already mentioned. It can become xenophilia or its most visible manifestation, exoticism. We can see this historically and convincingly in the Crusaders' fascination with Arab civilization (Maalouf 1999), through Jean-Jacques Rousseau's 'noble savage' and Orientalism's interest in faraway Eastern cultures (Said 1997), and in the more-recent popularity of presentations by great explorers. As Sylvie Vincent (1990) wrote:

> Xenophilia and exoticism represent the interest we feel for the stranger who is far away. For example, it can be said that Quebecers are more impressed by the Inuit they never see than by the occasionally-seen Aboriginal peoples much observed by their forebears.
>
> (p. 389)

In his research, Jean-Pierre Dupuis (2011) has found that xenophobic reactions are directed more often at foreigners who differ little from a country's nationals, and at those from other regions who take up residence in urban centers. Dupuis (2011) shows that Quebecers may hold such feelings for English speakers, and/or – in an extended heterophobia – the French, Italians, Jews and sometimes even Aboriginal peoples. In reality, these attitudes appear as heterophobia accentuated by a fear of losing economic, social, cultural or political status. Many Quebecers perceive immigrants as 'job stealers', Jews as thieves in general, Aboriginals as spoiled children receiving unjustified privileges from the government, and so forth. Furthermore, when a social crisis erupts, minorities and non-mainstream groups can quickly become scapegoats. Unfortunately, the history of the world is rich with examples of this phenomenon: the scapegoat allows a group to preserve its image, and to expel everything disliked about oneself to the fringes. It serves as a division that helps the individual or group deal with internal stresses, a psychic and social defense mechanism.

This comparison with the other also serves as a way to define oneself and, depending on the others present, to affirm or reject certain elements. This is how some Quebecers, confronted with Aboriginals, affirm their belonging to a civilized world to differentiate themselves from 'the savages'. When meeting people from France, some Quebecers will accentuate their American side and their naturalness to distinguish themselves from French intellectualism and snobbish mannerisms (Arcand and Vincent 1979). In this last example, the Aboriginal becomes one of the elements of the Quebecer's identity; in other words, 'the margin moves according to the identity the center wishes to give itself' (Vincent 1990, p. 389).

Once a group has ranked and ordered other social groups, the next step – differentiation – takes place by seeking rational justifications. Such rationalizations are social constructions, yet not entirely predetermined; they may alter following a game-changing event. The innate fears underlying such rationalizations may also become amplified or perpetuated by powerful individuals for their own purposes, acting through institutions – government, media, schools, think tanks, and so forth. Rational justifications for differences between human groups notably arose in the eighteenth and nineteenth centuries, when the idea of race started to become part of biology and other sciences. According to Vincent (1990), following the work of Flem (1985), the signifier 'race' appeared in France in the sixteenth century. It came from the Italian word *razza*, which means 'species' or 'kind' from the Latin *ratio* or 'reason', 'order of things', 'category' and 'species'. The modern conception of racial ranking expanded rapidly in the nineteenth century; evolutionists provided its theoretical basis. Social Darwinism and hereditary laws gave the world an explanation for the 'superiority' of Westerners and whites over the rest of the world, a superiority that rooted itself in biological differences. The latter took on the role of principal marker for racial differentiation, overtaking the cultural differences that dominated earlier discourse. Henceforth superiority resulted from genetics. During the twentieth century, the Nazi experience – guided by such views – showed where such beliefs take us (Enriquez 1983). In the West, racism became 'scientific' in conjunction with religion's decline and the rise of reason and science (Delacampagne 1983; Flem 1985), and with the West's constant effort to legitimize its social domination (Jacquard 1985). This brings us to racism's social functions.

Racism has two main social functions. The first defines the self through a positive comparison with another; the second justifies the domination that follows. Thus many Westerners define themselves vis-à-vis other peoples, e.g. Aboriginals, Africans, Arabs, Asians, etc., believing the 'superior' Western civilization legitimizes their conquests, their use of slavery and colonialism – the famous 'white man's burden' that Rudyard Kipling wrote about in the nineteenth century. The rationales follow:

> I am not responsible because it [our difference] is determined by biology. They are others because nature ordains they cannot be me. In fact, they are responsible for my oppressing them because of their natural incapacity to be me, to do as I would. The oppression I exert against myself by oppressing part of humanity – of which I am the

measure and the meaning – is their fault and due to their hereditary incapacity to be what I am.

(Guillaumin 1979, p. 42)

In other words, as Memmi (1982, pp. 98–99) defined it, 'racism is the generalized and definitive assignment of value to real or imaginary differences, for the benefit of the accuser and the detriment of his victim, to justify violence or privilege'.

The stereotype provides a category of thought that filters perceptions of the world and orients behavior accordingly. According to Rocheblave-Spenle (1970, p. 10),

> a stereotype is a cliché, a preconceived idea that directs the expectations of a group's members; it essentially determines their opinions, targets a particular group, arises from a dispute or conflict, varies from one culture to another and is learned during social interaction.

All scholarly works show that stereotypes are a permanent feature of all groups. Institutionalized racism springs from the combination of prejudices and the power to make them operative in an institutional setting on a daily basis. Some painful and tragic historical examples include the colonial period, the African-Americans' situation before the Civil Rights Movement, apartheid in South Africa, discrimination against Jews in Europe in the 1930s and during World War II, and the plight of Aboriginals in Australia until the late 1960s.

Many organizations may practice institutional racism: businesses, unions, associations, schools, universities, churches, hospitals, police, transit companies, media, and even the state and its judicial system. Such racism may be deliberately enacted, as with apartheid in South Africa, or occur passively without active collusion, simply because 'others' are invisible and discrimination not explicitly outlawed. Organizations help maintain social differences through their discriminatory practices, controlling access to many services – health, education, justice, welfare, as well as to housing and employment, while maintaining a negative image of the groups being discriminated against. In other words, institutional racism is a form of racial prejudice integrated within the frameworks and procedures of primary institutions, companies and social welfare systems. It allows discrimination against ethnic minorities and maintains the socially-dominant majority's privileges and benefits; it is an extreme form of intercultural relations. In addition to institutionally-perpetuated racism, many misunderstandings between members of different cultures arise from their inability to comprehend each other's worldviews or points of reference. This lack of understanding can also lead to prejudices, conflicts and forms of racism, as we shall now see.

Sources of intercultural misunderstanding

As social animals, humans live more or less in relation to other humans. That is how humans construct themselves over time and what they live with every day. Rituals and communication processes make these social relations possible, whether in interpersonal or intergroup settings.

Spoken human communication uses three types of elements: textual, co-textual and contextual. Textual elements refer to words, register and discourse. Co-textual elements concern para-verbal aspects – intonation, timber, intensity, speed, accent – and gestural ones – mimicry, eye movements, posture, gestures – that accompany speech. Contextual elements include space and time markers, body marks (scars, hair or skin color, tattoos) and affiliation markers (clothing, insignia, decorations); all of these aspects affect the communication context.

Indispensible rites for every interaction, interpreted differently

Connection with another person does not simply happen; it demands rituals that are highly codified by each culture. For example, even though in all cultures people greet one another before starting a conversation, the greeting itself takes various forms. Such rituals encompass more than just traditional greetings; they touch every aspect of social life. The sociologist Erving Goffman (1973, 1974) provides an analysis of what happens during these daily interactions. He argues that these rituals are indispensable for maintaining social ties because they allow everyone to save face during an interaction. Without a minimum of politeness, manners and civility, there is no collective life to speak of, and we probably would not want to start relationships with people who never say 'hello', who close a door in our face, or who step on our toes without saying they are sorry. This idea of 'face' is essential for understanding all of the rituals that we use in these types of situations. We also have a repertoire of faces to beg pardon when we commit a gaffe, and excuses and gifts that perform a similar function to mend hurt feelings.

All cultures have a more or less strongly present notion of 'face'. Rituals that contribute to its preservation can vary from one place to another, and what passes for good manners and civility can differ from one case to another. For instance, in Chinese culture, making a noise while eating shows that one likes the food, while such noises would be considered very impolite in Western cultures. Knowing a culture's rituals and manners before entering into relations with its people is vital to avoid misunderstandings or even potential clashes. In all cultures, causing your conversational partner to lose face is a serious thing, but the framework of symbolic interpretation often varies from one world to another. The first elements of a meeting can contribute to or reinforce prejudices. Holding a fork in a certain way, or giving out a business card in a different way, can make one person think the other is ill-bred. The Chinese always use two hands to present business cards. So when a newly-arrived American consultant started a meeting by offering his own one-handed – as if dealing playing cards – none of his Chinese interlocutors would accept one. In a transaction, such observed behaviors might lead the Chinese to think of Americans as uncivilized – barbarians – even though the Americans are doing everything 'right' according to their own social and cultural references. China specialists often relate an anecdote from the eighteenth century about an English ambassador who arrived at court and did not want to bow before the Chinese emperor, as that would be a sign of submission and humiliation in his English culture. However, not bowing to the emperor would insult the Chinese, so the Chinese functionaries had to draw on all of their ingenuity to find a greeting ritual acceptable to both parties, lest a conflict break out between the two countries.

Textual communication elements

Human communication rests on a uniquely human faculty – language, manifested by using one or several natural languages, e.g. English, French, German, Spanish, Arab, Chinese, Japanese. Each language system draws on words (a lexicon), sounds (phonetics) and syntax (grammar). Arranging these three elements makes it possible to create sentences and construct what we call a text. The precise construction depends on the speaker's language and can vary, of course; linguists estimate there are more than 6,000 languages spoken world-wide (Hagège 1985, 2005). That is why passage from one language to another will vary in its complexity, especially when the syntax and phonetics differ greatly from the speaker's mother tongue. In general, this means a French person finds it easier to learn a Latin-based language than an Asian or Germanic one.

A speaker's difficulty pronouncing words, or a strong accent can create a negative impression on his or her conversational partner. As an illustration, we refer to the term 'barbarian' mentioned earlier, which means 'someone who speaks Greek poorly' in Greek. We can also point to how many Americans in the United States interpret a British-English accent as haughty, associating it with the stereotype of a snob, or how Quebecers may envision a snobby, affected Frenchman when they hear a continental French accent. In intercultural communication, words can also pose problems for two primary reasons: the same word can signify two different things, and speakers often assume that the structure and locutions of their mother tongue should apply to other languages – a phenomenon we will discuss below as 'lingocentrism'.

When the meaning of words differs from one world to another

Since the foundational work of Ferdinand de Saussure, one of linguistics' foremost contributions has been to show that two elements, the sign (word) and the signified (concept), compose every signifier (Hagège 1985). In everyday life, that means the words I use may not have the same meaning for the person with whom I speak. Illustrations abound of semantic misunderstandings between people who belong to the same linguistic and cultural universe, such as between French people. The same types of misunderstandings also arise between people who share a linguistic system, but who live in different worlds, e.g. the French and the Quebecers. The latter 'lunch' in the morning, eat 'dinner' at mid-day and have 'supper' in the evening, while at the same hours of the day the French have a 'small lunch', followed by 'lunch' and 'dinner'. It is easy to see how misunderstandings may arise! We see the same types of misunderstanding between the British and the Americans: George Bernard Shaw noted at the turn of the twentieth century that they were 'two peoples separated by a common language'. The many variants of English language dictionaries remind us of the lexical differences between Great Britain and other English-speaking countries – the United States, Canada, Australia, New Zealand, India, and others. Of course, we see the same kinds of misunderstanding between people who belong to different linguistic *and* cultural universes. According to recent research (Chevrier 2000), German-speaking Swiss and French engineers do not appear to give the same meaning to the word 'quality'. The former associate quality with reliability, while the latter link it to ingenuity. It is not surprising they have difficulty understanding one another, and that preconceived ideas about the other provide the source of the problem, reinforcing existing prejudices – in this case, that the French lack rigor and that the Swiss-Germans are slow (Chevrier 2000).

When our national linguistic systems follow us into another language

Another great cause of misunderstandings and failures in intercultural communications arises from 'lingocentrism' (Geoffroy 2001). What does this neologism mean? It refers to the worldview that arises among speakers of a 'native tongue', rooted in a theory of language tacitly constructed and shared by almost everyone in the same linguistic group.

Table 1.1 Types of semantic transfer

Type	Key idea	Example
Lexical	Words that look the same in both languages	In French, the word 'versatile' means 'unpredictable, volatile, changeable' or even 'lunatic' and is pejorative, reserved for describing persons. Its definition in English is completely different, i.e. flexible, having diverse aptitudes or multiple uses, is not pejorative, and can be applied to persons or things.
Syntactic	Tense or gender use	In English, inanimate objects have no gender, as they do in French, causing confusion when English speakers transfer to French.
Prosodic	Intonation	In English, the phrase, 'What do you mean?' can have a different meaning depending on which word(s) carry an inflexion; the phrase can signify a question, disbelief, exasperation or even despair.

Therefore, transfers from one's maternal language to a foreign one use forms that feel like equivalents, but which the listener-recipient interprets quite differently.

In other words, when the French speak English, they risk using French forms of words whose meaning will be completely different for their English interlocutor. Geoffroy (2001) observed this phenomenon in his research on communication between French and British executives. His study noted two kinds of transfer: semantic and pragmalinguistic, i.e. involving speech-act rules, conventions and practices (see e.g. Clark 1979). Semantic transfers occur when a foreign language is insufficiently mastered, resulting in vocabulary, syntax and/or intonation mistakes (see Table 1.1).

Pragmalinguistics refers to situations where the speaker orients his speech to produce an effect on his interlocutor. In English, obligation may be expressed in several ways, including 'have to', 'must' and 'should'. Faced with this diversity, foreign speakers of English – especially the French – often choose to use the word 'must'. For a native English speaker, a French person using 'must' instead of 'have to' tends to reinforce the stereotyped perception that the French are arrogant, because 'must' infers a power relationship between the speaker and anglophone listener, i.e. an imposed opinion. The word 'but' is also a source of miscomprehension. In French, the equivalent word is used as a transition, marking a more direct contact with the listener by signaling the speaker is taking his turn at speaking, expressing his personal position or adding a supplemental element. By using 'but' to start their turn at speaking, a French person speaking English inadvertently reinforces the British or American stereotype of the French as arrogant 'loudmouths'.

When words help build personal relationships

Personal relationships are built on the words we use. The way we address and interact with people influences the markers and perceptions of our relationship with them. Subtle differences in address lead to substantial misinterpretations. For instance, in French, others are addressed most often with the formal *vous* or the informal *tu* for 'you', although other possibilities include *Monsieur, Madame*, a last name, first name or nickname, each signifying a certain distance or closeness to that person. In English, 'you' is a neutral term; addressing someone in Great Britain or America by their first name, nickname or diminutive does not signify a close or personal relationship, as it does in French. In English, these forms are informal and cordial without being intimate. The French often unconsciously interpret their use according to the French system. Confusion can also arise when the French speak English, where a professional title with a last name provides information about someone's function, not an honorific status, as it does in French. The great diversity of modes of address in French can disturb Britons or Americans, because each mode refers not only to the type of relationship one has with the person in a given context, but also to the history of this relationship (Guigo 1994). In this way, some people can use the informal *tu* form among themselves even if their ages differ, while others use *vous* even while addressing one another by their first names, and still others use *Monsieur* or *Madame* and the formal *vous* form, all depending on their closeness to and history with their conversational partners.

Politeness also takes on different forms in different languages. Geoffroy (2001) found that in British English, words expressing sincerity, loyalty and esteem have great importance, while the French express feelings with other nuances and qualifications. Britons use many indirect formulations known as 'dubitives', i.e., to guess, to suppose, to believe, to think, and they make use of expressions such as, 'I am afraid' to introduce negative news or outcomes. In comparison, the French use far more direct expressions; this can shock Britons. In his very detailed analysis of verbal exchanges between French and British executives, Geoffroy (2001) showed that linguistic competence does not necessarily mean social and cultural competence.

Mastering a language is a necessary but insufficient condition to succeed in intercultural relations. Knowledge of cultural references remains essential. Every speaker of a foreign language and every native speaker should be sensitive to the idea of lingocentrism. That would help attenuate the listener's initial (negative) reactions and assist the speaker in understanding how his or her approximations pose problems. Managers who live in multilingual contexts and in work environments that often favor English should be more aware of the effects of lingocentrism, because the resulting misunderstandings can greatly affect social dynamics.

Co-textual communication elements

Co-textual elements comprise all of the para-verbal aspects – intonation, timber, rhythm, accent, intensity – and gestural ones – posture, mimicry, eye movements – that accompany a text. During an interaction, more than words are exchanged, of course. People use intonation, timber, intensity, speed; they reveal their accent. These co-textual elements vary according to culture; some cultures encourage speakers to show passion when they talk, while others do not. Accents sometimes constitute a phonetic obstacle to comprehension. For a speaker who learned English in Oxford, a Texas accent may prove disconcerting. In the same way, continental French speakers may initially have trouble understanding Quebecers' speech, just as Quebecers might find it difficult to understand French youth from the Parisian *banlieues* or housing projects. These para-verbal variations can lead to misunderstandings, especially when cultures use these elements in opposite ways. Phonetics is a marker contributing to the perception of others, and may give pretext for prejudice, as young people from the *banlieues* can attest.

Gestures and mimicry, for example postures and more or less intense facial expressions, also help convey a text. Some cultures – Latin, Middle Eastern, African – use many gestures, while others – Nordic, Germanic and British – use fewer. Sometimes non-verbal expressions surpass verbal ones in importance, as in some Asian and Aboriginal cultures. Everyone learns how to use the body expressively within the 'native' cultural framework (Le Breton 1998). Problems can arise when interlocutors belong to opposite worlds, as when a member of a culture that maintains strong eye contact interacts with someone from a culture that avoids direct looks (Hall 1979). The latter person may easily feel invaded or harassed, and at the same time see confirmed a prejudiced view of the other. Many Westerners have historically stereotyped Asians as 'inscrutable'; this perception is rooted, in part, in cultural differences related to non-verbal aspects of expression.

Contextual communication elements

Interactions always take place in a given context; space and time surround every relationship. These elements help construct an interrelation and its meaning. For instance, a boss summoning a subordinate to his or her office has a different effect than a boss visiting the subordinate's office. The time we spend with someone and the moment in which we connect with another affects how both will act and what will be said. Other aspects create context, particularly body and kinship or affinity markers. Here again, it matters if an interlocutor wears an earring, has red hair, tattoos or light or dark skin; the way people dress and their accessories carry meaning. Cultural frameworks also influence these aspects. A recent anecdote describes how the French chief executive of a large industrial group visited the United States; he explained to his American interlocutors that the red French Legion of Honor insignia he wore was the equivalent of an American CEO's stock options. In doing so, he responded in an indirectly-stated cultural way.

Another example comes from the many French discussions about whether to wear or not to wear the Islamic face-veil, or *niqab*, to school or to public-sector workplaces. The French conception of republican laicism, or the secular control of political and social institutions, has a strong influence on the debate (Laborde 2008; Bowen 2010). In the Arab world, or in Great Britain or the United States, the face-veil clearly does not have the same significance, so we can easily deduce how much misunderstanding exists on the subject. For most non-Muslim French, wearing an Islamic face-veil to a public school violates rules about schools' religious neutrality. For most Britons and Americans, prohibition of face-veils seems to be an attack on individual liberties. For most Muslims around the world, it appears to be a rejection of Islam. Different social and political frameworks determine how each culture interprets the face-veil using its own references – the French Republic, individual rights or society's religious character. When some frameworks oppose others, differing interpretations may understandably lead to conflict. In this way, most French expect resident Muslims to assimilate into French culture, subsuming some aspects of *sharia* and accepting laws that defend secularism and separate the religious and non-religious spheres of social and political life (Weil 2005). We also note that some countries (e.g. Holland, Denmark and Great Britain) that have accommodated *sharia*-based demands for separate public-life rules for Muslims now question their position on the subject.

As Hall (1984) reminds us, our culture's interaction context may be relatively rich or poor. Rich context exchanges include elements of pre-programmed information specific to the receiver and the milieu; the transmitted message carries minimal information. We see this in Japan's Noh theater, where actors' movements are almost imperceptible to Western eyes. Poor-context exchanges create the opposite situation: messages must include all information to make up for contextual insufficiencies. Unlike communication in poor contexts, communication in rich contexts is economical, rapid, effective and satisfying, but requires agreed-upon conventions established in advance. For Hall (1984), while no culture falls exclusively at one end of the spectrum or the other, some have richer interaction contexts than others. He finds Asian, Latin and North African cultures context-rich, and German, Nordic and American cultures context-poor. This helps us understand the problems that may arise when interlocutors from opposite contexts interact. An anecdote about an Air France co-pilot at JFK airport in New York illustrates this: annoyed by the many checkpoints and controls, he joked that he had a bomb in his shoe. He was surprised when an American airport-security officer took him out of the line. He had behaved with the 'rich-context' assumption that a guard would take his word situationally, as would happen in France, while the officer had responded in a 'poor-context' fashion, assuming that a co-pilot's words should be respected to the letter. The pilot was arrested, but freed before his trial; he faced up to 7 years in prison. One does not joke in the same way on each side of the Atlantic; jokes also depend on context. Again, we can see how such differences may lead to misunderstandings or even serious conflicts. In the above case, 350 people had to spend the night in a hotel, waiting for a different co-pilot to arrive the next day, before they could depart for Paris.

Cohabitation and one's own cultural connection

Group living requires a certain number of shared elements – language, rules, beliefs, values. These elements are learned and interiorized in such a way as to become natural for people in a given group. We all learned how to speak a language, how to sit at a dinner table, and how to express our emotions in certain ways. Thus we come to believe that those ways are natural; only when we meet people from other cultures do we discover the singularity of our way of living. Other worlds are possible and their existence inevitably leads us to question ourselves. In fact, we learn much about ourselves through this comparison with the other. Our relation to what is foreign, exotic or different is an integral part of creating our identity (Joly 1990; Todorov 1995; Fernandez 2002). Anthropology, ethnology, geography and comparative history greatly help us understand the differences we encounter. Each discipline reminds us in its own way that we maintain different connections with language, space, time and others. Thus, the business management practices we can observe often have these same connections, and the intercultural communication that we have been discussing exists within much larger anthropological frameworks.

A special relation to language

The human faculty of language and its concrete expression – speech – possess several functions, including seven primary ones:

- An information function that affects all pronouncements, such as 'the weather is fine', 'the plane just landed', or 'the meeting is in room 212'. This function is the basis for all of the information we transmit daily.
- An expressive function refers to individual and collective expressions. Illustrations include phrases such as, 'I believe, I think, I admit, we find', that express the subject speaking as either a single person (i.e. me, I, Mr Smith or Ms Jones), or as a member of a collective (i.e. we, the union representatives, or representatives of an organization, a staff level, an ethnic group, etc.).
- A representation function that allows us to think, or to make representations of the world. Without language, thought cannot exist. Even mathematics, which appears to be the most developed formal language, needs natural language to exist as such.
- A symbolic function that touches symbolic activity; language lets us give meaning to what we do. This function is especially important in analyzing practices in intercultural situations. We will return to this a little later.

- An action function that was brought to light by language philosophers who showed that language served as actions. Phrases such as, 'I'm going to do this', 'I promise you will be promoted', do not simply state something, they signify an action will follow. They are what we call 'speech-acts' (see e.g. Austin 1962). Since business management is a world very much focused on action, speech acts are very frequent and numerous. Furthermore, the credibility of a person who performs such acts rests on fulfilling the commitments he or she has made: we can understand how very meaningful being a 'man of his word' is in human relations.
- A relational and affinitive function that allows connections to others and develops a sense of belonging. I create connections through language; the fact that I speak the same language as my conversational partner, or that of the group I live with, allows me to belong to a linguistic region.
- A poetic function that refers to the poetic character of language. It appears when language becomes the object of speech, an arrangement of words and phrases that result in poetry and literature. That is why there is no culture without poetry – it gives expression to the imagination and to dreams. Every society, whether in oral or written tradition, has poets and storytellers who allow its members to enjoy language games and to create a literary universe.

While these principal functions exist in every linguistic and cultural universe, we must take note of each society's distinct relation to language and speech, particularly in conversational style and the connection the speaker maintains with his or her own tongue.

Different styles of conversation

In her work on comparative ethnology, Raymonde Carroll (1987) describes the different styles of conversation she observed in the United States and France. In her view, American conversation resembles a jazz session, where the goal is to exchange thoughts through speaking informally. Order is determined by the amount of time needed to explain something. 'Discordant notes' refer to interruptions – an excited tone, suddenly loud voices or laughter over trivialities. According to Carroll, French conversation is entirely different and resembles fireworks. The rhythm of the speakers defines its order. Discordant notes may come from laborious explanations, an absence of variety or long replies. In the first case, speakers listen to one another and express themselves in turn on a precise topic. In the second case, participants discuss things in a lively way, intervening whenever they think they should, taking on topics that vary greatly during the conversation. As we can see, this presents two very different styles that can provoke misunderstandings or even aggressive reactions. For Carroll (1987), the subjects of American conversation correspond best to what French people consider 'serious' conversation.

Why do such differences exist? In large measure, history provides an explanation. For the French, coming from an aristocratic culture, conversation was first and foremost an art; one had to distinguish oneself in its practice. Innumerable books show how court life and (more broadly) salons played a role in establishing rules for conversation (Fumaroli 2001). The bourgeoisie's rise followed this courtly pattern. Many novels illustrate the importance of knowing how to converse and the role played by women, in particular, in felicitous conversational customs. For instance, a good hostess had to place guests at the dinner table according to an informed calculus that accounted for the conversational interests of each. Many Americans, mostly from lower socioeconomic classes, have a completely different experience (Hertsgaard 2002); a traditional aristocracy based on monarch-granted titles never really existed in America and – except for a small elite – conversation was never an art. The interlocutor's subject, and the respect shown him or her, is more important in a pointedly democratic culture than the brilliance of the discussion. This explains why the French applauded the form as much as the content of the speech given by their foreign affairs minister, Dominique de Villepin, at the United Nations during the run-up to the Iraq War; the Americans, notably the Republicans, had a different response. The French found that Villepin executed the canons of French discourse with style, suitable citations and striking phrases. The Americans saw yet another manifestation of French arrogance and snobbishness in the speech.

A special relation to one's spoken tongue

The relationship that the French and the Americans have to their language provides another explanatory element. For most Americans, it is a communication tool above all; a functional and instrumental conception of language dominates in the US. However, uneven levels of schooling due to income inequalities often create marked differences in the American public's language use and appreciation. This explains, for example, why a presidential candidate in the United States must not appear too intellectual or speak in too artful a way. If a candidate does so, he or she risks being perceived as a snob by less-advantaged or less well-educated Americans – more numerous than the elites; the candidate thus has an interest in speaking like the Everyman. An example of this arose in the 2004 election, when the Democratic candidate and wealthy elite member John Kerry was characterized as an East Coast snob, and even 'French-looking', since he spoke the language fluently.

Historically, another conception of language prevails for the French: the language is a treasure, so important that an academy dedicated to it was founded in the seventeenth century. All French residents are expected to speak the language correctly; students from all socioeconomic classes undergo the same strict language classes in schools, and even foreigners learning the language are held to high standards (this should be kept in mind with the example of Nicolas Sarkozy!). Every politician and public personage remains conscious of the language's importance, which is why many great French politicians have maintained close relationships with writers and literature. While the hypothetical American presidential candidate must avoid a too-cultivated 'elitist' or 'intellectual' speech, a French counterpart who was careless about language usage would risk disqualification for the job. This reveals the aristocratic sources of such an attitude – the mind gets its pleasure from its sensitivity to the language. In the country of Louis XIV, of literary salons and sanctifying speech, it remains inconceivable that public officials would not know how to express themselves artfully.

The importance given to speech helps us understand why the French tend to correct their conversational partners – whether French or foreign – when they commit speech errors. This sometimes leads foreigners see the French as nit-picking grade-school teachers, when they simply want to help foreigners to speak French as well as possible. A long-running French spelling and dictation championship provides proof of the popularity of proper language use; it was created in 1985 by Bernard Pivot, a host of cultural television shows. By contrast, Americans have unsurprisingly developed a greater tolerance of linguistic errors; a nation of immigrants prioritizes good communication, in a context where many interlocutors have just arrived and language is primarily a communication tool.

Given French regard for the aesthetic and poetic functions of their language, we can better grasp why intercultural exchanges between the French and foreigners sometimes pose problems. As Dupuis (2005) noted, the different relationship to language, speech, conversational style and word use remains a point of tension between French and Quebecer executives who work together. These unique, socially and historically rooted connections with language sometimes cause intercultural relations to stumble.

A special relation to space

The relationship to space provides another key element for understanding culture and human behavior. Each society and human group has its own territory, a particular geography that influences how people live together; it affects shelter, food, sociability, habits, mentalities and attitudes to nature. The most striking illustrations of the different ways geography influences human customs appear in the differing lifestyles of indigenous tribes, such as the Inuit in the Canadian Arctic, the Yanomamö in the Amazon rainforest or the Mongolians in the Gobi desert.

Space is not merely physical. It is also a repository of history, of important events and vestiges of the past that mark the land: memorials, burial grounds, traces of ancient roads. Successive waves of immigration have crossed such spaces, helping constitute current populations. Space's historical aspects help explain why Europe's culture differs from that of North America, Africa or Asia; a French person's space differs greatly from that of a Canadian or Brazilian. While physical space dominates the North American experience, historical space models the European (and French) experience. It should come as no surprise that a recent survey (Sciences Humaines 2011) showed that the French retain a strong attachment to their region of origin, and revealed their unwillingness to move very far away from it. Such attitudes are understandable in a country where history has deep roots and the landscape changes every few kilometers. It is equally understandable that Americans, as immigrants from all over the world, strongly marked by a history of spatial conquest and the myth of the frontier, prove more geographically mobile than the French. American space seems less invested with history (at least to European eyes) and housing is more standardized, which also facilitates movement from one place to another; the deep historical and social roots that attach the French to their territory prevent the same degree of mobility.

Connection to one's space also matters at a personal level and in daily life. Everyone needs a protected space of one's own – the well-known, invisible but well-delineated 'personal bubble' that surrounds each individual, answering a need to mark one's territory by some sort of appropriation. This space provides the distances that regulate our social relations – intimate, personal, social or public. The American anthropologist Edward Hall and other social scientists clearly show how this connection to space remains fundamental for every human being, but also how much group culture influences territoriality (Hall 1984; Fischer 1990, 1997). Some cultures allow people to touch more easily and to look into each other's eyes without feeling invaded, for example Mediterranean, Latin and African cultures. Others, for example Scandinavian, Germanic, British or American, resist touching strangers or maintaining long eye contact, feeling both to be an invasion of personal space. The way a Parisian bistro is organized provides a classic example of these different spatial expressions; the tables generally face the street so customers can watch the street spectacle and passers-by can check out the seated customers. Such a system is possible only in a culture favoring visual contacts (Hall 1984).

The same type of see-and-be-seen system exists in French public parks, on the subway and on trains, but in many other countries, people do not look directly at one another in public places. This means, for example, that women from cultures that frown upon such looking may experience it as harassment, while in the opposite case, women might find the averted eyes a sign of disinterest. I have heard many French and Italian women complain that no one notices them in America, while American women often feel the opposite way when in Italy or France. What can you tell people from southern cultures who find northerners too distant? Again, we can see how potential misunderstandings and conflicts may arise between people who do not belong to the same spatial world; where some feel invaded by the lookers and see incivility, others perceive the lookers as interested and polite.

We can also understand why some cultures reject certain ways of arranging space, such as open-plan offices. Despite their invention by two Germans after World War II, open plans did not succeed in Germany. The inventors went to the United States, where numerous organizations noticed and adopted their office plans (Fischer 1990). This difference in receptivity arises from Germans' and Americans' different relationship to personal space; the former prefer closed spaces while the latter are comfortable with open ones (Hall 1984). We can see how social and cultural patterns influence the conception of space and work spaces: areas for social interactions or layouts can create problems when they do not consider vital cultural attitudes toward personal space. Since space plays a large role in building and maintaining social ties, it must be taken into account, as must cultural relations to time.

A special relation to time

A movement in space is always a movement in time. But just as human actions take place in a spatial and temporal framework, the relation to time varies according to cultural parameters. As many studies show (Hall 1966; Hofstede and Hofstede 2004), human beings do not always have the same perception of time. Large differences exist between hunter-gatherers' sense of time and that of agricultural societies, industrial societies and present-day ones (Gasparini 1990; Kamdem 1990; Sue 1994; Aubert 2003). Similar gaps exist in today's world; humans do not share a common temporal imperative. Different ones rule the farmer in Burkina Faso, the shop owner in Bombay, a Guarani Indian in the Amazon rainforest, a bus driver in the mountains of Peru, a financier on Wall Street, a farmer's wife in Provence or a supermarket cashier in London. Even in the age of globalization, different conceptions of time exist, depending on a society's organization and level of development. They illustrate the diversity and plurality of conceptions and conditions of living.

According to Hall (1966), humans follow two major ideal types in time use. In the first, known as monochronic, people generally do only one thing at a time, emphasizing timelines, schedules, and achievements, focusing primarily on the task at hand, communicating without referring to context, and pushing punctuality to the extreme. Monochronic cultures are found notably in North America, Northern Europe and Germany, Switzerland and Austria. Monochronic time is linear and segmented, like a road or ribbon that unfurls from the past toward the future, and seems tangible, like a commodity; time can be saved, spent, wasted, lost and found, or hurried, delayed, slowed or fleeting (Hall 1966, p. 24). The dominance of this type of time in the nineteenth-century West allowed industrial society to emerge. To industrialize, all traditional societies have had to adapt to it, more or less. Historians have shown that adaptation was sometimes difficult; the first workers coming into factories from the countryside had to learn the discipline of working at an industrial rhythm, something completely new to them (Gasparini 1990).

Hall's second ideal type of relationship to the use of time, the polychronic, is characterized by multiple activities taking place at the same time, by giving priority to human interactions and context, by a relative punctuality, and by a facility for changing programs and planned projects. Polychronic uses of time are found in Latin, Mediterranean and African cultures. 'Polychronic time can be represented by a point more than by a ribbon or a road, and this point is sacred' (Hall 1966, p. 22). This conception of using time is primarily found in traditional societies. It rests on the idea that human interactions are more important than interactions with material objects. Time becomes subordinated to whatever people consider essential at the moment they interact.

These two systems – monochronic and polychronic – are very different and extreme opposites; it is easy to understand how their meeting can pose problems. For example, many Americans and other Westerners feel irritated when they travel or work in primarily poly-chronic countries. They thereby lose sight of the importance of relationships and context in this type of system. This brings us to the last major relation – with the other.

A special relation to the other

Every organization, no matter what type – company, administrative, cooperative, charitable association, union – possesses a division of labor and a hierarchy. Every leadership unit implements systems for hiring, selection, remuneration and supervision. While numerous factors may influence these elements, we will examine those that come from the spheres of national or regional culture. One of the most important issues concerns the meaning people give their conduct and the categories that help them interpret what is happening. Culture, defined as a worldview and set of references, makes intelligible whatever we observe in a given organization. For example, what categories account for the workplace behavior of a French person, a Dutch person or an American? Philippe d'Iribarne attempted to define them in his now-classic 1989 study, *La Logique de l'honneur* (The Logic of Honor). The research he undertook in three factories in three different countries reveals that work relations, whether horizontal or vertical, depend on three different logics: honor in France, contracts in the United States, and consensus in the Netherlands.

The logic of honor

A logic of honor prevailed in the French factory that Iribarne studied. Within this context, each profession was guided by a set of rights and duties. Group membership assumed con-formity to a particular mode of conduct, and carried responsibilities not always determined through formal procedures. Iribarne found that the French worker or executive tended to act according to what he or she believed was fair in given circumstances. Their assessment fol-lowed their group's norms. Relations to hierarchical bosses varied depending on whether the boss respected subordinates' autonomy and rank. Bosses were accepted as superiors insofar as they showed themselves deserving of the position. In French hierarchical relations, Iribarne observed bosses who did not deserve the title, the 'wannabe bosses' or *petits chefs*. The defer-ence shown to one's boss was related to the attitude of the bosses. In the French model Iribarne describes, the subordinate does not like his or her boss to interfere with their job; such interfer-ence feels like a vote of no confidence, and the subordinate's concept of the profession alone should guide his or her behavior. That is why the French in Iribarne's study detested being treated like servants, a dreadful role. We can imagine the effect of such an attitude in service businesses. Iribarne found that a French person who voluntarily provides a service would have a hard time submitting to a customer who treated him or her like a valet. In other words, while the French will render service, they find it imperative not to be servile in doing so.

Informal adjustments were another important aspect of community life in the French factory observed by Iribarne (1993). Each employee would do what was needed according to his or her personal reading of the situation, which made coordination difficult. That was why a network of personal relationships existed, allowing people to make adaptations as needed. Cooperation at work was founded on a number of services rendered that were more like gifts and reciprocations. Nevertheless, this system was not conflict-free: in French culture, Iribarne observed that workplace conflicts might take the form of violent verbal exchanges. This emotional engagement showed how attached employees remained to their ideas and their work. Iribarne revealed how a cultural obligation to be moderate, to not exceed implicit limits, regulated French employees' responses. If that failed, the boss would be asked to arbitrate conflicts.

As we can see, this logic of honor is related to historical experience. France is an old country; its social order emerged in the medieval period as three orders or estates – those who fight (nobles), those who pray (clergy) and those who work (peasants) (Le Goff 2003). This ranking follows categories from noble to base: whoever is at the summit is considered noble while whoever is below that is considered not noble. In Ancien Régime France, this conception of coexistence was set by the monarchy and court life (Elias 1974). This logic of rank and its associated aristocratic categories was maintained as France became a democracy. Today, the republican French state never hesitates to ennoble its members through new rankings and ritualized trials, such as competitions to enter the so-called 'Great Schools' (*Grandes Écoles*) (Bourdieu 1989). The opposition of noble to base regulates social relations between and within groups and categories of people. Every group has this kind of hierarchy. To be considered worthy of the honor attached to one's profession or trade, the French tradesman or professional has to respect its rights and duties.

The logic of contracts

The logic of contracts that Iribarne (1993) observed in an American factory is quite different. It rests on the idea that social relations are contractual, similar to a customer–vendor relationship, and references the market rather than the dignity of a profession or trade. In the American company that Iribarne observed, a subordinate worked for his or her immediate boss, who set the direct subordinates' objectives, judged their work quality, and could order them to do things. Such work contracts have no bias toward an established hierarchy, are based on a relationship between equals, and must ensure a degree of equity given their importance in defining the work relationship. Thus an American contract is usually very detailed and uses clauses that anticipate all of the problems that might arise during its execution. The factory that Iribarne studied had many rules and procedures that had to be followed; several were quite detailed to reduce arbitrariness and ensure equity. The contract was explicit; highly objective procedures were used to see if it was performed correctly or not. If not, a complete legal system could be called on to litigate any dispute. As the press sometimes observes and as the French sociologist Michel Crozier (1980) noted more than 30 years ago, this can lead to an escalation in litigation.

Iribarne observed that even though each American's freedom is – a priori – unlimited, and even if contractual relations can temper deviations, a spirit of community also plays a significant role in maintaining equitable work relations in the United States. American society originated with a community of men and women who came from Europe for religious, economic, political and social reasons. Upon arriving in America, they sought to build a society of equals founded on moral principles, obviously drawn from religion, where status based on inherited hierarchy was banished. Some vestiges of this history remain, such as the importance American firms often assign to moral values and to concepts of equity and fairness, leading to the proliferation of ethics and business conduct charters and plans (Pesqueux 1998; Pasquero 2000). Even though this commitment to morality sometimes goes astray, it nonetheless dominates American society (Etzioni 1988): personal interest and morality are not opposed as they are in France. The logic of contracts differs greatly from one where honor plays the central role; both types arise as products of specific social and historical experiences, as does the logic of consensus.

The logic of consensus

A logic of consensus operated in the Dutch factory studied by Iribarne (1993). In this world, the boss was a peer, at the same level as everyone else, having no special status. When he or she had to make a decision, Iribarne observed that the Dutch boss spent the day talking with subordinates to gain their agreement; they did the same in return, constantly seeking consensus in a convivial way. Decisions were made through long discussions that needed to engage each collaborator; this was a world of equals where the majority had to respect minority opinions. This kind of group consensus-making has some limitations, of course. Strong social pressure is brought to bear to achieve an agreement, and to restrict more aggressive displays of opinion. Iribarne found that the process could lead workers to withdraw, as manifested by high levels of absenteeism and employee turnover. Like the other two logics, this one draws on the Netherlands' experience and history, which are the products of an egalitarian association between different-sized groups of various origins. The Dutch Republic (1581–1795) was constructed on a model of consensus, and contemporary society has kept the same structure and spirit, as have workplace relations.

The three logics – honor, contracts and consensus – must not be judged according to a standard criterion: we are not saying one is better than the other. Each is capable of achieving good or bad results. The interest of this analysis springs from the way it shines light on the symbolic framework within which each employee evolves. That makes it possible to read certain behaviors at work that would otherwise be difficult to understand. This ethnographic approach, supported by observation and extensive interviews, allows us to avoid what are sometimes over-simplistic ideas about how workplaces function, because it accounts for the complexity of attitudes by drawing on political culture and social history. It also allows us to illuminate areas of possible tension between different cultures, and to unpack some of the assumptions and prejudices that can emerge from such intercultural relations, shedding new light on stereotypes – such as the hierarchical French person, haughty in their relation to customers, or the individualistic American, for example (Iribarne 2004).

The history of intercultural relations

In this last section of this chapter, we would like to address an issue that intercultural management studies often fail to emphasize: the historical nature of relations between peoples. When we look at history, we see that intercultural connections in professional and social lives may not be new experiences for the respective peoples involved. The weight of history lurks in the background, whether one likes it or not. To forget history, pushes a key dimension for understanding relations into the shadows – one that will re-emerge when relations hit a rough patch, since the past may well color interpretations of the situation.

While historical examples of cultural misunderstanding abound, three cases prove especially helpful for this discussion: France's relations with Americans, with the French Quebecers and with North Africans. These examples draw usefully on the present writer's research and cultural perspective while providing a uniform history on one end of the comparison. Moreover, each illustrates relationships in a particular context: (1) two independent countries; (2) a mother country and its extension in a new world; and (3) colonized and colonizer countries.

French–American relations: more than 200 years of ups and downs

The start of the 2003 Iraq War put America's government in opposition to most of the world, and also highlighted strained relations with France, which – along with Germany – formally opposed American policy within the United Nations Security Council. In the United States, this episode resulted in many 'anti-French' articles in magazines, newspapers and on television shows (Chesnoff 2005). It led to an attempted boycott of French products and to changing the name of french fries and french toast to 'freedom fries' and 'freedom toast' in the restaurant that serves Congress, as well as in several others across the United States. Germany escaped this level of opprobrium even though it held the same position on the war as France. Traditional politics underlie such reactions, as does the relatively weak demographic weight of Americans of French descent versus those of German origin. However, the history of relations between the two countries does not explain everything; many criticisms of the French reaction to America's stance on Iraq centered on the lack of gratitude and unwillingness to help America when needed, given America's rescue of France during World Wars I and II. Such a reckoning of the historical balance sheet is necessarily selective, and omits several other significant events that the French might perceive as equally or more significant: the crucial French aid during the Revolutionary War, to say nothing of more recent support in the first Gulf War and in Afghanistan. French responses to 9/11 carried a particular symbolic weight by French cultural standards: President Jacques Chirac visited New York – the first world leader to survey the devastation after the destruction of the World Trade Center – and an editorial in the French newspaper *Le Monde* pronounced 'We are all Americans now' after that tragic event.

The strain over the Iraq invasion exposed recurring undertones in the relationship between France and the US: it was not the first time their governments had clashed. At the birth of the United States, historians recall the tension between French military officers and George Washington and other Americans; the former were perceived as arrogant snobs by the latter. During World War II, relations between President Roosevelt and General de Gaulle were very poor; as France's president, de Gaulle did all he could to distance himself from the Americans whenever he thought it necessary, taking France out of NATO for this reason. Since the beginning of the plan for a European Union, the French have campaigned for a powerful Europe that is both independent from and allied to the United States.

The source of this critical attitude springs from two opposing models of universality. Historically, the American model aligns with a democratic experience which, over time, has made it seem a land of possibility for many poor, persecuted immigrants suffering from famine and war in other parts of the world. The experience of continental conquest also contributes to the model. And where a free-market economy has large support, government assistance seems undesirable; socioeconomic inequalities are tolerated and religion plays a visible role in daily life (Micklethwait and Wooldridge 2004). The French model of universality draws on a different context, while sharing some elements with the American model.

Born out of the French Revolution, France's experience was deeply influenced by its long aristocratic history (Iribarne 2006), its centralized monarchy and the influence of French culture on the world. As an ancient nation, proud of its past, France has always sought to preserve its ranking in the world in some way, despite its gradual decline and lessening influence. This attitude has a way of irritating – understandably – its closest allies.

A mutual fascination, especially within some social circles, further complicates relations between France and the United States. While most in the United States can conjure only a vague image of France, if not a total misapprehension, in some American intellectual and cultural circles France still has a good image and represents a certain art of living. For example, when a few American congressional representatives called for a boycott of France, Cornell University organized a 'France Week' as its response to the 'French-bashing' that had become popular, particularly among Republicans. In France, a large coterie of America admirers exists; and despite the United States' often-negative image, many French regularly make it a basis of comparison for their own world.

These two historical experiences affect the way each culture tends to view 'otherness' and the relationship to differences. In the French context, the French Republic serves as the guarantor of liberty, equality and national solidarity, without alluding to the various communities that constitute it. Hence there is no national statistical measure of ethnic origin and most researchers, despite recent debates about diversity, do not want one. This color-blind conception of the French citizen explains why the French approach discrimination and racism differently than do Americans. In France, a large majority overwhelmingly favors assimilation, while different ways of adapting to American life are accepted in the United States. Thus, racism toward blacks remains weak in France compared to the United States, with its long history of African slavery and citizenship previously based on skin color, white or black. French citizenship has never been defined in terms of skin color; however, France's colonialism and its wars in North Africa contribute to more negative attitudes among the French toward North Africans, particularly Algerians, for similar historical reasons and especially because of certain Islamic ideologies and practices, such as wearing the *niqab*, or forbidding certain foods. The differences between France and the United States must be understood as the products of a unique history and narrative.

French–Quebecer relations: a complicated history

French and French–Quebecer relations have greatly expanded in the last 40 years. At the beginning of the 1960s, agreements signed by the Quebec premier Jean Lesage and the French government helped knit together ties that had weakened over the preceding two centuries. The British conquest of Canada in 1760, and ensuing changes in French Canada and in France, somewhat attenuated French–Canadian relations. France and Quebec also took different directions; over the last 40 years their renewed relationship, although very warm, has led to incomprehension and misunderstandings, several of which endure. Three indicators suggest the effects of these differences. The first comes from media surveys that show that a very high percentage of French citizens who emigrate to Quebec seem to return to France after a few years abroad; precise numbers are difficult to determine, but some surveys show 50 percent returning after two years (Saire 1995; Dupuis 2005) The second draws on a few research studies that examine Quebecers' rejection of 'paternalistic' French expatriates who in turn find it difficult to adjust to Quebecois norms (Saire 1995; Dupuis 2005). The third is illustrated by the oft-used expression 'damned French' current in Quebec. These three things would have us believe that French–Quebecer intercultural relations are less simple than they might first appear. What appears most important in understanding this complicated relationship from an anthropological point of view? It seems to us that, once again, history can shed light on these questions.

In spite of a shared language and, in most cases, a common demographic origin, Quebec was shaped by experiences very different from the French ones. The Quebecer community originated in what used to be New France (1524–1763), but today's citizens descend from a pioneer community that experienced its mother country's retreat – or abandonment – in 1763, followed by the arrival of the British. This founding community lived through the creation of the Canadian nation, and constituted the basis for what was known until the 1960s as French Canada; since then it has affirmed its Quebecer identity. This history forged a collective personality distinct from the French one. Among its central differences, we note that it belongs to the American continent, that French speakers are a minority, and that the Catholic Church has played a defining role.

Their experience of the American continent has left Quebecers with an egalitarian social organization and a special connection to nature, space, language and time. As a minority, the French-speaking community has internalized a feeling of vulnerability and a long-term anxiety about survival. Historically, the Quebec Catholic Church was pronatalist and strongly ultramontane;[1] it opposed secularism, the idea of the French Revolution, and the subsiding of the French-Catholic demographic; it mistrusted the modern-day French. As Dupuis (2005) showed so well in his study, the idea that the French may threaten French-Canadian identity was widespread among the clergy for a century. Compared to the many Quebecers who grew up in an egalitarian and working-class context dominated by the Church, the French from higher socioeconomic classes or 'noble' families seem very different, and reflect a fundamentally aristocratic, republican and secular culture. These types of French people usually love arguing in an artful style and happily find fault with daily events; many working-class Quebecers see only critics, crybabies and snobs, a view shared by many Americans, as we saw earlier. The French tend to distinguish themselves through rank and the logic of honor (Iribarne 1993, 2006) while Quebecers try to remain members of a group and submit to the logic of consensus. These different ways of functioning create misunderstandings or even conflicts. Clashes occur frequently between French and Quebecers of modest and working-class means, and also among business executives working in French-speaking factories in Quebec, as Dupuis' study (2005) shows; one may note, however, that Quebecer executives working in France do not seem to suffer the same ostracism.

Social and historical backdrops always stand behind face-to-face intercultural relations. One may reduce the distance between background and foreground through the devices and symbolic frameworks used to interpret speech and action. In French–Quebecer relations, problems arise from the fact that both interlocutors speak French, but in different ways. Similar traps exist for Britons and Americans, Spaniards and Latin Americans, and Brazilians and Portuguese. However, France – the linguistic parent country – has the greater number of speakers, unlike the other examples. For Quebecers, sharing the French language with France raises the issue of which norms and standards to follow – an inexhaustible source of argument throughout Quebec's history. Even if the arguing appears to have quieted and a norm has been adopted that rejects the working-class French-Canadian dialect and too-French-sounding phonetics, many language traps still await French and Quebecers in conversation. Beyond the language – and through it – a different mode of coexistence also comes into play.

Historically, the French come from an aristocratic society where the logics of honor and of rank largely affect their ways of reacting to things. In this context, the opposition of noble and base constitutes a key to understanding French behavior. Many Quebecers, using American references and a Dutch-like mode of consensus, do not comprehend these categories; many misunderstandings result and understandable strains arise at work or in daily life. In the world of business management, there is a pressing need to address these differences on each side of the Atlantic, to prevent unthinking reactions along with their damaging consequences. At a time when French and Quebecers interact more frequently than ever, serious thinking about their intercultural relations grows more urgent. A review of history is absolutely necessary to understand what unites and what distinguishes these transatlantic cousins.

French–North African relations: between tragedy and fascination

In 2005, a year after a nationwide debate about banning Islamic face-veils in schools, riots took place in the French suburbs known as *banlieues*, the housing projects and ghettos that surround major cities. Primarily populated by immigrants from the northern Maghreb region of Africa – Morocco, Algeria and Tunisia – and their descendants, the projects burst into violence, shocking international observers. The riots also drew attention to the state of relations between the French majority and the minorities of North African descent and other immigrant youth. Many American and British commentators proposed burying the French model of integration and copying theirs. Although political considerations colored many of the commentaries, notably following France's position on the Iraq War, the issue of French–North African relations had been first revived following other less violent protests, such as the marches in 1983 and 1984 by second-generation North Africans for equality and against racism. Social integration and assimilation (the stated goals of policy and the communities themselves) remain especially complex for many reasons, including the varied origins of immigrants and their children – Moroccan, Algerian, Tunisian – and their broad social demographics, for example shop owners, intellectuals, blue- and white-collar workers. Their highly variable degrees of integration and success are also factors. Many feel excluded, while others succeed very well, and some – great athletes, singers, entertainers and comics – become symbols. In addition, many marry spouses of other origins: France has one of the highest rates of first-generation inter-ethnic marriages of any country (Todd 1993).

So where lies the problem in these relations? Observers see several factors, including a too-great concentration of immigrants in certain areas, namely the ghetto *banlieues*; hiring discrimination against first-generation immigrant fathers, resulting in a lack of economic integration; little visible immigrant presence in the major political parties; and a retreat, for some, into fundamentalist Islam (Kepel 2012a, 2012b). All of these factors add obstacles to success in school and socioeconomic integration. For the French Republic, these difficulties pose an unprecedented problem, since the French model of integration appeared quite successful prior to the 1960s. In the past, and in spite of the ambient xenophobia that surrounded them, immigrant parents and their children had a strong desire to become French. Schools and other public institutions played a large role in the assimilation process, one that still exists for many young immigrants – especially those of North African origin – who play by establishment rules. Many immigrant parents living in France illegally, try to prevent their children's deportation so that their offspring may become educated French citizens. What has changed is the social and cultural distance that some first-generation immigrants and their immediate descendants maintain vis-à-vis the French majority's culture (Lagrange 2010; Kepel 2012a, 2012b). Their use of slang, incivility toward others and conspicuous religious behavior shocks the majority of French citizens who prefer to coexist in a republican manner; these 'un-French' behaviors exacerbate problems with youth integration into everyday life.

Past and present histories join to increase the difficulty (*Le Monde* 2004). For example, the Algerian War of Independence (1954–62) spurred much racist and xenophobic behavior toward Algerian immigrants right after the French president Charles de Gaulle declared Algeria an independent country. On the French side, losing Algeria as a colony provoked its own share of trauma, particularly for French émigrés forced to return to mainland France after independence, and those nostalgic for empire. On the Algerian side, colonial history and the war remain part of the backdrop in relations with the French. The outrage of Algerians and others (including many French intellectuals) at a law passed in the French National Assembly in 2005, recognizing the 'positive role' of colonization, illustrates how history's deep scars affect contemporary events and re-emerge whenever relations are strained. When participants in history – in this case French officials – stifle history's tragedies, it affects ordinary relations as well as official ones. However, history weighs differently on different countries; neither Morocco nor Tunisia – both former French colonies, but exempt from wars of independence and direct French control – have the same troubled relations with France. These differences contribute to a more peaceful relationship and a more positive view of the French, who, in turn, have a more positive opinion of Moroccans and Tunisians than of Algerians.

Over the last 15 years, other factors have affected the situation of Algerian immigrants and French Muslims: the growth of a militant, fundamentalist strain of Islam in the Muslim world, and the Algerian Civil War (1992–present) between the government and various Islamist rebel groups. These events have had repercussions nearly everywhere in the West, especially France, which counts the largest Arab and Muslim population in Europe. The terrible images coming out of Algeria and other countries have fostered highly negative views among Westerners, both of the nations and Islam itself. A minority of French Muslims challenged secularism over the face-veil issue – clashing with republican French ideals and French citizens, who widely support the law against wearing the veil in certain public places. On a larger scale, in 2006, the international controversy over 'blasphemous' cartoons of Muhammad, published in the Danish newspaper *Jyllands-Posten*, revived the question of religious satire's place in the public sphere. Obviously, intercultural relations between French citizens of North African origin and those with older ties to France can also be very harmonious, as many cases amply illustrate. Such harmony requires efforts and compromise on both sides – less resistance to secularism and French law among immigrants, more meritocracy and less exclusion in French institutions (Laborde 2008; Iribarne 2010; Kepel 2012).

As we have seen, intercultural relations between distinct groups involve historical elements that may help mutual understanding. If we do not keep history in mind, important things can escape us; alternatively, history can be used to clarify words and deeds that would otherwise be incomprehensible. Management in an intercultural context must not forget this, because – in addition to the elements cited here – the history of relations between peoples provides the framework for interpreting current relations, even if that past usually remains invisible to those interacting with one another.

Conclusion

Employment and management practices seen in Europe and elsewhere are closely tied to worldviews. An analysis that draws on an action's symbolic framework may help clear up tensions that arise around what different cultures mean by 'decisions', 'ethics', 'qualifications', 'competency', 'quality', and so forth. By accumulating examples from different societies, such analyses can help build a typology of cultures, showing the dynamics between each country's – or even each sphere of civilization's – own values (Iribarne 1998; Dupuis 2004). Understanding comes from seeing the singular way articulations occur between key elements of each culture. Even references shared by several Western and European cultures, such as 'individual', 'equality', 'liberty', 'community', will take on a specific meaning within a culture under study. This is what research into intercultural management endeavors to show, by looking at cultures as worldviews with specific sets of references.

Such an approach has much merit in a globalized world of international management practices. In contrast to the monolithic notion that there is only one way of managing – a single 'best practice' – it breathes life into a healthy cultural pluralism, enriching business thought. This is an important issue for European – and other – countries dealing with an invasion of American-inspired business management tools. In European companies, it means paying more attention to this issue within one's own national workplace, and remembering that proximity does not always mean similarity (*Futuribles* 2002; Sorge and Harzing 2003). The arrival of new European Union members and current problems in this domain should increase interest in questioning many such assumptions.

Developing countries, often viewed as incapable of developing high-performance management practices for cultural reasons, also have a fundamental interest in this issue, since field research shows that taking into account a culture's specific worldview often proves critical for success in business modernization (Iribarne 2003, 2010). Cultural diversity, vitally important to so many, depends on intercultural dialogue and respect for differences; the world of business management cannot ignore these issues. On the contrary, given anthropology's centrality to present-day transformations, its study should be obligatory for all business students and managers. Their future social and economic performance depends on a broader understanding of the world's many cultures, since an abstract, universal form of business management does not exist.

Note

1 According to the definition given in Leichtenberger, *Encyclopédie des sciences religieuses* (1882):

> The character of Ultramontanism is manifested chiefly in the ardour with which it combats every movement of independence in the national churches, the condemnation which it visits upon works written to defend that independence, its denial of the rights of the state in matters of government, of ecclesiastical administration and ecclesiastical control, the tenacity with which it has prosecuted the declaration of the dogma of the pope's infallibility and with which it incessantly advocates the restoration of his temporal power as a necessary guarantee of his spiritual sovereignty.
>
> (Benigni 1912)

References

Adler, N. (1986). *International dimensions of organizational behavior*. Boston: Kent Publishing Company.
Amadieu, J.-F. (2003). *Le Poids des apparences*. Paris: Odile Jacob.
Amado, G., Faucheux, C. and Laurent, A. (1998). Changement organisationnel et réalités culturelles. Contrastes franco-américains. In J.-F. Chanlat (ed.), *L'Individu dans l'organisation. Les dimensions oubliées* (pp. 629–62). Sainte-Foy: Les Presses de l'Université Laval.
Arcand, B. and Vincent, S. (1979). *L'Image de l'Amérindien dans les manuels scolaires du Québec ou comment les Québécois ne sont pas des sauvages*. Montreal: Hurtubise HMH.
Aubert, N. (2003). *Le Culte de l'urgence. La société malade du temps*. Paris: Flammarion.
Austin, D. (1970). *Quand dire c'est faire*. Paris: Seuil.

Austin, J. L. (1962). *How to do things with words.* 2nd edn 2005. Cambridge, MA: Harvard University Press.

Balandier, G. (1991). *L'Afrique ambiguë.* Paris: Plon.

Benigni, U. (1912). Ultramontanism. In *The Catholic Encyclopedia* (vol. 15). New York: Robert Appleton Company. http://www.newadvent.org/cathen/15125a.htm

Bourdieu, P. (1989). *La Noblesse d'état.* Paris: Éditions de Minuit.

Bowen, J. R. (2010). *Can Islam be French? Pluralism and pragmatism in a secularist state*, Princeton, NJ: Princeton University Press.

Carroll, R. (1987). *Évidences invisibles.* Paris: Seuil.

Césaire, A. (2005). *Nègre je suis, nègre je resterai.* Paris: Albin Michel.

Chanlat, J.-F. (1998). *Sciences sociales et management. Plaidoyer pour une anthropologie générale.* Paris: Eska.

—— (2002). Le manager à l'écoute des sciences sociales. In Michel Kalika (ed.), *Les Défis du management* (pp. 59–82). Paris: Éditions Liaisons Sociales.

Chanlat, J.-F. (ed.) (1998). *L'Individu dans l'organisation. Les dimensions oubliées.* Paris: Eska.

Chen, A. (2004). *Histoire de la pensée chinoise.* Paris: Gallimard.

Chesnoff, R. Z. (2005). *The Arrogance of the French: Why they can't stand us and why the feeling is mutual.* New York: Sentinel.

Chevrier, S. (2000). *Le Management des équipes interculturelles.* Paris: Presses Universitaires de France.

—— (2003). *Le Management interculturel.* Paris: Presses Universitaires de France.

Clark, H. H. (1979). Responding to indirect speech acts. *Cognitive Psychology*, 11, 430–77.

Crozier, M. (1964). *Le Phénomène bureaucratique.* Paris: Seuil.

—— (1980). *Le Mal Américain.* Paris: Fayard.

Cuche, D. (1996). *La Notion de culture dans les sciences sociales.* Paris: La Découverte.

De Custine, N. (1975). *Lettres de Russie. La Russie en 1839.* Paris: Livres de Poche.

Delacampagne, C. (1983). *L'Invention du racisme.* Paris: Fayard.

Desjeux, D. and Taponier, S. (1994). *Le Sens de l'autre.* Paris: L'Harmattan.

De Tocqueville, A. (1835). *De la démocratie en Amérique.* Paris: Gallimard (new edn, 1985).

Dubar, C. (2000). *La Crise des identités.* Paris: Presses Universitaires de France.

Dufour, M. and Chanlat, A. (1985). *La Rupture entre l'entreprise et les hommes.* Paris: Éditions d'Organisation.

Dupriez, P. and Simons, S. (eds) (2002). *La Résistance culturelle.* Brussels: De Boeck Éditeur.

Dupuis, J.-P. (1998). Anthropologie, culture et organisation: Vers un modèle constructiviste. In J.-F. Chanlat (ed.), *L'Individu dans l'organisation. Les dimensions oubliées* (pp. 533–51). Paris: Eska.

—— (2004). Problèmes de cohérence théorique chez Philippe d'Iribarne. Une voie de sortie, *Management international*, 8 (3), 21–30.

—— (2005). Être 'un maudit français' en gestion au Québec. *Gérer et comprendre*, 9 (81), 51–61.

—— (2008) Culture et gestion au Québec: entre cultures latine, anglo-saxonne et nordique. In E. Davel, J.-P. Dupuis and J.-F Chanlat (eds), *La gestion en contexte culturel: la gestion en contexte interculturel: problémaliques, approches et pratiques* (pp. 1–45). Québec: Les Presses de l'Université Laval.

Eibl-Eibesfeldt, I. (2002). *Éthologie et biologie du comportement.* Paris: Diffusion Operts.

Elias, N. (1974). *La Société de cour.* Paris: Flammarion.

Enriquez, E. (1983). *De la horde à l'état. Psychanalyse du lien social.* Paris: Gallimard.

Etzioni, A. (1988). *The moral dimension: Toward a new economics.* New York: Free Press.

Fanon, F. (2002). *Peau noire, masques blancs.* 2nd edn. Paris: Seuil.

Fernandez, B. (2002). *L'Identité nomade.* Paris: Anthropos et Economica.

Fischer, G.-N. (1990). Espace, identité et organization. In J.-F. Chanlat (ed.), *L'Individu dans l'organisation. Les dimensions oubliées*, Paris: Eska.

—— (1997). *Psychologie des espaces de travail.* Paris: A. Colin.

Flem, L. (1985). *Le Racisme.* Paris: M. A. Éditions.

Francfort, I., Osty, F., Sainsaulieu, R. and Uhalde, M. (1995). *Les Mondes sociaux de l'entreprise*. Paris: Desclée de Brouwer.

Fuentes, C. (1994). *Le Miroir enterré. Réflexions sur l'Espagne et le Nouveau Monde*. Paris: Gallimard.

Fumaroli, M. (2001). *Quand l'Europe parlait français*. Paris: De Fallois.

Futuribles (2002). Les Valeurs des Européens. Les tendances de long terme. *Futuribles*, 7–8, 277.

Gancel, C., Rodgers, I. and Raynaud, M. (2002). *Successful mergers, acquisitions and strategic alliances*. New York: McGraw Hill.

Gasparini, G. (1990). Temps et travail en Occident. In J.-F. Chanlat (ed.), *L'Individu dans l'organisation. Les dimensions oubliées* (pp. 199–214). Paris: Eska.

Geoffroy, C. (2001). *La Mésentente nationale. Voyage au cœur de l'espace interculturel francoanglais*. Paris: Grasset and *Le Monde*.

Girin, J. (1998). Problèmes du langage dans les organisations. In J.-F. Chanlat (ed.), *L'Individu dans l'organisation. Les dimensions oubliées*. Paris: Eska.

Goffman, E. (1973). *La Mise en scène de la vie quotidienne*. Paris: Éditions de Minuit.

—— (1974). *Les Rites d'interaction*. Paris: Éditions de Minuit.

Guigo, D. (1994). *Ethnologie de la vie de bureau*. Paris: L'Harmattan.

Guillaumin, C. (1979). *L'Idéologie raciste, genèse et langage actuel*. Paris: Mouton.

—— (1984). Avec ou sans race? *Le Genre Humain*, no. 11, 'La société face au racisme', 215–22.

Hagège, C. (1985). *L'Homme de paroles: Contribution linguistique aux sciences humaines*. Paris: Fayard.

—— (2005). *Combat pour le français*. Paris: Odile Jacob.

Hall, E. (1966). *La Dimension cachée*. Paris: Seuil.

—— (1979). *Au-delà de la culture*. Paris: Seuil.

—— (1984). *Le Langage silencieux*. Paris: Seuil.

Hampden-Turner, C. and Trompenaars, F. (2000). *Building cross-cultural competence*. New York: John Wiley & Sons.

Hertsgaard, M. (2002). *L'Amérique expliquée au monde entier*. Paris: Stock.

Hofstede, G. (1980). *Culture's consequences: International differences in work-related values*. Beverly Hills: Sage.

—— (1994). *Vivre dans un monde multicultural*. Paris: Éditions d'Organisation.

—— (2002). *Culture's consequences: Comparing values, behaviors, institutions and organization across nations*. London: Sage.

Hofstede, G. and Hofstede, G. J. (2004). *Cultures and organizations: The software of the mind*. New York: McGraw-Hill.

Inglehart, R., Basanez, M. and Moreno, A. (1998). *Human values and beliefs*. Ann Arbor: University of Michigan Press.

Iribarne, P. d' (1993). *La Logique de l'honneur*. 2nd edn; 1st edn 1989. Paris: Seuil.

—— (2003). *Le Tiers monde qui réussit. Nouveaux modèles*. Paris: Odile Jacob.

—— (2004). Face à la complexité des cultures, le management interculturel exige une approche ethnologique. *Management International*, 8 (3), 11–20.

—— (2006). *L'Étrangeté française*. Paris: Seuil.

—— (2008). *Penser la diversité du monde*. Paris: Seuil.

—— (2010). *Les immigrés de la République*. Paris: Seuil.

Iribarne, P. d' (ed.) (1998). *Cultures et mondialisation*. Paris: Seuil.

Jacquard, A. (1985). *Éloge de la différence*. Paris: Seuil.

Joly, A. (1990). Être cadre à l'étranger. In J.-F. Chanlat (ed.), *L'Individu dans l'organisation. Les dimensions oubliées* (pp. 457–506). Paris: Eska.

Jullien, F. (1996). *Traité de l'efficacité*. Paris: Grasset.

Kamdem, E. (1990). Temps et travail en Afrique. In J.-F. Chanlat (ed.), *L'Individu dans l'organisation. Les dimensions oubliées* (pp. 231–55). Paris: Eska.

—— (2002). *Management et interculturalité en Afrique. Expérience camerounaise*. Paris: L'Harmattan.

Kepel, G. (2012a). *Banlieue de la République. Société, politique et religion à Clichy-sous-Bois et Montfermeil*. Paris: Gallimard.

Kepel, G. (2012b). *Quatre-Vingt Treize*. Paris: Gallimard.

Laborde, C. (2008). *Critical republicanism: The hijab controversy and political philosophy*. Oxford: Oxford University Press.

Lagrange, H. (2010). *Le déni des cultures*. Paris: Seuil.

Lamont, M. (2002). *La Dignité des travailleurs. Exclusion, race, classe et immigration en France et aux États-Unis*. Paris: Presses de Sciences Po.

Langaney, A. (1981). Comprendre l'autrisme. La science face au racisme. *Le Genre Humain*, 1, 94–106.

Laurent, A. (1983). The cultural diversity of western conceptions of management. *International Studies of Management and Organization*, 12 (1–2), 75–96.

Lautier, F. (1999). *Ergotopiques. Sur les espaces des lieux de travail*. Toulouse: Octarès.

Le Breton, D. (1998). *Anthropologie des emotions*. Paris: Presses Universitaires de France.

—— (2006). *La Saveur du monde. Une anthropologie des sens*. Paris: Métaillé.

Le Goff, J. (2003). *L'Europe est-elle née au Moyen Âge?* Paris: Seuil.

Le Monde (2004). France, Algérie: Mémoires en marche. 28 October.

Lévi-Strauss, C. (1960). *Tristes Tropiques*. Paris: Plon (new edn, 2000).

—— (1961). *Race et histoire*. Paris: Gonthier.

Lichtenberger, F. (1881). Ultramontanism. In *Encyclopédie des sciences réligieuses*, ed. G. Fischbacher, Paris.

Linton, R. (1967). *Le Fondement culturel de la personnalité*. Paris: Dunod.

Maalouf, A. (1999). *Les Croisades vues par les Arabes*. Paris: Livre de Poche.

Management International (2004). Cultures nationales et gestion. S.I. *Management International*, Spring.

Martin, D., Metzger, J.-L. and Pierre, P. (2003). *Les Métamorphoses du monde. Sociologie de la mondialisation*. Paris: Seuil.

Mauss, M. (1968). *Sociologie et anthropologie*. Paris: Presses Universitaires de France.

Memmi, A. (1957). *Portrait du colonisé*. Paris: Gallimard (new edn, 1985).

—— (1982). *Le Racisme*. Paris: Gallimard.

—— (2004). *Portrait du décolonisé*. Paris: Seuil.

Micklethwait, J. and Wooldridge, A. (2004). *The right nation: Conservative power in America*. New York: Penguin Press.

Mutabazi, E. (2004). Le Management des équipes interculturelles. L'expérience des équipes afro-occidentales en Afrique. *Management International*, Spring, 31–40.

Osty, F. (2002). *Le Désir de métier*. Rennes: Presses de l'Université de Rennes.

Pasquero, J. (2000). Éthique et entreprise: Le point de vue américain. In M. Côté and T. Hafsi (eds), *Le Management aujourd'hui. Une perspective nord-américaine*. Paris: Economica.

Paz, O. (1990). *Le Labyrinthe de la solitude*. Paris: Gallimard.

Pesqueux, Y. (1998). La référence à la valeur actionnariale: Perspectives éthiquese. In *Le rapport moral sur l'argent dans le monde* (pp. 307–16). Paris: Association d'Économie Financière.

—— (2000). *Le Gouvernement de l'entreprise comme idéologie*. Paris: Ellipses.

—— (2004). *L'Entreprise multiculturelle*. Paris: L'Harmattan.

Rocheblave-Spenle, A. M. (1970). *Les rôles masculins et féminins, les stéréotypes, la famille, les états intersexuels*. Paris: Éditions Universitaires.

Said, E. (1997). *L'Orientalisme: l'Orient créé par l'Occident*. Paris: Seuil.

Saire, P.-O. (1995). *L'Acculturation des cadres français au Québec*. Montreal: HEC Montréal.

Saussure, F. de (1978). *Cours de linguistique générale*. Paris: Payot.

Schneider, S. and Barsoux, J.-L. (2003). *Managing across cultures*. New York: Prentice Hall.

Senghor Sedar, L. (1988). *Négritude et civilisation de l'universel*. Paris: Grasset.

Sorge, A. and Harzing, A. W. (2003). The relative impact of country-of-origin and universal contingencies on internationalization strategies and corporate control in multinational entreprises: Worldwide and European perspectives. *Organization Studies*, 24 (2), 187–214.

Sue, R. (1994). *Temps et ordre social*. Paris: Presses Universitaires de France.

Tap, P. (ed.) (1986a). *Identités collectives et changements sociaux*. Paris: Privat.

—— (1986b). *Identités collectives et organizations*. Paris: Privat.

Todd, E. (1984). *Structures familiales et développement*. Paris: Seuil.

—— (1993). *L'Invention de l'Europe*. Paris: Seuil.

Todorov, T. (1995). *La vie commune: Essai d'anthropologie générale*. Paris: Seuil.

Trompenaars, F. (1994). *L'Entreprise multiculturelle*. Paris: Éditions Maxima.

Trompenaars, F. and Hampden-Turner, C. (2004). *Managing people across cultures*. Chichester: Capstone Publishing Ltd.

Vincent, S. (1990). Racisme et hétérophobie dans les organizations. In J.-F. Chanlat (ed.), *L'Individu dans l'organisation. Les dimensions oubliées*. Paris: Eska.

—— (2002). Racisme et hétérophobie dans les organizations. In J.-F. Chanlat (ed.), *L'Individu dans l'organisation. Les dimensions oubliées*. 2nd edn. Paris: Eska.

Webber, R. A. (ed.) (1969). *Culture and management*. Homewood, IL: Irwin.

Weber, M. (2003). *L'Éthique protestante et l'esprit du capitalisme*. Paris: Gallimard.

Weil, P. (2005). *La République et sa diversité, immigration, intégration, discriminations*. Paris: Seuil.

Winnicott, D. (1965). *The maturational processes and the facilitating environment: Studies in the theory of emotional development*. Madison, CT: International Universities Press.

Zweig, S. (1997). *Le Monde d'hier. Souvenirs d'un Européen*. Paris: Belfond.

2 Intercultural analysis in management

Decompartmentalizing the classical approaches

Jean-Pierre Dupuis

Translated from the French by
Nancy Dunham

Introduction

For nearly 30 years, researchers (Hofstede, 1980; Laurent, 1983; d'Iribarne, 1989; Trompenaars, 1994, to name but a few) have studied international management practices from a comparative perspective. Their studies aim to better understand the practices and attitudes of corporate leaders, managers and employees in the different countries and cultures of the world, first in a context of the internationalization of firms, then in a context of the globalization of economic exchanges. These two phenomena have resulted in more and more people working in cultures other than their own, a situation that has caused its share of difficulties. Indeed, the experience has revealed that, contrary to what many Western executives believed, management is not a fixed and universal set of rules and practices but rather a mosaic of local practices, as these studies have shown and tried to explain. Usually, the so-called national culture has been the principal explanatory vector. Thus, if management practices in different countries do not conform to management theory as developed in the United States, it is because the individuals who make up each of these societies have their own way of seeing the world and interacting with one another (their culture), and consequently they are not content to reproduce a Western or American management model: they transform it, appropriate it, infuse it with their culture.

In this chapter, we will present the knowledge on cultures revealed by the two main research approaches in this field to see what they teach us about management in a cross-cultural context. To do this, we will examine the works of two of the authors most representative of these approaches, Geert Hofstede and Philippe d'Iribarne.

In the late 1960s and early 1970s, Hofstede used questionnaires to conduct expansive surveys on employees' behaviours and attitudes at work in different countries or cultures of the world. This approach gained acceptance following the publication of *Culture's Consequences: International Differences in Work-Related Values* in 1980. We will examine the strengths and weaknesses of this now dominant approach, along with the criticisms made against it. This questionnaire approach has been adopted by many researchers in different cultural contexts and has largely inspired others (Schwartz, 1992; Trompenaars, 1994) who have sought to identify other important dimensions in order to understand cultures.

Some with perspectives critical of and opposed to Hofstede's approach have proposed quite another approach. This is the case with Philippe d'Iribarne, the most well-known researcher in this field in the French-speaking world. He also attempts to define the relationships between national culture and management, but through the use of more ethnographic studies (see his major works of 1989 and 1998). His approach is interesting because it is both a radical alternative solution to the dominant perspective and an articulate critique of Hofstede's works. We will also examine the strengths and weaknesses of this approach.

Like most approaches in cross-cultural management, these two approaches focus on national culture. In our chapter, in addition to examining this aspect through the works of Hofstede and d'Iribarne, we will show that along with national culture there are also local, regional and cross-national cultures that have just as much influence on management practices. We will show that it is important to take these cultures into account in management, despite the small amount of knowledge specifically produced for this purpose. Finally, in the last part of the chapter, we will address the question of using this research and knowledge to analyse cross-cultural management and work situations. More specifically, we will propose an integrated use of these approaches in order to draw the most benefit from each.

The dominant perspective: Geert Hofstede's approach

Hofstede's works on cross-cultural management have so profoundly influenced the field that they have become the obligatory reference. Within the space of 10 years, the book *Culture's Consequences* (1980), which presents the results of a vast survey carried out in IBM subsidiaries around the world, was the subject of some thirty reviews and was cited more than 1,000 times in specialized journals. Moreover, other researchers adopted Hofstede's research design in whole or in part in more than sixty studies, by and large confirming the results of his analysis (Sondergaard, 1994). Hofstede himself, in the second edition of his book, published in 2001, reviewed a considerable number of surveys that had used his model.

Hofstede's survey initially involved more than 72 IBM subsidiaries and 116,000 questionnaires administered in two rounds in 1968 and 1972.[1] He retained only about fifty units (a unit is either a subsidiary or a group of subsidiaries from the same cultural region)[2] for the presentation and analysis of his results, eliminating the subsidiaries in which fewer than fifty people were surveyed and where it was not possible to form groups of people on the basis of their culture. The strength of his work lies in several elements, notably sampling size, the attention to controlling variables other than national culture, validation of results by comparison with those of other surveys, the anthropological foundations of his concept of culture and its operationalization through four 'universal' dimensions.

With respect to sampling size, it is important to emphasize the rarity of a study that relies on such an impressive number of respondents from around the world. Hofstede's decision to study subsidiaries of the same corporation in different countries helps to control variables other than national culture, which ensures a certain homogeneity in the profile of the people surveyed with respect to training, education and social class. Hence, it is difficult to attribute the country differences that emerge from the survey to anything other than national culture. Hofstede compares his results at length with those of existing surveys. The comparison not only validates his results but also explains certain more aberrant data (for example, some countries' scores on one of the indices). It also fuels the discussion on the conclusions the author draws with regard to consequences for management. Indeed, without these surveys he would have much less to say on management itself. In this respect, the 1980 work, like its 2001 second edition, is a wealth of erudition, as Chapman (1997) remarked, which largely explains its success.

The dimensions he retained to operationalize his concept of culture derive from a work on data collected in his previous surveys and from an attentive reading of anthropological and sociological texts, particularly those of Clyde Kluckhohn, Alex Inkeles and David Levinson.

Hofstede identified four dimensions that relate to universal truths of societal life, specifically to problems that all human groups must cope with during their lives (see Table 2.1). These four dimensions are Individualism (versus collectivism), Power Distance (large or small), Uncertainty Avoidance (weak or strong) and Masculinity (versus femininity).

In Hofstede's work, 'the variation of country scores along these dimensions shows the position each society takes with regard to these problems'[3] (Bollinger and Hofstede, 1987, pp. 155–56). The scores are calculated based on responses to the questionnaires and the results are given on a scale from 0 to 100, where the higher the score, the more the country is influenced by this dimension. We present Hofstede's results by country on each of the dimensions in Table 2.2.

Hofstede believes the consequences of these cultural differences are important for management, and indeed for 'any social and institutional organization in a country' (Bollinger and Hofstede, 1987, p. 95). They explain the differences that we find in how individuals and organizations are managed in the world. Thus, for example, a high power distance index means that the managers tend to centralize, that the organization is pyramidal, that there is a lot of supervision and that the employees have few qualifications. In contrast, a low index indicates a tendency towards decentralization, a flattened pyramid and less hierarchical supervision (Bollinger and Hofstede, 1987, p. 98).

Similarly, a high or low index on the individualism dimension (a low index indicates high collectivism) produces different consequences: 'the relationships between employers and employees are forged on a moral basis in collectivist cultures, while they are forged on the basis of personal calculation in individualist cultures' (Bollinger and Hofstede, 1987, p. 132); 'Decisions can be taken either by prioritizing personal relationships [high collectivism], or by putting everyone on an equal footing [high individualism]' (Bollinger and Hofstede, 1987, p. 134).

Table 2.1 The fundamental problems faced by human beings and the corresponding dimensions

Fundamental human problems	Description	Dimensions
The relation between individuals and their congeners.	In some societies 'the ties between individuals are extremely loose' and in others they 'are extremely tight' (p. 12).	Individualism (versus collectivism)
How society deals with the fact that people are unequal.	'Some societies try to play down these inequalities in power and wealth as much as possible; others accept them.' (p. 12)	Power distance
How society deals with the fact that time runs only one way [...] and we have to live with uncertainty because the future is unknown and always will be.	'Some societies socialize their members into accepting this uncertainty [...]. Other societies socialize their people into trying to beat the future.' (p. 14)	Uncertainty avoidance
How society organizes the division of roles between the sexes.	'We can classify societies on whether they try to minimize or maximize the social sex role division.' (p. 16)	Masculinity (versus femininity)

Note: Here I used the French summary of the 1980 work that was published in the *Revue Française de Gestion* in 1987, see Hofstede (1987). To read the author's more substantial development of these dimensions, consult the original 1980 edition (Hofstede, 1980, pp. 44–50 and pp. 312–14). I also use the French adaptation of the 1980 edition written by Bollinger in 1987, see Bollinger and Hofstede (1987), in the rest of the text.
Source: After Hofstede (1987).

Table 2.2 Scores by country

Country index values	Power distance	Uncertainty avoidance	Individualism	Masculinity
Argentina	49	86	46	56
Australia	36	51	90	61
Austria	11	70	55	79
Belgium	65	94	75	54
Brazil	69	76	38	49
Canada	39	48	80	52
Chile	63	86	23	28
Columbia	67	80	13	64
Costa Rica	35	86	15	21
Denmark	18	23	74	16
Ecuador	78	67	8	63
Finland	33	59	63	26
France	68	86	71	43
Great Britain	35	35	89	66
Greece	60	112	35	57
Guatemala	95	101	6	37
Hong Kong	68	29	25	57
India	77	40	48	56
Indonesia	78	48	14	46
Iran	58	59	41	43
Ireland	28	35	70	68
Israel	13	81	54	47
Italy	50	75	76	70
Jamaica	45	13	39	68
Japan	54	92	46	95
Malaysia	104	36	26	50
Mexico	81	82	30	69
Netherlands	38	53	80	14
New Zealand	22	49	79	58
Norway	31	50	69	8
Pakistan	55	70	14	50
Panama	95	86	11	44
Peru	64	87	16	42
Philippines	94	44	32	64
Portugal	63	104	27	31
Salvador	66	94	19	40
Singapore	74	8	20	48
South Africa	49	49	65	63
South Korea	60	85	18	39
Spain	57	86	51	42
Sweden	31	29	71	5
Switzerland	34	58	68	70
Taiwan	58	69	17	45
Thailand	64	64	20	34
Turkey	66	85	37	45
United States	40	46	91	62
Uruguay	61	100	36	38
Venezuela	81	76	12	73
West Germany	35	65	67	66
Yugoslavia	76	88	27	21
Arab Countries[a]	80	68	38	53
East Africa[b]	64	52	27	41
West Africa[c]	77	54	20	46
Average	57	65	43	49
Standard deviation	22	24	25	18

Notes: [a] Arab countries: Saudi Arabia, Egypt, United Arab Emirates, Iraq, Kuwait, Lebanon and Libya.
[b] East Africa: Ethiopia, Kenya, Tanzania and Zambia.
[c] West Africa: Ghana, Nigeria, Sierra Leone.
Source: Hofstede (1980).

The author suggests that in the uncertainty avoidance dimension, a high index means 'low ambition for career advancement, and a clear preference for senior hierarchical leaders who are specialists in the activity they manage, a preference for large organizations rather than small ones, a tendency to avoid competition [and conflicts] [...] resistance to change' (Bollinger and Hofstede, 1987, p. 113). Finally, for the masculinity dimension, a high index means a work approach focused more on confrontations, conflicts and self-actualization through one's career, as opposed to femininity, shown by a low index pointing to greater focus on cooperation, humanization of work, group spirit.

The country positions on the various dimensions and the interaction between these dimensions have repercussions on management practices (leadership, organization and motivation). For example, according to Hofstede (1987, p. 18) leadership practices are linked to the individualism and power distance dimensions. In individualist societies such as the United States, the leader's qualities are 'based on the presumed needs of individuals who seek their ultimate self-interest' (Hofstede, 1987, p. 18) while in collectivist societies, leadership 'is a group phenomenon' (Hofstede, 1987, p. 18) in which loyalty to the group is very strong.

Moreover, participation in leadership is possible, even desirable in the United States, a country where power distance is close to the middle zone, although decisions remain the responsibility of the leader who keeps the initiative. In countries with higher power distances, such as many Third World countries, as well as France and Belgium, subordinates generally refuse to participate in leadership. They expect their leaders to act as autocrats, so that, by their own behaviour, they make it difficult for leaders to lead in any other way. Participative management is very rare in France and Belgium (Hofstede, 1987, pp. 18–19).

Geert Hofstede proposes that, while leadership is rooted mainly in the dimensions of individualism and power distance, organization (the fact of organizing) is rooted in the dimensions of power distance, and uncertainty avoidance and motivation in the dimensions of individualism, uncertainty avoidance and masculinity (Figure 2.1 summarizes Hofstede's model). For example, the achievement-based motivation (performance premiums) dominant in American society indicates a low score on the uncertainty dimension and a high score on the masculinity dimension while the security-based motivation (job security) of several European countries indicates a high score on the uncertainty dimension and a low score on that of masculinity.

The interaction of these various dimensions in a culture and in organizations gives rise to diverse configurations of management and organization. Hofstede (1987, p. 14) speaks of the well-oiled machine, typical of Germanic countries, the human pyramid, typical of Latin countries, the family, typical of several Asiatic countries, and the village market, typical of Anglo countries, to illustrate the variety in organization models. Hofstede's data thus permitted him to group countries on the basis of minimal variations on several dimensions in relation to all the other countries. The result of the groupings reveals broad culture areas (Hofstede, 1980, p. 336), cultural clusters already known and defined in popular and scientific literature. However, he was careful to distinguish between developed and less developed areas, wealth being a factor that seems to produce strong variation in the individualism index score (wealth producing high individualism). Hence, he distinguishes Latin (developed and less developed), Anglo, Asian (developed and less developed), Near Eastern, Germanic and Nordic (Northern Europe) cultural clusters in which the countries in each cluster present similar scores on the four indices[4] (see Table 2.3). The countries within each of these clusters usually have a great deal of similarities in terms of management practices.

This broad cultural breakdown has been adopted by several authors to present cultures and their relation to management (see, for example, Hickson and Pugh, 1995). Philippe d'Iribarne,

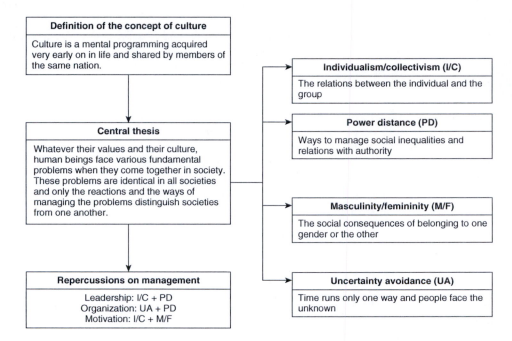

Figure 2.1 The Hofstede model (1987)
Source: Based on Hofstede (1987), prepared by Luc Audebrand.

an author critical of the Hofstede's method, arrives, after several qualitative field surveys, at very similar groupings. These are 'traditional categories: European cultures, which include Germanic or Anglo-Saxon cultures, Maghreb cultures, black African cultures, and other well-known cultures' (d'Iribarne et al., 1998a, p. 293).[5] This point of contact on the traditional categories clearly shows the permanence of these broad regional cultures and the obligation to examine them more closely, as we will do further on.

Critiques of Hofstede's approach

Hofstede (1980, 2001) relies heavily on other studies to present and discuss the consequences of a high or low index. This is often presented as a strength of his study, but it is also one of its main weaknesses. In effect, he refers to other studies not only to validate his results, but also to put flesh on their bones, because his research instrument ultimately provides him with few indications about what is really happening in the subsidiaries he studied. He obtains many responses to questions on important subjects and themes, but he cannot bring them to life except by taking concrete examples from other studies. One might even be inclined to think that these other studies do not validate Hofstede's, but rather the opposite, that his study validates the others. However, it is important to acknowledge the synthesizing aspect of his study that, in a certain way, encapsulates and surpasses all the others by its scope and erudition.

The use of statistical indices to describe a culture and to predict its consequences for management is highly contestable. This approach has been widely criticized by the supporters

Table 2.3 Comparison of the broad cultural clusters using data from the Hermes (IBM) study conducted by Hofstede

Cultural worlds	Power distance	Uncertainty avoidance	Individualism	Masculinity
Developed Latin world (Belgium, France, Argentina, Brazil, Spain, [Italy])	high	high	average to high	average
Less developed Latin world (Columbia, Mexico, Venezuela, Chile, Peru and Portugal)	high	high	low	low to high
Developed Asian world (Japan)	average	high	average	high
Less developed Asian world (Pakistan, Taiwan, Thailand, Hong Kong, India, Philippines and Singapore)	high	low to average	low	average
Near Eastern world (Greece, Iran, Turkey, [Yugoslavia])	high	high	low	average
Germanic world (Austria, Germany, Switzerland and Israel)	low	average to high	average	average to high
Anglo world (Australia, Canada, Great Britain, United States, Ireland, New Zealand, [South Africa])	low to average	low to average	high	high
Nordic world (Denmark, Finland, Netherlands, Norway and Sweden)	low	low to average	average to high	low

Source: Based on Hofstede (1980, p. 336, figure 7.12).

of less positivist approaches. British anthropologist Malcolm Chapman (1997) is surprised, for example, by the use of the questionnaire on attitudes to identify and define cultures, a majority of anthropologists having rejected this method at the end of the 1950s.[6] This forceful criticism has not prevented supporters of this approach from continuing to dominate the field. It explains why Hofstede deals at length with the methodology, discusses the interpretations, increases the number of references to other studies to reinforce his thesis and discredit others (that of cultural convergence, for example) and extensively evaluates certain cultural elements, such as mother tongue influence in some societies where more than one language exist side by side (as in Belgium and Switzerland for example). These discussions were reopened, continued and enriched in a second book (Hofstede, 1991) that uses the same data while adding new information drawn from more recent surveys, again with the aim of validating the first study and of convincing people of its relevance. Supporters and users of Hofstede's approach responded by trying, for example, to 'sharpen' their methodology, exercising greater care in the construction of the questionnaire and in sampling selection (see, for example, Cavusgil and Das, 1997, who list the problems and propose solutions; see also Tayeb, 1994; Nasif et al., 1991; Punnett and Whitane, 1990).

Other critics, such as Thomas (2002), retain mainly the individualism–collectivism dimension to explain cultural differences among countries, notably with respect to management practices. They find the other dimensions much less convincing. Thomas also makes this observation about authors such as Schwartz (1992) and Trompenaars (1994) who developed similar models, but who take into account more dimensions than does the Hofstede model. It is true that the move from traditional societies to modern societies is chiefly a move from collectivist societies to individualist societies and that it is often these differences, between modern Western societies and the traditional societies in the rest of the world, that these studies observe. We will come back to this point further on.

D'Iribarne (1997) is one of the researchers who most forcefully showed the theoretical and methodological weaknesses of Hofstede's approach. Surprised by the high scores of his own country, France, on the power distance and uncertainty dimensions, he tested his approach against Hofstede's and compared the results. According to d'Iribarne, the idea that, based on a high score on the power distance dimension, France can be considered a country without a democratic tradition, even more authoritarian than Iran or South Korea, where power is concentrated in the hands of a handful of people who control and impose their diktat on a submissive and silent majority, corresponds little to the French reality. Indeed, Hofstede does not write just about management, he also writes about how societies function. He generalizes his results to society in general, and not just to the workplace.

But, says d'Iribarne, is Hofstede really talking about power distance or is he talking about hierarchical distance, as the French translation for the term suggests? (The French translation for power distance is *distance hiérarchique*.) According to d'Iribarne, the notions of power and hierarchy do not refer to the same reality. Thus, in France there is a large distance between hierarchical levels, but does that mean a real inequality of power? Does it mean that power is concentrated at the upper levels of the hierarchy? Not at all, believes d'Iribarne, and several studies that he cites in support (by Michel Crozier, by Jean-Louis Barsoux and by Peter Lawrence, among others) show that French managers have a great deal of difficulty exercising authority, influence and power over their employees. In fact, the index built by Hofstede teaches us more about hierarchical distance, and especially about the symbolic aspects, notably prestige, connected with it, than about the exercise and distribution of power in this society and in its organizations. He believes that several countries, such as Indonesia (Bali in particular) and India, are in this situation, in other words, countries where the difference between hierarchy and power is fundamental. In fact, he says, as renowned German sociologist Max Weber pointed out nearly a century ago, the distinction between power and prestige is a characteristic that is found in many societies.

In the case of uncertainty avoidance, d'Iribarne emphasizes the fragility of the index and of Hofstede's interpretation. D'Iribarne believes the responses to the three questions used to build the index on this dimension could just as easily be interpreted in a different or even completely opposite way. For example, the question on stress: while, for Hofstede, high stress at work means strong uncertainty avoidance, for d'Iribarne (1997, p. 43), it could just as well mean the opposite, the existence of weak uncertainty avoidance, since the degree of stress is not controlled in high-stress societies. If we accept this interpretation, France should be rated as having low rather than high uncertainty avoidance. Hofstede did not choose this interpretation, a choice which d'Iribarne disputes.

Like Chapman (1997), we may conclude that Hofstede's entire approach should be rejected because of its methodological weaknesses. Or we can see Hofstede's dimensions and indices as an interesting but imperfect tool to convey the reality of each country or region. The latter hypothesis requires a consistent effort to refine the indices and the questions that support them. Specialists who use this method are working to do just that, and

Hofstede himself has endeavoured to perfect his questionnaire since his famous survey. It also requires that the results be interpreted by drawing on other surveys, other data, in particular those using different methods. Hofstede is doing this too, by reading and using the works of several authors who have a different approach. In addition, historical and ethnographic surveys are required to understand, more diachronically and more thoroughly, the culture of the societies and organizations being studied. To a large extent, this is what a researcher like Philippe d'Iribarne is doing, but it is important to stress that his is a radically different approach. He puts flesh on Hofstede's skeletal construct, as Hofstede candidly remarks:

> The two approaches are complementary – mine is more quantitative, d'Iribarne's more qualitative. I provided a skeleton for the countries he studied, and he provided the flesh. The skeleton I proposed is a worldwide structure in cultural differences among countries.
>
> (Hofstede, 1999, p. 39)

Finally, Philippe d'Iribarne reveals one of the weaknesses of Hofstede's approach, that these cultural dimensions are based on just a few questions within a closed questionnaire. Is that sufficient to describe a culture and its principal dimensions? To ask the question is to answer it. It is obviously an interesting, even a daring strategy, but it is certainly not sufficient.

The historical and ethnographic approach of Philippe d'Iribarne

Since the mid-1980s, Philippe d'Iribarne has developed a very different approach that is based on the study of organizations in different countries and that enables him to show in greater detail the cultural logics at work. In his most well-known study, *La Logique de l'honneur* (The Logic of Honour) (1989), he analyses three subsidiaries of a multinational organization that adopted an American-style management model which he describes as follows: '[one that] accurately and explicitly defines everyone's responsibilities, clearly formulates their goals, allows them freedom to choose methods, carefully evaluates their results and rewards or disciplines them based on their successes and failures' (d'Iribarne, 1989, p. 131).

His study involved three production plants belonging to a parent company, one plant in France, one on US soil and one in the Netherlands. Through observation and interviews with the personnel, he sought to understand how the organization functions in each plant. The comparison of the three subsidiaries owned by one multinational featured the same conditions as in Hofstede's study, in other words, control of the elements other than national culture (same type of production, same management model, same training requirements for employees, for example).

In his survey, he observes important differences in the management methods of the three plants, despite the existence of an officially shared management model. He shows that cultural logics based on fundamental contrasts are at work in each of the cultures[7] and that they explain the differences observed. He identifies these logics by drawing on field data and on their interpretation based on an understanding of the country's history and culture. Thus, facts that were difficult to explain using traditional organization theories, such as the persistence of what at first seem to be averaging behaviours, become meaningful in a historical perspective of the country culture.[8]

In the United States, organizations function according to the logic of the contract, which implies two imperatives, 'free' and 'fair'. In d'Iribarne's own words:

> Everyone must have the possibility to act freely, while being legally bound by the contract, the terms of which they value above all else [free]. And they simultaneously agree to be loyal to a moral imperative of fairness, which requires that a just weighing of individual merits be combined with the respect due to any person [fair].
>
> (d'Iribarne, 1989, pp. 159–60)

The functioning of American organizations relies on significant control to ensure strict compliance with the rules 'of the contract' on the part of both managers and employees. Concretely, this means, for example, scrupulous respect for the chain of command, clearly defined tasks and goals and an evaluation on the basis of these quantified goals, which allows everyone to fulfil their contract in a spirit of equality and honesty. A deviation from these rules may be severely punished and may even lead to an employee's dismissal. To appreciate the power of this principle, one simply has to recall the dismissal of 11,000 air traffic controllers under Reagan, for non-compliance with their contract.

In France, organizational functioning is not at all based on contract logic, even in organizations that adopt American-style management (written rules and goals), but rather on a logic of honour. All the employees in the organization see their work as a set of duties to accomplish. It is custom that assigns 'the particular category to which one belongs (the duties of one's status)' (d'Iribarne, 1989, p. 27). It is these duties, more than the written definition of the tasks, that will serve as references in the execution of their work. In concrete terms, this means more flexibility, that is to say more informal adjustments in the organization since the employees themselves solve a great many of the problems because it is their duty – a question of honour – to see that the work is accomplished beyond the written rules and regulations that determine their task.

This type of functioning – based on duties specific to each status, informal adjustments, a certain moderation in open confrontations, the ability of legitimate leaders to intervene in case of crisis, and cooperation that leads people to do more than their duty in support of those with whom they have good personal relations – is not unique to the Saint-Benoît plant. And, even beyond the French industrial world, it defines, in a remarkably enduring manner over the centuries, a French way of living together (d'Iribarne, 1989, p. 55).

In effect, the specific duties of each employee are duties specific to each status in the organization. In other words, there are managers' duties and duties for maintenance employees or machine operators. The organization is therefore, in reality, organized according to a system of workstations (each one a status) with specific corresponding duties.

In the Netherlands, organizational functioning is based on the search for consensus beyond hierarchical and authority relations. Disciplinary action is limited, discussion being the chief means to correct a situation or to convince employees of the value of an orientation.

Two characteristics of life in Dutch society ensure that this duty to explain, to explain oneself, to listen and to seek agreement sufficiently influences individuals to bring about effective cooperation: first the great importance attributed to what others think, and second the place accorded to factual data (d'Iribarne, 1989, p. 216).

As d'Iribarne explains, the Dutch model is radically different from the two other models:

> What dominates is not the demand to be justly judged and rewarded, on the basis of one's personal merits and faults, nor the demand to act in compliance with the duties

and privileges that custom assigns to the group to which one belongs. It is instead the desire to reach agreements among peers, based on an honest examination of the facts, without which no one is in a position to impose his or her will.

(d'Iribarne, 1989, p. 222)

The organizational game rules, and thus the strategies of the various actors, therefore vary in the three organizations according to each culture's specific social rules. Table 2.4 indicates the main differences in the management logics of the organizations on the basis of these cultural logics. Hence, the sense of duty, the hierarchical relations, the perception of control, the definition of responsibilities and the quality of the cooperation within the organization vary according to national contexts. Moreover, problems specific to these contexts and methods to regulate these problems are also identified within the organizations. Philippe d'Iribarne explains these differences by the different lifestyles and ways of relating to others in the different countries. In France, society is more hierarchical and features a system of social groups ('estates') inherited from the Middle Ages. In the United States, society is more egalitarian and is governed by the contract among citizens. In the Netherlands, society is also more egalitarian and is dominated by the search for consensus. Thus, for d'Iribarne (1989, p. 272) culture is a context, it provides a referential frame of meaning: 'A national culture cannot be reduced to a collection of independent dimensions. It is a set of characteristics possessing a certain coherence.' In this context, management methods and innovation methods must fit with the country's national culture: 'You don't play games with the major principles that govern your country's culture' (1989, p. 201).

Philippe d'Iribarne explains the French workplace system and the logic of honour that governs organizational functioning as a way of living together that has its roots in Indo-European culture and in the estates-based society of the Middle Ages (the three estates being the clergy, the nobility and the third estate)[9] which the French Revolution (citizens equal before the law) did not manage to eradicate in day-to-day relations among the French. In this estates-based system, the logic of honour (see Box 2.1) prevails and the contrast between noble (pure) and vile (impure) is at the heart of this logic. Indeed, every position ('estate') holder – worker, technician or manager – has a noble idea of his/her work and objects to any debasement of that position by too much interference from others in that field of action.

In the United States, the way people work together originated with the first emigrants, the pious merchants, who founded the United States of America. The ultimate example is the colonists travelling aboard the *Mayflower* who first settled in New England in 1620. The Mayflower Compact, signed by the 41 men aboard, established a form of local government in which the colonists agreed to abide by majority rule and to cooperate for the general good of the colony. These merchants belonged to the upper middle classes, shared largely similar conditions and were guided both by puritan ideals and merchant values of honesty. American society was built in the image of the lifestyle of these pious merchants, that is to say around a merchant, contractual logic (honest exchange) and a highly affective community life (community of the faithful).

In the Netherlands, organizational functioning arose out of a society built on ever-renewed compromises. The country was formed as the result of an agreement – the Union of Utrecht of 1579 – among seven provinces to expel the Spanish invaders. A decentralized, federal system was set up that prohibited one province or city from holding a hegemonic position over the others. The French, who occupied the country from 1795 to 1813, abolished this federal system. In the mid-nineteenth century, a consociational democracy was introduced, founded on a pillarization of the society. This democracy stemmed from the refusal of major

Table 2.4 Cultural logics of management and national culture

Country		France	United States	Netherlands
Characteristics of the traditional society		Estates-based society, hierarchy of pure and impure, noble versus vile, values of distinction and unselfishness, monarchic estates (logic of honour).	Act of 1620: contract form, sacred nature of contract, honest market values, pious merchant heritage, executives as delegated authorities.	Functioning of the Union's political institutions: mix of independence and spirit of compromise, *pillarization*, rejection of hegemonic positions.
Typical cultural logic		Logic of honour	Logic of the fair contract	Logic of consensus
Characteristics of the cultural logic	*Sense of duty*	Perform duties dictated by custom (p. 27)	Faithfully respect the terms of the contract (pp. 27, 176)	Seek agreement, and respect agreements reached (p. 257)
	Hierarchic relations	Plurality of relations (p. 38); opacity in relationships (p. 47)	Similar to a client–supplier relationship (p. 256)	Great resistance to pressures (p. 213); transparency in relationships (p. 215)
	Perception of control	Aversion to control (p. 46)	Control of results accepted (p. 158)	Control perceived positively (p. 215)
	Definition of responsibilities	Individual interpretation of responsibilities (p. 45)	Meticulous codification of rights and duties by the superior (p. 138)	Established after discussions (pp. 211–12)
	Disciplinary actions	No disciplinary action admitted to (protection of honour) (p. 24)	Right to discipline based on contract (p. 148)	Strongly rejected (pp. 209, 241)
	Quality of cooperation	Depends on the quality of the personal relationships (pp. 52–55)	Relatively high given the specific nature of the duties (pp. 132–40)	High given the attention accorded to what others think (p. 216)
	Problem	Open conflicts, verbal violence (pp. 28–29)	Arbitrary, subjective aspect (p. 137)	Disengagement, poor treatment of material, absenteeism and turnover (pp. 221–22)
	Regulator	Principle of moderation with informal adjustments (pp. 29, 35)	Mores underlying procedures (honesty, fairness, good faith, etc.) (pp. 141–43, 152)	Precise organization, factual data, predictability, discussion (p. 216)
Management logic		French-style management: know what hurts and denigrates and respect the importance of honour (pp. 98–99)	American-style management: treat staff in accordance with American political values of equality (pp. 185–87)	Consensus management: listen, talk, consult, explain. Refrain from verbal violence. Avoid unpredictable behaviors (pp. 243–44)

Source: Based on Philippe d'Iribarne (1989), compiled by Isabelle Fréchette.

Box 2.1 Honour according to Montesquieu

What is honour? It is, says Montesquieu, 'the prejudice of every person and every rank'. What each group considers as honourable or contrary to honour is not defined by reason, or by law, or by the prince. It is a 'prejudice'. It depends on 'a man's own caprice', and not on another's will. Only a tradition can prescribe it. It is 'less what one owes to others than what one owes to oneself'; it is 'not so much what draws us to our fellow citizens as what distinguishes us from them'. It is intimately linked to pride in one's 'rank' and to the fear of forfeiting it. It strongly prohibits us, when we have been placed in a rank, 'from doing or allowing anything that may make it appear that we hold ourselves inferior to that same rank'. And this is equally true for the privileges linked to the rank as for the duties it imposes. To renounce the former, to run away from the latter, is also on attack on one's honour.

(d'Iribarne, 1989, p. 59)

---

social groups (orthodox Calvinists, Catholics and socialists) to accept the 'growing' domination of the liberal Protestant bourgeoisie. It was 'constituted of four very different groups, which consider themselves fundamentally equal and which refuse to accept the domination of any one group or even of the majority over the minority, while being committed to reaching compromises with one another' (d'Iribarne, 1989, p. 225). Each of these four groups, or blocks, or pillars, of Dutch society 'will develop its own institutions (schools, health care institutions, political parties and later, radios and televisions)' (d'Iribarne, 1989, p. 226). The political system of proportional representation and a system of ongoing concerted action among the large blocks reflected this diversity and this attitude of tolerance and compromise. This system lasted until the 1960s; since then, the large blocks have substantially crumbled, but the spirit of consensus remains and is manifested through the relationships maintained among the interest sectors of Dutch society (agriculture, salaried workers, employers, and others). This desire to work in a spirit of consensus is still found in organizations.

Strengths and weaknesses of d'Iribarne's approach

Three major elements form the strength of d'Iribarne's survey (1989): first, the field study, focusing on life in three plants, draws attention to numerous aspects of organizational functioning; second, the use of the country's and the society's history to understand the culture and to identify cultural logics at work in the organizations; and third, as Barbichon (1990) noted, the comparative analysis of three cases that goes beyond a simple two-term juxtaposition, which is likely to caricature the cultures compared in this way. D'Iribarne's three-way comparison requires the researcher 'to introduce other terms, new dimensions of classification and explanation' (Barbichon, 1990, p. 180 [translation]), to transcend binary thinking (good versus bad organization; open versus closed organization).

Nonetheless, d'Iribarne's work (1989, 1998b, c) does not escape criticism, even of these strong elements. For example, each case is not given the same breadth of treatment, the French case being the most developed, the Dutch case the least developed. The comparison begins with the French case and the primary aim is to clarify that case; however, the author does not shrink from making generalizations about the other cultures as well. As Barbichon (1990) points out, studies of American and Dutch organizations in the three societies

(France, the United States, the Netherlands) would have been a good test of d'Iribarne's interpretation and would have enabled him to extricate himself from this initial bias. But rather than test his first results in this manner, Philippe d'Iribarne preferred to expand his method to other societies and other organizations (see his 1998 [b, c] work which presents several surveys conducted in new countries). Understandably, as he himself says, he is trying to build a classification of cultures,[10] probably in response to that of Hofstede, and, to do so, he needs to increase the number of cultures covered by his surveys. But what he gains in breadth, he inevitably loses in depth, further exposing his generalizations to criticism.

Thus, his portrait of how American society and organizations function does not always correspond to that found in other qualitative surveys. For example, Lamont (1995, pp. 54–59) shows not the rigidity of the rules and the contract, but the pervasiveness of values pertaining to conviviality, conflict avoidance, team spirit and workplace flexibility among American managers and professionals, at least in their relationships with one another. These behaviours noted by Lamont (1995) can be explained by the strong feeling of identification with the community with its fervent emotional tone that d'Iribarne spoke of (1989). However, in the ideal American organization, contract and emotional community are equally balanced and d'Iribarne (1989) seems to neglect this point in his analysis.

Furthermore, the fundamental contrasts he identifies are not always evident (Dupuis, 2004). While the contrast between noble and vile in France is clearly evident and seems quite stable in his analysis, that is not the case for the contrasts in the United States and the Netherlands. In the case of the United States, he uses several contrasts that are rooted in different realities, such as those between contract and community, between individual and community, between liberty and equality, between strong and weak, between free and fair. We believe the contrast between strong and weak best conveys his thinking, but the designations are unstable and they are not always rooted in a real contrast, notably between liberty and equality or between free and fair. In the case of the Netherlands, while we agree some contrasts are apparent, such as those between individual and community, between consensus and conflict, between dominated and dominant, the author does not refer to any of them as being a fundamental, structuring contrast. To our way of thinking, the contrast between unity and diversity, which appears only as a section subtitle, best conveys his ideas.

In fact, in later works d'Iribarne introduces even more ambiguity about the value of his approach and the knowledge uncovered. For example, in a comparative France–Sweden study (d'Iribarne, 1998b), in which he analyses a merger bid between a French firm and a Swedish firm, the logic of honour (and its underlying noble–vile contrast) gives way to a new logic – the dynamic of ideas – characteristic of the French culture. Does this logic replace the other? Is it in addition to the other? In combination with the other? D'Iribarne says nothing on the subject and we have to wonder about the value of the initial logic revealed in his 1989 study.

As well, we clearly feel in his more recent works that, although he does not abandon the ideal of cultural logics and fundamental contrasts, he qualifies his position when he says that there are several ways to be subordinated without losing face, of thinking about and experiencing liberty, of giving meaning to disciplinary actions and challenges (d'Iribarne et al., 1998a, pp. 281–93). This is assuredly a path to explore, but it weakens the idea of defining a culture by one or two fundamental contrasts since the same contrast or contrasts can in some way be found in other cultures. Nevertheless, the question remains of the centrality of a contrast for one culture in relation to others. We might in fact think that, for some societies, certain contrasts are central while, for other societies, they are more peripheral. This perspective would bestow (or re-bestow) relevance on an approach based on fundamental contrasts.

However, it requires more extensive study and work. For now, his model is more unstable, unlike that of Geert Hofstede, which has remained very rigid since the 1980 work, probably also because it is more open to discussion and interpretation.

The openness of d'Iribarne's model to hybrid forms of management

A good example of this openness is the research carried out by d'Iribarne (2003a) in Third World cultures in which he shows, through case studies of organizations, that it is possible to combine modernity and tradition with regard to management. Indeed, one of the weaknesses of the comparative studies of Hofstede (1980, 2001) and d'Iribarne (1989, 1998b, c), in the first versions of their work, is that they assume that cultural context wholly determines the management practices within organizations. Thus, the multinational organizations that these two authors studied, even though they adopt an American-inspired universal management model, see this official management style being flooded by management practices based on the host country's national culture. In this context, by force of circumstance, the actual management style is more reflective of the local culture, and the official management model is merely superficial, sometimes existing only on paper. Yet, in these studies on Western organizations entrenched in the Third World, d'Iribarne (2003a) shows that the multinational's management style is not completely subjugated by the local culture but that a hybridization occurs between the local culture and the so-called universal practices. This viewpoint is more consistent with the findings of contemporary anthropologists, who clearly show that the influence of the West in the rest of the world does not result in the outright adoption of the Western lifestyle, but in the creation of hybrid practices and even hybrid cultures (see Inda and Rosaldo, 2002, for several examples). Let us examine one case in more detail, that of the French organization Danone in Mexico.

The Danone group is the market leader in fresh products in Mexico, with a market share of the order of 40 per cent. The two plants studied by d'Iribarne (2001, 2003b) are remarkably successful, a fact he felt ought to be explored and explained. In fact, he observed a clever mix of modern management and traditional Mexican culture. In terms of modern management, the organization has shortened its chain of command, removing echelons and bringing the organization's directors and employees into closer contact. In the same spirit, the organization practises an open door policy, which encourages the Mexican workers to talk with their managers, whereas prior to this there was no dialogue, as in the majority of Mexican organizations. The company has also introduced the use of the familiar form of 'you' among managers and employees and abolished the executive dining room in order to create a single dining room for all, again in the hope of bringing managers and employees closer together. Finally, the organization has promoted the formation of more autonomous and more responsible work teams. These measures are usually associated with modern participative management. They have been successfully introduced in the organization because they are accompanied by measures rooted in Mexican culture.

In fact, according to d'Iribarne, the organization displays a very un-modern model of cooperation and integration based on the idea of the family. Not an authoritarian family in which 'the father scolds, frightens, causes mistakes to be made' (d'Iribarne, 2001, p. 13) but a family of brothers, 'somewhat modified compared to real families' (p. 13), where friendship and mutual aid dominate. This family is a place where not only the organization, but everyone grows and develops thanks to 'the support received, especially from the organization and one's superiors' (d'Iribarne, 2001, p. 7). This feeling of trust and security and this climate of personal and collective growth create a very strong, very emotional bond with the organization, even total identification on the part of employees: 'These manifestations of strong bonds are directed toward the "whole" created by all the organization's personnel and not toward the managers' (d'Iribarne, 2001, p. 9). A notable example of this family attachment is the 'Let's Build Their Dreams' programme for the community's children in difficulty that, as it were, strengthens and expands the Danone family.

In effect, Danone's strength is to have combined economic association and social progress in Mexican cultural terms. In its organizations around the world, Danone is trying to develop a social component and, according to d'Iribarne (2003b, p. 47, note 14), the Mexican project was defined 'after having studied what Danone subsidiaries were doing in other countries with respect to corporate patronage, protection of endangered species, cultural sponsorship, and so on. It [the programme chosen] appeared to be the best adapted to Mexican society.' This programme creates a vast community that transcends the organization's borders and that everyone is proud to belong to. In this way, Danone's Mexican organization contrasts strongly with

> the usual operational style employed in Mexican organizations, as it appears through the experience, in other organizations or in the past in Danone, of the people we met, [and which] is characterized by strong individualism. Peers cooperate poorly, even amongst those who are part of the same work team, superiors are authoritarian and distant, entry-level workers are seldom given responsibilities and are not considered deserving of the organization's trust. Unions maintain a mistrustful attitude toward the company. This situation is even more frustrating because everyone has a deep desire to achieve his or her full potential, to grow, and feels blocked in this desire. This relationship style contrasts strongly with that found in the family, where people pay attention to one another, help one another, support one another, in both their desire for security and their desire to grow.
>
> (d'Iribarne, 2003b, p. 54)

Danone thus managed to reproduce in the workplace, at least in part, the practices and values of the Mexican ideal family. Of course, the experience is not perfect. For example, employees believe that the organization has progressed only part-way along the path and that there is still much to accomplish. D'Iribarne (2001, p. 14) himself points out 'this did not lead them to a great deal of individual autonomy in their work, but it did promote the development of a strong collective autonomy at the core, an autonomy that also fosters the implementation of an effective way of functioning'.

Other examples documented by d'Iribarne show a similar approach. For example, in the case of a French organization in Morocco, d'Iribarne (2003c) explains the organization's success by the implementation of a total quality management (TQM) programme that proved to be in accordance with the Muslim workers' culture, particularly with teachings of the Koran (transparency, simplicity of relationships, for example). In effect, he shows that the organization was able to benefit from this favourable situation thanks to the 'leadership style of the director general, the emphasis placed on specifications, and [good] training policies' (2003c, p. 83). D'Iribarne (2003c, p. 89) writes:

> The highly ritual aspect of the TQM, the increase in the number of 'specifications', which have to be followed to the letter in order to remain TQM […] fits in well with the fact that respect for ritual obligations holds an important place in the definition of 'a good

Muslim'. Good Muslims scrupulously attend to their five daily prayers, having appropriately purified themselves, and faithfully observe Ramadan.

These examples of successful cultural encounters between modern management practices and traditional cultures are obviously somewhat idealized by d'Iribarne (2003a), but they have the advantage of showing other paths for organizations rather than the imposition of their management model or total adaptation to the local culture. A successful approach involves the creation of hybrid and very often innovative management practices that borrow from the cultures of the host countries. These hybrid practices also reconcile two apparently contradictory movements observed by some specialists: that pertaining to the development of universally held best practices and that pertaining to the affirmation of a people's identity and culture.

What knowledge of culture is gained?

Hofstede's approach (1980, 2001) is of interest because it gives us an overall vision of a very large number of cultures from around the world and in particular the ability to compare them on the same dimensions (the four dimensions) and from the same database (the IBM survey). The knowledge produced is general and somewhat skeletal but it is enriched by the use of other studies, both qualitative and quantitative. They give us relevant information on management in these cultures. D'Iribarne's approach (1989, et al. 1998a) is to examine cultures in greater depth by trying to identify the cultural logic specific to a country (a nation), but his scope is more limited, covering fewer countries, and his approach is less systematic, not always dealing with organizations and cultures in the same way (sometimes he emphasizes certain aspects of management, other times the overall dynamic of the organizations).

Both approaches shed additional light on cultures in that Philippe d'Iribarne's fleshes out the cultural structure identified by Geert Hofstede, at least for the countries covered by his surveys. They both arrive at regional typologies of cultures identifying broad culture areas in the world: Anglo(-Saxon), Latin, Maghrebian, Asian to name a few. As well, they specifically studied the differences within Western Europe, both researchers' native region, presenting the differences among the cultures in this region of the world: Anglo(-Saxon), Germanic, Latin, Scandinavian, for example. These typologies make it possible to distinguish different management models among the cultural regions. They are therefore a corpus of knowledge that enables us to understand cultural differences and to comprehend in part their repercussions on management.

However, we believe it is important to reposition these works in a framework that transcends the national context, in order to better measure their significance and to use them more effectively.

Beyond national cultures

The broad regional breakdowns outlined by both authors are a first step in this direction. They show that beyond national differences there are broad areas that share a certain number of cultural characteristics and that therefore it is possible to approach them as cultural entities in themselves. One of the principal ways to understand a national culture is to see its affiliation with a wider culture area. But, beyond even that, there is, as we have already stated, a broad cultural breakdown at the global level, this being the divide between modern societies and traditional societies, which sociologists and anthropologists revealed a long time ago, and which overhangs national breakdowns and the breakdown of broad culture areas. Fundamental differences are revealed with regard to several dimensions of culture and to the relations the individuals have with one another in these societies (see Table 2.5). These differences can be observed in respect to organizational management. For example, traditional societies are more collectivist and local populations react badly to individualist management models (control, motivation and individual rewards systems). Or for another example, business or work contracts in traditional societies rely more on trust than on written texts that define each person's obligations, the latter procedure being rooted more in the attitude of mistrust typical of modern societies.

It should be noted, however, that within so-called modern societies it is possible and quite common to find more traditional living spaces (rural areas for example), and inversely to find modern living spaces (very often large cities) in traditional societies. The cultural breakdown between traditional societies and modern societies is not a simple breakdown between the modern West and the rest of the world. For a modern organization with urbanite managers, to locate in a rural setting in Canada can be as confusing as locating in Mexico. In Mexico, in the capital or along the US border, for example, organizations can find employees who have experience of North American companies and who participate in an urban and modern lifestyle. On the other hand, in a rural setting, in Canada or elsewhere, these employees are more difficult to find. This is the experience of many manufacturing companies who choose to build a plant in a rural area of their own country or in the Third World because of the low labour costs. In these cases, managers may be surprised by the collectivist aspects of life both within the plant and beyond its walls.

This first broad breakdown of human groups transcends national cultures and teaches us about broad cultures (traditional or modern) that have a set of diametrically opposed values and practices (behaviours) which it is important to know about. A second broad breakdown further illuminates the knowledge produced by cross-cultural management researchers such as Geert Hofstede and Philippe d'Iribarne. It presents and organizes in a different way the knowledge on cultures that they gathered. This breakdown highlights two major cultural dynamics that have dominated the world for several centuries and that, in our opinion, continue to influence it. They are the dynamic of liberty and equality and the dynamic of honour and hierarchy.

The former promotes strong individualism, values of liberty, equality and democracy, and tends to reduce power distances (symbolic or real) in the society. This dynamic is

Table 2.5 First broad cultural breakdown of human groups

Dimensions	Modern societies	Traditional societies
Nature of the human being (perception of the human being)	Bad; cannot be trusted	Good; can be trusted
Individual's relationship with nature (relation with the world)	Domination	Harmony or submission
Individual's relationship with others (personal relations)	Individualism	Collectivism
Principal activity style	Act, do	Be
Concept of time	Future-oriented	Past-oriented
Concept of space	Distinction between private space and public space	No distinction between private space and public space

Source: Adapted from Adler (1994, pp. 22–23).

spreading in the world. Starting in Northern Europe, it has conquered a large part of Europe and moved to North America and Oceania (Australia, New Zealand). The expansion and domination of the capitalist system around the world nourishes and transports it to the four corners of the globe, where it is compared with other cultural dynamics, in particular the dynamic of honour and hierarchy (see Figure 2.2 on the migration of cultural values and dynamics). The latter dynamic, which dominated the old economic world (the pre-capitalist world), was organized around patriarchal societies and their values of hierarchy and honour (importance of saving face). These values reigned across the Mediterranean world and as far as East Asia (Burton et al., 1996). The silk and spice trade route crossed that vast expanse and made these often nomadic societies the masters of the world in that immense economic trading zone.[11] In fact, patriarchal societies controlled and regulated trade all along the route. This dynamic was transported, in its Spanish and Portuguese version, to Latin America where it took on a distinct character following contact with the indigenous peoples.

These two major dynamics transcend the national cultures that often serve as reference points for discussing the relation between culture and management, as in the surveys by Hofstede and d'Iribarne that we have presented. This second broad breakdown of the cultural differences in the world profoundly influences national, regional, local and organizational sub-sets. Other dynamics exist at this level but they are more marginal and most

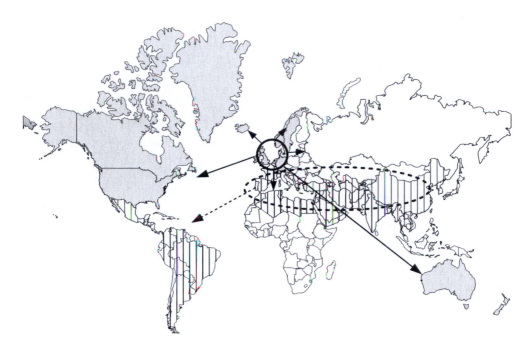

Figure 2.2 Map of the migration of cultural values and logics

    Notes: Grey: the logic of liberty and equality, high individualism, and small power relations (symbolic or real) are spreading around the world. The circle illustrates the origin of this logic and the arrows pointing outward, its spread across the world.

    Lined: The logic of honour, the importance of saving face, large power distance (symbolic or real) dominated the old economic world (pre-capitalist) and correspond to the culture area of traditional patriarchal societies, illustrated by the dotted ellipse.

    Source: Constructed on the bases of Hofstede (1980), d'Iribarne (1989, 1998), Hickson and Pugh (1995) and Burton et al. (1996).

importantly, they have been less studied in cross-cultural management. We are thinking in particular of the circulatory dynamic that according to Rwandan researcher Evalde Mutabazi (2000) includes all of black Africa. Other logics, such as that of Russia and Eastern European countries (Ukraine, Poland and others) for example, need to be explored and documented. Nevertheless, these two dynamics are key to understanding today's world and the various cultural confrontations seen both in the world and in organizations.

It is certain, however, that this breakdown diminishes the reality, over-simplifies it; but it helps us begin to understand the fundamental cultural differences in the world. It must be supplemented by more detailed analyses to better convey national, regional, local and organizational contexts, and, on that score, the works of Hofstede, d'Iribarne and others are all useful. In fact, this breakdown allows us to place a large number of the culture areas identified by these two authors into one or the other of the two cultural dynamics (see Tables 2.6 and 2.7). Thus, the Anglo(-Saxon) (England, Australia, Canada, United States), Germanic (Germany, Austria, Switzerland, the Netherlands) and Scandinavian (Sweden, Denmark, Norway) worlds belong to the major dynamic of liberty and equality, as does a country such as France, which belongs to this dynamic while still being part of the dynamic of honour and hierarchy, as d'Iribarne (1989) shows in his book *La Logique de l'honneur*. In contrast, other surveys by d'Iribarne (1998b, c) show the full importance of the modern values of liberty and equality, notably his comparative France–Sweden survey in which the French demonstrate their penchant for liberty as compared to the Swedes who are resolutely egalitarian. In fact, the demarcation line that separates the two dynamics in Europe passes right through the centre of France.

In these worlds and countries, the perpetual tensions between the values of liberty and equality are the cornerstones of life in these societies. These tensions are embodied for example in the conflict between the political parties on the right that value liberty and those on the left that promote equality. According to several observers, it is clear, for example, that in the Anglo world, the value of liberty predominates, while in the Germanic and Scandinavian worlds, equality usually takes precedence. The Anglo world's emphasis on liberty is reflected by the greater liberty allowed to entrepreneurs and executives in the management of their organizations (for example, fewer regulations affecting organizations and easier dismissal)

Table 2.6 The cultural dynamic of liberty and equality

Common core		
Characteristic principles		*Repercussions on management*
High individualism		Autonomy and responsibility
Pressure for equality		Small power distance
Cooperation		Value the participation of all
Conflict avoidance		Clear procedures or mechanisms
Separation of private life/work life		Impersonal management
Broad cultural areas (regional varieties)		
Anglo world	*Germanic world*	*Scandinavian world*
England, Australia, Canada, United States	Germany, Austria, Switzerland, the Netherlands	Denmark, Finland, Norway, Sweden

Source: Constructed on the basis of Hofstede (1980), d'Iribarne (1989, 1998), Hickson and Pugh (1995).

Table 2.7 The cultural dynamic of honour and hierarchy

Common core		
Characteristic principles	*Repercussions on management*	
Authoritarianism	Centralization of power; large power	
Importance of saving face (honour)	distances	
Non-separation of private life/work life	Deference in work relations ('being subordinate without losing face')	
	Personal/paternalistic management	
Broad cultural areas (regional varieties)		
Latin world	*Arab world*	*Asian world*
Southern Europe	North Africa	Central Asia
Central America	Near East	South Asia
South America		East Asia

Source: Constructed on the basis of Hofstede (1980), d'Iribarne (1989, 1998), Hickson and Pugh (1995).

than that allowed in the Germanic or Scandinavian worlds, or in France, where organizations live with more constraints and where employees benefit from greater protection at work.

What differentiates these worlds, besides the greater emphasis on liberty or equality, is often the central role of another value within the society. For example, in the liberty and equality dynamic, the importance of the laissez-faire value for the Anglo world, consistent with and strengthening the value of liberty, differentiates it from the Germanic world where the emphasis is more on state intervention and order. In France, it is clearly the omnipresent idea of honour in society that influences the country's cultural dynamic.

The Latin (Southern Europe, Latin America), Arab (North Africa and the Near East) and Asian worlds (Central Asia and East Asia) belong to the dynamic of honour and hierarchy. In these worlds, hierarchy, whether symbolic or real, occupies a central place and determines authoritarian work relations and a substantial centralization of power. The importance of saving face is very strong. Individuals cannot and must not be publicly humiliated. This being so, relations are very formal and demands are made by indirect means that do not offend people's sensibility. As d'Iribarne et al. (1998a) say, subordinates may have to submit to the authority of the organization's managers but they must be able to do so without losing face. As such, communication is achieved more through context, through non-verbal signs and through respect for formal rituals, than through the American-style honest and direct approach. As well, in these worlds, no distinction is made between private life and work life. As a result, personal, family and professional relations mix together, which always surprises people from worlds belonging to the liberty and equality dynamic in which great care is taken to separate private and professional lives.

Here again, what differentiates these worlds is how each one combines honour and hierarchy, and other values that orient the cultural dynamic of each world in one direction instead of another. In the East and Southeast Asian worlds for instance, the quest for virtue, extolled by Buddhist philosophy in particular, is opposed to the search for truth, a veritable obsession in Christian religions, the Catholic world (including Latin countries) or the Muslim world (including Arab countries) for example, according to Hofstede (1991). Thus, while Asians are able to reconcile different positions, to move from one position to the other depending on the circumstances and the stakeholders, the same is not true of the other groups. These differences are rooted here in a greater contrast: that between the Western world and the Eastern world (the Far East).

Within the national culture

We wanted to show that beyond national cultures there are broader cultural dynamics and culture areas that assemble cultures in large groups sharing a certain number of cultural characteristics. This excursion into the broader groups should not make us forget that within national cultures, cultural diversity also exists, and that it is important to take it into account. This internal cultural diversity is based theoretically on several factors: existence of cultural and linguistic minorities, geographic isolation, different natural settings, distance from the country's power centres, to name a few. Let's examine some of these factors.

The existence of cultural and linguistic minorities necessarily introduces diversity in a society, although the dominant culture can ignore this or these minorities. Nevertheless, for the people living in this society, the cultural attitudes and behaviours may not correspond exactly to those identified in studies on national cultures that generally focus on the dominant culture. In Canada, for example, Hofstede's celebrated study (1980) did not include French Canadians for methodological reasons (a single culture per nation). Yet, several studies (see Dupuis, 2002, for a presentation of these) show there are differences between English-speaking North Americans, including English Canadians and French Quebecers, with respect to management. The latter have a more community-based management style, more focused on equality, participation, accommodation and some form of consensus, that places Quebec in the same category as the small societies of Northern Europe such as Belgium, the Netherlands and Sweden for example (Dupuis, 2002).

Canada's case is not an exception, but rather the rule. Such cultural diversity is found in several European countries – Belgium (the Flemish and the Walloons), Spain (Catalans, Basques), Switzerland (German-, French- and Italian-speaking), the former Yugoslavia (Serbs, Croats, Slovenians, Muslims, Macedonians), for example – and in the United States. In the latter case, there are differences between the large East Coast, Southeastern, Midwest, Southwest, Northwest and West Coast regions. These differences refer not only to contrasting geographic spaces but also to different populations. The Northeast was first settled by immigrants from England while the Southwest has a large population that originated in Mexico and Central American countries. In the nineteenth century, a population arriving from the Scandinavian countries settled in the Northwest, while a very large German immigration occurred in the Midwest during the same period. A large part of the black American population still lives in the Southeast. The West Coast is still a land of immigration, from within and outside the US, which makes it a particularly dynamic region. Thus, people in the different regions of the United States do not enter into relationships in the same way, no more than they do business in the same way. For instance, 'the concept of time [...] is substantially different: in the South and the West. In terms of accuracy [...], people's attitude is far more tolerant than on the East Coast. In short, "monochronism" is much less absolute' (Hall and Hall, 1990, p. 125 [translation]), meaning that the pace of life is slower, that people take the time to talk and get to know one another and that lateness is more accepted. Business and management are done in a more relaxed atmosphere and people are just as important as the tasks to be accomplished.

In Asia, cultural and linguistic minorities are also present in most countries. Thus, in China, the 8 million Uygurs, who represent a large portion of the population of Xinjiang, are Muslims of Turkic descent. They do not have the same values and attitudes as the Han Chinese who make up the majority of China's population. They want more autonomy, or even independence to better defend their culture and their traditional institutions, which are threatened by the arrival of millions of Han from the east (Philip, 2006). They are not the only minority in China. More than 150 have been listed, although the Chinese government officially recognizes only about fifty, the most important of these being the Manchu, Hui, Miao, Yi, Tujia, Mongolian and Tibetan groups that all have between 4 and 8 million members.[12] India, to take another example, includes, besides the Hindu majority, several large cultural groups such as Sikhs, western Muslims and Dravidians, each of which speak their own national language (Sikh, Urdu or Dravidian). In fact, there are more than eighteen official languages and 1,600 dialects spoken in the country.

In Africa, each country is a veritable cultural mosaic, comprising from a few to several hundred cultures on the same national territory. For example, Cameroon has more than 100 ethnic groups (Kamdem, 2002, p. 257) in which more than 270 languages are spoken, in addition to English and French that have the status of national languages, for a population of nearly 17 million people. These groups exhibit important differences in regard to their social, political and economic organization. For example, a strong contrast exists between the groups originating in the Semi-Bantu territory (such as the Bamenda, Bamileke and Bamum) and those originating in the Bantu territory (notably the Douala, Bakoko, Bakweri, Bassa, Batanga and Malimba). The former, who reside chiefly in the southwest and west of the country, 'live in a very hierarchic and highly centralized monarchic-style social organization' while the latter, whose territory covers almost the entire centre and south of the country, 'have a traditional social organization based on lineage and the clan, relatively informal, highly decentralized and with little hierarchy' (Kamdem, 2002, p. 260 [translation]). Understandably, these differences, particularly those pertaining to the presence or absence of a strong hierarchy or strong centralization, have implications for the management of people and organizations. In addition, we find in Cameroon a group, the Bamileke, highly reputed for its entrepreneurial attitudes and behaviour,[13] who do not have the same relationship with money and business as other Cameroon groups, or Africans in general. According to Dogmo (1981, in Kamdem, 2002, p. 263), this situation 'leaves no one indifferent, creating jealousy among some, admiration and respect or desire among others'. Here again, it is understood that doing business with the Bamileke, with their strong business sense and work ethic, will be different from working with other groups that are less focused on these values.[14]

In Latin America, the presence in many of the countries of large Amerindian populations alongside European descendants may hugely influence national cultures, not to mention the slavery heritage that has created large black populations. Hence, according to Lemogodeuc and his associates (1997, p. 112), we can distinguish three broad culture areas in South America: an Afro-Latin area in the Caribbean located in a low tropical region and with poor productivity (northeastern Brazil is also an Afro-Latin area); a Euro-Latin area represented by Argentina, Uruguay, Costa Rica, the far south of Chile and southern Brazil which occupies a low and temperate region; and a mixed-culture area with enclaves of exclusively indigenous populations in Mexico, Guatemala, the Andes and the Amazon basin.

So, within several countries, there are often regions that are more Europeanized and regions that have stayed closer to Amerindian values, influenced by a large black population. That said, working with descendants of Europeans, or with Amerindian or highly mixed populations, is not the same thing. The dynamic of honour and hierarchy, which we spoke of for Latin America and which comes from Europe, was grafted onto the collective and community logics of the Amerindians, or onto the more egalitarian African logics, giving rise to syncretic, hybrid practices that influence this broad culture area. Therefore, we have on the one hand, a Brazilian-style feudal management, derived from the Portuguese organization of the territory, and on the other hand, a highly community-based management such as that involving a large number of black culture organizations in the city of Salvador de Bahia (Joly, 1996, 2004; Dantas, 1994).

Apart from these cultural and linguistic minorities, there may be regions or groups belonging to the majority culture, but that are in more distant geographical areas far from the power centres, that develop local or regional cultures that differ on certain points from the dominant culture of the country. We often find in these areas a breakdown between modern societies (large urban centres) and traditional societies (rural areas). The south of France or of Italy versus the dominant north, Abitibi or the Saguenay versus the urban area of Montreal in Quebec, or the Andean plateau region versus Lima in Peru. Hence, in many countries, there may be culture differences between populations living in mountain regions versus plain regions, in tropical forest versus savannah, in desert versus coastal regions. Climate and geography here dictate the methods of organization, interaction and exchange that may be sharply contrasting.

An author such as Philippe d'Iribarne (1993) is very aware of these differences. He says, in regard to France, that there can be as many differences between local and regional organizations as there can be between organizations in France and those in other countries.[15] However, he did not work on these internal differences but rather on the differences between nations. Anthropology possesses a wealth of data on these more local or regional differences and cultures, but unfortunately few researchers have made use of this material in the field of cross-cultural management. To have a more detailed knowledge of cultures, and of local and regional varieties of national cultures, and to be more effective when we do business or manage organizations in these contexts, we must use and develop this knowledge. There is still much to be done by researchers in cross-cultural management.

The importance of cross-cultural knowledge

Cross-cultural knowledge teaches us about cultures and, at the same time, helps us to understand them, and in particular to understand the attitudes and behaviours of the people who belong to these cultures. But is this knowledge reliable, or valid, or universal? To answer these questions, it is important to remember a few things about cultures. First, cultures are not stable entities that have a set content once and for all. On the contrary, cultures are all dynamic, constantly moving and endlessly renewing. Certainly there is the idea of a solid core that gives meaning to the concept of culture. But, as several authors have shown, it is possible to write several scenarios on the basis of this core. Philippe d'Iribarne (1989) shows for example that the France of the Ancien Régime (pre-revolutionary) and the France of the Republic (post-revolutionary), which differ greatly with respect to political power, social organization and other dimensions, share the same cultural core, namely the logic of honour based on the noble versus vile contrast, that we find alive and well in day-to-day interactions within the society and its organizations. Moreover, onto this logic of honour was grafted a logic of ideas originating in the Age of Enlightenment, in which reason dominates and reshapes, as it were, the traditional idea of honour. This provides us with a better understanding of modern-day France.

Second, it is also important to know that the existence of a culture does not necessarily imply that all the members of the society share its dominant values or its key shared references. Members know about these values or references but some may strongly oppose them. For example, some nostalgic French citizens may see the glory of the past in former values typical of the Ancien Régime, not of the Republic. In Quebec (Canada), certain cultural values are contested by Quebecers of all cultural backgrounds, including the native French-speaking population. Some maintain that Quebecers are first and foremost Americans while others loudly proclaim the existence of a significant difference between Quebecers and other North Americans. Illustrating this point is the debate that opposes historians Gérard Bouchard and Yvan Lamonde (1995), ardent defenders of Americanicity, to define Quebecers' identity, and sociologist Joseph Yvon Thériault (2005), who believes Quebecers contribute an original point of view on America and its culture. The former try to prove their point of view by listing the many American behaviours adopted by Quebecers, while the latter instead draw attention to the singularity of the Quebec community in America. We find this tension between the American and Quebec models in the debates about the nature of Quebec's economic model and management practices (see on this subject Dupuis, 1995, 2000).

Furthermore, knowledge about cultures is not set in concrete but is relative knowledge that fluctuates according to the context and the actors. Thus, to Germans, Quebecers seem polychronic, as German researcher Christof Barmeyer (1994) has shown, while to Mexicans, Quebecers seem monochronic, as my own research has shown. So are Quebecers polychronic or monochronic? The answer is both simple and complicated: they are neither or, if you prefer, they are both at once! They are neither because, in and of themselves, Quebecers are not monochronic or polychronic, they are one or the other solely through the lens of their relationships with others. And since they have relationships with many others, they are necessarily both at once!

That being said, knowledge of cultures is reliable and valid, but only in context. However, this context is not, and cannot be, universal. In other words, this knowledge is not true all the time and everywhere, for everyone, either within a culture or between cultures. It is relative and, as such, it must be utilized prudently, as an initial exploration of the other, which must then be built on through direct, real interactions that are the result of the to-and-fro between action and thought. Which means that, when we meet people from another culture, we have to use this knowledge to try to understand them through who they are and what they do and say, but we should not confine them within the bounds of our knowledge of culture. They may confirm or overturn this knowledge, but we must not draw conclusions too quickly about either the truth or the falsity of the knowledge. One case does not make or break a body of knowledge or a theory. And above all, first contacts do not say everything about the individual standing before us, or about their culture. We need time to see things clearly. We have to take our time. Nevertheless, this knowledge does allow us to make hypotheses that we will be able to validate or invalidate through contacts and interactions, and that will help us to know the other. It is in this sense that this knowledge is useful, and not as final and definitive knowledge.

Let's take a more concrete example. A Canadian manager is preparing to go and work in France: will he find centralized, bureaucratic and hierarchical organizations as Hofstede's model predicts? And do the French managers behave in accordance with this type of organization? In both cases, we can answer maybe, but not necessarily. What Hofstede's model tells us, irrespective of the strong criticisms made in its regard, is that on average we will find this type of organization and these types of attitude and behaviour, but not necessarily, since there may be more or less pronounced deviations from this average. These deviations are linked to other factors, to the context as we mentioned above, but also to the different personalities that are found in a society, and to other cultural elements, such as the occupational culture or the regional culture, which will moderate the effect of the national culture. However, our Canadian manager will not be surprised to find these attitudes and these behaviours in his French counterpart. He must nevertheless avoid confining his counterpart to the caricatured model described by Hofstede and make room to build a cross-cultural dialogue, since the other can never be reduced to just his culture. He is above all a person who can make different choices from those that dominate in his culture.

The knowledge produced by d'Iribarne's approach must be considered and utilized in the same way. Knowledge is not always easily available. We do not have, at least in cross-cultural management, as much of this type of research on cultures. However, we can read the works of anthropologists who do research on cultures. They often bring to light the deep-seated logics of the cultures they study. In fact, identifying the distinctive meaning of each culture is the chief purpose of contemporary anthropologists. This knowledge of national cultures must then be put into context, on the one hand in regard to the internal diversity distinctive to each culture[16] and, on the other hand, by their affiliation with broader cultural sets (broad regional cultures). The national culture is thus an entry point into the culture of a society. It is not the only component.

In conclusion: linking cross-cultural analysis approaches to improve understanding and to improve management

The goal of this chapter was to examine the knowledge produced by researchers in cross-cultural management. What type of knowledge do they produce? What is the value of that knowledge? What are its uses? We have examined in particular two dominant models in the field of cross-cultural management, those of Geert Hofstede and Philippe d'Iribarne. These two models are highly representative of the field, and they differ both in the way they produce this knowledge and in how they present it. Hofstede's approach to culture is more statistical. He relies on a quantitative methodological instrument and his results are in the form of synthesized tables. D'Iribarne's approach to culture is more historical and relies on case study methodology. He presents his results in the form of short or long monographs.

The two approaches can be presented as complementary, as Geert Hofstede argues when he focuses on the similarity of some results, or as opposing, as Philippe d'Iribarne argues when he instead stresses the differences in the methodology. For our part, we have presented the works of these two authors as sources of knowledge on cultures, and as a means to analyse different management situations, and we have pointed out their strengths and their weaknesses. We believe they are useful to better understand cultures and the management that is practised within these cultures, as long as we do not assume they provide complete and definitive knowledge of cultures. We have tried to show that beyond and within national cultures there are other cultural elements that must also be taken into account. This knowledge has to be put into context to extract the most benefit from it, and it must be used as a hypothesis to explore cultures and the management logics practised within these cultures.

Notes

1 The questionnaires were administered to employees and the original aim was to evaluate their satisfaction at work. The discovery of country differences inspired the author to explore the cultural hypothesis as an explanation.
2 For example, the author grouped under East Africa the questionnaires from Ethiopia, Kenya, Tanzania and Zambia, and under West Africa those from Ghana, Nigeria and Sierra Leone; he grouped Saudi Arabia, Egypt, United Arab Emirates, Iraq, Kuwait, Lebanon and Libya under the Near East.
3 All quotations from Bollinger and Hofstede (1987) used in this chapter are translated from the French.

4 Hofstede grouped 'the countries within a small group of countries having identical levels of variables: the differences between countries in the same cluster must be minimal, while the differences between the countries in different clusters must be as great as possible'. The statistical technique used to form the clusters 'is a hierarchical cluster analysis displayed in a *dendrogram*' (Bollinger and Hofstede, 1987, p. 167).

5 All quotations from d'Iribarne used in this chapter are translated from the French.

6 He is referring here to the vast Human Relations Area Files project that, in his opinion, proved to be a failure.

7 D'Iribarne (1989, p. vi) writes in the preface to the soft cover edition of his book: 'The continuity of each culture, although it is influenced by many changes, stems from the stability of the system of fundamental contrasts on which it is built.'

8 The following presentation of d'Iribarne's book (1989) is based in part, but expands on, the presentation in Dupuis (1998, pp. 234–36).

9 Note that each large estate comprised

> in its turn many subgroups. Thus, wrote Tocqueville, 'to faithfully portray the estate of the nobility, one would have to distinguish the Nobles of the Sword from the Nobles of the Robe, the Nobles of the Court from the Nobles of the Provinces, the hereditary nobles from the recent; one would find in this small society almost as many nuances and classes as in the general society of which they were only one part'.
>
> (d'Iribarne, 1989, p. 62)

10 As clearly indicated by the title of Chapter XI: 'From a collection of case studies to a classification of cultures' (d'Iribarne et al., 1998a, p. 277).

11 According to Burton and others (1996), this zone includes North and Northeast Africa, the Middle East, South and Central Asia, most of China, and Vietnam.

12 www.paulnoll.com/China/Minorities/index.html (consulted 12 May 2006).

13 As evidenced by these figures collated by anthropologist Jean-Pierre Warnier (1993) and reported by Kamdem (2002, p. 262):

> In 1976, the members of the Bamileke ethnic community, estimated at 17.5% of the total population of Cameroon (residents and diaspora included) […] represented 58% of the nation's importers, 87% to 94% of market stall owners in Douala and Nkongsamba, 75% of cacao buyers, and 47% of Douala's local industrial products wholesalers. Moreover, they owned 80% of the city taxis in Douala and Yaoundé (the country's two main cities), 50% of the intercity transport busses, 29% of the road transportation fleet, and 75% of the hotels in Douala and Yaoundé.
>
> (Translation)

14 On management in Cameroon, also consult Kamdem and Chanlat (1994a, 1994b, 1995), and Jackson and Nzepa (2004).

15 He says for example: 'Just as a language makes it possible to build an infinite number of discourses, in which the language is nonetheless clearly recognizable, a culture makes it possible to build an infinite number of organizational forms, without ceasing to be recognizable' (d'Iribarne, 1993, pp. x–xi). Therefore: 'The coexistence of the unity of a culture and the variety of concrete models of organizational functioning is also easy to understand when culture is seen as a repository of meaning' (1993, p. ix). In fact, in the case of France, this means that 'the noble/common contrast influences French culture as a whole. But there is no consensus within this culture about what is noble and what is common. And the definition of what is noble is a particularly strategic issue in the country…' (1993, p. ix), hence the possibility of having a variety of organizational forms.

16 Anthropologist Ulf Hannertz (1992, p. 14) proposes this contemporary definition of culture 'as an organization of diversity'.

References

Adler, N., *Comportement organisationnel. Une approche multiculturelle*, Ottawa, Éditions Reynald Goulet, 1994.

Barbichon, G., 'L'ethnologie des organisations. À propos de *La Logique de l'honneur*', *Ethnologie Française*, vol. 20, no. 2, pp. 177–88, 1990.

Barmeyer, C., *Comprendre et conjuguer les différences culturelles: le management entre Québécois et Allemands*, Quebec, Government of Quebec, 1994.

Bollinger, D. and G. Hofstede, *Les Différences culturelles dans le management*, Paris, Éditions d'Organisation, 1987.

Bouchard, G. and Y. Lamonde (eds), *Québécois et Américains: la culture québécoise aux XIXe et XXe siècles*, Montreal, Fides, 1995.

Burton, M. L., C. C. Moore, J. W. M. Whiting and A. K. Romney, 'Regions Based on Social Structure', *Current Anthropology*, vol. 37, no. 1, pp. 87–123, 1996.

Cavusgil, S. T. and A. Das, 'Methodological Issues in Empirical Cross-cultural Research: A Survey of the Management Literature and Framework', *Management International Review*, vol. 37, no. 1, pp. 71–96, 1997.

Chapman, M., 'Social Anthropology, Business Studies, and Cultural Issue', *International Studies of Management and Organization*, vol. 26, no. 4, pp. 3–29, 1997.

Dantas, M., *De Bloco Afro a Holdin Cultural*, Salvador, Editora Olodum, 1994.

d'Iribarne, P., *La Logique de l'honneur. Gestion des entreprises et traditions nationales*, Paris, Seuil, 1989.

—— Préface, *La Logique de l'honneur*, Paris, Seuil, Éditions de poche, pp. i–xxxii, 1993.

—— 'The Usefulness of an Ethnographic Approach to the International Comparison of Organizations', *International Studies of Management and Organization*, vol. 26, no. 4, pp. 30–47, 1997.

—— 'Comment s'accorder. Une rencontre franco-suédoise', in P. d'Iribarne, A. Henry, J-P. Segal, S. Chevrier and T. Globokar (eds), *Cultures et mondialisation. Gérer par-delà les frontières*, Paris, Seuil, 1998b.

—— 'Coopérer à la Belge. La mise en oeuvre problématique d'un agenda électronique', in P. d'Iribarne A. Henry, J-P. Segal, S. Chevrier and T. Globokar (eds), *Cultures et mondialisation. Gérer par-delà les frontières*, Paris, Seuil, 1998c.

—— 'Un management moderne enraciné dans une culture traditionnelle. Les enseignements d'un success-story mexicaine', *Gérer et Comprendre*, no. 65, September, pp. 5–16, 2001.

—— *Le Tiers-Monde qui réussit. Nouveaux modèles*, Paris, Éditions Odile Jacob, 2003a.

—— 'Croître ensemble au Mexique', in *Le Tiers-Monde qui réussit. Nouveaux modèles*, Paris, Éditions Odile Jacob, 2003b.

—— 'Qualité totale et islam à Casablanca', in *Le Tiers-Monde qui réussit. Nouveaux modèles*, Paris, Éditions Odile Jacob, 2003c.

d'Iribarne, P., A. Henry, J.-P. Segal, S. Chevrier and T. Globokar (eds), *Cultures et mondialisation. Gérer par-delà les frontières*, Paris, Seuil, 1998a.

Dupuis, J.-P., 'Intégration des immigrants et conquête des marchés internationaux: le difficile apprentissage des différences culturelles', in J.-P. Dupuis and A. Kuzminski (eds), *Sociologie de l'économie, du travail et de l'entreprise*, Boucherville, Gaëtan Morin Editor, pp. 193–244, 1998.

—— Entre cultures latine, anglo-saxonne et nordique: les Québécois en économie, en affaires et en gestion, Montreal, École des HEC, Cahier de recherche no. 00-29, October, 2000.

—— 'La gestion québécoise à la lumière des études comparatives', *Recherches Sociographiques*, vol. XLIII, no. 1, pp. 183–205, 2002.

—— 'Problèmes de cohérence théorique chez Philippe d'Iribarne: une voie de sortie', *Management International*, vol. 8, no. 3, pp. 21–30, 2004.

Dupuis, J.-P. (ed.), *Le Modèle québécois de développement économique. Débats sur son contenu, son efficacité et ses liens avec les modes de gestion des entreprises*, Cap-Rouge et Casablanca, Presses Inter Universitaires, 1995.

Hall, E. T. and M. R. Hall, *Guide du comportement dans les affaires internationales: Allemagne, États-Unis, France*, Paris, Éditions du Seuil, 1990.

Hannerz, U., *Cultural Complexity. Studies in the Social Organization of Meaning*, New York, Columbia University Press, 1992.

Hickson, D. J. and D. S. Pugh, *Management Worldwide: The Impact of Societal Culture on Organizations around the Globe*, London, Penguin Books, 1995.

Hofstede, G., *Culture's Consequences: International Differences in Work-Related Values*, Beverly Hills, CA, Sage, 1980 (French adaptation: D. Bollinger and G. Hofstede, *Les Différences culturelles dans le management*, Paris, Éditions d'Organisation, 1987).

—— 'Relativité culturelle des pratiques et théories de l'organisation', *Revue Française de Gestion*, no. 64, September–October, pp. 10–21, 1987.

—— *Cultures and Organisations. Sofwares of the Mind*, London, McGraw-Hill, 1991 (French translation: *Vivre dans un monde multiculturel. Comprendre nos programmations mentales*, Paris, Éditions d'Organisation, 1994).

—— 'Cultural Constraints in Management Theories', *Academy of Management Executives*, vol. 7, no. 1, pp. 81–94, 1993.

—— 'Problems Remain, But Theories Will Change: The Universal and the Specific in 21st-century Global Management', *Organizational Dynamics*, vol. 28, no. 1, pp. 34–44, 1999.

——. *Culture's Consequences: International Differences in Work-Related Values*, new edition, Beverly Hills, CA, Sage, 2001.

Inda, J. X. and R. Rosaldo, 'Introduction. A World in Motion', in J. X. Inda and R. Rosaldo (eds), *The Anthropology of Globalization*, Malden MA, Blackwell, 2002.

Jackson, T. and O. N. Nzepa, 'Cameroon. Managing Cultural Complexity and Power', in T. Jackson, *Management and Change in Africa. A Cross-cultural Perspective*, London and New York, Routledge, 2004, pp. 208–33.

Joly, A., *Le Dirigeant féodal: le lien d'homme à homme dans la grande entreprise brésilienne: leçons pour l'Amérique du Nord*, Montreal, École des HEC, Cahier de recherche, Centre d'études en administration internationale, 1996.

—— *Fiefs et entreprises en Amérique latine*. Sainte-Foy: Les Presses de l'Université Laval, 2004.

Kamdem, E., *Management et interculturalité en Afrique. Expérience camerounaise*, Sainte-Foy, Les Presses de l'Université Laval, Paris, L'Harmattan, 2002.

Kamdem, E., and J.-F. Chanlat, *Dynamique socioculturelle et management de l'entreprise camerounaise: le cas FEUBOIS*, Montreal, École des Hautes Études Commerciales, Centre d'Études en Administration Internationale, 1994a.

—— *Dynamique socioculturelle et management de l'entreprise camerounaise: le cas de la compagnie ABC*, Montreal, École des Hautes Études Commerciales, Centre d'Études en Administration Internationale, 1994b.

—— *Dynamique socioculturelle et management de l'entreprise camerounaise: le cas de la BNDC*, Montreal, École des Hautes Études Commerciales, Centre d'Études en Administration Internationale, 1995.

Lamont, M., *La Morale et l'argent. Les valeurs des cadres en France et aux États-Unis*, Paris, Métailié, 1995.

Laurent, A., 'The Cultural Diversity of Western Conceptions of Management', *International Studies of Management and Organization*, vol. 13, nos. 1–2, pp. 75–96, 1983.

Le Petit Robert des noms propres, Mayflower, A. Rey (ed.). Revised edn, corrected and updated in March 1999, p. 1346, Paris, Dictionnaires Le Robert, 1994.

Lemogodeuc, J.-M. (ed.), *L'Amérique hispanique au XXe siècle. Identités, cultures, sociétés*, Paris, Presses Universitaires de France, 1997.

Mutabazi, É., 'L'expérience multiculturelle des entreprises africaine', Symposium: 'El Análisis de las Organizaciones y la Gestión Estrategic: Perspectivas Latinas', Zacatécas, 11–14 July 2000.

Nasif, E. G., H. Al-Daeaj, B. Ebrahimi and M. S. Thibodeaux, 'Methodological Problems in Cross-cultural Research: An Update Review', *Management International Review*, vol. 31, no. 1, pp. 79–91, 1991.

Philip, B., 'Chez les indépendantistes ouïgours', *Le Devoir*, 16 August 2006.

Punnett, B. J. and S. Whitane, 'Hofstede's Values Survey Module: To Embrace or Abandon?' *Advances in International Comparative Management*, vol. 5, pp. 69–89, 1990.

Schwartz, S. H., 'Universals in the Content and Structure of Values: Theoretical Advances and Empirical Tests in 20 Countries', in M. P. Zanna (ed.), *Advances in Experimental Social Psychology*, San Diego, CA, Academic Press, 1992.

Sondergaard, M., 'Hofstede's Consequences: A Study of Reviews, Citations and Replications', *Organization Studies*, vol. 15, no. 3, pp. 447–56, 1994.

Tayeb, M., 'Organizations and National Culture: Methodology Considered', *Organization Studies*, vol. 15, no. 3, pp. 429–46, 1994.

Thériault, J. Y., *Critique de l'américanité: mémoire et démocratie au Québec*, Montreal, Éditions Québec Amérique, 2005.

Thomas, D. C., *Essentials of International Management: A Cross-cultural Perspective*, Thousand Oaks CA, Sage Publications, 2002.

Trompenaars, F., *L'Entreprise multiculturelle*, Paris, Éditions Maxima, 1994.

3 An interactionist approach to intercultural management analysis

Olivier Irrmann

From comparison to interaction in intercultural analysis

A great deal of effort has been dedicated by management scholars to the description and codification of nationally determined business systems, cultures and management styles. The classical approach to culture in the fields of management and strategy could be defined as *cartographic* and is based on the measurement of so-called 'cultural dimensions'. The project is to draw a map of cultures – along a set of measurable variables – and try to place every national business system and management style on a graph that could describe and codify this culture, preferably on a two by two grid.

As the experience of international contacts became more common, through students' international exchanges, exports, and cross-border mergers and acquisitions, we realized that organizations around the world were working in different ways and that we were not completely understanding our foreign colleagues and partners, creating a perception of distance we needed to interpret.

The cartographic approach to culture has led to the growing popularity of the concept of cultural distance. The rationale is that cultural distance is generating difficulties in the implementation of foreign direct investment, the international management of human resources, and project management. This is a very attractive proposition for both practitioners and researchers. It would be enough to measure that distance, be aware of cultural work-related differences and as a consequence be able to better manage organizations and business at the international level. With the strategic choice of culturally similar partners, such distance could be reduced and problems would be avoided.

Comparing scores of cultural dimensions (with the influential models of Geert Hofstede, Shalom Schwartz and Edward T. Hall, among others) would give everyone a relative position on the cultural map, the ability to position the others, and allow predictions about what might happen during the intercultural encounter. A difference in terms of power distance would trigger conflicts about ways to manage, the best way to organize a company and proper management style. A difference in terms of task orientation versus person orientation would mean divergences about how to lead teams, reward performance and provide personal feedback. Even the vision of the proper goal of the organization can vary around the world, from profit-making to patriotism and the preservation of family interests, reflecting multiple interpretations of what an exemplary leader is supposed to do (Hofstede et al., 2002). The main idea is that knowing where we are on the map of cultural dimensions will allow us to better plan and manage the intercultural relationship.

The first to really question this hypothesis were negotiation specialists. Negotiating is one of the most common activities in both the business world and everyday life. In a series of laboratory experiments that measured negotiators' cultural dimensions and video-recorded all of their conversations, Adler and Graham (1989) noticed something peculiar in the negotiators' behaviour. During the interaction – while negotiating and bargaining – negotiators were no longer behaving as predicted by their cultural profile. Each party was adapting its behaviour according to the situation, making an effort to understand the other, changing strategies for convincing, or suddenly becoming less cooperative than predicted by observations made in intracultural settings. Adler and Graham (1989) concluded that in intercultural research we must forget the cross-cultural comparison fallacy.

The cross-cultural comparison fallacy is also felt in international mergers and acquisitions and in the management of alliances and joint ventures. Practitioners and researchers identified culture as one of the main reasons behind the high failure rate of these operations, estimated to lie between 40 per cent and 70 per cent. None of the multiple studies on the topic focusing on macro-level measures of national culture scores could find meaningful reasons for such a high rate of failure. For mergers and acquisitions the mode of integration and the level of acculturation – in other words, the way the two firms were to be reorganized together and how one culture would have to yield to another – are the main identified causes of failure, but how and why, no one really seems to know. It is ironic that in 25 years of extraordinary expansion in the numbers of mergers and acquisition transactions, the failure rate has remained very high, suggesting that not much has been learned about these complex intercultural organizational events.

The concept of cultural distance has been widely used to try to explain the high failure rate of international corporate acquisitions, with the hypothesis that a larger cultural distance would create more problems and lower performance. Some works actually showed that cultural distance would have a negative impact on performance following the acquisition of foreign firms (Datta and Puia, 1995). Others (Morosini et al., 1998) found on the contrary that national cultural distance was positively associated with some dimensions of perceived performance by top managers. More in-depth studies on acquisitions between different groups of countries showed that there would be a directional dimension in the perception of cultural difference (Very et al., 1993; Very and Lubatkin, 1997; Very et al., 1996) and that this influence could be positive, negative or neutral. A French company buying an American firm would not trigger the same cultural dynamics as an American firm buying a French one, all things being equal.

For alliances and cross-border acquisitions, many multinational managers and CEOs are actually insisting on the fact that it is precisely cultural difference that brings value, triggers innovation and generates market value. Different organizational routines help identify better management practices, give a better understanding of markets, bring new competences and a whole new relationship network to exploit. Differences can be sources of both problems and solutions in management; what is important is to understand the mechanisms by which this difference can generate either conflict or cooperation in intercultural teams.

In order to fully understand intercultural contacts, we need to focus on the contact itself, that is on interaction between people. People are not walking the streets with a backpack full of cultural dimensions ready to deploy during the intercultural contact. The perception of culture and of cultural differences is assessed and perceived while in contact with the other, trying to communicate – orally, in writing, face-to-face or not – with another person, in a language which is often not our native one, with strategies to convince that may work in our language but not necessarily in another.

In management, interpersonal contacts occur around tasks to be done, around work, but all these tasks are certainly not magically coordinated by the sheer power of the organizational structure or the inner motivation of employees. Language and communication play a major role in organizational life and in the practice of management. Management is essentially a communicative activity. Already in the 1970s, Henry Mintzberg followed managers during their whole working day, trying to understand the nature of managerial work. He found that on average they spent 78 per cent of their time in oral communication, either negotiating or requesting and transmitting information, opinions, orders (Mintzberg 1973, 1975). The situation is even more complex today with virtual teams and the multiplication of information technologies that force us to practise other modes of communication, such as e-mail, phone conferencing, videoconferencing, instant messaging and all their derivatives (Tengblad 2002). At the end of the day, the essence of management is to communicate efficiently.

Communicating efficiently: the concept is seductive but misleading. How can we efficiently communicate and convince in very culturally diverse environments? This is not a trivial task and the question forces us to examine what is the reality of intercultural contacts in the business world. What does it mean to communicate in an environment which is more and more international and multicultural?

Throughout this chapter we will see how misunderstandings can emerge between people even when their communicative goals and intentions are identical. In the first part we will review different types of deviations in communication, differences from a standard usage of the language that can generate incomprehension and a lack of trust in the interlocutor. We will then see how these deviations materialize in the practice of communication in an international context: when you need to convince, communicate signs of credibility, obtain something or give orders. Finally, we will delve deeper into the sources of such dissonance, some of them coming from surface elements in the mastery of language, some being more deeply anchored in a communicational culture and rarely identified in the practice of management. We will review a few tools that come from applied linguistics that will allow us to shed light on some communicative cultural dissonances in management. Finally, we will see how this analysis can be applied in a case study of a Franco-Finnish corporate acquisition.

Deviations in intercultural communication

Communicating efficiently requires that the decoded intention is as close as possible to what was intended to be communicated. Miscommunications are unavoidable, both in a native or foreign language, but when using a foreign language the risk of misunderstanding is higher, as we observe a set of deviations from the standard use of the language.

Linguists distinguish between three major components in the mechanics of language. The first one is syntax, which is the study of the rules that govern the ways words are combined to form correct sentences. The second component is semantics, which is the study of the meaning of linguistic expression (words and sentences). Finally, pragmatics is the study of the aspects of meaning and language use that are dependent on the speaker, the addressee and other features of the context. The basic grammatical competence of a speaker is related to the knowledge and mastery of the first two components. The pragmatic competence of a speaker refers to the ability to use the language effectively in context, in order to achieve a specific purpose. The three elements are closely interrelated. Semantics studies the transmission of meaning through grammatical mechanisms (therefore syntax) and lexical components (words we know) of a language. The meaning of sentences and discourse is always decoded by passing them through the filter of contextual information and linguistic cues, in other words according to rules of pragmatics. When we learn progressively to master our native language, the three dimensions of syntax, semantics and pragmatics are combined together and we do not realize that they are separate elements. When learning the grammar of a foreign language, it is generally semantics and syntax that we study; rules of pragmatics remain generally in the shadows. As we use a different language to communicate, we mostly use rules of pragmatics coming from our own mother tongue, hoping that the same style of sentences, the same way to formulate a request, the same way to manifest interest and the same negotiation tactics as in our native system will function identically in the other language system. In most cases, this 'pragmatics transfer' – applying rules of pragmatics coming from a specific language (for instance French spoken in France) to another language (say, British English) – rarely occurs without problems and creates a number of misunderstandings and conflicts. In fact it is not even necessary to speak a different language in order to experience problems of pragmatics. Francophones from three different parts of the world can have very different communicational cultures and accordingly experience difficulties in negotiating together.

The first kind of deviation from the standard use of a language has to do with problems of vocabulary, grammatical competence and pronunciation. Participants search for appropriate expressions, correct definitions and interpretations. Generally the conversation continues to flow, even if all the lexical items are not fully understood, as there is a considerable amount of corrective activity initiated by the speaker or the listener, or cooperatively by both. The corrective activity can be either direct, 'Do you mean cubic tons?' or 'Pardon? What was that?', or indirect, through testing comprehension later in the conversation by a request for clarification or confirmation. Too much deviation at this level can cut communication short, but even a very basic level of fluency can be enough for conducting a transaction. The channel of communication used plays a major role, as the corrective activity can be easily generated in face-to-face conversation or on the phone, but becomes impossible with written material. Too much deviation in a written message or commercial brochure can have a devastating impact on the perception of credibility and make potential partners run away.

The second kind of deviation comes from a lack of knowledge of the whole array of language subtleties, the meaning of specific understatements, and the most adapted scripts for convincing people in a specific context. It is mostly an unidentified deviation, coming from different rules of pragmatics. As none of the communicators are conscious of the type of language issue that is at play, there is no corrective activity during the exchange, and it leads to miscommunication, negative perception, and the feeling of 'culture shock'.

Whatever language we use, whether our native language or a foreign one (with parties using more often a non-native language for both of them), the way we encode our intentions and decode others' plays an important role in the perception of our business partners. In intra-cultural situations, knowledge of deep communicative and socio-cultural norms has been acquired through a slow process of cultural socialization, learning the rules of the game at home, at school and at work. In multi-cultural situations, we are no longer able to master these communication codes, and the lack of knowledge about facts and conversational norms related to social, cultural and business backgrounds can lead to *pragmatic failures* (Thomas 1983). In its most basic form, a pragmatic failure generates the feeling that we do not understand what is meant by what is said, even if the words do make sense. In its more complex form, the non-comprehension of conversational pragmatic rules will often lead to the perception that we – or the interlocutors – are impolite, ignorant, incompetent, difficult, unreliable. What is often labelled as culture shock is no more than a communicational shock, where different communication styles are clashing. Activities such as discussing, criticizing, negotiating, getting information, leading, communicating trustworthiness – in other words, managing – are all language-based activities, using different language strategies, with different pragmatic rules from context to context.

Trust is generated from repeated interaction between people comparing their expectations and the outcomes of their relationships. Every disappointing gap between expectation and outcome contributes to mistrust. On the other hand, when expectations from one side are rewarded by positive outcomes from the other side, then trust is progressively built. This is a dynamic process where interaction takes centre stage (see Box 3.1). Perceptions are important for creating and sustaining trust. This perception of the other is often influenced by their style of communication, and it has an impact on the level of trust we give and on the quality of further professional relationships.

The impact of a good comprehension of language strategies is extremely important in business, even though it is generally overlooked and underestimated. In a classic study of the evolution of a cooperative alliance, Doz (1996, p. 65) showed how the alliance between the two multinationals Alza and Ciba-Geigy rapidly failed, among other things because of issues of working style communication between teams. Confronted with what they considered to be a meandering and time-wasting decision-making process at Ciba-Geigy, Alza personnel began to bypass Ciba's hierarchy and communicate directly with scientists and managers in charge of the development of their common project. By doing so, they alienated a large part of Ciba's middle management in the process, as they were viewed as making 'constant criticism and attacks on people who were their best friends'. Alza people wanted to find a more effective way to proceed, but could not find the appropriate behavioural and communicational script for addressing criticisms and remarks within a team with different cultural backgrounds. It is unlikely that Alza personnel wanted to create a conflict. Their intention was to create a more dynamic relationship and a more effective process, but it was interpreted as an inadmissible disregard for rules, in a style that was much too aggressive. Such a pragmatic failure as we mentioned earlier had an effect on the perception of the business partner, created an atmosphere of mistrust, and the alliance was terminated much more rapidly than planned – there were also other reasons, but this one played an important role in the process.

Box 3.1 Different forms of trust

Trust is a frequently used concept that can lose its meaning when used too broadly to describe very different realities, particularly in business. John Child (2001) reminds us that in practice there are many forms of trust:

- *Trust based on calculation*: this is the kind of trust that can be found at the beginning of a relationship, when a risk is taken without much information by estimating that it is worth it. Partners give each other the benefit of trust (rather than the benefit of the doubt) and embark on the process of getting to know each other.
- *Trust based on mutual understanding*: this kind of trust is created by people who have worked together over a long term; it is based on mutual knowledge and common experience among the partners.
- *Trust based on bonding*: this kind of trust arises when partners come to appreciate each other, and create a psychological bond and a strong personal relationship. In the business world it can come from relationships maintained for a long period of time. It can take the form of an alliance. John Child gives the example of the Royal Bank of Scotland the Spanish bank Banco Santander who, thanks to a relationship that extended over a decade, learned enormously from each other in terms of organizational efficiency and quality of customer service.

In the following section we will review how language is used in practice to communicate credibility, to convince, to gain compliance. They are all culturally and linguistically relative strategies. In other words, the way to communicate efficiently and convincingly varies from language to language and from culture to culture, with culture being defined at the national, regional, organizational or occupational (communicating as an engineer or as a salesperson) level.

The pillars of intercultural communication in business and management

Specialists in intercultural communication tend to have an idealized vision of the goals of communication. It is often stated that the goals of good communication are to understand another culture, express empathy and respect for that culture, learn something during the inter-cultural contact and improve relationships across cultures. Those are certainly noble enter-prises and could be goals in themselves, but intercultural communication in business is something much more down to earth. We shift from a system that puts values first (doing what is right) to a system that puts action first (doing what is efficient), though both systems could be combined. In the reality of intercultural business contact, in management, what is necessary is to convince and build an image of credibility (for instance during business negotiations), to read the signs of credibility (necessary when estimating the risks of a business relationship), and gain compliance or give orders (for instance when managing a foreign subsidiary).

Convincing

A large part of international business is constituted by sales and negotiation activities. Convincing the other party is one of the main goals of communication in this context. Every culture, and often every region, has its own combination of strategies for convincing, for building an argument, for defending an opinion and a bargaining position, and for which tone to take in order to sound convincing.

In his in-depth analysis of verbal negotiation tactics, John Graham (1985, 1996; Graham et al., 1994) showed how negotiators of different nationalities used differently, with a higher or lower frequency, specific verbal and non-verbal bargaining strategies (see Table 3.1 for the full list of verbal strategies). The results showed that negotiators used surprisingly similar bargaining behaviours across cultures. Negotiations in the ten cultures studied comprised primarily information exchange tactics – questions and self-disclosures.

Variations across cultures were much greater when comparisons included non-verbal and paraverbal behaviours. The biggest differences were observed in terms of what Graham calls values and decision-making process (see Table 3.2). Anglophone Canadians tended to never use threats, but this was sometimes the case with French negotiators. Strategies of recommendation were much rarer among French negotiators than among Mexican ones. Using commands ('You must absolutely do…') as a tactic was twice as frequent with anglophone Canadians than with francophone Canadians. The use of 'No' as a communication tool was ten times more frequent with French negotiators than with Japanese negotiators. Japanese negotiators tended to person-alize the exchange much less than their francophone Canadian counterparts (twice as much 'You' used by French Canadians than by Japanese). On the other side, francophone Canadians were hardly ever silent, while the Japanese would use silence as a way to communicate.

The goal is the same for every negotiator/bargainer: using a set of verbal tactics for convincing the other party (Usunier, 1996b), but the path taken for reaching that objective

Table 3.1 Verbal negotiation tactics and linguistic aspects of language and non-verbal behaviour

Verbal negotiation tactics (the 'what' of communication)	
Commitments	Promise: A statement in which the source indicated his intention to provide the target with a reinforcing consequence which source anticipates target will evaluate as pleasant, positive or rewarding.
	Commitment: A statement by the source to the effect that its future bids will not go below or above a certain level.
Prescriptions	Recommendation: A statement in which the source predicts that a pleasant environmental consequence will occur to the target. Its occurrence is not under the source's control.
	Command: A statement in which the source suggests that the target perform a certain behaviour.
Admonitions	Threat: Same as promise, except that the reinforcing consequences are thought to be noxious, unpleasant or punishing.
	Warning: Same as recommendation, except that the consequences are thought to be unpleasant.
Reward	A statement by the source that is thought to create pleasant consequences for the target.
Punishment	Same as reward, except that the consequences are thought to be unpleasant.
Positive normative appeal	A statement in which the source indicates that the target's past, present or future behaviour was or will be in conformity with social norms.
Negative normative appeal	Same as positive normative appeal, except that the target's behaviour is in violation of social norms.
Question	A statement in which the source asks the target to reveal information about itself. It can take the form of (a) clarification, (b) request for information, (c) initiations.
Self-disclosure	A statement in which the source reveals information about itself, (a) in response to other's questions, (b) unsolicited.
Linguistic aspects of language and non-verbal behaviours ('how' things are said)	
Structural aspects	No's: The average number of times the word 'no' was used by each negotiator per 30 minutes of negotiation.
	You's: The average number of times the word 'you' was used by each negotiator per 30 minutes of negotiation.
Non-verbal behaviours	Silent periods: The average number of conversational gaps initiated by each negotiator, 10 seconds or greater, per half hour.
	Conversational overlaps: The average number of interruptions by each negotiator per half hour.
	Facial gazing: The average number of minutes each negotiator looks at partner's face, per 10-minute period.
	Touching: Incidents of bargainers touching one another (not including handshaking).

Source: Adapted from Graham (1996); Neu and Graham (1994); Angelmar and Stern (1978).

is different. A French negotiator competent in their own culture will use verbal strategies that are more aggressive, actively use interruption, say 'No' to mean that they are not convinced, and frequently use the word 'You' in order to personalize the discussion. The anglophone Canadian negotiator competent in his or her culture will be as little aggressively

Table 3.2 Sample of measures of frequencies in use of verbal and non-verbal negotiation tactics by negotiators

	Japan	USA	Canada FR	Canada EN	Mexico	France
Verbal tactics						
Promise	7	8	8	6	7	5
Threat	4	4	3	0	1	5
Recommendation	7	4	5	4	8	3
Warning	2	1	5	0	2	3
Reward	1	2	1	3	1	3
Punishment	1	3	2	1	0	3
Engagement	15	13	8	14	9	10
Self-disclosure	34	36	42	34	38	42
Question	20	20	19	26	27	18
Command	8	6	5	10	7	9
Structural and non-verbal elements						
No	1.9	4.5	7	10.1	4.5	11.3
You	31.5	54.1	72.4	64.4	56.3	70.2
Silence	2.5	1.7	0.2	2.9	1.1	1
Conversational overlaps	6.2	5.1	24	17	10.6	20.7
Facial gazing	3.9	10	18.8	10.4	15.6	16

verbal as possible (no threats or warnings), actively interrupting their interlocutor and actively using 'No' during the process. The Japanese negotiator will have a lower-key strategy for convincing, comprising positive promises, recommendations and commitments. He will hardly ever use a direct 'No' and will avoid personalization of the 'You', while actively using silence as a communication tool.

None of these tactical configurations is more efficient than the other; they are all powerful in their own context, but can become totally irrelevant in another context. The real danger is to try applying ready-made recipes or to think that our own stratagems will work every-where. To be convincing in an intercultural context means having to relativize twice. First of all, there are numerous tactics for convincing someone and their efficacy is relative to the local context and the person we are trying to influence. We should therefore be trained to convince by using different negotiation and bargaining modes. Then, we have to realize that when we are not convinced, it may be because the strategies applied to us are not efficient. We may also try to understand what kind of negotiation strategy our interlocutor is trying to use with us. Becoming exasperated during an international transaction is often a symptom of bad intercultural communication. The example from Box 3.2 shows how even the way to manipulate silence can have an impact on the ability to convince.

National culture is not the only element that influences strategies for convincing. Occupational cultures and generational cultures play an important role, as they come with their preferred style of discourse (Scollon and Scollon, 1995). An information technology project manager trying to sell a product to a buyer from a multinational does not only face a national or language barrier. In the line of fire, there is also the discourse of a young IT spe-cialist in his or her twenties manipulating technological innovation arguments that may be impressive in his or her own universe but are hardly convincing for the baby-boomer seated on the other side of the desk who grew up in a culture of a large industrial multinational company, where robustness and reliability play the major role. The cultural referents and symbols to be manipulated are not the same at all.

Box 3.2 The francophone seller and the Scandinavian buyer

It is tempting to consider intercultural communication problems only as the consequence of 'exotic' encounters with people from very distant parts of the world. But within the same geographical area, the pragmatic rules of conversation can also differ greatly. For instance, within the European Union, Finns actively use silence as a mode of communication, while silence is often considered as a passive mode in most Indo-European languages. The following example illustrates how this difference can lead to a seller–buyer interaction that unfolds in a less and less favourable atmosphere.

The story takes place during a meeting organized in Finland by the local chamber of commerce between a French seller and a Finnish industrial buyer strongly interested in the line of products presented. At the beginning of the meeting, the seller started his sales pitch with a confident attitude, and a presentation that was rather lengthy, according to the attentive buyer. The end of the presentation was followed by a short period of silence, interrupted by the seller resuming his pitch, in a slightly less comfortable fashion, in front of a buyer who was by now really suspicious and totally silent. The meeting was a failure and no contract was concluded (Irrmann, 1999).

To understand this meeting and the root causes of its failure, even though all the ingredients for a success were present, we need to consider the divergent interpretations of silence as a mode of communication (Jaworski, 1997; Tannen and Saville-Troike, 1985) and rules of interaction. The French seller started the sales pitch and was expecting to build his presentation around questions and interruptions from the buyer, interruption being a classical mode of showing interest in many Latin languages. The Finnish buyer was communicating his respect and interest by not interrupting his interlocutor, a behaviour in line with verbal interaction rules in Finland where it is extremely impolite to interrupt a speaker. The seller, confronted by extremely limited verbal and non-verbal feedback, interpreted this as a sign of scepticism on the part of the buyer and carried on with his presentation in a continued attempt to be convincing. When the pitch ended, the short period of silence was too long for the seller, and was interpreted as a danger signal, prompting him to try to save the meeting with a renewed attempt to trigger the buyer's interest. The buyer, rudely interrupted during his (silent) evaluation of the size of the purchase he could conclude, started to have doubts about the quality of the product. The seller seemed quite unsure about his product, otherwise why would he talk so much? The question of a few seconds of silence was enough to derail the meeting.

Building an image of credibility and interpreting the signs of credibility

The raw material for all relationships in management is credibility. Most managerial activities, beyond the technical side of tasks, aim at building an image of credibility and reading the signs of credibility displayed by others. There are three important vehicles of credibility: personal credibility, institutional credibility and status credibility (Usunier, 1996a, 1996b ch. 15). They are all culturally relative and there is a high probability of misunderstanding messages of credibility that are sent and received.

Personal credibility is related to the characteristics of the individual. Physical traits can be vectors of credibility. Western countries tend to idealize an image of a leader who is male, young, fit, tall, with a low voice. On other latitudes, the typical image of credibility and respect is held by an older male, bold, with a beard if possible, and well-nourished. These physical symbolic codes play a role in the initial building of credibility at the early stages of interaction. It can be a minor role, but it is still a factor to take into account. None of them is incompatible with exercising power in the business world, but they are still a barrier to take into account from the onset.

Another important aspect of personal credibility is mediated by the communication style. Some cultures consider that a competent communicator should be low-profile, presenting arguments as suggestions and understatements, being modest and a good listener. At the other end of the spectrum, a competent communicator can be seen as an incisive speaker, having high self-esteem, and trying to convince through verbal brilliance. These two styles, once again, can both be extremely efficient, but using the wrong communication system in a foreign environment can create difficult situations. The failure of the cooperative venture between Volvo and Renault in the 1990s (their strategic alliance lasted from 1990 to 1994) was partly due to differences in communication styles between the Swedish and French teams, the former using a logic of consensus in their negotiations and the latter a logic of incisive and combative debate. French teams felt they were successful during discussions as they won the debate, while Swedish teams considered the decisions taken to be neither justified nor acceptable (d'Iribarne, 1998 for an analysis of the Francoh-Swedish work relationships). French teams thought they were credible, Swedes saw them as not credible and extremely authoritarian.

Institutional credibility is related to the organizations people represent or the institutions they belong to. The firm, its name, its size, its reputation, can evoke a very strong image that is going to lend a certain aura to the person representing the company. The very large multinationals have a certain advantage in this game. But, again, the symbols of credibility are very variable. In some cases making profits can be seen as a positive sign, in others it is rather the connection with the government or the ability to win large contracts. These institutional symbols need to be handled carefully, and the power of evoking an employer can vary a lot. The image and reputation of firms such as ABB, Infosys, Tata, Research in Motion or Outokumpu varies greatly depending on the industrial culture of partners and the geographical area. Once a top manager, wanting to convince me of a company's credibility, said simply: 'It's a company that belongs to the first lady's [the spouse of the head of state] brother.' In this particular context he did not need to elaborate further: he had sufficiently proved that this company was an important partner.

Institutional credibility is not restricted to the corporate world. Belonging to clubs or associations is in itself a powerful vehicle of credibility. Most non-profit business clubs play this role. Belonging to a national chamber of commerce is an excellent way to get known in many Asian countries, to the extent that membership is often stated on the business card. In some places it is common practice to state *en passant* that you are member of an exclusive club or to mention the university that you attended. These symbols can be important as they can allow quick connection with some networks, but they can also be completely useless. Knowing which university you studied at is of limited importance to a Dane, while Americans will be more likely to discretely flash their alumni ring to show who they are.

The game of images continues with *status credibility*. Building an image of credibility requires communicating about power and status. It's often done indirectly, with behaviour considered as 'normal' and in line with the rank of the person in the company. Some cultures (organizational and national) value external signs of power: corner offices on top floors of building, view to the parking for assistants and view to the city skyline for directors, personal secretariat, corporate cars, etc. Interpersonal behaviour can also be influenced by the difference in term of status. In cultures that value power distance, formality and distance with a superior is also communicated through language. It is considered normal to behave as 'a boss' and therefore to communicate 'bossily', as it is normal for a subordinate to communicate as a subordinate. In egalitarian cultures such as the Nordic and the Scandinavian, such behaviour is not acceptable and communicational distance cannot exist. To behave as a boss would be seen as an unbearable mark of arrogance – arrogance being considered a negative trait – and therefore a mark of social incompetence.

Divergence in terms of status credibility can create a shock of images that can trigger important problems. For instance, French managers are often considered as arrogant since they do what is most effective in their own cultural context: they openly display marks of status and competence in order to be taken seriously by others. The markers of status are rather complex and it is a difficult task to discover which one to use and to communicate about, and when they should be forgotten altogether. In an egalitarian environment, one should not attribute too much importance to external signs of status. In this kind of environment, it is difficult to know who is important because no one is supposed to be important. Danish managers refer to the *Jantelagen*, or law of Jante – with reference to a classic Danish novel – which is a tacit norm of social behaviour according to which no one should ever think or communicate the feeling that he or she is someone special or superior to others. This rule is widespread in Nordic countries and in some areas of the Netherlands. Consequently, talking in a superior manner (or being perceived as considering others from a higher level) in Denmark or Quebec can dramatically decrease credibility. The excessively formal tone of a teacher or an executive in that environment is perceived as a form of disdain. To remark in a meeting that a candidate is 'extremely brilliant' can therefore either be seen as a proof of high personal qualities (in a context where verbal talent is seen as important) or considered as an important handicap (in *Jantelagen* type of country).

Gaining compliance or giving orders

Getting something done, being obeyed, giving orders, is after all one of the main goals of a manager, locally or internationally. There are different compliance-gaining strategies that are more or less applicable according to the cultural environment (Sullivan and Taylor, 1991; Sullivan et al., 1990). The two main categories of compliance-gaining strategies are the *hierarchical logic* and the *strategy of reasoning*, the first one being an appeal to higher authority – influencing by relying on the chain of command, using the higher levels in the organization to back up requests, expecting undisputed submission – and the latter relying on explanations to support requests, stating the objective merits of a point of view, and being ready to accept a rebuttal grounded in logic. This recalls the notions of power distance and hierarchy that are common in cultural analysis, but we are not so much interested here in knowing whether or not this particular work-related value exists in the cultural group, but rather in knowing whether influence through hierarchy is considered as one of the legitimate modes for gaining compliance or whether reasoning is considered the normal mode.

An illustration of the clash of compliance-gaining strategies is provided by the case of a Finnish industrial company acquired recently by a French group. French engineers asked their Finnish colleagues to supply them with details of the production costs of one of their major products. The Finnish teams replied that they did not want to give this information and asked for what reason the French headquarters would need the data. A stupefied engineering team at the headquarters turned to their managing director, trying to get the information through the hierarchical lines, thinking that the lack of cooperation of their Finnish colleagues meant that they didn't understand that they were now part of the same firm. The managing director of the firm asked his counterpart, the Finnish manager of the Finnish unit, for access to the information and received confirmation that the subsidiary saw no reason why it should release such critical data. We can observe here the expression of two different compliance-gaining logics. The issue is not so much about a lack of cooperative willingness or resistance to sharing information, but rather about the right way to ask. French teams tend to turn rather quickly to a hierarchical logic, while Finns follow a logic of reasoning and explanation. Generally, parties are not aware of their use of a specific strategy, and use it in good faith and interpret any deviation from their own norm as a sign of abnormal behaviour.

In her analysis of a French automobile factory in Slovenia, Globokar (1996) showed how a faulty comprehension of the dynamics of compliance, motivation and control had initially generated serious tensions between French managers and Slovenian staff. Later on, the implementation of a more appropriate management and communication framework, giving ample freedom to the Slovenian factory workers and the chance to talk directly and without constraint to the unit manager, therefore allowing the development of a collective competence through shared speech, helped create an impressive rise in productivity and quality. By contrast, the implementation in another part of the factory of a system based on hierarchy and centred on the technical competence of the unit manager, that relegated workers to the role of executants without the possibility of a dialogue about the content of their work, created a feeling of demotivation and renewed tensions between work units. Slovenian workers also had to learn how to become 'interlocutors' in the French sense of the word, becoming more incisive in their verbal exchanges, daring to put forward their points of view and actively asking questions.

The two other major compliance-gaining logics are the *bargaining strategy* – using negotiation and exchange of favours as well as invoking the social norms of obligation and reciprocity – and the *coalition strategy* – leveraging social pressure and mobilizing other people to support requests. These modes of obedience and compliance are often found in Quebec where the patient construction of a consensual decision is generally preferred to a war of position, and where there is always a way to find informal arrangements to solve conflicts ('il y a moyen de moyenner'). This form of action following a 'communitarian' model (as labelled by Segal, 1991, 1998) differs from the American model by the active search of a consensus, but shares with it the values of direct communication and conviviality in work relationships (for a complete review of works on Quebecer management style, see Dupuis, 2002). These values of openness in communication are a reason why the logic of explanation is also widespread in Quebec – 'come and explain to me your problem, we'll find a solution' – and even more so with the new generation of employees who have been socialized in a mode of overt negotiation with authority.

The sources of communication dissonance in intercultural management

We have just reviewed the spaces of intercultural management, the activities that structure the realities of interaction in business: convincing, transmitting credibility, and finally getting things done and gaining compliance. During these acts of intercultural management, cultural dissonances can appear for several reasons. The sources of these dissonances can be found in the ways we speak a language and in the way we use specific communication tactics to reach our goals. When deviations from the norms of a native and competent speaker do appear, dissonances can occur and lead to poor cooperation and negative perception of the other, and generate numerous pragmatic failures. Intercultural competence is consequently shaped by the different levels of knowledge and mastery of languages, and the ability to master different communicational registers.

Deviations at the surface level

The first type of deviation comes from varying level of mastery of the surface features of the language, such as syntax, grammar and pronunciation. They are the raw materials that allow one to communicate in another language and to understanding people using that language. Language can be spoken in different contexts with different levels of fluency: everyday language, business language, technical language. These are categorizations found in a classic language course, based essentially on acquiring a specific vocabulary and mastering some aspects of grammar and syntax. Even those speaking a language fluently can create considerable deviation when using a term in the wrong context. I participated in a meeting between engineers from a large multinational, where a European programmer triggered a shock among his North American colleagues by stating that 'that piece of software really sucks', a phrase often heard on TV but incredibly impolite in normal conversation. At that level, numerous little misunderstandings can interfere with the conversation, but they are generally identified quite quickly and corrected during the interaction.

Developing a language-centred intercultural competence means also taking into account the ability to understand the different ways of pronouncing the same language: understanding English spoken in southern India is a very different skill from understanding that spoken in northern Britain. Films made in Quebec that are shown in France are often subtitled, and many British movies are difficult to understand for North American audiences. In an experiment carried out among firms in the London area, an analysis of telephone calls showed that many foreign callers were confused by expressions like ''s-ringin-fer-yer' ('it's ringing for you'), 'putin-yerfru' ('putting you through') and 'lines-bizi-ye-old?' ('the lines are busy, will you hold?') (Crick, 1999). One-third of calls failed at the first point of contact and foreign callers reported various rebuffs, including muffled nervous laughter, long silences and responses enunciated with a high level of decibels (as if talking louder would help comprehension).

The ability to understand the dynamics of a multilingual conversation with speakers who have different levels of language fluency is certainly one of the first intercultural competences to develop. One needs to keep in mind that in many situations, the conversation will often involve up to three or four different languages, considering the number of multilingual speakers in many countries. A classic situation is presented in Table 3.3 below, which is an excerpt from an analysis of a business meeting in Asia between three multinational managers (Babcock and Du-Babcock, 2001).

Speaking a language fluently, or understanding speakers from different region, is still no guarantee of good communication. Convincing people from another linguistic/cultural world is still a challenge and deviations at a deeper level can still occur. Three francophones from different areas can experience intercultural conflict, as we'll see in the next section.

Table 3.3 Language proficiency of the speakers at a business meeting

Speakers	*Language proficiency*		
	Japanese	English	Chinese
Divisional manager (Japanese multinational)	Native	Fluent	Elementary
Regional manager (Taiwanese multinational)	Elementary	Intermediate	Native
Country manager stationed in Japan (Taiwanese multinational)	Fluent	Elementary	Native

Deviations coming from the deep structure of a language

Structure of argumentation

Patterns of argumentation – the way in which arguments and evidence are presented – can be the source of cultural dissonance. Every language, or language group, has a way to structure a convincing argument. A typically Western pattern is to present the main point and then introduce supporting elements later on. A more Asian pattern is to present the background of the topic before proceeding to the main point. These two patterns are often confused with a direct or indirect style of communication. This is not the case: each form is as direct and incisive as the other, but in different ways.

   Ron Scollon and Suzanne Wong Scollon, two eminent specialists of communication in the Asian context, illustrate well this difference in the following excerpt (Scollon and Scollon, 1995, p. 2). In a meeting between Hong-Kong Chinese business people and English-speaking North Americans, one of the Chinese team members might say the following:

> Because most of our production is done in China now, and uh, it's not really certain how the government will react in the run-up to 1997, and since I think a certain amount of caution in committing to TV advertisement is necessary because of the expense … So, I suggest that we delay making our decision until after Legco makes its decision.

The Western executive would rather expect the following utterance:

> I suggest that we delay making our decision until after Legco makes its decision. That's because I think a certain amount of caution in committing to TV advertisement is necessary because of the expense. In addition to that, most of our production is done in China now, and it's not really certain how the government will react in the run-up to 1997.

The result of these different discourse strategies can lead to stereotypes like the 'inscrutable' Asian who is perceived as imprecise and vague, or the 'rude' Westerner perceived as too frank, impolite and even brutal.

What can be communicated and in which way

Every culture has a set of rules regarding what is considered proper communication, what can be said or not, and in which style it can be uttered. The ethnographer of communication Donal Carbaugh (Carbaugh, 1988) has studied in depth the cultural rules of American (United States) discourse by viewing a year of broadcasts of a well-known US talk show. Among the cultural rules of American discourse he distinguishes, two are particularly useful to understand the peculiarities of US communicational culture (Carbaugh, 1988, pp. 21–40):

- Individuals have the right to state almost any opinion, as a form of expression of their individual rights.
- When stating a position or opinion, one should speak only for oneself and not impose one's opinions on others.

These rules are found beyond the studios of TV talk shows, and permeate much of American communicational culture. When someone criticizes a project or an idea in the United States, the presenter often answers 'Your point is very well taken' and does not fuel the debate further.

It is a way to acknowledge someone else's point of view and still defend one's own. Both have the individual right to say what they want but will certainly not try to convince the other, nor impose one's own opinion on the other(s).

In education and training, a classic technique in the United States is to ask the opinion of all participants, note their ideas on the flipchart or whiteboard, organize and structure the ideas, and present this as the final output in terms of knowledge to be retained. Everyone would be shocked if the trainer or the consultant were to explain ex-cathedra what needs to be known and reject others' opinions. There is an obligation to acknowledge different ideas equally, and to choose between the competing solutions by using a so-called 'objective' criterion. The criterion is generally expressed in terms of measure (implementation costs, speed of implementation) or in terms of group preference (where the group takes a vote).

In this context, the style of adversarial debate common in other communicational cultures would be seen as shocking, and as part of a tendency to impose one's opinion on others. The French, who really enjoy debate, are generally extremely frustrated by the lack of response from their American partners and do not realize that their attempt to convince is doomed to fail. Conversely, American speakers tend not to realize, first, that this approach allows them to demonstrate their own competence in a much stronger fashion, and second, that it is mainly a rhetorical game that often has only a symbolic role, independent of the final decisions that will be taken at the end of the meeting.

The three cultures of a meeting

There are also cultural rules about the right settings in which to convince. The most traditional setting is the meeting, and it may seem that the role played by a meeting is rather obvious. But again, if the meeting is a well known organizational event, what happens in it can be very different. Three cultures of a meeting can be broadly defined, three visions of what is supposed to happen when people meet face-to-face for a period of time.

The first way of seeing the meeting is as a stage for decision making and problem solving. In this case, the meeting tends to unfold with a set agenda, a tight timetable, decisions taken together issue by issue, and tightly implemented later on. The goal is that after the meeting decisions will have be taken and may be implemented immediately, or that problems will have been solved and a chain of responsibilities defined. We find here the traditional logic of problem resolution adopted in some negotiation processes.

A second view is of the meeting as a stage for exchange of ideas and debate. Here, there is also a set agenda but with a much more flexible timetable. The meeting is a stage for a battle of ideas and opinions, where proposals and solutions identified are only various hypotheses among others. This kind of meeting is common in cultures with a strong oral tradition and where overt communication is important for being visible within the organization. Taking a turn in the conversation is not always with the intention to provide a solution, but rather to express one's right to expression on the topic. The goal of the meeting is to have ideas expressed in a forum, or to test ideas, and some of the decisions taken here will not be implemented at all, the place for the final decision not necessarily being the meeting that just occurred. It is common to discover that the minutes of such a meeting bear no resemblance to the discussion that took place in it.

A third variation of the meeting is one where the encounter is a largely ritualistic way to ratify decisions that have already been taken, with a small part open to improvisation during the event. The presence of officials in the meeting is necessary so that no one can claim not to have been informed, but actually there is no problem to be solved during the event.

It would be ridiculous to try to start to negotiate or discuss during such a forum, as it is simply not the right place nor the right moment for it. In some cases the meeting will end before all of the issues have been made official and when some open questions (still to be negotiated) are pending. In some instances the final decisions are then taken after the official meeting, often in a less formal context, during a big dinner, for instance. However, these decisions still symbolically belong to the meeting that just ended, and have as much value as if the debates had taken place during the formal meeting itself.

Deviations in the culture of the communication channel

Miscommunications can also emerge from different perceptions and expectations regarding the message medium, the channel used to transmit information and communicate. An audit of preferred use of communication channels could be a useful instrument for international companies, as the choice of medium is representative of certain social and cultural practices.

Face-to-face conversation is still an essential way to convey information and establish relations. Even virtual teams operate efficiently only if their members periodically meet face to face. Something fundamental is happening when people are physically co-located. The dominance of orality is also present in telephone conversation (taken in the wide sense of the term, as speech can be broadcast via a traditional telephone operator or by the more recent Internet servers) where communication is synchronous but there is no opportunity – or very little – to give non-verbal feedback. Written information plays also an important role, often as an asynchronous medium with e-mail and classic postal mail. Mixed forms have also appeared where written communication can become relatively synchronous with the emergence of instant messaging services within organizations (and not only in the form of chat between friends).

All communication channels are present in most organizations and can be used in an efficient manner by everyone, but divergences regarding the preference for a channel remain very large. Managing in a multinational company necessitates a rich and targeted use of different media channels, and employees may realize that they are not all equally powerful around the world.

The fact that electronic mail (e-mail) is a ubiquitous form in all communication flows today can make us forget that it is not valued equally by all groups for all purposes. First of all, does the reception of an e-mail oblige the receiver to reply or not? Is it a genuine communication tool, or just an accessory in order to inform people that may be possibly interested in the information, in the same way as a message on a noticeboard works, but that actually no one uses to discuss serious issues?

In the subsidiary of a large Scandinavian industrial group, engineers were using e-mail as their main mode of communication for resolving technical issues. When there was a malfunction on a machine, the standard procedure was to ask for an e-mail message with pictures taken of the parts of the machine in question, and the problems were generally solved within 2 hours, without having to talk to the customer nor visit their premises. To make a phone call in such a case was not really useful as the reply was generally 'send us an e-mail'. The relationship with their South American colleagues was not very good. The e-mails from the Scandinavian teams remained unanswered, and the problems were never satisfactorily solved. An audit revealed than in many of the South American subsidiaries, e-mail was considered to be a second-class communication channel, not to be used for important issues. If the message was sent only by e-mail, it meant that the issue was neither important nor a priority. Something important was necessarily communicated by telephone first, and then possibly by sending supporting information by e-mail. The telephone is not necessarily the most efficient way to communicate – particularly with large time zone differences – but it can, however, remain a necessity for solving specific issues or establish cooperative links within a team.

I also saw European executives extremely shocked to receive some important information by telefax. For them the telefax was a communication channel dedicated to suppliers, therefore to unimportant partners. According to them, any important information should have been transmitted via a special meeting or by traditional mail using official paper signed by a leading authority. The senders of the message saw the fax as an economical and efficient way to sent that information from a distant unit and were extremely surprised to hear that their gesture had been badly received.

Deviations due to the cultural scenarios for action

In parallel to the growing integration of international markets, there is also a growing diversity in modes of management, organizational structure and local workforce behaviours (Guillén, 2001, 1994). Everyday life management in the enterprise requires a very high level of adaptation and many national models are very deeply integrated in everyday practices. The study carried out in Europe by Michael Segalla and his colleagues (Segalla et al., 2000) shows that the logic that drives human resources management decisions varies a lot from country to country. Their study of 900 decision makers focused on decision-making scenarios about recruitment, promotion, compensation and staff reduction in five countries: Germany, Spain, France, the United Kingdom and Italy. On all dimensions there were found to be important differences over what was considered to be an appropriate type of decision. Two major dominant logics exist – the market logic (decisions based on objective performance indicators) and the group logic (decisions linked to the logic of belonging and fidelity to the group) – but each country has a profile of logic that varies according to the type of decision to be taken. German managers, for instance, tend to have a group logic for recruitment and workforce reduction, but a market logic for promotion and compensation. Each culture has a set of expectations about what employers and employees can or cannot demand from each other, and both logics can be present for the same group, according to the type of decision to be taken. Again, one size does not fit all, and unmet expectations can trigger serious conflicts in multinationals or acquired firms.

The preferences for a particular type of interpersonal leadership are also very diverse among employees. Some groups prefer a coaching approach to leadership, while others feel more comfortable with a directing approach. Regarding interpersonal communication from leaders, preference can go from high to low intensity, from frequent pep-talks to 'silent coaching'. In her analysis of interpersonal leadership preferences among 17,000 employees of a Swedish multinational, Lena Zander (1997) distinguishes eight major clusters of preferences for interpersonal management along the two dimensions of interpersonal communication and management (Table 3.4).

In the first group where preference goes to a coaching approach, employees from the North American group (USA and Canada) want their leader to communicate intensively and make them proud of their work (pep-talk coaching), while the Anglo–Australian–Dutch group prefers a more personalized type of communication, taking an interest in their personal life (personalized coaching). With those appreciating a coaching approach but with a lower intensity of interpersonal leadership, the Nordic countries group prefers a high level of empowering (empowering coaching) and displays a high reluctance to direct supervision

Table 3.4 Preferences for a type of interpersonal leadership

Intensity of interpersonal leadership	Focus of interpersonal leadership	
	Coaching	*Directing*
High	USA and Canada Pep-talk coaching	Spain (Brazil) Pep-talk directing
	Great Britain, Australia and the Netherlands Personal coaching	Austria Communicative directing
Low	Denmark, Norway and Sweden Empowering coaching	Philippines Personal directing
	Finland Silent coaching	Japan, Germany, Switzerland, Belgium and France Empowering directing

of work, with Finland showing a preference for even more minimal communication (silent coaching).

In the second group, there is little interest for coaching and preference for a classic style consisting of supervision and direction. A first cluster of countries wants high intensity of communication with their leaders, with employees from Spain and Brazil wanting to be made proud of their work (pep-talk directing) and the Austrians wanting frequent communication (communicative directing). The last group indicates a preference for directing but with less intense interpersonal communication. Employees from the Japan–Germany–Switzerland–Belgium–France country group prefer an empowering style with frequent control of achievements and review of objectives. They are much less attracted by a personal style of communication (empowering directing). The group of employees in the Philippines is the one that tends to prefer a more personal communication for being directed (personal directing).

This complexity is a challenge for international management: things seemingly as simple as rewarding, criticizing, motivating, firing and recruiting necessitate in reality a very high level of global management competences. Of course, it is always possible to ignore these subtleties, but such a course of action paves the way for crisis and conflicts.

Cooperative forms of internationalization, such as alliances and joint ventures, are the theatre of even more complex intercultural interactions, as it is necessary to combine different management and interaction styles into a functional whole, leveraging differences to innovate while avoiding destructive conflicts. In their study of a German–Japanese joint venture, Brannen and Salk (2000) showed how a common work culture was formed in the venture little by little, in a relatively unpredictable way, with improvised and negotiated solutions between partners. In this type of organization, the success of the joint venture depends on the ability of organizational members to adopt a certain form of diplomacy, accept its own limits (such as being aware that only 85 per cent of what is communicated will be understood, or that headquarters' control system will necessarily diverge), and finally on the capacity to be innovative with work and communication modes. For instance in the joint venture, German and Japanese teams progressively invented a form of compromise between the two national cultures of decision making: shorter meetings with fewer people involved, co-directors having more freedom to make decisions without going through the group discussion phase, and finally co-directors being in charge of their own national group whenever a conflict emerged and needed to be resolved. An interactionist approach to culture is essential when dealing with such situations. It would be unrealistic to adopt a complete uniformity of management modes, as this would lead to the loss of valuable employees and an inability to exploit the potential value of the alliance. It would also be a mistake to try and select a partner according to their organizational or working culture, as in most of the cases an alliance is made for reasons of technological complementarity or access to new markets and resources. It is therefore necessary to develop and improvise new ways to work together, to convince, to be credible and gain compliance by leveraging different logics of action and different types of communication and conflict resolution modes.

This is the realm of symbolic communication. The conflicts over logics of action and management, such as those analysed by d'Iribarne and his team (1998) (logic of honour versus logic of contract and logic of community) are due to a lack of knowledge of the different repertoires – in other words the scenarios and the symbolic images to be used – for motivating, gaining compliance, rewarding and criticizing, obtaining information. The comparative approach helps us understand where those different logics come from, knowing in which values they are possibly anchored and why they are efficient in some environments. The interactionist approach would rather focus on understanding how these logics can conflict, how to use in an 'efficient' manner different communication modes in order to avoid dissonance with other communication types, and how to create hybrid systems of communication modes anchored in different logics of action. The logics and cultural scripts can correspond to deeply anchored values, but again, if cultural conflicts are often perceived and interpreted as conflicts about values, in most cases they originate in a lack of communicational competence and a lack of knowledge of existing cultural scripts. This lack of competence frequently takes the form of a complete ignorance, as training in intercultural management and communication remains the exception in organizations, so strong being the illusion of universality in management and negotiation techniques. As illustrated in Box 3.3, this illusion of universality can make the acquisition of a foreign company quite painful, even for experienced teams.

Developing intercultural competency means mastering the deep elements of language and communicational culture, so to give us the ability to fine tune our messages according to our intentions and apply a set strength to our utterances. This competence is essentially acquired through experience with our cultural and, later on, professional socialization. With the first professional experience comes the realization that the world of the firm does not always follow the same rules as the social world beyond it. Employees need to identify these rules and 'learn the ropes' of efficient communication within the organization where they work. Information may be gathered or communicated via formal channels (hierarchical lines, official written material) or informal channels (direct and transversal contacts with colleagues, grapevine communication), and there are tacit rules about what can be said or not in the company. These rules may profoundly differ in two different organizations, whether based in the same or in different countries. 'Corporate culture' differences are generally identified because of differing rules of internal communication, and may actually be not much more than a set of interaction and communication rules. Professions have also cultural rules for communication: sales people talk, engineer talk and consultant talk are all rather different from each other. This is one of the reasons why moving from one industry or profession to another can be difficult, both for managers and for leaders. Then, on top of that, come the issues of language pragmatics that present an extra challenge for communication in the intercultural context. In the vast majority of cases, in intercultural management we navigate in automatic pilot mode without realizing that our ways of acting, reacting,

---

Box 3.3 A Canadian–European acquisition

A few years ago a large Canadian company acquired a French competitor. The operation was so well coordinated that it gained approval from the European Commission in an unprecedentedly short timespan.

Shortly after the transaction, the management of the integration process made the front pages of the French press, which reported an extremely aggressive management style on the part of the acquiring company's teams, who displayed constant bad faith and a refusal to negotiate with the 'partenaires sociaux' (social partners) – in other words the trade unions.

Canadian managers showed their goodwill by implementing a set of initiatives for helping their European colleagues undergo the integration process, such as providing English-language training to be optimally prepared for their 're-hiring' interviews, which were to be conducted in English as part of the firm's global policy. Wanting to proceed quickly with the integration process so as to reduce uncertainty, they had a classic attitude towards trade unions, using a combination of the fait accompli and confrontation.

Tensions emerged rapidly and led to the mass departure of experienced executives, who declared officially that they could not bear to see the destruction of a gem of French industry. On another front, the difficult relationship with the trade unions had the opposite effect to that expected, and actually extended the period of uncertainty.

How could two groups with positive intentions find themselves in a situation of explosive conflict so quickly?

First of all, there were two different visions in play about the nature of the work relationships, with one group seeing it as contractual (the logic of contract as labelled by d'Iribarne) and the other as a professional and community model (the logic of honour).

Next, different understandings of the role of trade unions definitely played a part. Trade union representatives were treated roughly as, through an Anglo-Saxon prism, trade unions are mostly seen as enemies of the organization to be opposed, and if possible to be avoided at all cost (large corporations are often suspected of simply closing down subsidiaries where a trade union would have been created). In a more European logic, trade unions are partners to be taken into account, often unwillingly, but to be taken into account anyway. The expectations in terms of relationships with top management are very different from one continent to the other. The tone adopted by the acquiring firm was particularly aggressive, in strong contrast with expectations, and it triggered a cycle of negative emotions that lengthened considerably the negotiation period with the unions and thus made decision making much more difficult.

---

communicating and leading can be executed in a very different fashion, with different styles, and much more efficiently.

Practices versus ideals: a call for innovation in intercultural management

With all the different ways to operate, whether in negotiation or playing the status game or different convincing strategies, there is a difference between 'what is' the dominant management and communication style and 'what should be' the ideal practice as dreamed or imagined by those working in organizations. In the most recent studies of the cartographic traditions, particularly in the GLOBE project (House et al., 2002; House, 1998), this dichotomy is taken into account and assessed in the measures of work-related values, with sometimes large differences between practices and expectations. The experience of a Mexican subsidiary of the multinational Danone analysed by d'Iribarne (2002) illustrates well the fact that Mexican employees confirm that hierarchy is extremely present in Mexican corporations, but that its exercise is often considered by the same workers to be a detestable practice. The hierarchical logic can be efficient and dominant in many countries, but it is not always a good vector of dynamism and innovation. Many young Europeans are moving to Anglo-Saxon countries at the beginning of their career precisely because they find 'classic' hierarchical management styles difficult to tolerate anymore. More and more Japanese and Chinese graduates choose to start their careers in a foreign firm, as these tend to offer quicker promotion opportunities.

It is therefore possible to go against the existing practices, as long as the potential impact is assessed. What is counter-productive is to think that a good practice at home can be a good practice somewhere else, or even to consider that a dominant practice in a country is a good practice. Cultural innovation can and should exist, but unexpected conflicts should be avoided.

Understanding misunderstandings: a model of cultural dissonance

We are often in situations beyond our area of cultural expertise, where things are going to happen that we do not understand. When we no longer get the point of a message, in a meeting or in a written document, an automatic reaction is to be shocked, exasperated, or attribute incompetence or lack of credibility to the other. A rule of thumb is: when you feel bothered, insulted or experience unease that you cannot fully understand, you'll most likely find the reason at the level of intercultural communication.

Rather than speaking of culture shock – shocks generally being considered as unavoidable and deeply anchored in people's values – we should talk about 'cultural dissonance' that usually stems from a communication dissonance. The model presented here (Figure 3.1) sums up the different facets of that dissonance.

Cultural dissonance can materialize in behaviours within or between organizations, as described on the right-hand side of the figure ('Consequences of dissonance'). Organizational conflicts, lack of interpersonal trust, information retention, are often triggered by a communication dissonance. It is rare for anyone in a joint venture to be considered totally unreliable, but we might often interpret that person's communication or management style as reflecting someone not to be trusted. As we saw earlier in the Ciba-Geigy and Alza case, a good intention communicated the wrong way can be negatively interpreted. Members of an organization explain this dissonance – this so-called culture shock – by attributing it to cultural differences (not very precisely defined) or to a bureaucratic or hierarchic style, and generally consider that there is nothing to be done about it. One needs to be careful not to put too much face value on this first interpretation, as the source of dissonance is to be found in much deeper layers than the generic 'culture' label.

The sources of communication dissonance (left-hand side of Figure 3.1) can be found in different deviations from cultural norms of the language that we reviewed earlier. The easiest to identify are surface deviations from the native language norm: accent, syntax, grammar, fluency. Then there enter into play rules of pragmatics that dictate the way language is used in order to convince and not to offend during a debate: structure of the argumentation, ways to address contradictions, preferred channels of communication. Finally come deviations from the way language is use to generate action and the culturally acceptable scenarios for action. These elements are often considered as simply management techniques, but we

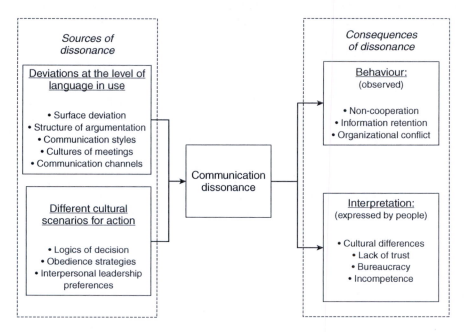

Figure 3.1 A model of intercultural dissonance

should never forget that all these techniques use language as their primary tool, so they belong to the realm of communication. When using a wrong compliance strategy, or a communication style poorly adapted to the local leadership's preferences, there is the risk of generating a strong communication dissonance. These communication strategies have been identified by the managers as efficient through their education, socialization, and personal and professional learning. Actually, nothing prevents us from using other communication modes, whatever our personal preferences might be. The francophone or Hispanic manager may perfectly well have a personal preference for adversarial debates, but in a Scandinavian environment they will have to learn how to communicate in a softer way, more in accordance with a logic of coalition. What we describe as a different culture is often nothing more than a different way to communicate.

But at the end of the day, is it worth it? Wouldn't it be possible to do international business without having to learn about complex modes of communication and management? After all, it seems that a vast majority of managers and businesspeople are doing transactions, managing and making profits without wondering too much about intercultural competences. This is of course often the case, but the hidden cost of unidentified cultural faux-pas is without a doubt horrendous.

Let's take a a look at the incident experienced by a very large communications company whose general manager triggered a communication dissonance that cost his firm close to 6 million US dollars of revenue per year and the termination of a 14-year-old joint venture with one of China's leaders in media and communications. The Chinese vice-chairman of the joint venture, also head of a large advertising agency in China, was going to London to discuss with his British colleague the management problems faced for the past few months by the joint venture. There was an enormous divergence between the two managers in terms of what a 'frank' discussion about issues to solve was supposed to be. A few weeks later the Chinese general manager was pronouncing the end of the 14-year-old joint venture and announcing an alliance with the direct competitor of his previous ally. In an interview with the British newspaper the *Financial Times* the Chinese manager stated

> I have met a lot of people but never met anyone as rude as [name of the chief executive of the British group]. I went to London to tell him about the problems and he dealt with me very rudely in the discussion. Because of this kind of attitude, we have been forced to cease cooperation with him. We have instead looked for a more understanding partner with whom to develop the Chinese market.

The revenues from that joint venture represented only a little more than 1 per cent of the activities of the British group in China, which still amounts to 6 million US dollars in a market growing at 120 per cent per year. Nice invoice for a communication mistake.

Contrasting two approaches: for and against the classic analysis

The classic cultural analysis can be useful for studying and understanding relatively simple phenomena in a well-defined context, such as the comparison of top managers' behaviours. This type of analysis quickly reveals its limits as soon as the situation becomes more complex and involves the coordination of many organizational actors, or when we study complex, company-wide processes – in fact every time we analyse a process rather than compare discrete situations.

A deeper analysis, following d'Iribarne, makes us understand the deep historical sources of behaviours within the organization. The analysis of 'logics of action' is extremely valuable and allows us to compare different systems of action and realize that the levers of managerial influence and action are very diverse. However, this historical analysis does not necessarily shed light on the unfolding of managerial actions and does not always help in designing new intercultural systems.

Understanding the historical and institutional sources of cultural misunderstanding is very instructive but it puts us in a situation of interpretation of differences. Trying to understand how *perceptions* of difference emerge is putting us in a logic of action. For instance, reading the examples given by Dupuis on the theme of the 'damn French' (Dupuis 2004, 2005), it is quite clear that when Quebecer managers use such stereotypes in their speech, it is always following a communication event perceived as improper, in other words a situation of communicative dissonance. The initial problem is not so much the existence of the stereotype of the damn French, but the fact that breaking the communication rules will trigger a symbolic defence, in the form of the evocation of the stereotype.

The experience of a Franco-Finnish corporate acquisition

In order to illustrate the limits of a dimension-based cultural analysis and show what a communication and interaction-centred approach could bring, let's consider a real case of a Franco-Finnish corporate acquisition. The complete study and its model are presented in detail in other works (Irrmann, 2005, 2006). This case is based on an in-depth analysis of the acquisition by Frantech (pseudonym), a French group in the industrial ventilation industry, of the Finnish firm Fintech (name disguised), operating in a very profitable niche market in the same industry. The acquisition gave Frantech a consolidated position in a growing market by acquiring one of the industry leaders, and brought new opportunities for an activity representing only 10 per cent of its turnover but a large share of its profits.

The classical cultural analysis

An analysis using Hofstede's cultural dimensions (1981) can help to construct a hypothesis on the challenge of integrating this new unit of the firm (Table 3.5).

The first striking difference is about power distance. In the traditional literature on management styles, French firms are generally considered as having a high level of hierarchy with a paternalist management style, while the Nordic firms (Scandinavian) would have a flat hierarchy and a very consultative style. Lawrence and Edwards (2000, p. 42) give the following description of the French management style: 'the hierarchy is more self-conscious, predominates, and there is less mixing across ranks or levels. A French employee who has a problem will be more inclined to pass it up to the next level for resolution.' On the other side, Lindell and Arvonen (1997) describe the Nordic management style (including Finland) as managers having 'high trust of subordinates' managing with 'friendliness' and 'taking care of subordinates'. The crossing of power distance and uncertainty avoidance made by Hofstede places France on the pyramid model quadrant and Finland on the well-oiled machine, which corresponds to the kind of metaphors used by other popular authors who write about management in these countries.

One could thus expect conflicts over management style, with one side having a very hierarchical and bureaucratic style and the other a decentralized and flat hierarchy system.

The mirror image phenomenon

In the Frantech–Fintech case, we observed a very interesting mirror effect in the perception of management style. Fintech employees were certainly describing French management as extremely bureaucratic, with a desire to control everything and refusing to communicate horizontally. But each and every Finnish employee was describing their own style using the auto-stereotype of an egalitarian manager, talking straight and informally, and able to make a decision quickly without having to go through the whole hierarchy for authorization – all things that were impossible for the French, according to them.

But the French managers were actually saying exactly the same thing about their Finnish colleagues. The discourse was generally the following: 'here we have a culture of horizontal communication, without many hierarchical differences'. The communication problems between the units were attributed to the excessive hierarchy present in the Finnish organization where everything had to go through the managing director. Finns were described as 'extremely bureaucratic', with a mentality of 'Big boss, small boss and even smaller boss; they look at each other before they say anything at all. No one can obtain anything from them.' Finnish executives were seen as not wanting to discuss anything directly with their

Table 3.5 Analysis using Hofstede's cultural dimensions

	Power distance	*Individualism collectivism*	*Uncertainty avoidance*	*Masculinity femininity*
France	68	71	86	43
Finland	33	63	59	26

colleagues, and always using the official hierarchical line. According to the interviewees, this attitude was not well received in France, where informality and direct discussion across hierarchical levels were said to be promoted at all levels.

It is clear that just comparing the cultural dimension does not allow us to understand what happens in the reality of the intercultural contact. It does not mean that these differences would not play a role, but rather to acknowledge that the notion of cultural differences – actually the comparison of work-related values, which is what Hofstede (1981) actually measures – is far from playing the major role it is credited for in intercultural work relationships.

Analysis of the critical incidents

In the Frantech–Fintech case, the interviews conducted helped to track the sources of difficulties in communication and showed that most of the perceived problems came from an inability to efficiently communicate between groups. What is interesting is that the label put on the problem is often misleading.

For instance the label of bureaucracy and hierarchical distance often appeared as the result of a misunderstanding about the right way to convince the other.

Many meetings were conducted in a tense atmosphere, as both parties were using their own modes of convincing, in perfectly good faith. The French teams were using a communication strategy where speech played an important role. With this style, one expresses aloud the thinking process, can interrupt others in their talk in order to show interest, and silence is clearly a danger sign. The conception of a meeting is that of a forum for displaying ideas and verbal brilliance, where rhetorical skirmishing is the goal. Finnish teams were using a strategy of communication where one expresses only the result of the thinking – one says only what one thinks and believes in – and where it is absolutely forbidden to interrupt someone who is talking. Silence is a mark of polite interest and respect. The culture of meetings is one of sharing ideas but particularly of finding common solutions which, once decided upon, are very rapidly implemented. A person's status does not play any role in these discussions, and the discussion cannot be an oratorical joust.

In these conditions, the very 'dominating' verbal attitude of the French was considered by the Finns as the mark of an unbearable authoritarianism which refused to listen to others. On the other side, the French teams considered the 'passive' attitude of their colleagues as proof of their immobility, which they interpreted as stemming from a very bureaucratic system. This perception was reinforced by the feeling that one could never discuss alternative solutions, since once a decision was taken it was generally applied in an inflexible manner.

The strategic consequences of communication dissonance

In the Frantech–Fintech case the poor quality of communication between the two firms resulted in an extremely limited integration of activities and exchange of knowledge. While strategic analysis showed that some activities managed from France would benefit from joining the much more important network of the Finnish unit, teams remained separated without benefiting from synergies and unable to exchange market and technical knowledge. The integration plan failed because of a lack of communicational competence on both sides. Because of its peripheral geographic position and its language mastered only by a few foreigners, the Finnish unit could not easily be coerced by firing local top and middle managers and replacing them by staff from the French headquarters. The status quo was maintained with management at arm's length and limited collaboration. This frustrated both parties, as they saw the potential of collaborating but could never agree on common activities. The issue was not about cultural differences but about cultural interactions.

Conclusion: understanding intercultural dissonance for better communication, interaction and intervention

Managing in an intercultural environment is much more complex than a simple exercise of comparative cultural cartography. The comparison of work-related values and the comprehension of major logics of action is a good start for understanding how organizations function and how they are managed in different cultural universes. But the big challenge is to navigate through all these different modes of action and learn how to communicate, motivate and convince across cultural universes. For that, one has to look at the cultural interaction, the one reflecting the reality of work in intercultural and international contexts in the business and organizational world. We saw how communication and use of language plays a major role during that interaction. At the end of the day, in many cases, cultural distance is probably nothing more than an inability to communicate ideas in an efficient way across boundaries. By conducting an in-depth analysis of the difficulties appearing in alliances and international mergers such as those mentioned above, one notices that in no way did the managers involved on both sides have bad faith or wanted to harm their colleagues. However, it is often about perceptions. Intentions are the same: collaborate and work together, but the result is reciprocal mistrust. Attending to the big categories of dissonance we talked about, and their sources, can help us to defuse similar situations. Talking about dissonance rather than cultural dissonance is one of the ways to advance our comprehension and our mastery of the intercultural.

A final metaphor that may illustrate what intercultural competence is about is provided by the skill of driving a car. Knowing how to drive a car in Germany may not help you in France or in the United States. Beyond the basic control of the vehicle, what leads to a safe driving is informed expectations about others' behaviour, the rules for crossing each other's path (the number one source of accidents between the Germanic driving culture and the Latin driving culture), and the tacit rules of behaviour. All local drivers know that in New York or Palermo, a green light does not necessarily protect you and that you may expect a taxi to jump out in front of you even if your light has been green for half a minute; expecting the same rule in Stockholm is a recipe for accidents. Similarly, in all driving schools around the world, everyone learns how to negotiate a crossing by imagining the central point in the intersection. But in some countries you learn that you have to go beyond that point and then make your turn, while in other countries you learn that you should turn in front of that central point. Both rules allow cars to turn harmoniously provided that both drivers follow the same rule. Put face to face an American driver (turning in front of the central point) and a Latin driver (turning after the central point) and you have an accident.

In the same fashion, learning basic management techniques is like learning how to manoeuvre a vehicle. The crucial point is to manage the balance with other organizational actors (the other vehicles), your colleagues, your clients, your competitors, your contacts, your potential customers. What is important is to develop the ability to interact, judging when you should change your communication strategies in order to convince, appear credible, be obeyed or request a service from someone. Looking at a map – comparing cultural dimensions – can be useful for finding your way, but the moment of truth comes on entering the cultural vehicle and driving it. It is at that moment that one realizes that interacting with someone is more difficult than simply comparing oneself to the other. Pragmatic communication is a skill for driving in different communicational and cultural worlds. One cannot learn all the possible cultural scripts existing in the business world; however, it is possible to develop your communication skills and therefore your interaction skills in order to move around in the best possible way in an intercultural situation – and to drive without major accidents in the majority of the world's organizational cities.

References

Adler, N. J. and Graham, J. L. 1989. Cross-cultural interaction: the international comparison fallacy. *Journal of International Business Studies*, 20: 515–37.

Angelmar, R. and Stern, L. W. 1978. Development of a content analytic system for analysis of bargaining communication in marketing. *Journal of Marketing Research*, 15(February): 93–102.

Babcock, R. D. and Du-Babcock, B. 2001. Language-based communication zones in international business communication. *Journal of Business Communication*, 38(4): 372–412.

Brannen, M. Y. and Salk, J. E. 2000. Partnering across borders: negotiating organizational culture in a German–Japanese joint venture. *Human Relations*, 53(4): 451.

Carbaugh, D. 1988. *Talking American: Cultural Discourses on Donahue*. Norwood, NJ: Ablex Publishing Corporation.

Child, J. 2001. Trust – the fundamental bond in global collaboration. *Organizational Dynamics*, 29(4): 274.

Crick, D. 1999. An investigation into SMEs' use of languages in their export operations. *International Journal of Entrepreneurial Behaviour and Research*, 5(1): 19.

D' Iribarne, P. 1998. Comment s'accorder: une rencontre franco-suédoise. In P. d'Iribarne, A. Henry, J.-P. Segal, S. Chevrier and T. Globokar (eds), *Cultures et mondialisation: gérer par delà les frontières*. Paris: Seuil.

—— 2002. Motivating workers in emerging countries: universal tools and local adaptations. *Journal of Organizational Behavior*, 23(3): 243–56.

Datta, D. K. and Puia, G. 1995. Cross-border acquisitions: an examination of the influence of relatedness. *Management International Review (MIR)*, 35(4): 337.

Doz, Y. L. 1996. The evolution of cooperation in strategic alliances: initial conditions or learning processes? *Strategic Management Journal*, 17(7): 55.

Dupuis, J.-P. 2002. La gestion québécoise à la lumière des études comparative. *Recherches Sociographiques*, 43(1): 183–205.

—— 2004. Être un 'maudit Français' en gestion au Québec – un portrait et une interprétation. *Cahiers de recherche HEC Montréal*, 04–03: 1–47.

—— 2005. Être un 'maudit français' en gestion au Québec. *Gérer and Comprendre*, 81(September): 51–61.

Globokar, Tatjana. 1996. Intercultural management in Eastern Europe: an empirical study of a French-Slovenian plant. *International Studies of Management and Organization*, 26(3): 47–59.

Graham, J. L. 1985. Cross-cultural marketing negotiations: a laboratory experiment. *Marketing Science* (4): 130–46.

—— 1996. Vis-à-vis international business negotiations. In G. Pervez and J.-C. Usunier (eds), *International Business Negotiations*. Oxford: Pergamon, 1996.

Graham, J. L., Mintu, A. T. and Rodgers, W. 1994. Explorations of negotiation behaviors in ten foreign cultures using a model developed in the United States. *Management Science*, 40(72–95).

Guillén, M. F. 2001. Is globalization civilizing, destructive or feeble? A critique of five key debates. *Annual Review of Sociology*, 27(1): 235.

—— 1994. *Models of Management: Work, Authority, and Organization in a Comparative Perspective*. Chicago: University of Chicago Press.

Hofstede, G. 1981. Culture and Organization. *International Studies of Management and Organization*, 11(4): 15–41.

Hofstede, G., Van Deusen, C. A., Mueller, C. B., Charles, T. A. and Business Goal Network. 2002. What goals do business leaders pursue? A study in fifteen countries. *Journal of International Business Studies*, 33(4): 785–803.

House, R. J. 1998. A brief history of GLOBE. *Journal of Managerial Psychology*, 13(3/4): 230.

House, R., Javidan, M., Hanges, P. and Dorfman, P. 2002. Understanding cultures and implicit leadership theories across the globe: an introduction to project GLOBE. *Journal of World Business*, 37(1): 3–10.

Irrmann, O. 1999. Intercultural business interaction: French–Finnish aspects. In M. Lauristin and L. Rahnu (eds), *Intercultural Communication and Changing National Identities*. Tartu, Finland: Tartu University Press and Nordic Network for Intercultural Communication.

—— 2005. Communication dissonance and pragmatic failures in strategic processes: the case of cross-border acquisitions. In G. Szulanski, J. Porac and Y. Doz (eds), *Advances in Strategic Management, Vol. 22: Advances in Strategy Process Research*, pp. 251–67. New York: JAI Elsevier Science.

—— 2006. *Intercultural Communication and the Implementation of Cross-Border Acquisitions*. Helsinki, Finland: Helsinki School of Economics Press.

Jaworski, A. (ed.) 1997. *Silence: Interdisciplinary Perspectives*. Berlin: Mouton de Gruyter.

Lawrence, P. and Edwards, V. 2000. *Management in Western Europe*. London: Macmillan Press.

Lindell, M. and Arvonen, J. 1997. The Nordic management style in a European context. *International Studies of Management and Organization*, 26(3): 73–91.

Mintzberg, H. 1973. *The Nature of Managerial Work*. New York: Harper and Row.

—— 1975. The manager's job: folklore and fact. *Harvard Business Review*, 53(4): 49.

Morosini, P., Shane, S. and Singh, H. 1998. National cultural distance and cross-border acquisition performance. *Journal of International Business Studies*, 29(1): 137–58.

Neu, J. and Graham, J. L. 1994. A new methodological approach to the study of interpersonal influence tactics: a 'test drive' of a behavioral scheme. *Journal of Business Research*, 29(2): 131–44.

Scollon, R. and Scollon, S. W. 1995. *Intercultural Communication*. Oxford/Cambridge: Blackwell.

Segal, J.-P. 1991. Les pièges du management interculturel: une aventure franco-québécoise. *Gestion*, 16(1): 17–25.

—— 1998. Le frère déplace le frère. Un épisode de la vie d'une usine québécoise. In P. d'Iribarne, A. Henry, J.-P. Segal, S. Chevrier and T. Globokar (eds), *Cultures et Mondialisation: Gérer par delà les Frontières*. Paris: Seuil.

Segalla, M., Fischer, L. and Sandner, K. 2000. Making cross-cultural research relevant to European corporate integration: old problem – new approach. *European Management Journal*, 18(1): 38–51.

Sullivan, J. and Taylor, S. 1991. A cross-cultural test of compliance-gaining theory. *Management Communication Quarterly*, 5(2): 220–39.

Sullivan, J. J., Albrecht, T. L. and Taylor, S. 1990. Process, organizational, relational, and personal determinants of managerial compliance-gaining. *Journal of Business Communication*, 27(4): 331.

Tannen, D. and Saville-Troike, M. (eds) 1985. *Perspectives on Silence*. Norwood: Ablex.

Tengblad, S. 2002. Time and space in managerial work. *Scandinavian Journal of Management*, 18(4): 543–65.

Thomas, J. 1983. Cross-cultural pragmatic failure. *Applied Linguistics*, 4: 91–112.

UNCTAD. 2005. *World Investment Report 2005: Transnational Corporations and the Internationalization of R and D*. New York and Geneva: United Nations.

Usunier, J.-C. 1996a. Cultural aspects of international business negotiations. In P. Ghauri and J.-C. Usunier (eds), *International Business Negotiations*: Oxford: Pergamon.

—— 1996b. *Marketing Across Cultures* (3rd edn). London: Pearson Education (Prentice Hall/ Financial Times).

Very, P., Calori, R. and Lubatkin, M. 1993. An investigation of national and organizational cultural influences in recent European mergers. In P. Shrivastava, A. Huff and J. Dutton (eds), *Advances in Strategic Management*, pp. 323–43. London: JAI Press.

Very, P. and Lubatkin, M. 1997. Relative standing and the performance of recently acquired European firms. *Strategic Management Journal*, 18(8): 593.

Very, P., Lubatkin, M. and Calori, R. 1996. A cross-national assessment of acculturative stress in recent European mergers. *International Studies of Management and Organization*, 26(1): 59–86.

Zander, L. 1997. The license to lead – an 18 country study of the relationship between employees' preferences regarding interpersonal leadership and national culture. Stockholm: Institute of International Business (IIB), Stockholm School of Economics (published dissertation).

Part II

Issues

4 The international manager

Philippe Pierre

Translated from the French by
Suzan Nolan and Leila Whittemore

Introduction

Today, companies must optimize their resources for a population of managers boasting an intense geographic mobility. Related debates focus on the efficiency of recruitment, integration, the development of double careers, the opportune utilization of new information technologies (such as working remotely), and the influence of family members on the success of this mobility. However, few studies have explored the double movement by which international managers continue to act in the spirit of the community in which they were raised, while at the same time identifying with their professional roles and playing these roles in a personal and effective way, despite being outside of the context of their culture of origin (Hammer and Bennett, 1998).

For the German geologist who has been assigned to Africa for 6 years (recruited in Jersey with children studying in Paris and Los Angeles), for the English expert accountant (born in India and married to an Indonesian), or for the Gabonese financier (recruited in the United States on the behalf of a subsidiary of a major French oil company, for which he has already been working for 6 years), a stable definition of a sense of belonging, while increasingly more difficult to come by, seems free from multiple partnerships and is scattered across the globe. On whom does my career's longevity depend on, and with whom can I negotiate a minimum commitment for my professional future, given that both my mobility and the number of countries that I travel through are increasing, and that my family, friends, and relatives live on a number of different continents?

This chapter explores the socialization of managers who have been led to live in an important state of geographic and professional mobility, and who are stretched between several points of value that at times may be difficult to reconcile (cultures of upbringing, cultures of host countries, business cultures). At the basis of our approach lies a series of questions concerning both the cultural becoming of 'mobile' populations within businesses and their assumed ability to reconnect, to compartmentalize, or to foster dialogue between several cultural groups (Metzger and Pierre, 2003). Similarly, we also seek to understand both what culture 'is' and what it can 'do' by collectively considering the contrasts and the cultural traits that are selectively (strategically) used in order to organize their identities and interactions.

The results of our research that are presented in this chapter have been lived by the author: he was 'immersed' as both a researcher and a full-time employee for two large 'globalized' companies of French origin (one in the oil industry that we will call 'Alpha' and another in the cosmetics industry that we will call 'Gamma') (Pierre, 2005).[1] Through his experiences as an operational manager in areas of management such as international mobility, training, and recruitment, and his 5-year tenure as the director of human resources (which put him into direct contact with mobile managers from France and other countries), the author was able to observe scenes of daily professional life, which over the course of later analysis were understood to be real-life instances of multiple cultural codes conflicting within single individuals.

In observing expatriate managers, the question of their international business mobility has led us to understand the cultural variable of work, not per se, but in terms of novelty and the perceived gap that the disoriented individual perceives between the cultural environment that he has left behind and the environment of his destination. In our view, this perceived gap seems to be simultaneously related to one's general adaptation to the new living conditions brought about by international mobility (housing, food, children's education, spouse's employment, the possibility of finding time to relax and to take care of oneself), one's ability to adapt to new work environments, and (while often neglected by analysts,) one's ability to socially integrate in the host country, beyond the walls of the host company.

Moreover, we will explore the issue of identity production during periods of geographic displacement, which is linked to the cultural problem of business management. What consequences can international mobility have on managers' construction of their identity? To what extent can we speak of 'plural' or 'double' identities? Are we witnessing the emergence of an elite society of 'international managers' that carries with it its own cultural and professional way of experiencing international relations?

In this chapter, we will first underline the fact that the number of new actors involved in international mobility (originally from subsidiaries of the largest French companies) has increased significantly in the last 30 years. This emergence is related to a phenomenon of expatriate managers who, in their movement towards positions of upper management in the financial, administrative, or industrial sectors, desire to be treated equally alongside French expatriate populations.

This chapter will underline that within Alpha and Gamma, the globalized flows of a new type of personnel have led to particular social constructions of these individuals' identities, a situation which differs from both those concerning immigration (such as the sustainable expatriation in businesses during the 1960s), and those focused on the specific forms of mobility analyzed by sociologists in the 1980s (Sainsaulieu, 1988; Dubar 1991). It is our belief that for 'international managers', this complex process of identity production is not only at work in the workplace, but also sees itself played out in these individuals' personal and social lives. It follows that the degree to which these international managers adapt may differ according to their employment status (work adaptation), familial situation (adaptation to general living conditions), or social positioning (adaptation to social interaction with members of the host culture) (Cerdin, 1996). From this perspective, the paradox is that in reality, of these three spheres, the sphere of work is the least disrupted by an instance of international mobility. More specifically, in such a situation, the level of uncertainty that is attached to work is lower than that which is related to general living conditions, and even lower than the uncertainty that concerns relations with members of the host country.

One contribution of this chapter will consider the 'identity strategies' of 'globalized' firms, and in doing so will identify the possible range of positions taken by managers seeking to simultaneously articulate representations of two or more cultural frameworks. Due to both the radical fallback to their culture of origin and the impermeability of the foreign culture, the international manager is no longer recognized as being affiliated with his/her former cultural system. As a result, we have seen the emergence of a plurality of experiences that have come as the result of international mobility. If a business offers its members a number of possible strategies that can aide international managers in managing their cultural or ethnic differences, how can these strategies be imbedded in a career strategy and become 'worthwhile'?

In order to accomplish these tasks, this chapter is structured as follows. First, we will outline a number of recent and outstanding evolutions in the conditions of international mobility within large companies. Next, we will highlight managers' obligation to link multiple worlds: that of their country of origin, that of their work duties, the worlds both inside and outside the business, or the world containing their families, work partners, friends, etc. We will then demonstrate how international mobility is the 'business' of identity and at times, of the management of delicate gaps related to personal experience with integration-related stress. Some international frameworks seek to identify one ethnic or cultural group when such a choice presents itself as advantageous, privately bringing to life traditional alliances, and in many lived social business experiences, causing ethnic or cultural identifications to voluntarily dissolve. In these cases, such former identifications are seen as unrewarding, and other more positive identifications are chosen. Accordingly, we will identify five identity strategies, or rather, five ways of conducting oneself during processes of integration abroad, which are connected with three work resources (the asset of authority, the asset of community, and the asset of family). Finally, we explore the 'narrative' dimension of international managers' identity production.

An evolution in the conditions of international mobility

The obligation of international managers to be 'connected'

Within the companies that are experiencing a global expansion (which in this chapter we call 'globalized' firms), Gomez (2000) distinguishes between managers who operate on a transnational level (e.g. 'town squares', such as in New York, London, and Tokyo), those who operate on a multinational level (the author speaks of 'modern trading posts' and mentions cities such as Milan and San Francisco), and finally, those that operate on an international level (e.g. sites of production, such as Manchester or Lyon). The first set must learn to make decisions, at the highest level of the organization, about situations without necessarily taking local constraints into consideration, and must at the same time maintain the cohesion of the organized body of the organization. The others must have an understanding of the local characteristics of production areas that is based on more limited geographical parameters. As such, a certain 'pendular mobility' may at times lead managers to split their time between two or three different countries each week.

Companies must therefore define various contexts in which they can facilitate the acquisition of four types of more or less 'mobile' salaried workers: 'nomadic' executives, who occupy the top of the hierarchy and who live more than others in airplanes, are regularly asked to work on short- and medium-term projects of a global scale; 'mobile' managers, whose travel is more sporadic and mostly contained within a given geographical area; 'local' managers who direct foreign workers; and finally, 'local' managers who are living a form of 'static internationalization' without direct or extended face-to-face contact with foreign partners (but who do have a limited amount of contact with these partners that is mediated by new information technologies such as email).

While the image of 'brain drain' has long been employed in analyzing the unidirectional flows of highly qualified persons from under-developed countries towards rich ones (Nedelcu, 2004, p. 9), executives instead often refer to the image of the nervous system or the neural universe when justifying this 'beneficial' circulation of their human resources not only from the center to the periphery, but also among the peripheries themselves (subsidiaries, production facilities, research laboratories). While with the general integrated organization of the 1970s, each service is seen to work with a sole customer, in 'globalized' firms, the leading spheres rely on the effects of learning, the ability to resolve various problems associated with mobile personnel, and each service can conversely work for several services in relation to customers. For private interests, such processes are more officially a question of the mobility of the brain rather than leakage.

This global deployment of businesses leads to an activity-coordinated 'multi-site'. 'Networking', 'building bridges', and 'being a go-between' are all mediation qualities that are highlighted in this new type of manager, in contrast to other activities such as social control and discipline. The skills used are first local and circumstantial, but once internalized and understood by mobile managers, they become transferable and are truly personal experiences mobilized from a wide social capital. The managers' mobility allows them to share the experiences in and with different parts of the business, which is therefore above all an environment of permanent learning.

Identity affirmation in an intercultural context

Mutabazi (2001) notes that the research (which often brutally modifies and standardizes desired behaviors) that is oftentimes sought by company headquarters during international developments, mergers or takeovers frequently produces the reverse effect on local employees. Instead of accepting these behaviors, they tend to manifest their original identities, to hold firmly to values, and often oppose any lasting collaboration. At the smallest sign of weakness in controlling procedures, these 'traditional' values and national cultures (regional or local) can reappear, reinforcing themselves and breaking the unified social harmony (Delange and Pierre, 2004).

The affirmation of identity arises precisely when actors can no longer agree on the sense of the situation or on the roles that they are expected to endorse. What follows are several methods of constructing one's identification of self and of others, as well as multiple ways of constructing subjectivity, both social and psychic.

In the field of anthropology, studies have also demonstrated that through a complex process of identity deconstruction and reconstruction, individuals knowingly valorize the subcultural features of their 'ethnic' identity and subsequently gain recognition and other benefits as a result of said manipulations. Thus, the Moroccan or Chinese merchant knows how to occasionally accentuate their ethnicity and to emphasize specific symbols that manifest this identity (name, clan emblems, clothing, language, religion, life style, dietary habits or rituals) that function as connoted information for Western clients, thereby providing an adequate guarantee of their products or services. For example, from the Renaissance until the eighteenth century in France, architects, painters, and even transalpine theatre actors attempted to ensure their success by trying to appear 'Italian'. As such, the reason for life in the 'Hexagon' (i.e. France) was immediately placed under the sign of the exchange: it became a particular form of exoticism that ran counter to their accepted presence. Lyman and Douglass (1976) describe how Spanish Basques who had emigrated to the United States would adjust the definition of their ethnic identity during situations of interaction: when interacting with 'co-ethnic' individuals, they would define themselves as Biscayan, when interacting with French Basques, they would invoke a Spanish–Basque identification, and when interacting with non-Basques, they would identify themselves simply as Basque.

These situations imply that although actors are capable of acting on their own self-definitions when their identity is challenged, they mobilize (consciously, unconsciously, individually, collectively) certain resources and conduits according to both the variation of social situations and an accepted internal logic (Taboada-Leonetti, 1990, p. 49). In certain 'multicultural' situations, the conflict of codes of meaning and value formally informs individuals of when they should make decisions, keep a 'distance', establish themselves as actors, or connect with others based on their adaptability to a given context (Denoux, 1994, p. 264).

Moreover, this is above all in reference to foreigners from disadvantaged backgrounds (an immigration of labor that is bound to cause a shortage of domestic labor), and is built on reflections that cast new light on both the issue of interethnic relations at work (Camilleri, 1980; Taboada-Leonetti, 1982; Vinsonneau, 1993; Dasen, 1993) and the question of the 'bottom up' globalization of the economy and of corporate policies (Engbersen, 1999).

In effect, the majority of executives interviewed at Alpha and Gamma tended to hold as a general law of work behavior that very early on, most individuals are subject to contradictory social experiences when outside of their homelands, frequent instances of professional mobility, and have the tendency to reinforce their ability to cope with change and to establish an identity equilibrium. We are also a part of other research that has been conducted in social contexts other than 'globalized' companies. This research has highlighted other instances of personal experiences of acculturation through 'acculturative stress' (Berry, 1990), through the 'strategies' that a person can adopt in order to regulate perceived and experienced socio-cultural diversity (Camilleri and Malewska-Peyre, 1996), through the different types of 'psychological responses' to cultural contact (Furnham and Boschner, 1986), and through various types of 'acculturation'.

If we accept that both personal and professional trajectories can be marked by intergenerational continuity, within the majority of the international managers that we studied in these two companies, we found a common biographical disruption involving a deep questioning of previously constructed identities. While for the employee this evokes a 'world conquest' of material comfort and a greater feeling of freedom to act, geographic and functional mobility also has a dark side, which is made up of veiled conflicts between individuals of very distant cultures and identity crises that are difficult to interpret. This reality remains relatively unknown.

Even though training and support materials for mobile managers and their families are already put into place during transfers, executives often tend to 'overestimate' the integration capabilities of these managers in moving abroad. The accumulation of changes to one's lifestyle, environment, work or familial situation means that one's personal identity is increasingly forced to bear additional risks of otherness. At best, these difficulties are seen as breaks in 'life routines' (Black et al., 1992), and that a mental and behavioral 'programming' can be quickly acquired to counteract them. Utilization of the work of authors such as Hofstede (1987), Hampden-Turner (1991), Trompenaars (1994) or Black and Mendenhall (1991), the degree of adaptation within a new environment is often represented using a U-shaped curve, which presents a time axis (detailing that after a phase of euphoria, one either experiences a period of coming down or one 'takes control' of the situation) that necessitates that one prepare for a voyage via intercultural training sessions.

In the vast majority of cases, the dissonances of identity that affect international managers are supposed to be eliminated, or rather 'buried' under the common cultural reference to 'entrepreneurship'. Each manager must accept the tensions that result from the possible 'acculturative' shocks related to international mobility brought about by one's employment (e.g. families being broken apart by geographical distance, models for identification becoming blurred, one's double rejection in the professional world in the host country due to being 'foreign' and in the country of origin due to having become 'different', the progressive loss of both associative and religious social roots).

From this ideological perspective, the ideal of intercultural competence would be the 'global player' (or cosmopolitan manager), i.e. career managers that seek to develop greater flexibility while attempting to reduce the stress resulting from their actions abroad.

> For the most prominent managers, one must 'master oneself' or 'own oneself', an effort that is required throughout our contemporary societies, and which furthermore is surely in part the cause of the significant growth of industries based on self-image development, from the fashion, health, nutrition and cosmetics industries to the growing industry of personal development [...] including the emergence of new professions such as trainers.
>
> (Boltanski and Chiapello, 1999, p. 235)

Furthermore, our surveys illustrated that senior managers also feel a growing dissociation between the rationalities of each sphere of their lives (work, family, global society).

Five strategies of international managers

From a sociological point of view, identity can be defined as that in which the individual recognizes and is recognized by others. Dubar (2000, p. 109) holds that identity is the result of diverse processes of socialization that are both stable and temporary, individual and collective, subjective and objective, and biographical and structural, and that together build individuals and define institutions.

While all individuals face the same situation of acculturation, they will not all choose the same strategies[2] or develop identical processes for encouraging the other to recognize them in a way that suits them. Certain individuals tend to employ strategies of avoidance or of conflict moderation. On this point, Camilleri (1990) distinguishes between the conduits of those seeking to obscure the contradictions between original and new codes – some bind themselves to a unique cultural framework, while others practice alternating codes depending on the circumstances. Furthermore, Camilleri (1990) also cites differences in the conduits of those that face contradictions, i.e. heterogeneous frameworks – some employ a kind of artificial bricolage, while others synthetically bind features borrowed from different cultural codes. While the former do not necessarily feel compelled to justify their manipulation of their identities, the latter give the impression that they are able to remove themselves *from themselves*, creating a barrier between themselves and those that disturb or bother them.

The identity of international managers is established within a tension, an interaction between what is subjectively claimed by the subject and what is socially granted by the host environment. This identity is the result of the formation of professional and extra-professional spaces, in which individuals demand to be publicly judged as 'a certain type of person' so as to acquire a more valorized image. In this, there exists the possibility of a type of 'game' in the sense of Lyman and Douglass (1972), which plays itself out through the communication of clues and of ethnic roles. Furthermore,

> due to the fact that the information that is conveyed by these clues (physiognomic traits, skin color, accent) is often insufficient, actors can consciously provide additional

information, which allows them to control to some extent the presentation of a specific 'ethnic self'.

(Poutignat and Streiff-Fenart, 1995, p. 166)

For example, the existence of a black American manager born in India who has been working in Paris for 2 years (and who during said time has married a young French woman) strengthens the enigmatic character of identity construction within the context of a multicultural work environment. The 'we-subject' of his speech constantly oscillates between multiple instances of identification, evoking each 'we' rather differently: 'we foreign managers in France', 'we American geologists', 'we Anglo-Saxons of Alpha', or 'we, the blacks of the workplace'.

What made this manager like his colleagues was his 'high degree of differentiation' (Devereux, 1970), the difficulty he had relating to a 'nationality', and the fact that he saw himself as belonging to different identity-groups and that he sustained and nurtured different 'provinces of self'. Indeed, knowing a manager's identity on paper, or even their social status, does not permit us to predict their behavior.

How, then, can we account for these cultural bridges that have been established by this American manager, who was born in India and who does not hesitate in asserting that 'if for Americans, the country of India is the childhood of humanity, for Hindus, the United States is a country still in its childhood'? In such an instance, can he be seen as taking the side of the Hindus or of the Americans? Or is he experiencing a kind of identity duplicity in which he is able to identify with his 'two sides' simultaneously?

It is because international managers' construction of identity is not 'double' (between past and present, between the host country's culture and the culture of the country of origin) – but rather multidimensional – that it is difficult to predict the success of one's career abroad. Both immigrants and international managers alike have recalled that the subject is characterized not by an ability to preserve their identity, but rather, by their own subjective activities through which they (are often forced to) invent new configurations, which at times are in anticipation of events, while at others are attempts to make sense of the lived experiences of the workplace.

Because most individuals foster different attitudes that are not necessarily connected with one another, researchers and practitioners often deal with the 'intercultural' aspect of the issue of maintaining the desire for a certain unity of self. When talking about his identity, a Gabonese, Norwegian, or Italian expatriate, having been living in France, Luanda, or London for 3 years, will revisit his past, or will follow a particular logic that is the reverse of the immediacy of the company and the professional mobility that comes along with it. His 'demand' for identity is a 'demand' for stability, and often a 'demand' for acknowledgment of something that is lacking within his interactions with colleagues. Between permanence (the individual lives in a new universe as he did before), a split (the individual adopts thoughts, beliefs, and practices in relation to the dominant social universe), and mixture (each universe adds to his vision of the world and fosters a synthesis), the individual – especially in intercultural situations – does not hold an immediacy, simplicity, or primitiveness of self, but rather one that is mediated, constructed, complex, and 'belated' (Meyerson, 1948). It is always secondarily that the individual is able to comprehend the diversity of attitudes or attributes that he possesses and to begin the work of 'adjustment'.

These international managers can be represented through five types of identity strategies, which present various modalities of resistance or of openness to the ambient cultural milieu. Certain individuals will choose to radically fall back to their culture of origin. Others, on the contrary, will opt for the almost total permeability of the cultural milieu of the host country, a process that groups them into one of five types of identity conversion (the conservatives, the defensives, the opportunists, the transnationals, and the converted) (Pierre, 2000).

The conservatives

'Conservatives' understand international mobility as a 'parenthesis' within their careers. This is seen in the context of an eventual return to the subsidiary in the country of origin, where the manager will be 'converted' and permitted to take on a greater level of responsibility. Conservatives make a 'one-way trip'. During their experience on foreign soil, they wish to conserve the highest possible number of relationships with the culture and countries that they have left behind. They hope to protect themselves, and furthermore, the weight of their obligation to their parents and relatives back home emphasizes a great density of relations.

Conservative discourse is organized around the notions of honor, education, usage, family, loyalty, and the preservation of strong links. With their international mobility, conservatives appear to divide the social universe into two hemispheres: they fantasize about the 'inside' (i.e. family life, in most cases) as they seek to preserve the ways of thinking that they have inherited from native culture, and the 'outside' (i.e. the corporate world), in which they adopt the bare minimum of behaviors required by business life (without learning the language of the host country).

Through the facilitation of schools, businesses, churches, and association meetings, the contact between internationally mobile compatriots contributes both symbolically and materially to the establishment of a kind of 'ethnic space' that is articulated within the host company. The importance of conservatives' defense mechanisms therefore brings to light a key finding: an individual will not assimilate into this new human society as long as there is no guarantee of safety equivalent to that found in their country of origin, i.e. a guarantee that at the very least counterbalances the desire to regain the warmth of personal relationships and the secret of a meaningful history that they identify with their original community.

The defensives

Unlike conservatives, 'defensives' do not maintain a sense of inferiority in relation to the host society in which they work. Instead, they desire to defend their origins in the eyes of the new world that they find themselves in, in particularly vis-à-vis their colleagues. For defensives, international mobility must be 'awake' – they seek to defend an awareness of local ownership. These individuals find themselves needing to explain to their superiors their country of origin, their children's names, the reasons for their mobility, or even the history of their people.

Fully integrated into the company's business, defensives position themselves as 'foreigners' or 'outsiders' vis-à-vis the host society. As such, they are always finding ways to stand out. While the figure of the 'stateless' international financier or the 'European official' are foils for defensives, many of them do not hesitate to allow themselves to be considered as 'the American' or 'the Norwegian' of Port Harcourt or Libreville by forcing themselves into assumed cultural types. Defensives will first make an effort to maintain themselves, then will reinvent their difference, forming a difference seemingly 'cleansed' of the continual experience of self-depreciation. Defensives then attempt to put an end to the shame of the 'self-awareness' that they experience 'under the gaze of others'. They will demand, for example, the systematic appointment of local managers (and not expatriates) to the heads of subsidiaries worldwide, and will voluntarily refuse unique methods of performance evaluation or recruitment.

At the end of their careers, after numerous years of intense mobility, many defensives wish to return 'home', as if to symbolically ward off the fluidity of time spend in the 'globalized' company away from home. For these international managers, their 'roots' become more important than any eloquent professional success abroad. They become local entrepreneurs in terms of leverage and the 'intercultural' skills that their international mobility has fostered. An increase in association responsibilities or education, as well as entering into the political sphere, are all concrete possibilities by which one can more effectively and harmoniously equilibrate work, salary level, family life, and a sense of heritage.

Defensives are models of individuals with 'dual loyalties': immediately following retirement, they finish by practicing outside of the multinational firm. They cultivate activities (that are as militant as they are professional) in partnership with their home region or country, more often than not over the course of their final years of their career (Meyer and Hernandez, 2004, p. 42). Oftentimes, such activities have been physically abandoned for many years, sometimes for as much as three decades. By integrating themselves into networks dedicated to the transfer of skills (the South African Network of Skills Abroad is one example), they become leaders in animated networks of online newsgroups, they become involved with magazines, they attend parties of high symbolic value in order to consolidate community bonds, and they monitor any stock values, managers, diplomats, and alumni from the *grandes écoles* that may be able to help them down the line. At Alpha, certain members of the Association of Nigerians mobilized their experience and skills outside of the company in order to serve the country in the electrical engineering field during the privatization of the sector (Meyer and Hernandez, 2004, p. 49).

For those managers who travel very long distances every year, who rely on customized research network nodes and use of the Internet (Nedelcu, 2004, p. 79), 'the compression of time seems to expand space' (Fibbi, 2004, p. 66). For them, there is an imaginary space of return that is constructed on a translational scale and that accepts reports of non-market transfers, which differ from those that are cultivated in private business (Meyer, 2000). Defensives often simultaneously take part in economic networks and political or religious associations, while at the same time often disseminating universal democratic values that have come as the result of their transnational experiences. For them, this remote commitment is on the one hand an alternative to a physical return, as this would coincide with a high risk of occupational de-qualification in the absence of welcoming structures in the countries concerned. On the other hand, this allows these managers to cultivate a position of erudite authority that often protects them from certain political pressures.

Through their 'extraterritorial' status, defensives illustrate new forms of transnationalism in which identity is not only essentially conjoined with the present within the space of the 'globalized' business (Fibbi, 2004, p. 71), but also differentiates itself from a diasporic identity that 'tirelessly weaves together the continuity of being through a relation with the past'. At times, these international managers exploit the possibilities that are open only to those who occupy atypical positions (a 'semi-externality' – Fibbi, 2004, p. 72) in relation to the societies in which they live and the prospect of dual citizenship. By doing so, these managers cultivate a 'migratory knowledge', or more precisely, a 'circulatory capacity'.

The opportunists

The overall identity that we attribute to the 'opportunists' resembles first and foremost the young managers who are aware that they posses a degree that is rare and coveted within the organization, but who instead prove themselves to be specialists desiring to offset their 'poor training' through an avid display of enthusiasm and overworking. Opportunists' discourse is organized largely around the 'urgency on the ground', the acquisition of knowledge, and an incessant decision-making process that is based on a command of complex technical problems and sophisticated management tools. These individuals attempt to make their behavior 'synchronous' with what they understand as the code of conduct that has been approved by their interlocutors.

For example, if we consider how certain international managers alter between the usage of *tu* (informal) and *vous* (formal), their choice of topics of conversation associated with a particular culture, their use of 'Anglo-Saxon' gestures in public, and their use of body language associated with their home country during conversations with others from the same country, we can clearly observe their ability to play the game of 'proper social distance' in a given circumstance. Opportunists make an effort to reduce disharmony and to manage input–output roles, and such efforts are followed by a growing reflexivity that is specifically bound to the distance to said roles. Essentially, these are individuals who derive their meaning from immediate contexts more so than past experience.

Nevertheless, just as one does not abandon one frame of reference simply because one has adopted another that is under construction, it would be futile to consider opportunists as being ethnically and culturally 'empty'. Every hollow identity carries with it a controlled knowledge of behaviors, and suggests a minimal amount of learning of a particular cultural capital and a range of 'available' identities. Subsequently, any one choice of behavior is comparable to the migration from one mode of being to another.

The transnationals

Transnationals admit to being attached to individuals based on more than the passports that they hold, the places where they were born, or the societies that they have traveled through. Will, education, and common sense should be able to defeat racial discrimination, and the discourse of many of these managers calls for a 'necessary multilingualism', 'free enterprise', and the construction of a 'cosmopolitan' business spirit. For example, transnationals are highly favored in the development of intercultural training seminars and, through the languages that they practice, seek to foster 'an instrumental rapport that is a product of or effected by their conscience'. They value a management style based on 'evidence', and thus, whenever a change is proposed, the leader must be able to rely on objective systems of evaluation that are intended to avoid any cultural bias.

These transnationals also demonstrate that, much like the difference in prestige among business or engineering schools, the noble streams of internationalization differ from those that are less so; because their family life and history has instilled them with strong cosmopolitan values, transnationals are the heirs in whom the practices of career management reflect the dispositions acquired during childhood. These 'second generation' mobile managers therefore differ from local managers, who (like certain conservatives) live their mobility in a foreign land as if it were a reward or the well-deserved 'end of the road' for a career. Transnationals therefore often follow in the footsteps of their elders, and having been educated in transborder urban environments, they are frequently accompanied by their memories of childhood or adolescence. Each functional geographic movement constitutes a milestone in connection with an intense project of social advancement. The displacements of both these individuals and their ancestral predecessors are the result of identical residential journeys, as well as a shared loyalty to the places and societies that they have experienced.

The converted

The 'converted' strive to maintain the greatest possible level of similarity with those whom they consider to be in power, namely the executives. For example, mobility lived in France is seen as the culmination of a professional career, and mobility lived outside of France appears as a required period in which one is waiting to join the company's headquarters or become a part of one of its French establishments.

For this group of managers, individual identity seems to be based on the awareness of belonging to a powerful, internationally recognized company. The choice to seek naturalization, the search for a career entirely within the Hexagon, or the giving of French names to one's children all mark a partially conscious, and always imperfect, process of loss of one's native culture.

Seeking above all to be 'valued for who they are', the converted suffer from being positioned between a population that they have rejected, which itself designates them as members of a more general category (nation, skin color) and which is no longer their own, and an environment in which while introducing their own features, they have trouble being accepted. This stranger is in constant struggle with himself, realizing in a cruel way that the other's acceptance of us does not simply arise from an acute ability to reflect, but rather, it is a consummate art of detachment and tireless work of self. Behind the stereotyped figure that he is trying to adopt wherever he goes, the stranger constantly risks being 'betrayed' by the presence of the rejected self that he cannot fully control. The converted are best illustrated by the fact that assimilation never reaches completion, and that ethnicity refers not to a static state, but an ongoing process of social construction.

The prevailing direction of the conduct of the converted highlights a concept first introduced by Erikson (1972) – negative identity – which covers every trait that the individual learns to isolate and avoid. The converted therefore provide the best example of individuals seeking to reject part of their history in an effort to personally rewrite it. They believe in the possibility of carrying everywhere, in every country, the same lifestyle, but do not want to leave room for the 'cultural-factors' approach to business management. When asked to define themselves, the converted emphasize the community of age that brings them closer together with their colleagues, as well as the community of skills or of social status that collectively makes them 'managers'.

Three resources for integration while working abroad

The asset of authority

Human resources directors often place emphasis on the need to fairly estimate the duration of an international assignment, on the 'barriers' that are constituted by a spouse's work or child's education, and on the technical competence that protects managers in situations where mobility immediately fails. However, our work demonstrates not only the plural nature of the modalities of integration while working abroad, but also the fact that the socialization of international managers is primarily dependent on the degree of authority that they maintain in their work relations ('asset of authority').

During prolonged situations in which local staff and international managers must solve a common problem that may ultimately threaten the professional reputation or integrity of all, the most effective international managers are those who facilitate the integration of the dominant group, weaken stereotypes and consider their 'peers' to be their 'equals'. It is primarily this balance of power in the relationship that (a) allows for a better understanding of the other's cultural differences, (b) tends to restore dialogue to every type of communication breakdown, and (c) facilitates the integration of managers into their new environments. From this perspective, the most successful action strategies for managers are precisely those that rely on mediation and mobilization in the field of national resources.

In a seemingly paradoxical way, managers who radically define themselves as 'international' and who actually cultivate international lifestyles (multilingual, married to someone of another nationality, cosmopolitan friendships, international schooling for their children) are also those that most often systematically mobilize national resources in every dimension of social life, and who maintain the closest links with their country of origin. In fact, a supposedly 'global' culture can often work to the detriment of its employees' national identities.

The asset of community

In most cases, the success of international managers abroad depends equally on the presence or absence of a community of peers within the company, through which the individual can maintain a strong emotional bond with their community of origin ('asset of community'). This community is not necessarily made up of compatriots; many managers value and endorse the image of 'world citizens' (a concept that complicates the national boundaries of those that observe or manage such individuals), and are able to find knowledge in those places where the more privileged among them circulate. 'What good is it to live abroad in London, Tokyo or New York if one does not make friends from all countries?', a young marketing manager of Danish origin at Gamma declared to us.

The creation of a protean cultural, ethnic, and psychological intermediary space allows for conflicts arising from acculturation to be negotiated through a back-and-forth dynamic, and permits viable compromises between one's maternal language and the languages spoken within the company, the cultures of origin and the culture of the host country, and the professional culture of the globalized organization. This common attachment, lived mostly outside of the walls of the company, illustrates the interwoven nature of collective identity and of the individual identity of the international manager: by binding oneself to a unified collective, one invites others to connect with them, thereby giving meaning to their actions throughout the company. We must believe that our sense of identity truly lies in these rituals, these customary gestures, these reassuring spaces that give the impression of invariance during times of change.

Thus, at each stage of their mobility, certain privileged managers (transnationals) are able find their familial 'bearings' through their membership of clubs or international associations. These international bearings define a territory of symbolic exchanges, which ensures a certain unity of self, combats identity fragmentation, facilitates children's schooling, and can provide employment for one's spouse. Whatever their nationality, these individuals tend to group together and to take shelter within 'national colonies' in areas consecrated to their presence, (chosen or 'specific' suburban) places that may have been occupied by other colleagues or relatives that had come before them.

The asset of family

Breaking with the traditional role of expatriation 'en famille' as well as with the 'longue durée', our research illustrates that for the majority of international managers studied, there exists a concern about the 'consistency' of their career path, which with each consecutive step leads them in an attempt to balance a maximal integration into the company with an adequate level of familial organization ('asset of family'). In this, international managers accentuate the plasticity of their family unit in relation to the model of expatriation, in choosing (in contingency with their host country) whether they will leave unaccompanied or with their spouse, or with or without their children. Moreover, this plasticity is also accentuated by these managers' introduction (during each context of mobility) of a profound redistribution of roles and authority within the family.

In Figure 4.1, the symbols '+' and '+ +' represent the two levels of an international manager's ability to integrate into their new work environment. Conversely, the symbols '−' and '− −' represent low and very low integration into the company. We must also understand that the 'asset of authority' promotes the integration of international managers. We consider the 'asset of authority' to be all of the resources held when taking a post, and those related to effectively controlling one's position, hierarchical status, qualification in the organization, and feeling of being recognized as 'competent' over the duration of their employment. The 'asset of community' also promotes the integration of the international manager. For us, this asset takes into consideration all of the resources held by the international manager that come as the result of the communities that they are a part of (which are made up of not only fellow countrymen, but also of members of associations or networks) that are similar to communities that they were members of in their countries of origin. Such affiliations and social networks will carry a collective memory and will ultimately favor a specific cultural affiliation and social support that will become useful for the manager. By the 'asset of family', we are suggesting the ensemble of resources held by the international manager in the space of the family, which refers to factors such as the employment status of one's spouse and the plasticity of a family's organization, according to the type of geographic movement undertaken.

In Figure 4.1, the idea of *early adaptation* corresponds with the dimension of adaptation that begins and that takes place in the subsidiary of origin (an integral part of which is the role of experienced managers' testimonies after having returned home). This leads to a realistic understanding of one's responsibilities and the expected level of performance when taking a position abroad. Furthermore, a positive correlation exists between work integration and an *intercultural training* that is constructed not only around films, books and informational sessions with veterans about international mobility, but also around real situations that mobile managers can take first-hand experience from (role playing, short trips). It is also beneficial to have a high degree of participation from the manager's family during these training sessions (Landis and Bhagat, 1996).

Regarding the *personal dimension*, Mendenhall and Oddou (1985) classify individuals' capacity to adjust into three dimensions. From this perspective, the personal dimension includes capabilities that enable the mobile manager to maintain or strengthen their mental health, their psychological well-being, and their self-esteem. This consists of their ability to cope with stress, their technical skills, and their ability to replace activities that provided them with pleasure and support their well-being while in their country of origin with similar activities found in the host country. Moreover, the *relational dimension* encompasses one's capacity to interact with nationals of the host country. This includes one's willingness to learn and use the language of the host country, one's confidence in interaction with others and one's ability to develop relationships. The *perceptual dimension* includes one's ability to perceive, analyze the reasons for the behavior of foreigners, and to judge or behave ethnocentrically.

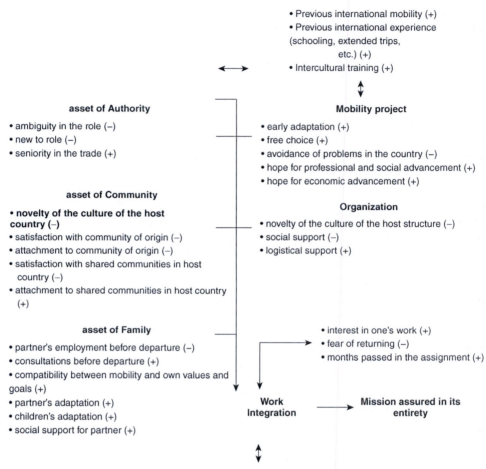

• Previous international mobility (+)
• Previous international experience
  (schooling, extended trips,
    etc.) (+)
• Intercultural training (+)

asset of Authority

• ambiguity in the role (–)
• new to role (–)
• seniority in the trade (+)

Mobility project

• early adaptation (+)
• free choice (+)
• avoidance of problems in the country (–)
• hope for professional and social advancement (+)
• hope for economic advancement (+)

asset of Community

• **novelty of the culture of the host country (–)**
• satisfaction with community of origin (–)
• attachment to community of origin (–)
• satisfaction with shared communities in host country (–)
• attachment to shared communities in host country (+)

Organization

• novelty of the culture of the host structure (–)
• social support (–)
• logistical support (+)

asset of Family

• partner's employment before departure (–)
• consultations before departure (+)
• compatibility between mobility and own values and goals (+)
• partner's adaptation (+)
• children's adaptation (+)
• social support for partner (+)

• interest in one's work (+)
• fear of returning (–)
• months passed in the assignment (+)

Work Integration ⟶ **Mission assured in its entirety**

IDENTITY STRATEGIES OF INTERNATIONAL FRAMEWORKS

asset of Authority	–	+	+	++	+
asset of Community	++	++	–	–	– –
asset of Family	– –	–	++	+	–
	Strategy of conservation and of fallback to original culture elements	Strategy of cultural claim and of affirmation of a sense of belonging to a group of origin	Strategy of borrowing and syncretic linkage of cultural elements	Strategy of synthetic articulation of cultural elements	Strategy of conversion to a culture of adoption
	Conservatives	Defensives	Opportunists	Transnationals	Converted

Legend: (+) positive influence on work integration / (–) negative influence on work integration

Table constructed with consideration of: J. S. Black, M. Mendenhall and G. Oddou (1991), C. Camilleri (1990), J. L. Cerdin (1996) and P. Pierre (2000).

Figure 4.1 Work integration and identity strategies of international managers

While a partner's employment prior to departure is a traditional barrier to the acceptance and the success of expatriation, for us, a spouse's employment (double careers in particular) does not carry with it a systematically negative influence. The social support of a partner relates to that individual's ability to adapt to their living conditions with the help of the company's actions concerning housing, food, leisure, healthcare, and administrative formalities. Community refers to the social fabric in a specific geographical area, including connections with friends, as well as the associative or civic role that the international manager plays in a particular group of people who share common goals. The issue of the 'asset of community' can be broken into three main dimensions: (a) the newness of the culture of the host country in relation to the country of origin, (b) the satisfaction with the community of origin and a similar community in the host country, and (c) the attachment to the community of origin and to the similar community in the host country.

Finally, logistical aide and social support concerns housing assistance, the completion of paperwork and other administrative formalities, the discovery of the region through short preparatory trips, and children's education. This assistance may be provided on site by either the organization in the host country, direct superiors or colleagues.

A situational manipulation of ethnicity in business

Racism and discrimination in globalized companies

To borrow Mayol's (1992) powerful image, many young managers from developing countries who became impatriates within Alpha seem to have 'one foot in the culture of their fathers and the other in that of their generation, but the second seems more entrenched than the first'. For these young elites, the society where they find strong attachments seems to eclipse the other, in which they are no longer fathers or elders who are actively formulating a cultural identity; instead, they are peers of the professional world. Their networks are therefore modernist (as opposed to their predecessors' networks of identity resistance), in that they are faced with the question of 'speaking like everyone else', entering into competition with other individuals in order to 'make a career in the company'.

'Before we are Africans, we are managers', a group of young managers strongly affirmed. For them, the 'right to fit in' seems to be more important than the right to be different. These managers state that the plurality of their affiliations is enriching, and that it allows them to exist in very different groups with a minimum distance without it being painfully disabling. The we-subject of their discourse constantly oscillates between several sites of identification, much as this young black manager based in Paris indifferently states: 'we, the foreign employees of Alpha' (denoting a minority status in contrast to both the French nationals within the company and to the country in which the company was founded, a status that is poorly distinguished in the host society), 'we, the Anglo-Saxons of the Alpha division at la Défense [Paris' major business district]' (emphasizing a micro-local solidarity, which is above all a linguistic system), or even 'we, the men of color of the company' (revealing an assignment of identity to a racial community that has been stigmatized and whose rights must be protected).

Globalized firms are also the scenes of everyday racism, even for managers of elevated social status and high incomes. If certain international managers hold recognized characteristics of status, or a particular diploma or technical experience, they subsequently will not have certain characteristics expected by the host environment (social capital, 'ethnic' origin or nationality, a good 'profile' for working in a particular way). On arrival, some international managers will suffer from various forms of discrimination, presumptions of 'incompetence' shaped and transmitted by a number of other managers who report them as having low work participation, and stresses of social life ('very different and very strong familial and dietary obligations, very unique and very respected social rituals, often practicing a double activity in addition to the salaried activity'). In these situations, skin color becomes an exterior sign, revealing alleged intellectual characteristics (Trutat and Obame, 1987, p. 35).

Within Alpha, it is particularly the non-work activities of a number of local officials in Sub-Saharan Africa – usually related to transport or cleaning companies – that draw the sharpest criticism from a small number of French expatriates, who see the possibility of these activities having negative effects on professional commitment. 'We do not take sufficient account of the African worker's extra-professional context. We need to know how to distinguish between the characteristics of each nationality', a French geologist for Alpha claimed in an interview. 'For an African, to be rational is to be relational; Nigerians have an innate sense of hierarchy', he continued,

> but are unable to take action or distribute information. They are never free; they are reluctantly penalized, fearing ancestral structures, the judgment of their elders or the recriminations of their brothers. Once you know this, you fix the problem by sharing the information right away or you risk being blamed. It is a problem of mental structures. It's not speaking negatively of them that I say that due to their temperament and the social constraints of their country, they cannot be trusted as much as French colleagues.

These racist criticisms of the relative inactivity of local subsidiaries do not hesitate to conflate 'physical causality' and 'mental causality'. They define a human being exclusively by the number of members in its respective affiliate groups. Such criticisms come in milder forms within other subsidiaries of Alpha, as illustrated by the remarks of a French human resources manager who has worked at Norwegian sites for 3 years:

> Norwegians begin working together when they are in school, and are therefore particularly good at everything concerning 'project teams'. This has nothing to do with the French who don't share their ideas with others. Nevertheless, they are accustomed to leaving the office at 16.00 while the expatriates are stuck there until 19.00. They do not have the same work dedication – they enjoy their spare time a bit too much.

Despite official recognition of the equal value of each subsidiary and each culture in the organization, a hierarchy of the prestige of ethno-cultural groups remains intact for a number of Alpha's employees. Intercultural confrontation cannot be considered independently of the 'national points of departure' of the company's actors. In the words of Wagner (1998, p. 3), in the context of comparable studies, 'international is far from signifying a-national, due to the fact that more nationalities can claim the appellation more easily than other groups'.

Everything happens as if the prestige of the country of assignment reflects on the career of the international manager who is appointed there. In this, career and geographic trajectories are both far from independent. With the international managers from Alpha, there was not strictly speaking a group that would require the legitimacy of 'international' competences, and that in doing so would efface its own specificities that were linked to 'national points of departure'. These are by and large the collective national histories that allow one to understand the differences in trajectories related to international mobility. This is due to the fact that in some national contexts, journeys abroad represent required steps for social success, while in others they are seen as risky choices that negate the possibility of rehabilitation, as well as the possibility of obtaining the most visible among national positions.

Wagner (1999) has noted the consistent hierarchization of national attributes in the population of international managers. She observes that the 'dominant' nationalities – those from the United States – show great ease in international circles. They are able to remain national while identifying as international, for their businesses, schools, associations and languages are both American and international. Other nationalities that have recently entered into the international sphere, the Japanese for example, behave with an 'international goodwill', which evokes the rise of the middle classes. Finally, the managers of dominated nationalities tend to repress anything that would evoke their national origins in order to better acculturate to Western international standards.

Manipulations of self and intracultural shock

When faced with discrimination and racist criticism, certain international managers will attempt to either accept these rejections, to accommodate and adapt to them, or to sublimate their own stigmata into a kind of 'transnational community of business managers'. For example, given the constrains of the social system, a number of managers at the petroleum company Alpha who come from Sub-Saharan Africa illustrate the problem with having a plurality of specific allegiances, an issue that has been surprisingly under-studied. These individuals are faithful members of religious orders by night, and through their employment of local dialects and traditional dress, express their animist beliefs. Within the multinational firm, they actively participate in the economic and political life of the country, speak English and French with their colleagues, train other employees in Anglo-Saxon management practices and standards, and thereby endorse (not without a certain degree of tension) another social role.

Depending on the situation and its interlocutors, these petroleum managers illustrate the principle of breaking (Bastide, 1955), i.e. the gap between the moments of public expression that consider themselves to be a 'native affectivity' and the ability to rationally judge industrial projects, to organize one's work according to a temporality defined as 'Western', and to enter into contract with colleagues according to relational codes that are wholly adapted to a 'modern' rationality. More than any other person, these 'ubiquitous' men and women seem to affirm the existence of a duplicity that is expressed in the following terms: they stay true to their community of origin while attempting to thrive in the organization that they depend on and which pays them.

As these international managers are inscribed in multiple, non-congruent registers, and in situations that are not fully coded or predictable, they effectively justify themselves and take a distance from their surroundings. Because international mobility is often a lived experience of heightened independence with regard to relational constraints involving one's group of origin, it is in opposition to the homogeneous nature of managers' plans prior to departure, thereby constituting 'a problem of consistency between original and new internalizations' (Berger and Luckmann, 1996, p. 192).

Forced to adopt the tastes and habits of a new environment, some international managers will therefore attempt to both partially and locally adjust a part of their psychological life to a temporality of professional order in order to preserve an intimate connection with what they see as the most 'authentic' part of themselves. For Berger and Luckmann (1996), these actors never seem to become fully immersed in their work, their culture or their interests without this 'reserve' appearing as an inability to socialize. The configuration of identity that comes as a result of primary socialization must therefore be reworked throughout one's life, offering the possibility of true identity strategies due to the non-coincidence between the 'self' and one's professional and social roles.

International mobility in business often appears to be a mythical experience, devoid of the observed fractures in identity or unhappy experiences of the cosmopolitan manager. Yet, this 'schema', which is promoted by most executives in companies (within which, as we have said, one finds that the socialization process for international managers essentially leads to full economic participation that is free from cultural denial and that does not necessitate the passage from one living environment to another free of antagonism), does not clarify the situations faced by those individuals whose intense professional activity forces them to instead take on renewed situations of 'cultural transplantation'.

Classically, a dissonance exists when an individual realizes that the reality that they see is different from their mental representation of that reality. International managers tend to seek to maintain an agreement between two planes: an idealized representation of how they will live as an expatriate and their actual lived realities. However, international mobility carries with it a number of risks, including the temporary inability to use 'social capital' (Bourdieu, 1980), and the 'inability to act in a satisfactory way on the environment that surrounds the expatriate' (Agard, 2004, p. 54). Based on the study of the comparability between these two different sources of capital (Bourdieu, 1992, p. 94), Agard speaks of 'temporary social disqualification' and 'social impotence' (Black and Mendenhall, 1991) in order to point out the discrepancy between the promotion of international mobility, the active passages that contribute to a 'balanced training', and the lived experience (organizational or social) of the mobile manager (Agard, 2004, p. 53). He explains that this impotence results in an inhibition – a fear of being misunderstood, ridiculed, in danger, or exasperated – when facing other actors (Agard, 2004, p. 416).

When their knowledge is put to the test, mobile managers may risk becoming, in the words of Sennett (2000), 'plants that get repotted too often'. Our work has led us to conclude that this temporary disqualification varies depending on the situation and types of resources possessed by managers. This has certainly been verified in certain individuals (conservatives or certain opportunists) who when abroad suddenly see the equilibrium between their professional life and family sphere shatter. However, for a percentage of mobile managers (transnationals, for example), the company offers a stable environment and such variations are less pronounced. Paradoxically, managers who are the most mobile from a geographic perspective are not necessary the most 'multicultural', the most apt at learning from others, or the most subjected to cultural difference. As in the European royal courts of the seventeenth century, when it was customary to (also) speak French, which permitted the sharing of the conditions of a common education for both those living there and strangers alike, some experienced international managers are able to be here, there, and in both places at the same time. For them, the company offers an environment that decreases both the tension and the risk of maladaptation.

Agard (2004, p. 294) rightly speaks of 'breathing moments' during which international managers are able to discuss their country of origin in the new environment that they find themselves in. He distinguishes between meetings among peers, among fellow citizens, brief trips to the country and the welcoming of family members or friends from home into the host country. We are in agreement with Agard (2004, p. 56) when he states that for certain managers, 'contrary to what is generally presented in the literature', the company would become a '"breathing space", a place where the expatriate's ability to act on their environment would still be operative, without fear of misunderstanding'. Similarly, the family becomes a location in which questions are asked (locations where it is necessary to invent, often with discomfort, new behaviors in order to adapt). Therefore, as highlighted by Agard, there is a need to devise new 'curves of acculturation', according to the social interactions and the experience of 'relational poverty' (Paugam, 1991, p. 6) to which they refer (Cerdin and Dubouloy, 2004, p. 964). Conversely, our work demonstrates that individuals who are the most sensitive to the realities of intercultural encounters (respect for others, active listening) feel that they have suffered a considerable 'culture shock' (Oberg, 1960) at the beginning of their journey, running the risk of an early return.

While forcing managers into various host environments, international mobility has led a number of them to recognize the impaired foreigners within themselves (be they loved or idealized), at times reformulating their feeling of acceptance in an act of affirmation. The art lies in mastering and in reading in others the incessant play of signs that define forms of civility, accepted competency, and the always-imperfect mastery of emotion. The man of this globalization, more than any other, 'knows to pay attention to others in searching for clues that will allow for the appropriate intervention in situations of uncertainty' and possesses 'the ability to control and modify self-presentation, that can stretch to a capability to improvise, or even lie without flinching if deemed necessary' (Bellenger, 1992).

In a dialectical process of mutual perception in which the forces of exclusion and assimilation confront one another vis-à-vis the host society, the one who travels to discover the world in turn discovers themself in its differences (Oberg, 1992). A culture not long ago familiar is itself made foreign by the expatriation. What is striking and surprising is one's internal reaction – in an experience of disorientation – to one's native culture, which was internalized beginning at a young age. Therefore, the cultural alterity is above all an inner reality, whose subjectivity and emotionality signifies that it is not only constructed in opposition to other exterior groups (people from a host of countries, foreign colleagues, compatriots and their families) but also in relation to the 'other' that one feels in oneself, the crossroads of allegiances that suddenly interfere with one another. Here, one can speak of 'self-shock' (Zaharna, 1989) as both a massive solicitation of the subjectivity of the disoriented subject, struggling with his own weaknesses, and a internalization of shock brought on by the differences that others carry.

In sum, while abroad the actor identifies himself in action with typifications of objectified social conduct, while at the same time re-establishing distance vis-à-vis these typifications, beginning at the moment when he reflects on his conduct and work after the fact while in a different location. This distance between the actor and his action may be maintained in his consciousness and projected onto future repetitions of lived situations. However, every hollow identity carries along with it a controlled knowledge of behaviors, and the migration of one mode of being to another. Furthermore, each suggests a minimal amount of learning of a particular cultural capital and a range of 'available' identities, distinguishing the heirs of international mobility (transnationals, defensives) from the less experienced (opportunists for example).

The time for clear affiliations in business

Travel narratives and life stories

As we know, artists have the ability to construct what one might call 'interpretive scenarios' based on their lives; however, this privilege is not limited to poets, musicians, writers and painters. We are thinking, for example, of how the identity construction of international managers may or may not resemble a bricolage in relation to these 'other interiors' – these ghosts of others that we all carry within us and that are revived in work conditions in foreign lands by reminding you of 'your skin color', 'your strange accent', or even 'your particular way of punishing or rewarding effort in your teams'. If such a bricolage lacks identity strategies, it will never be the result of conscious aims that are clearly expressed by international managers.

According to what modalities these individuals nurture, the relationship of 'non-congruence' between their own lives and the social reality that assumes the task of narrating events on the one hand, and the contingencies within a life's history on the other (Yanaprasart, 2006).

Due to the conditions that surround them, international managers find themselves forced to dwell, much more than others, on their backgrounds and their origins, and are required to provide every kind of authoritative entity (government authorities, banks, work colleagues, neighbors, police) with their dates of arrival, anniversary dates, birthdates, and the reasons for their stay (Vatz-Laaroussi, 2001). Migrants and international managers alike are required to construct a 'family memory'. Moreover, more than others, they demonstrate an interest in leaving traces (writings, photos, drawings, videos) in order to patiently build the history of their journey.

'The first moments my adaptation in Brazil were difficult', attested an Italian manager at Gamma, who today lives in France.

> I was left alone, and during my moments of relaxation, I would remember things that had been said by my relatives and my friends, and I would begin funny, distanced dialogues with them, sometimes aloud, sometimes in my head. I would relive conversations that had taken place months or even years before, sometimes playing multiple characters, but always giving myself the best part! I could see myself doing this, which intrigued me – I needed these dialogues to make myself feel better. I looked forward to meetings and would write in a notebook what I needed to remember about those that I loved and those that I worked with. I was making time to myself out of the time that was passing.

This testimony suggests that for international managers, walking and strolling outdoors during work time is itself a form of research, which is based on the mass movement of other bodies in the streets and cities, putting them one step ahead of strangers and providing them with the essence of a place while they are simultaneously consuming it. This way of walking, as if suspended, 'as if one had all the time of in the world', is in opposition to measured time (i.e. the time of the company's production process) and is often expressed as a necessity (Urry, 2005, p. 65). In this, it would be suitable to speak of the 'fable of life' that international managers create around figures limited to identification and to 'biographical illusion', in the sense that 'the individual must formulate it by pulling as many elements as possible from their own history' (Kaufmann, 2001, p. 168). Speech encourages distancing, rapprochement and remoteness. To speak is to access a representation of pleasure that appears strong among international managers.

For international managers,

> the acquisition of skills that address the universe of standards is no longer presented according the old problem of marginality, which signals being 'not yet from here and entirely from there', but instead according to an accepted meaning denoting one who is able to impose a sense of convenience on their comings and goings, their inputs and outputs, and between different worlds designated as being different.
>
> (Tarrius, 2000, p. 8)

International managers will not give up any element that has made them what they are; on the contrary, they will begin composing with this substrate. These additional integrations create a spiral made up of points of constant projection, but which moves away from the initial basic structure and is not designed as a development known as a linear change consisting of stages of both satisfactions and vexations (Reveyrand-Coulon, 1989, p. 342).

Faced with this permanent quest for self, which begins with the temporal events that constitute the 'self' (Binswanger, 1971), the actor's discourse is interesting because it is itself a practice that acts on the reality to which it refers: it is speech that acts as a system of meanings (Piolat, 1999). International managers' ability to 'put themselves into words' allows them to be understood and empathized with (Dubar, 2000, p. 203). Identifying with the words of administrative and public (defining multiple identities within the meaning of 'positions' in official categories) language is different to identifying with those of business language or the intimate words of everyday actions and conversations. What matters is the usage that individuals derive from their own categories and from the words coming from their experiences, like memories of their actions, and the parlance that they attain in multiple foreign languages with their spouses, parents, children, and friends.

Therefore, in intercultural contexts, international managers search more than any other employee for a meaningful possession of their own lives. This unity, which is unceasingly reconstituted, is based on the accumulation of historical meanings that reconsider the entirety of a lifetime. 'We would thus never value reading and writing our lives above living it!' said an Italian manager at Gamma, who also pointed out that 'the creation of something original within one's identity is a basic human need, and this need also affects international business managers, even if they are quickly likened to uniform global citizens, homogeneous, and identical'. Furthermore, as a marketing director at Gamma claimed:

> We all play with our identities. The time has come for clear affiliations in business. What does this mean? It means that nationality is not always situated where one believes it to be, but that it depends on the manner with which we observe those that have had experiences on multiple continents or in multiple countries since their childhood.
>
> I know a director in the makeup department of our group, whose colleagues attribute a Chinese identity to her – they do not understand why she has a limited understanding of skin bleaching products and of the market in China. The fact is that she has never worked there and does not speak the language. Her father is American and born in Hong Kong, and her mother was German and born in Munich – this young woman studied in England, France, and the United States. In fact, she acquired her main experience in cosmetics in Germany at the end of her studies, then in France while working with brands of Italian origin. Regardless of where she is, she claims that she feels perfectly 'adaptable', and says that she does not always understand the weight that speaking carries over writing in our group, and values Anglo-Saxon methods at work and in the areas of performance evaluation, reporting and organizing tasks. She is married to an American. Her last name and physical appearance seem to be 'Asian', but in reality I find it very difficult to attribute a certain nationality to her based on this.
>
> (Agard, 2004, p. 482)

This testimony illustrates that in large companies, the causality of linear cultural interpretation (which is supposed to be given by national origin, as this is now the main criterion of cultural differentiation) is constantly undermined by strategies of cultural production (Abdallah-Pretceille and Porcher, 1996). Globalized firms are thus becoming increasingly populated with individuals carrying multiple geographic referents. Having knowledge of cultural characteristics does not give one remote access to culture or to communication. According to Abdallah-Pretceille and Porcher (1996), 'by appealing to culture, the individual, like a text, says something other than the significance that comes as a result of a sum of statements'.

The fatigue and suffering of the intercultural manager

Where we least expect them, and even when they are found to be represented in different classes of work, international managers are examples of identity destabilization, registering themselves in the cultural and social changes of contemporary society, and thereby diminishing the rate of unionization, increasing the number of divorces, separations, and single-parent families, individualizing management methods related to the requirements of subjective employee mobilization, and promoting the emergence of different social times associated with flexibility, the reduction of work time, and mobility.

As we have mentioned, the 'globalized' firm relies on its nomads, i.e. its international managers, to break the demarcations between orders, devices, corporate bodies, and social classes, and to cultivate spaces open to the circulation of knowledge and skills. In such a productive, 'rhizomatic' world, nothing would hinder movement, and one would renounce having but one sole job or function. Work would come back to be sold and to sell itself in order to give 'added value' to the organization. For one's entire career, one must be able to clear paths in order to find preferential routes and connections without fixed points that will allow one to locate operating answers. A good geologist, for example, is the geologist who has traveled extensively and stored thousands of practical cases in different parts of the world, each consisting of diverse teams and varying climates.

In a world that demands that these managers build international links and exchange knowledge for productive purposes, every person is 'contactable' and every kind of contact is possible. This question of the constitution and mobilization of international networks illustrates managers' (official) obligation to remain detached from local affiliations and solely national ties, whereas their actual capacity does still does not always rest on professional international networks, due to the fact that such networks are difficult to establish at various levels of middle management (reduced duration of deployments, rotation, diversification of hiring procedures and career management practices). Therefore, the threat to international managers lies in 'fatigue, exhaustion, and the need address it, to constantly be organized, to "timmé" everything and to predict everything' (according to a Nigerian manager who has lived 5 years of international mobility in Paris during his 15-year career). For nestled within each instance of international mobility, especially those of short duration, there exists the risk of being not connected, but rather of being left in solitude. Recent studies have shown that for multinational firms faced with expatriation, there exists a failure rate of between 10 and 30 per cent for expected returns, with these firms also seeing less quantifiable declines in performance (Cerdin, 1999; Swaak, 1995).

The work of international managers and what makes them scarce in the organization is their knowledge of the organization and of those who compose it. This implies the endless task of interpreting local data in order to make it applicable and workable elsewhere, as well as the task of narrating experiences (in conjunction with consultants, colleagues) at conferences and training seminars (which international managers attend more than other employees). Therefore, in the 'globalized' company, the seemingly most stable properties of individual – such as sex or occupation, for example – are signs that are subject to interpretation and exchange during interactions. More and more, these properties are relational, and it is therefore necessary to discover the meaning given to them by actors (Boltanski and Chiapello, 1999). Resources that cannot be commoditized or contractualized (such as ideas) take on a great importance, as does information on the relationships of others, their health, their aesthetic and political preferences, their managerial habits, their tightly knit networks and those whom they are indebted to (Boltanski and Chiapello, 1999).

The emergence of reticular capitalism therefore appears to take part in a constant call to responsibility, to continuous investment, and to the 'corporate self' (Boltanski and Chiapello, 1999), ultimately increasing a feeling of anxiety. Moreover, it is striking to remark that this feeling of anxiety, of increased suffering, is experienced in a context of non-degraded physical stress, unlike other past experiences of displacement for 'migrant' populations, such as the industrial labor force of the 1960s (Sainsaulieu and Zehraoui, 1996; Sainsaulieu, 1988). As a manager of Norwegian origin explains:

> After dinner at the end of a workday, I always leave my hotel in order to walk and to release my stress. And well, for me, the urban territories that I walk through are enclosed territories. I intend to store up pieces of these cities that I'll take with me later on. I don't want to make contact with people. Besides, I don't have time, and when I go out, it's already too late. I rarely mention these moments when I go back home.

For international managers that have been taken out of their comfort zones, for those whose work intensity increases due to a lack of recreational time, there exists what Ricœur (1985, p. 422) calls 'the narrowing of the space of experience', i.e. the impossibility of appropriating the 'traditions' judged to be insignificant during routine interactions due to a lack of time. If you fail to find someone to explain these traditions to you, or to locate colleagues that can help you to decipher habits and customs, in reality, words fail to make them function. Suffering from various somatic failures, subjects are therefore subjected to a necessary metamorphosis: they must adapt to a new world without necessarily meeting reference groups, and they must live a demand for membership that is never granted (Nathan, 1994).

How can one develop the ability to change one's perspective while at the same time retaining one's sense of self? Renault has identified a new type of recognition denial that is unique to our society, which he calls fragmented or unsatisfying recognition.

> It is not only that the individual fails to recognize how he interprets the roles that he assumes (ignorance), but that these roles are superimposed on him, denying him the right to the personal unification that would allow him to feel recognized through those roles.
> (Renault, 2004, p. 193)

This would be a time of strong yet conflicting identifications: the individual is constantly emerging because he must personally produce a coherency and a series of adjustments that can no longer apply to the social system as a whole.

In return for their movements and their sacrifices, mobile managers seek fidelity from those who manage them, a fidelity that is valorized in terms of foresight and a steady growth of both income and status (hence the growing phenomena of 'expatriate support groups' and groups aimed at sponsoring the manager before and after his or her geographic mobility). If collectively, everyone within the 'globalized' firm is the guarantor of the firm's employability and competences, each individual also lives in fear of being disposed of, disconnected, or abandoned by those who are continually in motion. Indeed, there is a strong distinction between experts possessing specialized knowledge that is nevertheless highly transferable (i.e. imprecise), and other managers who are less subject to the obsolescence of their knowledge (Boltanski and Chiapello, 1999, p. 458).

International managers are threatened by the interference and friction between the disinterested sharing of common interests and the pursuit of economic interests, as well as between friendships and business relationships. How can one be somebody and be flexible at the same time? How can one possess permanence but also have a personality? Every concern among international managers forces them into a corner: they must be original, even 'exotic', but at the same time must remain sufficiently compliant. The foreigner must be interesting, must seduce, and must adapt to their work situation. At the same time, however, this stranger must also not disturb the existing order, and while their work response time becomes shorter and shorter, the time that is available for knowing the other in their difference becomes more compressed, largely for cost reasons (e.g. the phenomena of commuting or quasi-mobility).

Courpasson (2000) has developed the idea that for managers, obedience is an action: it is reflected, and individuals survive by reconstituting emotional niches and by ignoring guidelines or their bosses. This may be due to the fact that the individual has a growing sense of estrangement vis-à-vis both the social identities that make him or her a manager, as well as their social image. Furthermore, one of such a manager's main concerns is to ensure the correctness of his or her interpretation, insisting on the evocative power of music, smells, and other family objects from the country that has been left behind. Robert Demontrond (2000) highlights the state of nostalgia that many expatriates experience, which carries along with it a fear of losing what one has founded one's identity on. How, in other words, can one have both roots and wings, can one be 'authentic' while remaining 'true to oneself'?

A priori, the managerial vulgate banishes the presence per se of the subject in 'constant' relation with his or her origins. Their fidelity to tradition appears as rigidity, as a refusal to be connected to the company's internal 'network'. Nostalgia may, however, be compatible with a strong professional investment, and rather than forcing one to slip into a irremediable, pathological state, may in fact serve as a adjuvant, a kind of 'necessary' moment.

The danger that this displaced man faces is in fact that of a narcissistic identity, his complete attachment to a place, and his reflection in it, from which he cannot be pulled away lest he suffer or die. The vast majority of international managers claim that they must experience both this mourning as well as the particular notion that their culture of origin has been inherited, and furthermore, that it is in a perpetual state of reconstruction, an oscillation between what has already been seen and what remains to be discovered. From this perspective, it seems to us that the experience that awaits international managers is not one of bricolage, in which they themselves bring about such realizations, but rather, one of automation, of becoming an automaton. Baudoin (2003, p. 250) evokes the figure of the automaton to express the movement that the psyche makes in situations of high anxiety, conveying a purely objective character that is content to play its roles. The automaton lives experiences in a repetitive, mechanical fashion in order to protect itself. Furthermore, the author speaks of an interior uprooting as the body disappears.[3]

If the questions of labor law or of compensation remain the classic concerns of HR departments in the management of expatriation, spouses are subjected to a professional stress and a familial stress, which interact and provoke conflicts related to the roles that the two sides play (as well as career-related sacrifices when one goes abroad). The pace of life increases the repercussion and extension of these tensions into different spheres. Adler (1988) has demonstrated that the flow of stress is directed at the 'follower', who is forced to take up the responsibilities of domestic life while the 'director' is investing in new professional networks.

More often than not, we speak of 'identity embrittlement' when considering subjects facing job uncertainty or deskilling (Palmade, 2003). For a large majority of these employees, a weakening sense of self-unity corresponds to the relative dissolution of the structures that make sense of the spheres of work, society in progress, and family. Here, we can hear echoes of Max Weber's idea of the 'fragmentation of the soul', which he saw as resulting from the obligation to adapt to a instrumental capitalist rationality, which erected in value, also serves to weaken one's social grounding and collective affiliations. One must recognize a similar pathology in many international managers who, in failing to create opportunities for local or global commitments, develop a capacity for reflexivity (Giddens, 1991) and healing within community spaces and solid families.

Conclusions

Is the phenomenon of the intersection of cultures becoming more important in business than the existence of distinctive cultures? In the 'multicultural' firm, one must not only consider the nature of things – i.e. the fixed scale of classifications – but also what a given society does with such things in order to establish social classifications. Instead of a unique, central-ized *logos* for setting general policy, we must accept a multiplicity of decentralized *logoi* (Barloewen, 2003, p. 255). It is certain that adjacency with the foreigner has progressively become the norm since the 1970s, and that what matters now is 'not that which honors the sociopolitical conceptions that analysts have favored, but that which has brought to light new contexts of action' (Bastenier, 2004, p. 165). The time has come for the public expres-sion of the subjective rights of employees to be rooted in multiple national, regional, or even local cultures.

This chapter has brought us to see the identity of international managers as a 'prismatic' reality, that the majority of people, including their colleagues, refuse to acknowledge, thereby bogging down these subjects with an identity monism. Our investigations have revealed the expression of a reflexive component of 'mobile' managers involving ethnicity, a personal 'reserve' and a subjective autonomy that is representative of oneself, irreducible to borrowed or incarnate social roles. As such, the art of the international manager does not lie in being a 'chameleon', or in seeking out mimicry or imitation, but rather, in recognizing a part of identity creation (Delange and Pierre 2004); in this, we can understand international managers (depending on the context) as 'agents' socializing in different cultures, 'actors' playing a game and mobilizing strategies, 'subjects' that 'seek out themselves in incertitude', or 'authors' 'crafting a story about their world' (Dubar, 2004).

In a sense, international managers can be characterized not so much as a static state, but as a succession of states in the processes that allow them to create and to give meaning to themselves – processes that are in relation to the representation that creates and gives mean-ing to others – according to the multicultural contexts of work. If, in some way, we are only as much as we know about others, such a fact emphasizes the social essence that all things are multiple. International managers illustrate that the self consists of several individuals superimposed on each another. Alongside of so-and-so, one will lie, one will begin to play and to construct distinct roles that are adapted to one's interlocutor. These fabrications are oriented according to axes that do not mix. It is not the person that is multiple, but rather the reality that is imposed on that person and the continual construction of roles (Laurens, 2002, p. 249). Within the context of the problematic of the 'multicultural' firm, there exists that which connects people from different countries – the questions of a being whose privacy must also be able to deploy itself on the public stage and of a consideration of a need to be attached to individuals within a 'we' community. Without this, individuals create a derogatory image of themselves and of the company.

In our research practice, we capture the essence of the 'mobile' individual, less in terms of their 'cultural origin', what we know of it, their strategies for coping with their 'host culture', or what we know of these strategies, but rather in terms of their 'internal exile', that is to say their journey from one (imaginary) place to another, and how this journey fits into their professional, linguistic and emotional story. Into what network of significance does a given element fit? How does this element come to life in the 'mobile' manager's story? It would be useful for trainers (and for all those that develop along with international managers) to speak of education *à la* 'narrative coherence', or of education *à la* 'narrative identity' (De Carlo, quoted in Feldhendler 2003). Far too often, we represent the story of mobile work subjects as being a long process; however, to write about the intercultural in an interpretive work means to capture the 'moments' (Hess, quoted in Feldhendler 2003) that suggest something that is at once more complex.

We therefore consider intercultural space–time to be the sedimentation of intercultural situations experienced over a long period, which dismisses the idea of splitting the individual from society (Pierre, 2004). Moreover, we wish to consider the intrapsychic level of individual development by understanding it in terms of contextual influences and macro-social constraints. It is for this reason that within our work on management in an intercultural context, we mobilize a phenomenological approach, beginning with the psychosociological reality whose presence causes the observed individual to cease to function as a 'representation' of a culture. It would be important to bond culture to something other than collective representations, cultural traits, average values of a population, or any other 'universal' whose basis is neither individuals nor social groups, nor their relationships. Every social fact is a totality and every social fact is partially linked to conscious and unconscious representations of identity and culture, which actors temporarily give to themselves and others in connection with the balance of power, and the state of structural effects and ongoing conflicts (Martin et al., 2003).

Notes

1 The main conclusions and interview excerpts in this chapter are the result of large sociological surveys that were conducted in the companies of Alpha and Gamma over the course of 10 years (1993–2005). The first survey (2000) was an integral part of a successful doctoral thesis defense (Pierre, 2000). In that survey, 120 interviews were conducted with 'international' managers. Their mobility was therefore performed via a single employer within a diverse internal market, permitting them to occupy multiple positions and carry out various tasks. While working as a full-time employee at Alpha, the author was also a part of Gamma (1996–2005), where nearly 500 semi-structured interviews were conducted.

2 In accordance with Camilleri (1990, p. 49), we suggest that 'identity strategies' are the 'result of the individual and collective elaboration of actors', and that 'through their movements, [they] express the adjustments that are made day by day in relation to the various situations and issues that they raise (i.e. the aims expressed by the actors) and resources that come as a result of these elements'.

3 This is not a new phenomenon. The traumatic neurosis that manifests itself in lasting wounds, shame or sadness, fatigue, and nightmares for individuals who are studying, working, or carrying out military service, and that cannot be cured by medicinal therapies, was called a 'disease of nostalgia' during the seventeenth century. Later, the term 'pathopatridalgia' would be given to these symptoms, and is now considered to be a disease brought on by social misery. Ham (2003, p. 131) refers to the theories of 'structural homology' of the psyche and of culture, which gave way to the notions of 'ethnic unconscious' (which is linked to the repression that each culture imposes on social groups) and 'idiosyncratic unconscious' (which is linked to a 'single particular stress').

References

Abdallah-Pretceille, M. and Porcher, L. (1996). *Éducation et communication interculturelle*, Paris: Presses Universitaires de France.
Abdallah-Pretceille, M. (1999). *L'éducation interculturelle*, Paris: Presses Universitaires de France.

Adler, N. and Izraeli, D. (1988). *Women in Management Wordlwide*, New York: M. E. Sharpe.

Agard, J. Y. (2004). 'Ethnographie de la mobilité internationale. Le cas d'une multinationale française', Ph.D. thesis in sociology, University of Paris V Descartes.

Assoun, P. L. (2004). 'Jouissance du malaise', in Aubert, N., *L'individu hypermoderne*, Paris: Eres.

Aubert, N. (2004). 'L'intensité de soi', *L'individu hypermoderne*, Paris: Eres.

Barus-Michel, J. (2004). 'L'hypermodernité, dépassement ou perversion de la modernité?', in Aubert, N., *L'individu hypermoderne*, Paris: Eres.

Bastenier, A. (2004). *Qu'est-ce qu'une société ethnique?* Paris: Presses Universitaires de France.

Bastide, R. (1955). 'Le principe de coupure et le comportement afro-brésilien', Anais do 60 Congresso Internacional de Americanistas, Anhembi, vol. 1.

—— (1965). *Sociologie des maladies mentales*, Paris: Flammarion.

—— (1970). *Le prochain et le lointain*, Paris: Editions Cujas.

Baudoin, C. (2003). 'De l'instinct à l'esprit, Delachaux et Nestlé, 1970', cited by Romanens, C., *Maltraitance au travail. Les effets pervers du harcèlement*, Paris: Desclée de Brouwer.

Bellenger, L. (1992). *Etre pro*, ESF.

—— (1999). *Etre pro*, ESF, 1992, cited by Boltanski, L. and Chiapello, E., *Le nouvel esprit du capitalisme*, Paris: Gallimard.

Berger, P. and Luckmann, T. (1996). *La construction sociale de la réalité*, Paris: A. Colin.

Berry, J. W. (1990). 'Psychology of acculturation', in Bernam, J., *Cross-Cultural Perspectives*, Nebraska Symposium on Motivation, Lincoln: University of Nebraska Press.

Binswanger, L. (1971). *Introduction à l'analyse existentielle*, Paris: Editions de Minuit.

Black, J. and Mendenhall, M. (1991). 'The U-Curve adjustment hypothesis revisited: a review and theoretical framework', *Journal of International Business Studies*, Hampshire, UK. Second Quarter, 225–247.

Black, J., Gregersen, H. B. and Mendenhall, M. (1992). *Global Assignments: Successfully Expatriating and Repatriating International Managers*. San Francisco: Jossey-Bass.

Black, J., Mendenhall, M. and Oddou, G. (1991). 'Towards a comprehensive model of international adaptation. An integration of multiple theoretical perspectives', *Academy of Management Review*, 16 (2), 291–317.

Boltanski, L. and Chiapello, E. (1999). *Le nouvel esprit du capitalisme*. Paris: Gallimard.

Bosche, M. (1993). *Le management interculturel*. Paris: Armand Nathan.

Bourdieu, P. (1980). *Questions de sociologie*. Paris: Editions de Minuit.

—— (1992). *Réponses. Pour une anthropologie réflexive*. Paris: Editions du Seuil.

Breton, P. (1992). *L'utopie de la communication*, Paris: La Découverte.

Camilleri, C. (1980). 'Les immigrés maghrébins de la seconde génération: contribution à une étude de leurs évolutions et de leurs choix culturels', *Bulletin de Psychologie*, Paris, vol. 33, 347.

—— (1990). 'Identité et gestion de la disparité culturelle: essay d' une typologie' in Camilleri, C., Kasterzstein, J., Lipiansky, E.M., Malewska-Peyre, H., Taboada-Leonetti, I. and Vasquez, A. (eds), *Stratégies identitaires*, Paris: Presses Universitaires de France.

—— (1992). 'Cultures et stratégies: ou les mille manières de s'adapter', Paris, *Sciences Humaines*, no. 16, April, 21–23.

—— (1994). 'La psychologie, du culturel à l'interculturel', *Bulletin de psychologie*, Paris, vol. 48, January–April, no. 419.

Camilleri, C. and Malewska-Peyre, H. (1996). 'Socialization and identity strategies' in Berry, J. W., Dasen, P. and Saraswathi, T. S., *Handbook of Cross-Cultural Psychology, vol. 2*, Boston: Allyn and Bacon.

Camilleri, C. and Vinsonneau, G. (1996). *Psychologie et culture: concepts et méthodes*, Paris: A. Colin.

Cerdin, J. L. (1996). 'Mobilité internationale des cadres: adaptation et décision d'expatriation', Doctoral thesis in management science, University of Toulouse 1.

—— (1999). *La mobilité internationale. Réussir l'expatriation*, Paris: Éditions d'Organisation.

Cerdin, J. L. and Dubouloy, M. (2004). 'Expatriation as a maturation opportunity: a psychoanalytical approach based on "copy and paste"', *Human Relations*, 57 (8), 957–981.

Cohen-Emerique, M. (1999). 'Le choc culturel', in Lipianski, E. and M. Demorgon, J., *La formation en interculturel*. Paris: Retz.

Cohen-Emerique, M. and Hohl, J. (2002). 'Les ressources mobilisées par les professionnels en situations interculturelles', *Education Permanente*, Paris, no. 150, 113–125.

Corcuff, P. (1995). *Les nouvelles sociologies*, Paris: Nathan.

Courpasson, D. (2000). *Action contrainte. Organisations libérales et domination*. Paris: Presses Universitaires de France.

Dasen, P. (1993). 'L'ethnocentrisme de la psychologie', in Rey, M. (ed.) *Psychologie clinique et interrogations culturelles*. Paris: L'Harmattan.

De Carlo, M. quoted in Feldhendler, D. (2003). 'Approche dramatique du récit de vie: une démarche interculturelle', *Passerelles*, no. 27, 75–84.

Delange, N. and Pierre, P. (2004a). 'Pratiques de médiation et traitement de l'étranger dans l'entreprise multiculturelle'. *Esprit critique*, summer, 82–107.

—— (2004b). 'Compte-rendu de l'ouvrage de Philippe D'Iribarne: Le Tiers-Monde qui réussit. Nouveaux modèles'. *Revue Economique et Sociale*, no. 3, September, 129–135.

Delanoë, R. (1992). *Diversité et richesse des situations interculturelles, conséquences pour le management*, Management France. Paris: CNOF.

Delory-Moberger, C. (2000). *Les histoires de vie*. Paris: Anthropos.

Denoux, P. (1994). 'L'identité interculturelle', *Bulletin de psychologie*, Paris, 48, January–April, no. 419, 8–11.

Devereux, G. (1970). *Les facteurs culturels en thérapeutique psychanalytique*, Essais d'Ethnopsychiatrie Générale, Paris: Gallimard.

D'Iribarne, P. (1991). *La logique de l'honneur*, Paris: Le Seuil.

Dobry, M. (1990). 'Calcul, concurrence et gestion du sens', *La manifestation*, Paris, PFNSP.

Dubar, C. (1991). *La socialisation*. Paris: A. Colin.

—— (1992). 'Formes identitaires et socialisation professionnelle', *Revue Française de Sociologie*, Paris, 33, 505–529.

—— (2000). *La crise des identités*. Paris: Presses Universitaires de France.

—— (2004). 'Agent, acteur, sujet, auteur: de pareil au même?' *1er Congre's de L'AFS*.

Engbersen, G. (1999). 'Sans-papiers. Les stratégies de séjour des immigrés clandestins', *Actes de la recherche en sciences sociales*, 129, September, 26–28.

Enriquez, E. (2003). 'Caractéristiques spécifiques de la pulsion de mort dans les sociétés contemporaines et les organisations modernes', *O&S*, vol. 10, no. 28, 13–27.

Enriquez, E. and Haroche, C. (2002). *La face obscure des démocraties modernes*. Paris: Éditions Erès.

Erikson, E. (1972). *Adolescence et crise. La quête de l'identité*. Paris: Flammarion.

Fibbi, R. (2004). 'L'approche transnationale dans l'étude des migrations', in Nedelcu, M., *La mobilité internationale des compétences*. Paris: L'Harmattan.

Forse, M. (2000). 'Les relations sociales comme ressources', *Sciences humaines*, Paris, no. 104, April, 34–37.

Furnham A. and Boschner, S. (1986). *Culture shock: Psychological reactions to unfamiliar environments*, London: Methuen.

Giddens, A. (1991). *Les conséquences de la modernité*. Paris: L'Harmattan.

Gomez, P. Y. (2000), 'Monde global, cadres nomades. Réflexions sur le nomadisme dans les structures organisationnelles contemporaines', Document de travail, Lyon, EM Lyon.

Goodman, N. (1994). 'Cross-cultural training for the global executive', in Brislin, R. and Yoshida, T., *Improving Intercultural Interactions: Modules for Cross-Cultural Training Programs*. London: Sage.

Ham, M. (2003). L'immigré et l'autochtone face à leur exil, Grenoble: PUG.

Hammer, M. R. and Bennett, J. M. (1998). *The Intercultural Development Inventory (IDI) manual*, Portland: Intercultural Communication Institute.

Hampden-Turner, C. (1991). 'Vers une approche multiculturelle du bien-être et des valeurs', *Personnel*, Paris, no. 327, October, 45–53.

Hansen, M. L. (1938). 'The problem of the third generation immigrant', Augustana Historical Society, Roch Island.

Hess, R., cited by Feldhendler, D. (2003). 'Approche dramatique du récit de vie: une démarche interculturelle', *Passerelles*, no. 27, 87–98.

Hofstede, G. (1983). 'The cultural relativity of organisational practices and theories', *Journal of International Business Studies*, 14 (2), 75–89.

—— (1987). 'Relativité culturelle des pratiques et théories de l'organisation', *Revue Française de Gestion*, Paris, no. 64, September, 10–21.

Hofstede, G. and Bollinger, D. (1987). *Les différences culturelles dans le management*. Paris: Les Éditions d'Organisation.

Kaufmann, J. (2001). *Ego. Pour une sociologie de l'individu*. Paris: Nathan.

Landis, D. and Bhagat, R. S. (1996). *Handbook of Intercultural Training*. London: Sage.

Laurens, S. (2002). *La mémoire sociale, Identités et représentations sociales*. Rennes: PUR.

Lévi-Strauss, C. (1958). *Anthropologie structurale*. Paris: Plon.

Linton, R. (1986). *Le fondement culturel de la personnalité*. Paris: Dunod.

Lipiansky, E. M., Taboada-Leonetti, I. and Vasquez, A. (1997). 'Introduction à la problématique de l'identité', *Stratégies identitaires*. Paris: Presses Universitaires de France.

Lyman, S. M. and Douglass, W. A. (1972) 'Ethnicity: strategies of collective and individual impression management', *Social Research*, vol. 40, 344–365.

—— (1976). 'L'ethnie: structure, processus et saillance', *Cahiers Internationaux de Sociologie*, Paris, vol. 61, 197–220.

Marc, E. (1992). 'Les dessous de la communication interculturelle', *Sciences humaines*, Paris, no. 16, April, 67–74.

Martin, D., Metzger, J. L. and Pierre, P. (2003). *Les métamorphoses du monde. Sociologie de la mondialisation*, Paris, Éditions du Seuil.

Mayol, P. (1992). 'Radiographie des banlieues', Paris, *Revue Esprit*, Juin, 56–67.

Mendenhall, M. and Oddou, G. (1985). 'The dimensions of expatriate acculturation: a review', *Academy of Management Review*, 10(1), 39–47.

Metzger, J. L. and Pierre, P. (2003). 'En quoi le concept d'élite peut aider à analyser le processus de mondialisation?', *Recherches Sociologiques*, 34 (1), 95–115.

Meyer, J. B. (2000). 'The satellite: towards a local and global observation of the circulation of competence', in Charum, J. and Meyer, J. B., *International Scientific Migrations today*. New Perspectives, Bondy: IRD.

Meyer, J. B. and Hernandez, V. (2004). 'Les diasporas scientifiques et techniques: état des lieux', in Nedelcu, M., *La mobilité internationale des compétences*. Paris: L'Harmattan.

Meyerson, I. (1948). *Les fonctions psychologiques et les œuvres*. Paris: A. Michel.

Mutabazi, E. (2001). 'Multiculturalisme et gouvernance des sociétés africaines', Paris, *Sociologies Pratiques*, APSE, no. 5, 45–62.

Nathan, T. (1994). *L'influence qui guérit*. Paris: Odile Jacob.

Nedelcu, M. (2004a). 'Le saut paradigmatique: de la fuite à la circulation', in Nedelcu, M., *La mobilité internationale des compétences*. Paris: L'Harmattan, p. 9.

—— (2004b). 'Vers une nouvelle culture du lien: les e-pratiques locales et transnationales des migrants roumains hautement qualifiés', in Nedelcu, M., *La mobilité internationale des compétences*. Paris: L'Harmattan.

Noorderhaven, N. G. and Harzing, A. W. (2003). The country of origin effect in multinational corporations: sources, mechanisms and moderating conditions, Stuttgart: *Management International Review*.

Oberg, K. (1960). 'Culture shock: adjustment to new cultural environments', *Practical Anthropologist*, 7, 177–182.

Palmade, J. (2003). *L'incertitude comme norme*. Paris: Presses Universitaires de France.

Paugam, S. (1991). *La disqualification sociale. Essai sur la nouvelle pauvreté*. Paris: Presses Universitaires de France.

Pierre, P. (2000). 'La socialisation des cadres internationaux dans l'entreprise mondialisée. L'exemple d'un groupe pétrolier français', Ph.D. thesis in sociology, Institut d'Études Politiques de Paris.

—— (2003). *Mobilité internationale et identités des cadres. De l'usage de l'ethnicité dans l'entreprise mondialisée*. Fontenay-Sous-Bois: Sides.

—— (2004a). 'La vie professionnelle comme un récit. L'identité narrative des cadres internationaux dans l'entreprise mondialisée', *Migrations Société*, no. 93–94, May–August, 15–31.

—— (2004b). 'Mondialisation et constructions identitaires de cadres de l'industrie pétrolière', *Revue Française de Gestion*, 30 (148), 87–118.

—— (2005). 'Mobilité internationale et identités des cadres: pour une sociologie "immergée". Des usages de l'ethnicité dans l'entreprise mondialisée', www.EspacesTemps.net

Piolat, M. (1999). 'Les concepts de soi', *La construction sociale de la personne*, Grenoble, PUG.

Poutignat, P. and Streiff-Fenart, J. (1995). *Théories de l'ethnicité*. Paris: Presses Universitaires de France.

Raymond, H. (1982). 'Les samouraïs de la raison. Enquête sur la vie et les valeurs chez les cadres supérieurs de l'industrie', *Sociologie du travail*, Paris, no. 4, 378–402.

Reich, R. (1991). *L'économie mondialisée*, Paris: Dunod.

Renault, E. (2004). 'Reconnaissance, institutions injustice', *La revue du MAUSS*, Paris, no. 23, 180–195.

Reveyrand-Coulon, O. (1989). 'Quelques réflexions sur le devenir de l'identité de migrant', *Socialisations et cultures*, Toulouse: Presses Universitaires du Mirail.

Ricœur, P. (1985). *Temps et récit*. Paris: Éditions du Seuil.

Robert-Demontrond, P. (2000). 'Psychopathologie de l'expatriation: la nostalgie comme syndrome d'adaptation', XIème Congrès de l'AGRH.

Sainsaulieu, R. (1988). *L'identité au travail*, Paris: PFNSP, 1977, 2nd edn.

—— (1991). *Sociologie de l'entreprise et de l'organisation*. Paris: PFNSP/Dalloz.

Sainsaulieu, R. and Zehraoui, A. (1996). *Ouvriers spécialisés à Billancourt*, Paris, L'Harmattan.

Schein, E. H. (1985). *Organizational Culture and Leadership*. San Francisco: Jossey-Bass.

Schneider, S. C. and Asakawa, K. (1995). 'American and Japanese expatriate adjustment: a psycho-analytic perspective', *Human Relations*, 48, 1109–1127.

Sennett, R. (2000). *Le travail sans qualités*, Paris: Albin Michel.

Swaak, R. A. (1995). 'Expatriate failures: too many, too much cost, too little planning', *Compensation and Benefits Review*, 27 (6).

Taboada-Leonetti, I. (1982). 'Jeunes filles immigrées, une problématique spécifique', in Malewska-Peyre, H., *Crise d'identité et déviance chez les jeunes immigrés*. Paris: La Documentation Française.

—— (1990). 'Stratégies identitaires et minorités: le point de vue du sociologue', *Stratégies identitaires*. Paris: Presses Universitaires de France.

Tarrius, A. (2000). *Les nouveaux cosmopolitismes. Mobilité, identités, territoires*. Paris: Éditions de l'Aube.

Trompenaars, F. (1994). *L'entreprise multiculturelle*. Paris: Maxima-Laurent du Mesnil Éditeur.

Trutat, J. M. and Obame, J. A. (1987). 'Pour une politique de relève réussie de l'assistance étrangère par une main d'œuvre nationale', Paris, *Revue de l'ANDCP*, 45–56.

Uhalde, M. (2001). *L'intervention sociologique en entreprise*. Paris: Desclée de Brouwer.

Urry, J. (2005). *Sociologie des mobilités*. Paris: A. Colin.

Vatz-Laaroussi, M. (2001). *Le familial au cœur de l'immigration*. Paris: L'Harmattan.

Vinsonneau, G. (1993). 'Appartenances culturelles et subculturelles, inégalités sociales et variations des expressions identitaires. Etudes expérimentales réalisées parmi quelques populations en position sociale défavorable', Doctoral thesis, University of Paris V.

—— (1997). *Culture et comportement*. Paris: A. Colin.

—— (1999). *Inégalités sociales et procédés identitaires*. Paris: A. Colin.

Von Barloewen, C. (2003). *Anthropologie de la mondialisation*. Paris: Éditions des Syrtes.

Vrancken, D. and Kuty, O. (2001). *La sociologie et l'intervention*. Brussels: De Boeck.

Wagner, A. C. (1998). *Les nouvelles élites de la mondialisation*. Paris: Presses Universitaires de France.

—— (1999). *Les cadres internationaux en France: la formation d'une nouvelle culture*, Paris, Humanisme et Entreprise.

Weinshall, T. D. (1997). *Culture and Management*, London: Penguin Books.

Yanaprasart, P. (2006). *L'expatrié: un acteur social de la mobilité internationale. Cadres entre la Suisse et la France*, vol. 15. Berlin/New York: Peter Lang.

Zaharna, R. S. (1989). 'Self-shock: the double binding challenge of identity', *International Journal of Intercultural Relations*, 13 (4), 501–26.

5 International negotiations

Jean-Claude Usunier

Some researchers have questioned the very fact that cultural differences have an impact on international business negotiations, arguing that negotiation is negotiation irrespective of where and with whom it takes place. Zartman (1993, p. 19) has phrased it in strong terms:

> Culture is to negotiation what birds flying into engines are to flying airplanes or, at most, what weather is to aerodynamics – practical impediments that need to be taken into account (and avoided) once the basic process is fully understood and implemented.

However, there is now much empirical support for the view that culture has an impact on business negotiations (see for instance, Faure and Rubin, 1993; Graham et al., 1994; Leung, 1997; Brett and Okumura, 1998; Bazerman et al., 2000; Adair et al., 2001; Adler, 2002; Wade-Benzoni et al., 2002). Support comes also from authors actually involved in international negotiations (Foster, 1995; Cohen, 1997; Herbig, 1998; Schuster and Copeland, 1999; Saner, 2000). When negotiating internationally, one needs cultural knowledge and skills in intercultural communication. Many agreements have to be negotiated, drafted, signed and finally implemented: sales contracts, licensing agreements, joint ventures and various kinds of partnerships, agency and distribution agreements, turnkey contracts, etc. Negotiation is not only based on legal and business matters, hard facts which are often emphasized as being the sole important facts, but also on the quality of human and social relations, 'soft facts' which become of the utmost importance in an intercultural encounter. Goldman (1994) emphasizes for instance, the importance to the Japanese of *ningensei* which, literally translated, means an all-encompassing and overriding concern and prioritizing of 'humanity' or *human beingness* (see Box 5.1). According to Japanese specialists in international marketing negotiations:

> The North American and U.K. negotiators failed to communicate *ningensei* at the first table meeting. Rushing into bottom lines and demanding quick decisions on the pending contract, they also overlooked the crucial need for *ningensei* in developing good will... Hard business facts alone are not enough...*Ningensei* is critical in getting Japanese to comply or in persuading Japanese negotiating partners.
>
> (Nippon Inc. Consultation, quoted in Goldman, 1994, p. 31)

There are various kinds of 'distances' between the potential partners: physical distance certainly, but also economic, educational and cultural distance, which tend to inflate the cost of negotiating internationally. Difficulties in interacting, negotiating, planning common ventures, working them out and achieving them together are deeply rooted in the cultural, human

Box 5.1 Four principles of Confucian philosophy

Ningensei exemplifies four interrelated principles of Confucian philosophy: *jen*, *shu*, *i* and *li*.

1. Based on active listening, *jen* is a form of humanism that translates into empathetic interaction and caring for the feelings of negotiating associates, and seeking out the other's views, sentiments and true intentions.
2. *Shu* emphasizes the importance of reciprocity in establishing human relationships and the cultivation of 'like-heartedness'; in Mastumoto's (1988) words it is 'belly communication', a means of coding messages within negotiating, social and corporate channels that is highly contingent upon affective, intuitive and non-verbal channels.
3. *I*, also termed *amae*, is the dimension which is concerned with the welfare of the collectivity, directing human relationships to the betterment of the common good. 'The i component of ningensei surfaces in Japanese negotiators' commitment to the organization, group agendas, and a reciprocity (shu) and humanism (jen) that is long-term, consistent, and looks beyond personal motivation.'
4. *Li* refers to the codes, corresponding to precise and formal manners, which facilitate the outer manifestation and social expression of *jen*, *shu* and *i*. The Japanese *meishi* ritual of exchanging business cards is typical of *li*-coded etiquette.

(Adapted from Goldman, 1994, pp. 32–33)

and social background of business people. They are not related to a superficial variance of business customs, and simple 'empathy' is not enough for the avoidance of misunderstandings. In fact, people with different cultural backgrounds often do not share the same basic assumptions (see below), and this has an influence at several levels of international business negotiations: the behavioral predispositions of the parties; their concept of what is negotiation and what should be an appropriate negotiation strategy; their attitudes during the negotiation process which may lead to cultural misunderstandings and undermine trust between the parties; differences in outcome orientation.

Culture defined

Culture as learned and forgotten norms and behavioral patterns

Sometimes culture has a reputation for being rather vague, for being a somewhat 'blurred' concept. The Swedish writer Selma Lagerlöf defines culture as 'what remains when that which has been learned is entirely forgotten'. Depicted thus, culture may appear to be a 'rubbish-bin' concept. Its main use would be to serve when more precise explanations have proved unsuccessful. It would also serve as an explanatory variable for residuals, when other more operative explanations seem inadequate. Nevertheless, Selma Lagerlöf's definition does have the important merit of identifying two basic elements of cultural dynamics (at the individual level):

1. It is learned.
2. It is forgotten, in the sense that we cease to be conscious (if we ever have been) of its existence as learned behavior.

For example, if one has been told during childhood that modest and self-effacing behavior is suitable when addressing other people, especially at first contact – which is the case in most Asian cultures – one forgets about this and is easily shocked by the assertive, apparently boastful, behavior which may appear in other cultures. Although largely forgotten, culture permeates our daily individual and collective actions. It is entirely oriented towards our adaptation to reality (both as constraints and opportunities). Since culture is 'forgotten', it is mostly unconsciously embedded in individual and collective behavior. Individuals find, in their cultural group, pre-set and agreed-upon solutions which indicate to them how to articulate properly their behavior and actions with members of the same cultural group.

Basic definitions of culture

Culture has been defined extensively, precisely because it is somewhat all-encompassing. After having assessed its nature as learned and forgotten, we need to provide some additional definitions of culture. Ralph Linton (1947, p. 21), for instance, stresses that it is *shared* and *transmitted*: 'A culture is the configuration of learned behavior and results of behavior whose component elements are shared and transmitted by the members of a particular society.' However, we should not go too far in considering the individual as simply *programmed* by culture. At a previous point in his landmark book, *The Cultural Background of Personality*, Linton had clearly indicated the limits of the cultural programming which a society can impose on an individual:

> No matter how carefully the individual has been trained or how successful his conditioning has been, he remains a distinct organism with his own needs and with capacities for independent thought, feeling and action. Moreover he retains a considerable degree of individuality.
>
> (1945, pp. 14–15)

If individuals have some leeway, then what use is culture to them? According to Goodenough (1971), culture is a set of beliefs or standards, shared by a group of people, which help the individual decide what is, what can be, how one feels about it, what to do and how to go about doing it. On the basis of this operational definition of culture, there is no longer any reason why culture should be equated with the whole of one particular society. It may be more related to activities that are shared by a definite group of people. Consequently individuals may share different cultures with several different groups, a corporate culture with colleagues at work, an educational culture with other MBA graduates, an ethnic culture with people of the same ethnic origin. When in a particular situation, they will switch into the culture that is operational. The term 'operational', in this context, implies that a culture must be shared with those with whom there must be co-operation, and that it must be suitable for the task.

Goodenough's concept of 'operating culture' assumes that individuals are able to choose the culture within which to interact at a given moment and in a given situation. This is, of course, subject to the overriding condition that this culture has been correctly internalized during past experiences, that *it is so well learned that it can be forgotten*. Although the concept of operating culture is somewhat debatable, it does have the advantage of clearly highlighting the multicultural nature of many individuals in today's societies, including binationals, multilingual people and those who have an international professional culture or are influenced as employees by the corporate culture of a multinational company. In this respect, international negotiation between culturally different organizations results in creating a new operating culture, a common set of beliefs and solutions, which is especially the case in joint ventures (Brannen and Salk, 2000).

Significant components of culture

The following are some significant elements of culture that have an impact on international business negotiations.

Language and communication

The way in which people communicate (that is both emit and receive messages) and the extent to which their native language frames their world-views and attitudes directly affects international business negotiations (see for instance, Adachi, 1998). They require a dialogue, although partners may have different native languages, writing contracts in a foreign language (at least foreign to one side), using interpreters, trying to express ideas, concepts which may be unique to a particular language, etc.

Institutional and legal systems

Differences in legal systems, contractual formalism and recourse to litigation, express contrasts in how societies are organized in terms of rules and decision-making systems. The level of formality in addressing public and private issues has to be considered in any kind of negotiated partnership, including the discussion of joint-venture contracts, the registration of subsidiaries and the addressing of sensitive issues with the public authorities of the host country.

Value systems

The prevailing values in a particular society, and the extent to which they are respected in the everyday behavior of individuals, are important because they affect the willingness to take risks, the leadership style, and the superior–subordinate relationship. This is true for the relationships between negotiators within a particular team, antagonistic negotiation teams and the negotiators on both sides and those from whom they have received the mandate for negotiating.

Time orientations

Attitudes towards time and how it shapes the way people structure their actions have a pervasive yet mostly invisible influence. Differences in punctuality, reflected in everyday negotiation behavior, may probably appear as the most visible consequence, but differences in time orientations, especially toward the future, are more important as they affect long-range issues such as the strategic framework of decisions made when negotiating.

Mindsets

Whether called 'Mindsets' (Fisher, 1988), 'intellectual styles' (Galtung, 1981) or 'mental models' (Bazerman et al., 2000), another major difference concerns the way people reflect on issues. Do they prefer to rely on data, ideas or speech, and which combination of these? How does this influence the way they relate words and actions? Mindsets influence ways of addressing issues, of collecting information, of choosing the relevant pieces of information and of assessing their 'truthfulness', so that finally they influence the negotiation process and the resulting decisions.

Relationship patterns

These concern how the individual relates to the group(s); what the dominant family and kinship patterns are; and how relationships are framed (individualism/collectivism; patronage relationships). These patterns affect international business negotiations through the style of interaction between people, their decision-making process, and the way in which they mix human relationships and business matters (see Leung, 1997).

The influence of culture on some important aspects of business negotiations

Culture and negotiation: the academic literature

A large part of the academic literature on the influence of culture on international business negotiations uses a comparative and cross-cultural setting (see for instance Graham, 1985 or Wade-Benzoni et al., 2002). A laboratory experiment (e.g. the negotiation simulation by Kelley, 1966 or the sale of rights to a television station as in Tenbrunsel and Bazerman, 2000) helps in the comparison of negotiations between people of various nationalities. Nationality is used as a proxy and summary variable for culture. A basic description is made of the cultural traits of a specific nationality in negotiations, which is then contrasted with one or more different national groups. It is the basis for some hypotheses on either the process or the outcome of these negotiations, where the membership of a specific national group is one of the main explanatory variables.

It is advisable to be prudent before directly transposing data, on the behavior or negotiation strategies of people from a particular country, which have been collected during negotiations with their compatriots. Some traits may not recur when people are negotiating with partners of other nationalities. For instance, when Italians negotiate together, or with the French, they may not adopt exactly the same behavior and strategies as they do when negotiating with Americans. Adler and Graham (1989) address the issue of whether these simple international comparisons are fallacies, when and if researchers are trying to describe cross-cultural interactions accurately. They demonstrate that negotiators tend to adapt their behavior in intercultural negotiation. They do not behave as predicted by that which has been observed in intracultural negotiations. Therefore their behaviour as observed in intracultural negotiations can only serve as a partial basis for the prediction of their style and strategies when negotiating with people belonging to different cultures. Graham and Adler, for instance, show that French-speaking Canadians are more problem-solving oriented when negotiating with English-speaking Canadians than they normally are among themselves.

Hence, the word 'intercultural' in this text directly relates to the study of interaction between people with different cultural backgrounds. The word 'cross-cultural' relates to a research design that is generally comparative but may also be centered on the encounter/interaction.

General influence of culture on business negotiations

Culture has mostly an *indirect* influence on the outcome of negotiations (see, for instance, the models of McCall and Warrington, 1990, and Graham and Sano, 1990; see also Bazerman

Table 5.1 The impact of cultural differences on international marketing negotiations

1. Behavioral predispositions of the parties

Concept of the self	Impact on credibility (in the awareness and exploration phases)
Interpersonal orientation	Individualism versus collectivism/Relationship versus deal orientation
In-group orientation	Similarity/'Limited good concept'
Power orientation	Power distance/Roles in negotiation teams/Negotiators' leeway
Willingness to take risks	Uncertainty avoidance/Degree of self-reliance of negotiators

2. Underlying concept of negotiation/negotiation strategies

Distributive strategy	Related to in-group orientation/Power distance/Individualism/Strong past orientation
Integrative strategy	Related to problem-solving approach and future orientation
Role of the negotiator	Buyer and seller's respective position of strength
Strategic time frame	Continuous versus discontinuous/Temporal orientations

3. Negotiation process

Agenda setting/scheduling the negotiation process	Linear-separable time/Economicity of time/Monochronism/ Negotiating globally versus negotiating clauses
Information processing	Ideologism versus pragmatism/Intellectual styles
Communication	Communication styles/Degree of formality and informality.
Negotiation tactics	Type and frequency of tactics/Mix of business with affectivity
Relationship development	The role of 'atmosphere' as bearing the history of the relationship and facilitating transition

4. Outcome orientations

Partnership as outcome	Making a new in-group – 'marriage' as metaphoric outcome
Deal/contract as outcome	Contract rules being the law of the parties (litigation orientation)
Profit as outcome	Accounting profit orientation (economicity)
Winning over the other party	Distributive orientation
Time line of negotiation	Continuous versus discontinuous view of negotiation

et al., 2000). It works through two basic groups of mediating variables: the situational aspects of the negotiation (time and time pressure, power and exercise of power, number of participants, location, etc.); and the characteristics of the negotiators (especially personality variables and cultural variables). These two groups of factors, in turn, influence the negotiation process, which ultimately determines the outcome (Jolibert, 1988). However, it is my contention that culture also has an influence on the outcome orientation: certain cultures are more deal/contract oriented whereas others favor relationship development. This is further developed later in this chapter. A census of the impact of culture on international business negotiations is given in Table 5.1.

Behavioral predispositions of the parties

Who is seen as a credible partner?

Triandis (1983, p. 147) has emphasized three dimensions of the self-concept which may have a strong influence on the cultural coding/decoding process of credibility:

1. *Self-esteem*: the extent to which people think of themselves as very good or not too good;
2. *Perceived potency*: the extent to which people view themselves as powerful, able to accomplish almost any task; and
3. *Perceived activity*: the person sees him/herself as a doer, an active shaper of the world.

Since people generally live in homogeneous cultural settings (i.e. countries or regions within countries with one language, a dominant religion and shared values), they use the same cultural codes. But when people do not share the same codes, this may create problems for establishing credibility/trust. For example, a credible person may be considered by the emitter (coder) to be somebody showing a low self-concept profile (modest, patiently listening to partners, speaking little and cautiously, etc.); if, conversely, the receiver (decoder) considers a credible person as somebody with a high self-concept profile (showing self-confidence, speaking arrogantly, not paying much attention to what the other is saying, etc.), there will be a credibility misunderstanding.

A classic example is the misinterpretation by the Soviet leader Nikita Khrushchev of the credibility of the American President, John F. Kennedy. It was one of the main reasons for the seriousness of the Cuban Missile Crisis at the beginning of the 1960s. Kennedy and Khrushchev had held talks in Vienna, after the unsuccessful 1961 invasion of Cuba by US soldiers resulting in defeat at the Bay of Pigs. During their meeting, the young President Kennedy recognized that this attack had been a military and political mistake, which he regretted. Khrushchev saw this confession of error as a testimony of Kennedy's frank naivety and lack of character. He therefore inferred that it was possible to gain advantage by installing nuclear missiles in Cuba, which would be targeted at the United States. Their subsequent installation in 1962 led the world to the brink of nuclear war between the superpowers. The events which followed showed that Khrushchev had been wrong in evaluating Kennedy's credibility. Ultimately, Kennedy showed great firmness and negotiation skill.

Khrushchev's mistake may be explained by differences in the cultural coding of credibility. Whereas in the United States, reaching a high position while still young is positively perceived, Russians associate age with the ability to carry responsibilities. Moreover, the admission of a mistake or a misjudgment is also positively perceived in the United States. US ethics value frankness and honesty. There is the belief that individuals may improve their behavior and decisions by taking into account the lessons of experience. On the other hand, in the Soviet Union, the admission of errors was rare. It generally implied the very weak position of those who had been subjected to the enforced confessions of Stalin's show trials.

Signs of credibility

Personal credibility is decoded through the filter of numerous physical traits, which are not often actively taken into consideration as they seem to be only appearances, or because we tend to use these reference points unconsciously (Lee, 1966). Being tall may, for instance, be perceived as a sign of strength and character. Stoutness may be considered a positive sign for a partner in societies where starvation is still a recent memory. Where malnutrition is a reality for a section of the population, it is better to be fat, that is, well nourished and therefore rich- and powerful-looking. Naturally these signs have a relative value. Weight, height, age and sex cannot be considered as adequate criteria for selecting negotiators. Furthermore, people may, in fact, be largely aware of the cultural code of the partner. Each of these basic signs plays a role in the initial building of a credibility profile: age, sex, height, stoutness, face, tone and strength of the voice, self-esteem, perceived potency, perceived activity, etc. This profile is a priori because it only influences credibility in early contacts, that is, in the phase of awareness and at the beginning of the exploration phase (Scanzoni, 1979).

Interpersonal orientation

The reproach made to Western business people by the Japanese, quoted in the introduction to this chapter, illustrates differences in interpersonal orientation. The concept of *ningensei* has to do with the Confucian ethic which favors smooth interactions, underplaying conflict to the benefit of social harmony. For instance, the interpersonal sensitivity of Japanese people and their sincere interest in foreign cultures and people may make them friendly hosts at business lunches or dinners. As emphasized by Hawrysh and Zaichkowsky (1990, p. 42): 'Before entering serious negotiations, Japanese business men will spend considerable time and money entertaining foreign negotiating teams, in order to get to know their negotiating partners and establish with them a rapport built on friendship and trust.' But it should never be forgotten that Japanese negotiators remain down-to-earth: they are strongly aware of what their basic interests are. *Ningensei* is, in fact, typical of collectivist values of interpersonal relationships (see Box 5.1). A basic divide in the interpersonal orientation is the individualism–collectivism divide (for a review of its impact on negotiation behavior, see Leung, 1997 and Tinsley and Pillutla, 1998).

In-group orientation

Equal concern for the other party's outcome is not necessarily to be found across all cultures. Cultures place a stronger or weaker emphasis on group membership (the other party is/is not a member of the in-group) as a prerequisite for being considered a trustworthy partner. In cultures where there is a clear-cut distinction between the in-group and the out-group (according to age, sex, race or kinship criteria), people tend to perceive the interests of both groups as diametrically opposed. This is related to what has been called the concept of 'limited good' (Foster, 1965).

According to the concept of 'limited good', if something positive happens in favor of the out-group, the wealth and well-being of the in-group will be threatened. Such reactions are largely founded on culture-based collective subjectivity: they stem from the conservative idea that goods and riches are by their very nature restricted. If one yields to the other party even the tiniest concession, this is perceived as directly reducing what is left for in-group members. The concept of 'limited good' induces negotiators to adopt very territorial and distributive strategies. It is a view which clearly favours the idea of the zero-sum game, where 'I will lose whatever you may win' and vice versa. In Mediterranean and Middle Eastern societies where the in-group is highly valued (clan, tribe, extended family), the concept of 'limited good' is often to be found; it slows the adoption of a problem-solving orientation, since co-operative opportunities are simply difficult to envisage.

It has in fact been argued that members of collectivist cultures make a sharp distinction between in-groups and out-groups, a reason for that being that harmony enhancement is only viewed as possible with in-group members (see Leung, 1997 for a review of the empirical support). However, there is always some free room for negotiating insider/outsider status not only within but also across cultures: Merriam et al. (2001) present a number of case studies showing how people can gain status as partial insiders by leveraging on common features that transcend the borders of cultures, such as gender or professional cultures. Haugland (1998) demonstrates the role of a shared professional culture in blurring the in-group/out-group borders in an increasingly globalized world. His findings show that there is no significant impact of cultural differences on the international buyer–seller relationship in the context of the fisheries industries, whether trading partners of Norwegian exporters are

European or American (more in-group) or Japanese (more out-group). As he points out: 'It is not unlikely that industries or trades which are very international will develop a specific industry culture, serving the role of unifying persons and companies from different nations and ethnic groups' (p. 27).

Power orientation

One must distinguish between the formal power orientation on the one hand and the real power/decision-making orientation on the other. The first has to do with the display of status and how it may enhance credibility, especially in high perceived-potency societies. This involves the kind of meetings, societies, clubs, and alumni organizations which assemble potentially powerful people. Belonging to such circles gives an opportunity for socializing and getting to know each other. The simple fact of being there and being a member of a certain club is the main credibility message. The signs of formal power orientation differ across cultures; they may range from education and titles (English 'public' schools, French *Grandes Écoles*, *Herr Doktor*, etc.) to belonging to a particular social class or caste.

Real power orientation is a somewhat different issue. As illustrated in Box 5.2 with an African example, there may be wide differences between formal and actual influence on the decision-making process. When making contacts, in a cross-cultural perspective, people should be aware of the following:

1. Status is not shown in the same way according to culture;
2. Influential persons are not the same and individual influence is not exerted in the same way; and
3. The decision-making process differs.

Hofstede (1989), in his article about the cultural predictors of negotiation styles, hypothesizes that larger power distance will lead to a more centralized control and decision-making structure because key negotiations have to be concluded by the top authority. And, in fact, Fisher (1980) notes in the case of Mexico, a typically high power distance country

---

Box 5.2 The door-keeper

The story takes place in the corridor to the office of the minister of industry of the Popular Republic of Guinea. Whether you had an appointment or you came to request a meeting, you had to be let in by the door-keeper. Besides, the door was locked and he had the key. He was a little man, looking tired and wearing worn-out clothes; his appearance led foreign visitors to treat him as negligible and to pay little attention to him. When visitors had a lengthy wait while seeing other people being given quick access to the minister, they often spoke unreservedly to the old man who seemed to have only limited language proficiency. In fact, the door-keeper spoke perfect French and was the uncle of the minister, which gave him power over his nephew according to the African tradition. It was well-known that the minister placed high confidence in his uncle's recommendations. Thus, some foreign contractors never understood why they did not clinch the deal although they had developed winning arguments with the minister himself.

(Reported by Professor Gérard Verna, Université Laval, Québec.

Reproduced with permission.)

(score of 81 on Hoftsede's scale), one finds a relatively centralized decision-making, based on individuals who have extended responsibility at the top of the organization. They become frustrated when confronted by the Americans, who tend to have several negotiators in charge of compartmentalized issues:

> In another mismatch of the systems, the Americans find it hard to determine how much Mexican decision-making authority goes with which designated authority. There, as in many of the more traditional systems, authority tends to reside somewhat more in the person than in the position, and an organization chart does little to tell the outsider just what leverage (*palanca*) the incumbent has.
>
> (Fisher, 1980, p. 29)

Willingness to take risks

Negotiation activities are associated with risk-taking. Disclosing information, making concessions, or drafting clauses involves risk taking because there is always a certain degree of vulnerability to the other party's opportunist actions. As shown by Weber and Hsee (1998), cultural differences exist in the perception of risk rather than in the attitudes towards perceived risk. They studied how respondents from China, the USA, Germany and Poland differed in risk preference for risky financial options and found the Chinese to be the less risk-averse, with the Poles in the middle, and Germans and Americans showing the highest level of risk aversion. However, they show that attitudes towards perceived risk are shared cross-culturally, that is, people across cultures tend to be consistently willing to pay more for less risky options. What differs is the perception of risk itself. As emphasized by Weber and Hsee (1998, p. 1207): 'An understanding of the reasons *why* members of different groups (for example, different cultures) differ in preference or willingness-to-pay for risky options is crucial if one wants to leverage this differences into creative integrative bargaining solutions in inter-group negotiations.'

Risk taking is related to Hoftsede's cultural dimension of uncertainty avoidance, which measures the extent to which people in a society tend to feel threatened by uncertain, ambiguous, risky or undefined situations. Where uncertainty avoidance is high, organizations promote stable careers, produce rules and procedures, etc. 'Nevertheless societies in which uncertainty avoidance is strong are also characterized by a higher level of anxiety and aggressiveness that creates, among other things, a strong inner urge to work hard' (Hofstede, 1980). Hofstede points out that 'uncertainty avoidance should not be confused with risk avoidance…even more than reducing risk, uncertainty avoidance leads to a reduction of *ambiguity*' (1991, p. 116).

A high level of uncertainty avoidance is noted by Hofstede (1980) as being associated with a more bureaucratic functioning and a lower tendency for individuals to take risks. This may be a problem for business negotiators when they have received a mandate from top management. For instance, the bureaucratic orientation in ex-communist countries has imposed strong government control on industry. As a consequence, Chinese negotiators, for instance, tend not to be capable of individual decision-making. Before any agreement is reached, official government approval must be sought by Chinese negotiators (Eiteman, 1990). The same has been noted by Beliaev et al. (1985, p. 110) in the case of Russian negotiators:

> Throughout the process, a series of ministries are involved…Such a process also limits the degree of risk taking that is possible…the American who does see it from [the

Soviet] perspective may well interpret it as being slow, lacking in initiative and unproductive.

Tse et al. (1994) confirm this tendency in the case of Chinese executives, who tend to consult their superior significantly more than Canadian executives who belong to a low uncertainty-avoidance society.

Underlying concepts of negotiation and negotiation strategies

Integrative orientation versus distribution orientation

In business negotiations, the purchaser (or team of purchasers) and the vendor (or group of vendors) are mutually interdependent, and their individual interests clash. The ability to choose effective negotiation largely explains the individual performance of each party on the one hand, and the joint outcome on the other. In pitting themselves against each other, the parties may develop opposing points of view towards the negotiation strategy which they intend to adopt: distributive or integrative. In the distributive strategy (or orientation), the negotiation process is seen as leading to the division of a specific 'cake' which the parties feel they cannot enlarge even if they were willing to do so. This orientation is also termed 'competitive negotiation' or 'zero-sum game'. It leads to a perception of negotiation as a war of positions – territorial in essence. These are negotiations of the 'win–lose' type: 'anything that isn't yours is mine' and vice versa.

The negotiators hold attitudes and objectives that are quasi-conflictive. Interdependence is minimized whereas opposition is emphasized. At the opposite end of the spectrum is the integrative orientation (Walton and McKersie, 1965). The central assumption is that the size of the 'cake', the joint outcome of the negotiations, can be increased if the parties adopt a co-operative attitude. This idea is directly linked to problem-solving orientation (Pruitt, 1983). Negotiators may not be concerned purely with their own objectives, but may also be interested in the other party's aspirations and results, seeing them as almost equally important. Integrative orientation has been termed 'co-operative' or 'collaborative'. It results in negotiation being seen as an attempt to maximize the joint outcome. The division of this outcome is to a certain extent secondary or is at least perceived as an important but later issue. Here negotiation is a 'positive-sum game' where the joint outcome is greater than zero.

In practice, effective negotiation combines distributive and integrative orientations simultaneously, or at different stages in the negotiation process (Pruitt, 1981). The 'dual concern model' (Pruitt, 1983), explains negotiation strategies according to two basic variables: concern for one's own outcome (horizontal axis) and concern for the other party's outcome (vertical axis). This leads to four possible strategies (see Table 5.2). According to this model, the ability to envisage the other party's outcome is a prerequisite for the adoption of an integrative strategy. Problem-solving orientation can be defined as an overall

Table 5.2 The dual concern model

Concern for one's own outcomes *Concern for the other party's outcomes*	*Low*	*High*
High	Yielding	Integrative strategy
Low	Inaction	Contending

negotiating behavior that is co-operative, integrative and orientated towards the exchange of information (Campbell et al., 1988; Adler, 2002). Fair communication and the exchange of information between negotiators are important. 'Problem solvers' exchange representative information, that is, honest and objective data. There is no desire to manipulate the partner, as in instrumental communication (Angelmar and Stern, 1978). Exchanging representative information is considered a basic element in problem-solving orientation. Empirical studies (experimental negotiation stimulation) have shown that this orientation positively influences the common results of negotiation (Pruitt, 1983). Rubin and Carter (1990), for instance, demonstrate the general superiority of co-operative negotiation by developing a model whereby a new, more co-operative contract provides both the buyer and the seller with cost reduction, compared to a previous adversarial contract.

There are, however, some conditions; the first is the availability of cost-related data, the second is the release of these data to the other party during negotiation. The sharing of data is obviously conditioned by culture, language and communication-related issues. The adoption of an integrative strategy is facilitated by the following:

1. A high level of aspirations on both sides (Pruitt and Lewis, 1975);
2. The ability to envisage the future;
3. The existence of a sufficient 'perceived common ground', that is, enough overlap between the interests of the two parties (Pruitt, 1983).

Cultural dispositions to being integrative

Even though one may accept the superior effectiveness of integrative strategies, in as far as they aim to maximize the joint outcome, the problem of how this joint outcome is divided between the two sides remains largely unaddressed. When integrating the cultural dimension, three questions merit consideration:

1. Do the parties tend to perceive negotiations as being easier, and do they tend to adopt an integrative orientation more readily, when they both share the same culture?
2. Do negotiators originating from particular cultures tend towards an integrative or distributive orientation? Furthermore, do negotiators originating from cultures which favor a problem-solving orientation risk seeing their personal results heavily diminished by a distributive partner who cynically exploits their goodwill?
3. Do cultural differences and intercultural negotiation reduce the likelihood of integrative strategy?

Difficulties in being integrative in an intercultural negotiation situation

Generally, speaking, it seems more difficult to pursue an integrative strategy in an intercultural than an intracultural setting. Nationalistic feelings are easily aroused by conflicts of interest and the partner may easily be subjectively perceived as an 'adversary', occupying a different and rival territory. These negative feelings are often reinforced by an alleged atmosphere of 'economic war' which, for instance, results in 'Japan bashing' in the United States where the Japanese are considered to be unfair competitors. According to this view, a potential partner belonging to another country/culture would also be perceived as a global adversary.

There is general agreement in the existing literature that the results of negotiation are less favorable when the negotiation is intercultural as opposed to intracultural, all other things being equal (Sawyer and Guetzkow, 1965; Corne, 1992; Brett and Okumura, 1998; Bazerman et al., 2000). Van Zandt (1970) suggests that the negotiations between Americans and the Japanese are six times as long and three times as difficult as those exclusively between Americans. This increases the costs of the transaction for the American firms in Japan owing to the relative inefficiency of communication. Brett and Okumura (1998) show that intercultural US–Japanese negotiations result in significantly lower joint gains than intracultural US or Japanese negotiations (in which both national groups achieve similar joint gains). It seems that an explanation is that intercultural negotiators lack sufficient skills to adapt successfully and need a lot more clarifying statements than do intracultural negotiators (Adair et al., 2001). Another possible explanation is that American negotiators tend to use harder tactics, engaging in threats, demands, and sanctions, when there is more cultural distance with their partners' culture (Rao and Schmidt, 1998). The subjective satisfaction of the negotiators (measured by a questionnaire) in their result tends to be inferior for intercultural negotiation compared to intracultural negotiation (Weitz, 1979; Graham, 1985; Graham et al., 1994). However, recent empirical findings have contradicted this: in Brett and Okumura (1998), intercultural negotiators were more happy and satisfied with the negotiation than were intracultural negotiators. This can be explained either by the subjective reward effect of achieving an obviously more difficult negotiation task (i.e. intercultural as compared with intracultural negotiation) or by people being satisfied in both cultural groups by different – and not competing – outcomes (joint gains for Americans versus outcome parity for the Chinese, as in Tinsley and Pillutla, 1998).

Problem-solving depends on a collaborative attitude which is easier with a partner from the same culture. Negotiation partners' similarity, according to Rubin and Brown (1975), leads to more trust and an enhanced level of interpersonal attraction. As emphasized by Pornpitakpan (1999), greater similarity between two parties will induce greater interpersonal attraction. People need to evaluate others before entering into interaction: similarity facilitates accurate appraisal in the process of social comparison. As a result of similarity, each side tends to consider communication from the other as more representative, more honest and truthful: in other words, one party perceives that it transmits fairly objective information and does not try to unduly influence the other party, as is the case with instrumental communication (in the sense of Angelmar and Stern, 1978). The hypothesis that the similarity of the parties leads to a more favorable outcome was proposed by Evans (1963). Similarity facilitates awareness and exploration between parties. In fact, it is more a question of perceived similarity which leads to more co-operative behavior in negotiation (Matthews et al., 1972). If this similarity is perceived but not based on strictly objective indications (such as shared nationality, language or educational backgrounds), an asymmetric view of similarity may arise between the buyer and seller. For instance, many business people in the Middle East have a good command of either the English or French language and culture. Middle Eastern business people are often perceived by their American or European counterparts as being similar, whereas they may perceive their Western counterparts as different.

The role adopted in negotiation, buyer or seller, combines with perceived similarity: if sellers perceive a greater similarity, this can lead to a stronger problem-solving orientation on their part. Although appealing, similarity-based hypotheses have been poorly validated by the empirical study carried out by Campbell et al. (1988). No significant relationship was found among American and British buyer/seller pairs: similarity did not favor problem-solving orientation. In the case of the French and the Germans, the perceived similarity only led to a stronger problem-solving orientation on the part of the seller. However, in Campbell et al. (1988), the actual dissimilarity between negotiators was strongly reduced by the fact that all the simulated negotiations were intracultural.

In intercultural terms, there is the possibility of a misunderstanding arising from a perception of similarity which is not shared by both parties. For example, one can imagine a situation where a seller (American, for instance) perceives the buyer as similar (an Arab buyer who is very Westernized in appearance, who has a superficial but misleading cultural outlook because of his cultural borrowing). However, the reverse situation does not occur: the Arab buyer is aware that the American seller knows little about Arabic culture. In this case the seller will have a tendency to take a problem-solving orientation, because of fallacious perceived similarity, whereas the buyer may exploit the seller without feeling obliged to reciprocate, and ultimately maximize his personal outcome by adopting a distributive strategy. However, the dynamics of similarity (showing to the other side that one understands, and thus laying the foundation for an integrative attitude on both sides) can be reversed, more positively. Harris and Moran (1987, p. 472) cite the case of a US banker from the Midwest invited by an Arab sheik for a meeting in London. The banker demonstrates unusual patience and deep awareness of the other party's power.

> The banker arrives in London and waits to meet the sheik. After two days he is told to fly to Riyadh in Saudi Arabia, which he does. He waits. After three days in Riyadh, he meets the sheik and the beginning of what was to become a very beneficial business relationship between the two persons and their organizations began.

National orientations favoring the integrative strategy

The second question concerns the adoption of integrative strategies by some nationalities more than others. Studies tend to show that American business people show trust more willingly and more spontaneously than other cultural groups, and have a stronger tendency towards a problem-solving and integrative orientation (Druckman et al., 1976; Harnett and Cummings, 1980; Campbell et al., 1988; Tinsley and Pillutla, 1998). The level of their profits as sellers depends on the buyer responding positively by also adopting a problem-solving approach (Campbell et al., 1988). American negotiators have a stronger tendency to exchange representative communication, making clear and explicit messages a priority. This is in line with the American appreciation of frankness and directness and their explicit communication style according to Hall (1976). This is what Graham and Herberger (1983) call the 'John Wayne Style'. They often meet certain difficulties with cultures who take more time in the preliminaries: getting to know each other, that is, talking generally and only actually getting down to business later. As a result, Americans may not foster feelings of trust in negotiators from other cultural groups who feel it necessary to get to know the person they are dealing with (Hall, 1976). Graham and Meissner (1986) have shown, in a study comparing five countries, that the most integrative strategies are adopted by the Brazilians, followed by the Japanese. On the other hand, the Americans, the Germans and the Koreans choose intermediate strategies that are more distributive. This is consistent in the case of the Germans who, according to Cateora (1993), use the hard-sell approach, where the seller is fairly pushy and adopts an instrumental communication and a distributive strategy (Campbell et al., 1988).

The concept of integrative strategy is strongly influenced by the American tradition of experimental research in social psychology applied to commercial negotiation. As explained by Leung (1997, p. 648): 'In individualist societies, negotiation is seen more as a task than as a social process. The primary role of negotiators is to work out a solution that is acceptable to both sides.' It is also based on a 'master of destiny' orientation which feeds attitudes of problem resolution. As noted by Graham et al. (1994), the problem-solving approach appears to make sense to the American negotiators, but this framework may not work in all cases when applied to foreign negotiators. Americans tend to see the world as consisting of problems to be solved whereas Arabs, for instance, see it more as a creation of God. However, to our knowledge, there is no empirical study that has shown, for example, that the Arabs from the Middle East have a tendency to be more distributive and or less problem-solving oriented than the Americans.

A key issue in the integrative approach is whether parties should primarily strive for achieving a maximum joint gain or for reaching outcome parity between negotiators. Tinsley and Pillutla (1998) show that American negotiators consider problem solving as a more adequate strategy and are more satisfied with joint gain maximization than Hong Kong negotiators. When presented with co-operative instructions, Hong Kong negotiators tend to interpret them as meaning that they should strive for equality and display more satisfaction than Americans when the goal of outcome parity is reached. The tendency to search for equality in outcomes and to share the burden by allocating resources equally is confirmed in the case of Japanese as compared to American negotiators by Wade-Benzoni et al. (2002).

The dilemma about maximizing joint gains versus outcome parity is precisely where the 'double-bind' situation in negotiation is at its peak and where cultures offer simplified, preframed solutions to the paradox of having to co-operate at the risk of being taken advantage of. As emphasized by Bazerman et al. (2000, p. 297), cross-cultural negotiation research has provided data 'consistent with the generalization that members of individualist cultures are more likely to handle conflicts directly through competition and problem solving, whereas members of collectivist cultures are more likely to handle conflict in indirect ways that attempt to preserve the relationship'. Leung (1997) explains that 'disintegration avoidance' (DA) is at the very heart of Chinese negotiation behavior; as long as there is reason for maintaining the relationship, DA will result in a preference for conflict avoidance. However, when the conflict is perceived as caused by the other party's misbehavior, DA ceases to be effective and Chinese negotiators are more likely to recommend discontinuing the negotiation.

Box 5.3 Status distinctions

Americans, more than any other national group, value informality and equality in human relations. The emphasis on first names is only the beginning. We go out of our way to make our clients feel comfortable by playing down status distinctions such as clients and by eliminating 'unnecessary' formalities such as lengthy introductions. All too often, however, we succeed only in making ourselves feel comfortable while our clients become uneasy or even annoyed. For example, in Japanese society interpersonal relationships are vertical; in almost all two-person relationships a difference in status exists. The basis for such distinction may be one or several factors: age, sex, university attended, position in an organization, and even one's particular firm or company. Each Japanese is very much aware of his or her own position relative to others with whom he or she deals....The roles of the higher status position and the lower status position are quite different, even to the extent that Japanese use different words to express the same idea depending on which person makes the statement. For example a buyer would say *otaku* (your company), while a seller would say *on sha* (your great company). Status relations dictate not only what is said but also how it is said.

(Graham and Herberger, 1983, p. 162. Reproduced with permission.)

Ignorance of the other party's culture as an obstacle to the
implementation of an integrative strategy in negotiation

One of the most important obstacles to effective international business negotiation is the ignorance of all or at least the basics of the other party's culture. This is intellectually obvious, but is often forgotten by international negotiators. It refers not only to the cognitive ignorance of the main traits of the other party's culture, but also to the unconscious prejudice that differences are minor (that is, ignorance as absence of awareness). This favors the natural tendency to refer implicitly to one's own cultural norms, especially for the coding/ decoding process of communication (the self-reference criterion of Lee, 1966). Lucian Pye (1982, 1986) and Eiteman (1990) Tinsley and Pillutla (1998) in the case of business negotiations between American and Chinese people, and Tung (1984), Hawrysh and Zaichkowsky (1990), and Brett and Okumura (1998) for US–Japanese business negotiations, note the relative lack of prior knowledge of the American negotiators about their partner's culture. Before coming to the negotiation table, Americans do not generally read books, nor do they train themselves for the foreign communication style, nor learn about the potential traps which could lead to misunderstandings. As Carlos Fuentes states (in a rather harsh aphorism): 'What the US does best is understand itself. What it does worst is understand others' (Fuentes, 1986). French negotiators also tend to be underprepared in terms of cultural knowledge (Burt, 1984), whereas the Japanese seemingly try to learn a lot more than the French or the Americans about the other party's culture before negotiation takes place.

The negotiation and implementation (which often means ongoing negotiations) of a joint venture may last for several years. In this case, national cultures tend to disappear as the two teams partly merge their values and behavior in a common 'venture culture'. In order to improve intercultural negotiation effectiveness, it is advisable to build this common culture between the partners/adversaries right from the start of the negotiations. It means establishing common rules, communication codes, finding people on each side who will act as go-betweens and trying to agree on a common interpretation of issue, facts, solutions and decision-making. This must not be considered as a formal process; it is informal and built on implicit communications. Furthermore, it relies heavily on those individuals who have been involved in the joint venture over a long period of time and who get on well together.

Cultural misunderstandings during the negotiation process

If future partners do not share common 'mental schemes', it could be difficult for them to solve problems together. Buyer and seller should share some joint views of the world, especially on the following questions: What is the relevant information? How should this information be sought, evaluated and fed into the decision-making process?

An important distinction in the field of cross-cultural psychology opposes ideologism to pragmatism (Glenn, 1981; Triandis, 1983). As indicated by Triandis (1983, p. 148):

> Ideologism versus pragmatism, which corresponds to Glenn's universalism versus particularism, refers to the extent to which the information extracted from the environment is transmitted within a broad framework, such as a religion or a political ideology, or a relatively narrow framework.

This dimension refers to a way of thinking, an important element of the 'mindset'.

Ways of processing information: is there a common rationality between partners?

People differ in their ways of relating thinking to action: whereas the ideologists tend to think broadly and relate to general principles, the pragmatist orientation concentrates on focusing on detailed issues that are to be solved one by one. Pragmatists will prefer to negotiate specific clauses, in sequential manner. Conversely, ideologists see arguments in favor of their 'global way of thinking', when negotiating a large contract, such as a nuclear plant or a television satellite for instance: it is a unitary production, it is a complex multi-partner business, it often involves government financing and also has far-reaching social, economic and political consequences. Pragmatists will also find many arguments in favor of their way of thinking: the technicalities of the plant and its desired performance require an achievement and deadline orientation (pragmatist values).

Triandis hypothesizes that complex traditional societies will tend to be ideologist ones, whereas pluralistic societies or cultures experiencing rapid social change will tend to be pragmatist. This distinction may also be traced back to the difference between the legal systems of *common law* (mainly English and American) and *code law*. Whereas the former favors legal precedents set by courts and past rulings (case law) the latter favors statutory laws and general texts. These general provisions are intended to build an all-inclusive system of written rules of law (code). Codes aim to formulate general principles so as to embody the entire set of particular cases.

The ideologist orientation, which is to be found mostly in southern and eastern Europe, leads the negotiators to try and set principles before any detailed discussion of specific clauses of the contract. Ideologists have a tendency to prefer and promote globalized negotiations in which all the issues are gathered in a 'package deal'. The pragmatist attitude corresponds more to attitudes found in Northern Europe and the United States. It entails defining limited-scope problems, then solving them one after the other. Pragmatists concentrate their thinking on factual aspects (deeds, not words; evidence, not opinions; figures, not value judgments). They are willing to reach real-world decisions, even if they have to be down-to-earth ones.

Ideologists will use a wide body of ideas which provide them with a formal and coherent description of the world: Marxism or Liberalism for instance. Every event is supposed to carry meaning when it is seen through this ideologist framework. On the other hand, the pragmatist attitude first considers the extreme diversity of real world situations, and then derives its principles inductively. Reality will be seen as a series of rather independent and concrete problems to be solved ('issues'). These issues will make complete sense when related to practical, precise, and even down-to-earth decisions. Typically, ideologists will *take* decisions (*prendre des décisions*), that is, pick a solution from a range of possible decisions (which are located beyond the decision maker). Conversely, pragmatists will *make* decisions, that is, both decide and implement: decisions will be enacted, not selected. Box 5.4 illustrates how the pragmatist Americans can resent the ideologist French in international negotiations.

Communication may be difficult when partners do not share the same mindset. The most unlikely situation for success is an ideology-oriented contractor/supplier who tries to sell to a pragmatism-oriented owner/buyer. The ideologist will see the pragmatist as being too interested in trivial details, too practical, too down-to-earth, too much data oriented (Galtung, 1981) and incapable of looking at issues from a higher standpoint. Pragmatists will resent ideologists for being too theoretical, lacking practical sense, concerned with issues that are

Box 5.4 French ideologism

Rather imprecisely defined, the idea is that one reasons from a starting point based on what is known, and then pays careful attention to the logical way in which one point leads to the next, and finally reaches a conclusion regarding the issue at hand. The French also assign greater priority than Americans do to establishing the principles on which the reasoning process should be based. Once this reasoning process is underway, it becomes relatively difficult to introduce new evidence or facts, most especially during a negotiation. Hence the appearance of French inflexibility, and the need to introduce new information and considerations early in the game. All this reflects the tradition of French education and becomes the status mark of the educated person. In an earlier era observers made such sweeping generalizations as: 'The French always place a school of thought, a formula, convention, a priori arguments, abstraction, and artificiality above reality; they prefer clarity to truth, words to things, rhetoric to science...'

(Fisher, 1980; Zeldin, 1977)

too broad to lead to implementable decisions. In the first steps of the negotiation process, differences between ideologists and pragmatists may create communication misunderstandings which will be difficult to overcome during subsequent phases. Indeed, developing common norms will be fairly difficult, although it is necessary if partners want to be able to predict the other party's behavior. A frequent comment in such situations will be: 'One never knows what these people have in mind; their behavior is largely unpredictable.' An American (pragmatism-oriented) describes negotiations with the French (more ideology-oriented) in the following terms (Burt, 1984, p. 6): 'The French are extremely difficult to negotiate with. Often they will not accept facts, no matter how convincing they may be.'

Argument in negotiation: data, theory, speech and virtue

Galtung (1981) contrasts what he calls the 'intellectual styles' of four important cultural groups: the 'Gallic' (prototype: the French), the 'Teutonic' (prototype: the Germans), the 'Saxonic' (prototype: the English and the Americans) and the 'Nipponic' intellectual style (prototype: the Japanese). Saxons prefer to look for facts and evidence which results in factual accuracy and abundance. They are interested in 'hard facts' and proofs, and do not like what they call 'unsupported statements'. As Galtung states (1981, pp. 827–28) when he describes the intellectual style of Anglo-Americans:

> data unite, theories divide. There are clear, relatively explicit canons for establishing what constitutes a valid fact and what does not; the corresponding canons in connection with theories are more vague.... One might now complete the picture of the Saxonic intellectual style by emphasizing its weak point: not very strong on theory formation, and not on paradigm awareness.

Galtung contrasts the Saxonic style with the Teutonic and Gallic styles, which place theoretical arguments at the center of their intellectual process. Data and facts are there to illustrate what is said rather than to demonstrate it.

> Discrepancy between theory and data would be handled at the expense of data: they may either be seen as atypical or wholly erroneous, or more significantly as not really

pertinent to the theory. And here the distinction between empirical and potential reality comes in: to the Teutonic and Gallic intellectual, potential reality may be not so much the reality to be even more avoided or even more pursued than the empirical one but rather a *more real reality*, free from the noise and impurities of empirical reality.

(p. 828)

However, Teutonic and Gallic intellectual styles do differ in the role that is assigned to words and discourse. The Teutonic ideal is that of the ineluctability of true reasoning, *Gedankennotwendigkeit*, that is, perfection of concepts and the indisputability of their mental articulation. The Gallic style is less preoccupied with deduction and intellectual construction. It is directed more towards the use of the persuasive strength of words and speeches in an aesthetically perfect way (*élégance*). Words have an inherent power to convince. They may create *potential reality*, thus probably the often-noted Latin love of words.

Finally the Nipponic intellectual style, imbued with Hindu, Buddhist and Taoist philosophies, favors a more modest, global and provisional approach. Thinking and knowledge are conceived of as being in a temporary state, open to alteration. The Japanese 'rarely pronounce absolute, categorical statements in daily discourse; they prefer vagueness even about trivial matters…because clear statements have a ring of immodesty, of being judgements of reality' (Galtung, 1981, p. 833).

Communication and language

Needless to remark that cross-cultural communication processes are a key component of the influence of culture on international marketing negotiations. If negotiators want to promote an integrative approach, it is important for them to focus on sharing and seeking information. Communication has been shown to generate greater co-operation even among negotiation partners that display strong tendencies to self-interest (Wade-Benzoni et al., (2002). The language used for negotiation has its importance: the myth that any language can be translated into another language often causes English to be chosen as a central negotiation language and to add interpreters when proficiency is too low on one side.[1] As emphasized by Hoon-Halbauer (1999), in the case of Sino-foreign joint ventures, few Chinese can speak a foreign language and all oral communication between the Chinese and their foreign partners has to pass through interpreters: 'When a third person is involved no genuine, direct communication between two persons can take place. In other words, "heart-to-heart" talks are unlikely to take place' (p. 359). Furthermore, due to poor translation, it may be that only 30–40 percent of the actual content of what is said in Chinese is conveyed to the non-Chinese-speaking negotiation partners, resulting in the discarding of good ideas and suggestions made by the Chinese (Hoon-Halbauer, 1999).

There are semantic differences in the words used and many misunderstandings can arise from ignoring the precise meaning of key concepts for the negotiation; Adachi (1998) gives the example of noticeable differences in the use of the word 'customer' by Japanese and American negotiators. She shows that cultural connotations are a crucial aspect of conversation that needs careful attention in understanding the meaning beyond the mere one-to-one translations of words. Moreover, speakers of certain languages (i.e. high-context languages such as Japanese, Chinese or Arabic) use more contextual cues to decode messages. The role of high context versus low context communication has been described by Hall (1960; 1976).

When messages are exchanged, the degree to which they should be interpreted has to be taken into account as well as the cross-cultural differences in linguistic styles, involving the use of silence or conversational overlap (George et al., 1998). For instance, silence is a full form of communication for the Japanese, and Graham (1985) reports twice as many silences in Japanese interaction than in American. Westerners often have the impression that they 'do all the talking'. Low-context negotiators, such as Americans, tend to be explicit, precise, legalistic, and direct in communication, sometimes forceful and even appearing as blunt to the other party (USIP, 2002). In an empirical survey of Japanese and US negotiators, Adair et al. (2001, p. 380), show that direct and indirect communication patterns are consistent with Hall's theory of low-context versus high-context communication:

> The U.S. negotiators relied on direct information to learn about each other's preferences and priorities and to integrate this information to generate joint gains. They were comfortable sharing information about priorities, comparing and contrasting their preferences with those of the other party, and giving specific feedback to offers and proposals. The Japanese negotiators relied on indirect information, inferring each other's preferences and priorities from multiple offers and counteroffers over time.

In fact, the capacity to cope with very different communication styles is a key to successful international business negotiation. This is especially true for non-verbal communication. For instance, a lack of eye contact for the Americans is a signal that something is amiss and 'American executives reported that the lack of eye contact was not only disconcerting but reduced their bargaining performance' (Hawrysh and Zaichkowsky, 1990, p. 34).

Negotiators must be ready to hear true as well as false information, discourse based on facts as well as on wishful thinking or pure obedience to superiors. Frankness and sincerity are culturally relative values: they can be interpreted as mere naivety, a lack of realism, or a lack of self-control in speaking one's own mind. Furthermore, waiting for reciprocation when disclosing useful information for the other party, makes little sense in an intercultural context. Frankness and directness in communication are of substantial value to the Americans and to a lesser extent to the French, but not to Mexicans in formal encounters, nor to Japanese at any time (Fisher, 1980).

The issue of formality versus informality is a difficult one. Frequently, a contrast is made between cultures which value informality (e.g. American) and those which are more formal (most cultures which have long historical roots and high power distance). 'Informality' may be simply another kind of formalism, and the 'icebreaking' at the beginning of any typical US meeting between unacquainted people is generally an expected ritual. It is more important to try to understand what kind of formality is required in which circumstances with which people. Outside of formal negotiation sessions, people belonging to apparently quite formal cultures can become much more informal.

Due to increased global communication through the Internet and the extensive use of computer-mediated communication, in particular e-mail, as well as to the rise of business-to-business marketplaces, there is an increasing use of global electronic media in negotiating international deals.[2] Contrary to traditional negotiation which is assumed to be carried out almost exclusively via face-to-face communication, e-mail does not offer much of the non-verbal feedback which exists in other media. However, electronic communication is very useful for dispersed negotiations, when matters have to be discussed without incurring the high costs associated with face-to-face cross-border negotiation. Potter and Balthazard (2000) show that both Chinese and American managers prefer face-to-face over computer-mediated negotiation. However, both Chinese and Americans, negotiating intraculturally, do not perceive a significant difference between e-mail-based written negotiation and the same negotiation dealt with a web-based threaded discussion even though the latter method seems to allow for more continuous interaction. Ulijn et al. (2001), based on a study involving twenty participants, use speech-act theory and psycholinguistic analysis to show that culture affects non face-to-face communication as is the case of negotiation through e-mail. Kersten et al. (1999a; 2002) also find a number of cultural differences between managers from Austria, Ecuador, Finland and Switzerland who negotiate electronically.[3] Finally, e-mail communication is often mixed with face-to-face encounters; e-mailing is widely affected by prior personal acquaintance of the people involved: if negotiators have started with some face-to-face activity, computer-mediated negotiation will be largely facilitated and communication misunderstandings arising from the 'dry style' of e-mails may largely be avoided.

Negotiation tactics

Graham (1993) studied the negotiation tactics used in eight cultures, using videotaped negotiations in which statements were classified into twelve categories using the framework of Angelmar and Stern (1978). His results show very similar negotiation tactics across cultures, most of them using a majority of tactics based on an exchange of information, either by self-disclosure or questions (more than 50 percent in all cases). The Chinese score the highest in posing questions, which is consistent with Pye's comments about them: 'Once negotiations begin the Chinese seem passive. They simply ask questions, probe for information, and conceal any eagerness they may feel' (1986, p. 78). On the other hand, the Spaniards score the highest in making promises. The proportion of 'negative' tactics, including threats, warnings, punishment and negative normative appeal (a statement in which the source indicates that the target's behavior is in violation of social norms) is fairly low in all cases, never exceeding 10 percent of the information exchange. Finally cross-national differences are not great at the level of the type of tactics used, nor at the level of their frequency, but are more significant at the level of how they are implemented.

The use of theatricality, withdrawal threats and tactics based on time, such as waiting for the last moment to obtain further concessions by making new demands, are based on national styles of negotiation. Tactics are also related to the ambiguous atmosphere of business negotiations when implied warm human relations are supposed to be mixed with business. This relates to the divide between affective and neutral cultures (Trompenaars, 1993). Negotiations are always interspersed with friendship and enmity, based on personal as well as cultural reasons. *Atmosphere* can be considered as a central issue in the negotiation process: Ghauri and Johanson (1979) posit atmosphere as being of basic importance to the development of the negotiation process. Atmosphere has a double role, as a bearer of the history of the relationship and as main factor explaining the transition from one stage to the next. Atmosphere is characterized in a number of respects, namely the dynamics of conflict and co-operation, reducing or overcoming the distance between the partners, the power–dependence relation and, lastly, the expectations of the parties concerning future deals.

Emotions and conflict-handling styles in cross-cultural negotiations

Communication misunderstandings in intercultural negotiation quite often result in an increased level of emotions, that is, negotiators tend to depart from the rational and objective evaluation of issues at stake and to mix subjectivity and feelings with business matters.

Morris et al. (1998, p. 730) outline two types of misunderstandings that frequently arise between Asian and American negotiators:

> In one type of misunderstanding, U.S. managers make the error of reading silence of their Asian counterpart as an indication of consent… A different type of misunderstanding occurs when Asian managers make the error of reading an U.S. colleague's direct adversarial arguments as indicating unreasonableness and lack of respect.

Emotions such as anger result in negotiators being less accurate in judging the interests at stake, more self-centered on their own interests; it also has a general effect of reducing joint gains (Bazerman et al., 2000).[4]

Kumar (1997) makes a sharp distinction between positive and negative emotions in negotiation. Emotions contain both an element of affect and an accompanying physiological arousal. For him, positive emotions result in being more flexible in negotiations, as well as helping negotiators to be more persistent, especially since a positive affective state increases the confidence level of negotiators. However, a positive affective state may also heighten expectations and result in negotiators' disappointment with actual outcomes.

Negative emotions, on the other hand, may result in conflict escalation, that is, actors take matters personally when they should see them with a more distanced attitude. Likely consequences are the attribution to the other side of the responsibility for conflict, and possibly the discontinuation of the relation. While negative emotions may serve to inform the parties that an existing situation is untenable, they may also be snowballing and result in a negative conflict spiral (George et al., 1998; Brett et al., 1998). Negative spirals are partly based on selectively choosing those information cues which will confirm the negative feelings of a negotiators, leading her/him to an escalation of negative feelings toward the other party which are no longer based on hard facts. They also result from systematic reciprocation of contentious communication. Negative spirals are particularly likely to occur in cross-cultural negotiations due to differences at three levels: differences in internalized values and norms, differences in emotional expression and differences in linguistic styles (George et al., 1998). A conflict spiral appears as circular because it is based on repeated contentious communication whereby each side 'responds' to the other side's contentious communication by negative reciprocation (Brett et al., 1998).

The way to solve problems of negative spirals in negotiation has both to do with models of conflict resolution, and with strategic communication styles in negotiation which may help to manage discrepancies in process and outcomes of negotiation (Kumar and Nti, 1998), Tinsley (1998) shows that the Japanese, the Americans and the Germans use different models of conflict resolution. The Japanese tend to use what she calls the 'status model', that is, social interaction is viewed as governed by status and parties might solicit the advice of higher status figures to solve the conflict. The Germans display a preference for the 'regulations' model whereby conflict is seen as to be solved by applying standardized, universal and impersonal rules. Finally, Americans prefer the 'interest' model whereby parties exchange information on their interests, try to prioritize them and trade off interests. Another dimension of conflict resolution is whether people tend to avoid or to directly confront conflict. Morris et al. (1998) show that Chinese managers tend to display conflict avoidance whereas American tend to develop a competing style. Moreover, negotiators who come from more traditional societies, where the dimension of social conservatism is high, tend to be more conflict-averse (Morris et al., 1998; Kozan and Ergin, 1999).

Monitoring emotions in negotiation has to do with the avoidance of negative spirals but also with the avoidance of being too systematically conflict-avoidant. A number of communication strategies have been recommended for breaking negative spirals in cross-cultural negotiations. George et al. (1998) recommend that negotiators engage in what they call 'motivated information processing', that is, a process whereby information is selectively processed in ways that are supportive of motivational goals; motivation for certain outcomes, rather than affect, guides interpretation. Brett et al. (1998) show that a mix of reciprocation combined with non-contentious communication is likely to help break negative spirals in negotiations.

Differences in outcome orientation: oral versus written agreements

It would be naive to believe that profits, especially future accounting profits for each party, are the only possible outcome of the negotiation process. Other possible outcomes are listed in Table 5.1. The main reason for profits not being the sole possible outcome is that they are not really foreseeable. Basic differences in outcome orientation are generally hidden from the negotiation partners, generating increased misunderstandings. Another reason is that many cultures are relationship- rather than deal-oriented: as is described by Oh (1984) and Corne (1992) in the case of the Japanese, and Pye (1986) and Rotella et al. (2000) in the case of the Chinese, they prefer a gentleman's agreement, a loosely-worded statement expressing mutual co-operation and trust between the parties, to a formal Western-style contract. The most crucial element of preparation for a negotiation with the Japanese is drafting an opening statement which seals the start of a relationship, in which the Western side may have the opportunity to seize the moment and set the tone for the rest of the negotiation (Corne, 1992).

Asymmetry in the perceived degree of agreement

Agreements are generally considered as being mostly written. They are achieved by negotiation and by the signing of written contracts, which are often considered 'the law of the parties'. This is unfortunately not always true. Keegan (1984) points out that for some cultures 'my word is my bond' and trust is a personal matter, which he contrasts with the 'get-it-in-writing' mentality where trust is more impersonal. The former is typical of the Middle East, whereas the latter is to be found in the United States where hundreds of thousands of lawyers help people negotiate written agreements and litigate within the framework of these written agreements. This has to be qualified: it does not mean that people rely *entirely* on either an oral base (oaths, confidence between people, membership of a common group where perjury is considered a crime) or a written base. Exploring, maintaining and checking the bases for trust is a more complex process (Usunier, 1989). It entails various possibilities:

1. An agreement may be non-symmetrical. A agrees with B, but B does not agree with A. Various reasons may explain this situation: either B wishes to conceal the disagreement or there is some sort of misunderstanding, usually language-based.
2. People agree, but on different bases, and they do not perceive the divergence. They have, for instance, quite different interpretations of a clause or some kind of non-written agreement. Although much may be written down, some things will always remain unwritten. What is unwritten may, to one party, seem obviously in line with a written

clause, but not to the other. Moreover, if there is no opportunity to confront their interpretations, they cannot be aware of their divergent nature.
3.   The agreement is not understood by both parties as having the same degree of influence on:
     (a) The stability;
     (b) The precision and explicitness of the exchange relation.

Written documents as a basis for mutual trust between the parties

There is a fundamental *dialectic* in written agreements between *distrust* and *confidence*.
At the beginning there is distrust. It is implicitly assumed that such distrust is natural. This
has to be reduced in order to establish confidence. Trust is not achieved on a global and
personal basis but only by breaking down potential distrust in concrete situations where it
may hamper common action. Trust is built step by step, with a view towards the future.
Therefore *real trust* is achieved only gradually. Trust is deprived of its personal aspects.
Thanks to the written agreement, the parties may trust each other in business, although they
do not trust each other as people. Trust is taken to its highest point when the parties sign a
written agreement.
   On the other hand, cultures that favor oral agreements tend not to hypothesize that trust is
constructed by the negotiation process. They see trust more as a prerequisite to the negotiation of written agreements. Naturally, they do not expect this prerequisite to be met in every
case. Trust tends to be mostly personal. Establishing trust requires that people know each
other. That is probably why many Far Eastern cultures (Chinese, Pye, 1982; Japanese,
Graham and Sano, 1990; Tung, 1984; de Mente, 1987; Corne, 1992) need to make informal
contacts, discuss general topics and spend time together before they get to the point, even
though all this may not appear task-related.
   Subsequently, the negotiation process will be lengthy because another dialectic is at
work. Since people are supposed to trust each other, the negotiation process should not
damage or destroy the basic asset of their exchange relationship – trust. They will avoid
direct confrontation on a specific clause, and therefore globalize the negotiation process.
Local foes may be global friends, provided that trust as the basic asset of the negotiation
process is not lost.

The ambiguity of the cultural status of written materials

That one should always 'get it in writing' is not self-evident. The contrary idea may even
impose itself ('if they want it written down, it means that they don't trust me'). Regina
Traoré Sérié (1986, quoted in Ollivier and de Maricourt, 1990) explains, for instance, the
respective roles of oral communication (spoken, transmitted through personal and concrete
communication, passed on through generations by storytellers) and written materials (read,
industrially printed, impersonally transmitted, with no concrete communication) in the
African culture.

> Reading is an individual act, which does not easily incorporate itself into African cul-
> ture. Written documents are presented as either irrelevant to everyday social practices,
> or as an anti-social practice. This is because someone who reads, is also isolating him-
> self, which is resented by the other members of the community. But at the same time,
> people find books attractive, because they are the symbol of access to a certain kind of
> power. By reading, people appropriate foreign culture, they get to know 'the paper

of the whites'. As a consequence, reading is coded as a positive activity in the collective ideal of Ivory Coast society, since it is a synonym for social success. This contradiction between 'alien' and 'fetish' written documents encapsulates the ambiguity of the status of books in African society.

Do written contracts and the intervention of lawyers produce irreversible commitments?

In cultures where relationships are very personalized, confidence cannot be separated from the person in whom the confidence is placed. The basis for mutual trust is no longer the detailed written contractual documents, but a man's word, which is his bond. It is not 'just any word', but a special kind of word, which is heavily imbued with cultural codes (Hall, 1959; 1976). These words as bonds cannot easily be transferred from one culture to another. Adler (1980) describes the case of an Egyptian executive who, after entertaining his Canadian guest, offered him joint partnership in a business venture. The Canadian was very keen to enter this venture with the Egyptian businessman. He therefore suggested that they meet again the next morning with their respective lawyers to fill in the details. The Egyptians never arrived. The Canadian businessman wondered whether this was caused by the lack of punctuality of the Egyptians, or by the Egyptian expecting a counter-offer, or even the absence of available lawyers in Cairo. Adler (1980, p. 178), explains:

> None of these explanations was true, although the Canadian executive suggested all of them. At issue was the perceived meaning of inviting lawyers. The Canadian saw the lawyer's presence as facilitating the successful completion of the negotiation; the Egyptian interpreted it as signaling the Canadian's mistrust of his verbal commitment. Canadians often use the impersonal formality of a lawyer's services to finalize an agreement. Egyptians more frequently depend on a personal relationship developed between bargaining partners for the same purposes.

If agreements are mostly person-based, then their written base may be less important. Thus the demand for renegotiation of clauses by a Middle Eastern buyer in a contract already negotiated and signed, should not be seen as astonishing. It should not necessarily lead to litigation. Behind the demand for renegotiation is the assumption that, if people really trust each other, they should go much further than simple and literal implementation of their written agreements. This leads to the following question: to what extent should the contract signature date be considered as a time line which signals the end of the negotiation? (See Chapter 8.)

Different attitudes towards litigation

It is easy to understand that the function of litigation will be different for both sides. Recourse to litigation will be fairly easily made by those favoring written-based agreements as the ultimate means of resolving breaches of contract. The oral and personal tradition is less susceptible to recourse to litigation, because litigation has major drawbacks:

1. It breaks the implicit assumption of trust.
2. It breaches the required state of social harmony, especially in the Far Eastern countries, and may therefore be quite threatening for the community as a whole.

As David (1987, p. 89, author's translation) states:

> in Far Eastern countries, as well as in Black Africa and Madagascar…subject to the Westernization process which has been attempted, one does not find, as in Hinduism or Islam, a body of legal rules whose influence may be weakened by the recognized influence of other factors; it is the very notion of legal rules which is challenged. Despite authorities having sometimes established legal codes, it is well known and seems obvious that the prescriptions of these codes are not designed to be implemented literally. They should only be considered as simple patterns. The judge will be able to moderate their strictness and, moreover, it is hoped that this will not be necessary. The 'good judge', whether Chinese, Japanese or Vietnamese, is not concerned with making a good decision. The 'good judge' is the one who succeeds in not making any award, because he has been skillful enough to lead the opponents to reconciliation. Any dispute, as it is a threat to social harmony, has to be solved by a settlement through conciliation. The individual only has 'duties' towards the society. Recognition of 'subjective rights' in his favor is out of the question. Law as it is conceived in the West is seen as good for barbarians, and the occupation of lawyer, in the limited extent that it exists, is regarded with contempt by the society.

These remarks by a specialist in comparative law give a good idea of the differences of litigious tradition between the Far East and the West. In the field of contracts, the Western saying 'the contract is the law of the parties' dominates the practices of international trade. But this is, in part, window-dressing. When negotiating internationally, a set of written contracts is always signed. This is not to say that people choose either oral or written agreements as a basis for trust. The real question is rather: how should the mix of written and oral bases for trust, as they are perceived by the parties, be interpreted? People do not deal with conflicts in the same way. Negotiating together requires a capacity to envisage different ways of managing disputes. Not only differences in rationality and mental programs, but also differences in time representations, may lead to a partner 'who thinks differently' being considered a partner 'who thinks wrongly'.

The utmost caution is recommended when interpreting the bases of trust, whether written documents or oral and personal bonds. Even in the Anglo-Saxon world, where it is preferred to 'get it in writing', a number of business deals, sometimes large ones – in the area of finance, for instance – are based on a simple telex or fax, or a simple agreement between two key decision-makers. It would be a mistake to believe that personal relationships do not exist in places where written contracts are generally required. Moreover, in cultures where 'my word is my bond', it should never be forgotten that it is difficult to trust somebody who is not a member of the in-group, whether on a written or spoken basis. Therefore, trust has to be established (and monitored) on both bases, while at the same time keeping in mind a clear awareness of the limits of each.

Conclusion: negotiating shared cultures

The process of intercultural encounter in negotiation has been described as akin to a dance in which one party dances a waltz when the other dances a tango (Tinsley et al., 1999). There is, however, much adaptation in intercultural negotiation; negotiators tend to adjust to the other party's behavior in ways that derive significantly from what would be the stereotypical attitude in their native culture (Adler and Graham, 1989; Bazerman et al., 2000). It is naturally difficult to step out from one's own culture (Shapiro and von Glinow, 1999). However, negotiators exchange masses of information during a full negotiation and they process it in complex ways, ways that do not aim at an intellectual understanding of the beliefs and attitudes of the other party, but rather target mutual adjustment in view of maximizing outcomes. Negotiators therefore tend to adapt their behavior to the other party, at least to the extent they perceive as useful for smoothing the process and improving the outcomes. On average, cultural adaptation, provided that it is done properly – without naive imitation – is positively experienced by the other side. Pornpitakpan (1999) shows that neither the Japanese nor the Thais feel that their social identity is threatened by high adaptation coming from American sellers in sales negotiations. The Japanese buyers positively experience cultural adaptation by American sellers despite the marked tendency in Japan to make a clear-cut distinction between in-group members (*nihon-jin*) and out-group members (*gai-jin*).

Culture clash in negotiation may be strong at the very start, when negotiators expect behavior from the other side which normatively corresponds to what they are used to as well as to what they consider as the most appropriate for effective negotiation. Cultural adaptation is not necessarily symmetrical. For instance, Japanese negotiators tend to adjust to Americans by using more direct information-sharing and less indirect communication than in negotiations with their countrymen, whereas Americans adapt less to their Japanese counterparts (Adair et al. 2001). A common professional culture may also help overcome the barriers related to cross-cultural understanding (Haugland, 1998). That is why culture often appears as a relatively poor predictor of the negotiation process and outcomes, and should not be used directly to predict negotiation behavior (Tinsley and Brett, 1997).

In complex international negotiations, there is a mix of antecedent constructs, based on national cultures, individual characteristics of negotiators and organizational factors surrounding the negotiation (Money, 1998). Coalition building and emergent roles in the negotiation process transcend the borders of culture, leading to a redesign of the set of relationships. More extrovert negotiators and individuals who are proficient in the other side's language emerge as central figures in the negotiation process. Brannen and Salk (2000) show how a German and a Japanese company negotiate a common organizational culture within an international joint venture. This negotiated culture is not a blend of both cultures. It is rather an idiosyncratic whole, pragmatically defined for certain issue domains, containing parts of both parent cultures, but also new ways of doing that are specific to the common organization. Brannen and Salk take the example of problems related to working hours and summer vacations: the Germans tend to take three weeks vacation during the summer whereas the Japanese typically do not take more than five consecutive days of vacation, and this created conflicts between German and Japanese managers.

> There was no possibility of a negotiated outcome with regard to the length of summer vacation because of Germany's legal climate; Japanese simply continued to take vacation time off as they were accustomed while Germans continued as they had always done. Over time, however, negotiated outcomes did evolve with regard to socializing and the length of working hours though they were reached in a more idiosyncratic fashion. Certain German managers began to stay later at work while many of the Japanese worked fewer hours than they were accustomed to in Japan.
>
> (Brannen and Salk, 2000, p. 472)

Notes

1 Brannen and Salk (2000, pp. 473–75) give a detailed account of how language use is negotiated in the case of a German–Japanese joint venture:

> The negotiated outcome for language use [English as official venture language] was really the only one available. When a Japanese or German was confused or needed help, they would confer with members of their same cultural group in their mother tongue. This was done solely to expedite matters and clarify issues rather than as a means of excluding one or the other group from decision-making. One German manager spoke this way of the negotiation outcome: 'The work language is English. But, during discussion, they would sometimes speak Japanese and I thought this was a good thing because you know your own language better and can understand better and can discuss things more precisely. One has to be tolerant…'.
>
> (p. 474)

2 For a review and discussion of non face-to-face negotiations, see the section entitled 'The case against face-to-face communication in bargaining', in Bazerman et al. (2000, pp. 295–96).
3 Full electronic negotiation systems have been proposed, such as INSPIRE (Kersten and Noronha, 1997; 1999), and Negoplan (Kersten and Szpakowicz, 1998).
4 For a review and discussion of the role of emotions on negotiation behavior, see the section entitled 'Emotion and negotiation', in Bazerman et al. (2000, pp. 285–86).

References

Adachi, Yumi (1998), 'The effect of semantic difference on cross-cultural business negotiations: A Japanese and American case study', *Journal of Language for International Business*, vol. 9, no. 1, pp. 43–52.
Adair, Wendi L., Tetsushi Okumura and Jeanne M. Brett (2001), 'Negotiation behavior when cultures collide: The United States and Japan', *Journal of Applied Psychology*, vol. 86, no. 3, pp. 371–85.
Adler, Nancy, J. (1980), 'Cultural synergy: the management of cross-cultural organizations', in W. Warner Burke and Leonard D. Goodstein (eds), *Trends and Issues in OD: Current theory and practice*, San Diego, CA: University Associates, pp.163–84.
—— (2002), *International Dimensions of Organizational Behavior*, 4th edn, Cincinnati, OH: South-Western.
Adler, Nancy J. and John L. Graham (1989), 'Cross-cultural comparison: The international comparison fallacy?', *Journal of International Business Studies*, vol. xx, no. 3, pp. 515–37.
Angelmar, Reinhardt and Louis W. Stern (1978), 'Development of a content analysis scheme for analysis of bargaining communication in marketing', *Journal of Marketing Research*, vol. 15, February, pp. 93–102.
Bazerman, Max H., Jared R. Curhan, Don A. Moore, and Kathleen L. Valley (2000), 'Negotiation', *Annual Review of Psychology*, vol. 51, 279–314.
Beliaev, Edward, Thomas Mullen and Betty Jane Punnett (1985), 'Understanding the cultural environment: U.S.–U.S.S.R. trade negotiations', *California Management Review*, vol. XXVII, no. 2, pp. 100–112.
Brannen, Mary Yoko and Jane E. Salk (2000), 'Partnering across borders: Negotiating organizational culture in a German–Japanese joint venture', *Human Relations*, vol. 53, no. 4, pp. 451–87.
Brett, Jeanne M. and Tetsushi Okumura (1998), 'Inter- and intra-cultural negotiations: US and Japanese negotiators', *Academic Management Journal*, vol. 41, no. 5, pp. 495–510.
Brett, Jeanne M., Debra L. Shapiro, and Anne E. Lytle (1998), 'Breaking the bonds of reciprocity in negotiations', *Academy of Management Journal*, vol. 41, no. 4, pp. 410–24.
Brett, J. M., W. Adair, A. Lempereur, T. Okumura, P. Shilehirev, C. Tinsley and A. Lytle (1998), 'Culture and joint gains in negotiation', *Negotiation Journal*, pp. 61–86.
Burt, David N. (1984), 'The nuances of negotiating overseas', *Journal of Purchasing and Materials Management* (Winter), pp. 2–8.

Campbell, Nigel C. G., John L. Graham, Alain Jolibert, and Hans Günther Meissner (1988), 'Marketing negotiations in France, Germany, the United Kingdom and United States', *Journal of Marketing*, vol. 52, April, pp. 49–62.

Cateora, Philip R. (1993), *International Marketing*, 8th edn, Homewood, IL: Irwin.

Cohen, Raymond (1997), *Negotiating Across Cultures*, Washington, DC: United States Institute of Peace Press.

Corne, P. H. (1992), 'The complex art of negotiation between different cultures', *Dispute Resolution Journal*, vol. 47, pp. 46–50.

David, René (1987), *Le Droit du commerce international, réflexions d'un comparatiste sur le droit international privé*, Paris: Economica.

De Mente, Boye (1987), *How to Do Business with the Japanese*, Chicago: N.T.C. Publishing.

Druckman, D., A. A. Benton, F. Ali and J. S. Bagur (1976), 'Culture differences in bargaining behavior', *Journal of Conflict Resolution*, vol. 20, pp. 413–49.

Eiteman, David K. (1990), 'American executives' perceptions of negotiating joint ventures with the People's Republic of China: Lessons learned', *Columbia Journal of World Business* (Winter), pp. 59–67.

Evans, Franklin B. (1963), 'Selling as a dyadic relationship: A new approach', *American Behavioral Scientist*, vol. 6, May, pp. 76–79.

Faure, Guy Olivier and Gunnar Sjöstedt (1993), 'Culture and Negotiation: An introduction', in Guy Olivier Faure and Jeffrey Z. Rubin, *Culture and Negotiation*, Newbury Park, CA: Sage Publications, pp. 1–13.

Faure, Guy Olivier and Jeffrey Z. Rubin (1993), *Culture and Negotiation*, Newbury Park, CA: Sage Publications.

Fisher, Glen (1980), *International Negotiation: A cross-cultural perspective*, Yarmouth, ME: Intercultural Press, p. 50.

—— (1988) *Mindsets*, Yarmouth, ME: Intercultural Press.

Foster, Dean Allen (1995), *Bargaining Across Borders*, New York: McGraw-Hill.

Foster, G. M. (1965), 'Peasant society and the image of limited good', *American Anthropologist*, vol. 67, pp. 293–315.

Fuentes, Carlos (1986), cited in 'To see ourselves as others see us', *Time Magazine*, 16 June, p. 52.

Galtung, Johan (1981), 'Structure, culture and intellectual style: An essay comparing Saxonic, Teutonic, Gallic and Nipponic approaches', *Social Science Information*, Vol. 20, no. 6, 817–56.

George, Jennifer M., Gareth R. Jones and Jorge A. Gonzalez (1998), 'The Role of Affect in Cross-Cultural Negotiations', *Journal of International Business Studies*, vol. 29, no. 4, pp. 749–72.

Ghauri, Pervez N. and Jan Johanson (1979), 'International package deals – The role of atmosphere', *Marknad och Samhälle*, vol. 16, no. 5, pp. 355–64.

Glenn, E. (1981), *Man and Mankind: Conflict and communication between cultures*, Horwood, NJ: Ablex.

Goldman, Alan (1994), 'The centrality of "Ningensei" to Japanese negotiating and interpersonal relationships: implications for U.S.–Japanese communication', *International Journal of Intercultural Relations*, vol. 18, no. 1, pp. 29–54.

Goodenough, Ward H. (1971), *Culture, Language and Society*, Modular Publications, 7, Reading, MA: Addison-Wesley.

Graham, John. L. (1985), 'Cross-cultural marketing negotiations: A laboratory experiment', *Marketing Science*, vol. 4, no. 2, pp. 130–46.

—— (1993), 'Business negotiations: Generalizations about Latin America and East Asia are dangerous', *UCINSIGHT*, University of California–Irvine GSM, Summer, pp. 6–23.

Graham, John L. and Persa Economou (1998), 'Introduction to the Symposium', *Journal of International Business Studies*, vol. 29, no. 4, pp. 661–64.

Graham, John L. and Herberger, Roy A. Jr. (1983), 'Negotiators abroad: Don't shoot from the hip', *Harvard Business Review*, vol. 61, no. 4, pp. 160–68.

Graham, John L. and Meissner, Hans G. (1986), 'Content analysis of business negotiations in five countries', Working Paper, University of Southern California.

Graham, John L. and Yoshihiro Sano (1990), *Smart Bargaining: Doing business with the Japanese*, 2nd edn, Cambridge, MA: Ballinger.

Graham, John L., Alma T. Mintu and Waymond Rodgers (1994), 'Explorations of negotiation behaviors in ten foreign cultures using a model developed in the United States', *Management Science*, vol. 40, no. 1 (January), pp. 72–95.

Hall, Edward T. (1959), *The Silent Language*, Garden City, NY: Doubleday.

—— (1960), 'The silent language in overseas business', *Harvard Business Review*, May–June, pp. 87–96.

—— (1976), *Beyond Culture*, Garden City, NY: Anchor Press/Doubleday.

Harnett, Donald L., and L.L. Cummings (1980), *Bargaining Behavior: An international study*, Houston, TX: Dame Publications.

Harris, Philip R. and Robert T. Moran (1987), *Managing Cultural Differences*, 2nd edn, Houston, TX: Gulf Publishing Company.

Haugland, Sven (1998), 'The cultural dimension of international buyer–seller relationships', *Journal of Business-to-Business Marketing*, vol. 4, no. 4, pp. 3–33.

Hawrysh, Bryan Mark and Judith Lynn Zaichkowsky (1990), 'Cultural approaches to negotiations: Understanding the Japanese', *International Marketing Review*, vol. 7, no. 2, pp. 28–42.

Herbig, Paul A. (1998), *Handbook of Cross-Cultural Marketing*, New York: The Haworth Press.

Hofstede, Geert (1980), *Culture's Consequences: International differences in work-related values*, Beverly Hills, CA: Sage.

—— (1989), 'Cultural predictors of national negotiation style', in Frances Mautner-Markhof (ed.), *Processes of International Negotiations*, Boulder, CO: Westview Press, pp. 193–201.

—— (1991), *Cultures and Organizations: Software of the mind*, Maidenhead: McGraw-Hill.

Hoon-Halbauer, Sing Keow (1999), 'Managing relationships within Sino-foreign joint ventures', *Journal of World Business*, vol. 34, no. 4 pp. 344–71.

Jolibert, Alain (1988), 'Le Contexte culturel de la négociation commerciale', *Revue Française de Gestion*, November–December, pp. 15–24.

Keegan, Warren J. (1984), *Multinational Marketing Management*, Englewood Cliffs, NJ: Prentice Hall.

Kelley, Harold H. (1966), 'A classroom study of the dilemmas in interpersonal negotiations', in K. Archibald (ed.), *Strategic Interaction and Conflict*, Institute of International Studies, Berkeley, CA: University of California Press.

Kersten, Gregory E. and Sunil J. Noronha (1997), 'Supporting international negotiation with a WWW-Based system.', *IIASA Interim Report* IR-97-49, August.

—— (1999), 'Negotiation via the World Wide Web: A cross-cultural study of decision making', *Group Decisions and Negotiations*, vol. 8, pp. 251–79.

Kersten, Gregory E. and S. Szpakowicz (1998), 'Modelling business negotiations for electronic commerce', *IIASA Interim Report* IR-98-015, March.

Kersten, Gregory E., Sabine Köszegi and Rudolf Vetschera (1999a), 'The effect of culture in anonymous negotiations: A four countries experiment', *IIASA Interim Report* IR-99-023, July.

—— (2002), 'Effect of culture in anonymous negotiations: An experiment in four countries', *35th Annual IEEE Conference on System Science*, vol. 1, pp. 7–10.

Kozan, M. Kamil and Canan Ergin (1999), 'The influence of intra-cultural value differences on conflict management practices', *International Journal of Conflict Resolution*, vol. 10, no. 3, pp. 249–67.

Kumar, Rajesh (1997), 'The role of affect in negotiations: An integrative overview', *Journal of Applied Behavioral Science*, vol. 33, no. 1, pp. 84–100.

Kumar, Rajesh and Kofi O. Nti (1998), 'Differential learning and interaction in alliance dynamics: A process and outcome discrepancy model', *Organization Science*, vol. 9, no. 3, pp. 356–67.

Lee, James A. (1966), 'Cultural analysis in overseas operations', *Harvard Business Review*, March–April, pp. 106–11.

Leung, Kwok (1997), 'Negotiation and reward allocations across cultures', in P. C. Earley and M. Erez (eds), *New Perspectives on International Industrial/Organizational Psychology*, San Francisco: Jossey-Bass, pp. 640–75.

Li, Ji and Chalmer E. Labig, Jr. (2001), 'Negotiating with China: Exploratory study of relationship-building', *Journal of Managerial Issues*, vol. 13, no. 3, pp. 345–59.

Linton, Ralph (1947), *The Cultural Background of Personality*, New York: Appleton-Century.

McCall, J. B. and M. B. Warrington (1990), *Marketing by Agreement: A cross-cultural approach to business negotiations*, 2nd edn, Chichester: Wiley.

Markus, Hazel Rose and Shinobu Kitayama (1991), 'Culture and the self: Implications for cognition, emotion and motivation', *Psychological Review*, vol. 98, no. 2, pp. 224–53.

Matsumoto, M. (1988), *The Unspoken Way: Haragei – Silence in Japanese Business and Society*, New York: Kodansha International.

Matthews, H. Lee, David T. Wilson and John F. Monoky Jr (1972), 'Bargaining behavior in a buyer–seller dyad', *Journal of Marketing Research*, vol. 9, February, pp. 103–5.

Merriam, Sharan B., Juanita Johnson-Bailey, Ming-Yeh Lee, Youngwha Kee, Gabo Ntseane, and Mazanah Muhamad (2001), 'Power and positionality: negotiating insider/outsider status within and across cultures', *International Journal of Lifelong Education*, vol. 20, no. 5, pp. 405–16.

Money, R. Bruce (1998), 'International multilateral negotiations and social networks', *Journal of International Business Studies*, vol. 29, no. 4, pp. 711–27.

Morris, Michael W., Katherine Y. Williams, Leung Kwok, Larrick Richard, Mendoza M. Teresa, Bhatnagar Deepti, Li Jianfeng, Kondo Mari, Luo Jin-Lian and Jun-Chen Hu (1998), 'Conflict management style: Accounting for cross-national differences', *Journal of International Business Studies*, vol. 29, no. 4, pp. 729–47.

Munns, A. K., O. Aloquili and B. Ramsay (2000), 'Joint venture negotiation and managerial practices in the new countries of the former Soviet Union', *International Journal of Project Management*, vol. 18, no. 6, pp. 403–13.

Oh, T. K. (1984), 'Selling to the Japanese', *Nation's Business*, October, 37–38.

Ollivier, Alain and Renaud de Maricourt (1990), *Pratique du marketing en Afrique*, Paris: Edicef/Aupelf.

Pornpitakpan, Chantikha (1999), 'The effect of cultural adaptation on business relationships: Americans selling to Japanese and Thais', *Journal of International Business Studies*, vol. 30, no. 2, pp. 317–38.

Potter, Richard E. and Pierre A. Balthazard (2000), 'Supporting integrative negotiation via computer mediated communication technologies: An empirical example with geographically dispersed Chinese and American negotiators', *Journal of International Consumer Marketing*, vol. 12, no. 4, pp. 7–32.

Pruitt, Dean G. (1981), *Bargaining Behavior*, New York: Academic Press.

—— (1983), 'Strategic choice in negotiation', *American Behavioral Scientist*, vol. 27, no. 2, pp. 167–94.

Pruitt, Dean G. and Steven A. Lewis (1975), 'Development of integrative solutions in bilateral negotiations', *Journal of Personality and Social Psychology*, vol. 31, no. 4, pp. 621–33.

Pye, Lucian (1982), *Chinese Commercial Negotiating Style*, Cambridge, MA: Oelgeschlager, Gunn and Hain.

—— (1986), 'The China trade: Making the deal', *Harvard Business Review*, vol. 46, no. 4 (July–August), pp. 74–84.

Rao, Asha and Stuart M. Schmidt (1998), 'A behavioral perspective on negotiating international alliances', *Journal of International Business Studies*, vol. 29, no. 4, pp. 665–94.

Rotella, Mark, Charlotte Abbott and Sarah Gold (2000), 'Chinese Business Etiquette and Culture', *Publishers Weekly*, vol. 247, no. 25.

Rubin, J. Z. and B. R. Brown (1975), *The Social Psychology of Bargaining and Negotiations*, New York: Academic Press.

Rubin, Paul A. and J. R. Carter (1990), 'Joint optimality in buyer–seller negotiations', *Journal of Purchasing and Materials Management* (Spring), pp. 20–26.

Saner, Raymond (2000), *The Expert Negotiator*, The Hague: Kluwer.

Sawyer, J. and H. Guetzkow (1965), 'Bargaining and negotiation in international relations', in H. Kelman (ed.), *International Behavior*, New York: Holt, Rinehart and Winston.

Scanzoni, J. (1979), 'Social exchange and behavioral interdependence', in R. L. Burgess and T. L. Huston (eds), *Social Exchange in Developing Relationships*, New York: Academic Press.

Schuster, Camille P. and Michael J. Copeland (1999), 'Global business exchanges: Similarities and differences around the world', *Journal of International Marketing*, vol. 7, no. 2, pp. 63–80.

Shapiro D. L. and M. A. von Glinow (1999), 'Negotiation in multicultural teams: new world, old theories?', in *Research on Negotiation in Organizations*, vol. 7, Greenwich, CT: JAI.

Tenbrunsel, Anne E. and Max H. Bazerman (2000), 'Working women', in Jeanne M. Brett (ed.), *Teaching Materials for Negotiation and Decision Making*, Evanston, IL: Northwestern University, Dispute Resolution Research Center.

Tinsley C. (1998), 'Models of conflict resolution in Japanese, German and American cultures', *Journal of Applied Psychology*, vol. 83, pp. 316–23.

Tinsley C., J. Curhan and R. S. Kwak (1999), 'Adopting a dual lens approach for overcoming the dilemma of difference in international business negotiations', *International Negotiations*, vol. 4, pp. 1–18.

Tinsley, Catherine H. and Jeanne Brett (1997), 'Managing workplace conflict: A comparison of conflict frames and outcomes in the U.S. and Hong Kong', Paper presented at the Annual Meeting of the Academy of Management, Boston, MA.

Tinsley, Catherine H. and Madan M. Pillutla (1998), 'Negotiating in the United States and Hong Kong', *Journal of International Business Studies*, vol. 29, no. 4, pp. 711–27.

Traoré Sérié, Régina (1986), 'La Promotion du livre en Côte d'Ivoire', Paper presented to the conference on Marketing and Development, Abidjan (Ivory Coast), December.

Triandis, Harry G. (1983), 'Dimensions of cultural variation as parameters of organizational theories', *International Studies of Management and Organization*, vol. 12, no. 4, pp. 139–69.

Trompenaars, Fons (1993), *Riding the Waves of Culture*, London: Nicholas Brealey.

Tse, David K., June Francis and Jan Walls (1994), 'Cultural differences in conducting intra- and inter-cultural negotiations: A Sino-Canadian perspective', *Journal of International Business Studies*, vol. 25, no. 3, pp. 537–55.

Tung, Rosalie L. (1984), 'How to negotiate with the Japanese', *California Management Review*, vol. 26, no. 4, pp. 62–77.

Ulijn, Jan M., Andreas Lincke and Yunus Karakaya (2001), 'Non-face-to-face international business negotiation: How is national culture reflected in this medium?', *IEEE Transactions on Professional Communication*, vol. 44, no. 2, pp. 126–37.

USIP (United States Institute of Peace) (2002), *U.S. Negotiating Behavior*, Special Report 94, October, www.usip.org

Usunier, Jean-Claude (1989), 'Interculturel: La parole et l'action', *Harvard-L'Expansion*, no. 52, March, pp. 84–92.

Van Zandt, H. R. (1970), 'How to negotiate with the Japanese', *Harvard Business Review*, November–December, pp. 45–56.

Wade-Benzoni, Kimberly A., Tetsushi Okumura, Jeanne M. Brett, Don A. Moore, Ann E. Tenbrunsel and Max H. Bazerman (2002), 'Cognition and behavior in asymmetric social dilemmas: A comparison of two cultures', *Journal of Applied Psychology*, vol. 87, no. 1, pp. 87–95.

Walton, Richard E. and Robert B. McKersie (1965), *A Behavioral Theory of Labor Negotiations*. New York: McGraw-Hill.

Weber, E. U. and C. K. Hsee (1998), 'Cross-cultural differences in risk perception, but cross-cultural similarities in attitudes towards perceived risk', *Management Science*, vol. 44, no. 9, pp. 1205–17.

Weitz, B. (1979), 'A Critical review of personal selling research: The need for contingency approaches', in G. Albaum and G. A. Churchill Jr. (eds), *Critical Issues in Sales Management: State of the art and future needs*, Eugene: University of Oregon Press.

Zartman, I. William (1993), 'A skeptic's view', in Guy Olivier Faure and Jeffrey Z. Rubin, *Culture and Negotiation*, Newbury Park, CA: Sage Publications, pp. 17–21.

Zeldin, Theodore (1977), *France 1848–1945*, vol. 11, Oxford: Oxford University Press.

6 The effect of culture on business ethics

Philippe d'Iribarne

Translated from the French by
Suzan Nolan and Leila Whittemore

Introduction

Business ethics have emerged as a critical crossroads where the 'universal' and the 'local' intersect. Increasingly, multinational firms try to create a common culture and spirit to unite far-flung subsidiaries. Such firms create documents – codes of business ethics, conduct and professional practice – to give their employees guidelines and to demonstrate their leaders' principles. They set up ways to compel (greater or lesser) obedience to these guidelines, such as ethics training sessions and monitoring or enforcement tools. These codes cover many of the firms' everyday efforts to fight corruption, respect the rights of employees and promote social responsibility. However, as Herder (2000) noted in connection with religions, every universal message embodies a variety of local interpretations. This variety of constructs – in ways of being, values and customs – strongly influences ethics.[1] It affects behavior considered morally acceptable (or not), actions arising from a sense of duty, types of control considered legitimate, or even the very legitimacy of firms addressing ethics at all.

This variety poses problems when a company tries to develop a common ethic or set of ethics to promote employee integration: local managers must find the equivalents (or close approximations) of headquarters' benchmarks in other countries and cultures. One such problem arises when the approach to business ethics relies heavily on management tools, ethical codes and other measures that largely derive from an American context. Disseminating this approach worldwide requires that managers truly grasp how to accommodate the often-considerable differences between American ethical constructs and those found in other cultural contexts.

To demonstrate the variety of ethical constructs and the types of adaptation they require, we draw on research conducted in international corporations – specifically ones searching for ethical approaches that make the most of cultural diversity. In the first part of this chapter, we compare large cultural differences between two countries that initially appear close culturally – France and the United States – providing a particularly striking illustration of what is at stake. In the second part, we aim for insight into the effects of the diverse ethical constructs we see around the world. We address issues related to fighting corruption, illustrated by a case from Argentina, and the quality of relationships within a firm, illustrated by a case involving Malaysia and Jordan.

Varieties of ethical construct

The firm's role as an ethical actor in the United States and France[2]

Since the 1970s, the formalization of business ethics has expanded rapidly in the United States. In many other countries – France first and foremost – the concept often provokes criticism.

Patrick du Besset, president of the Association for Business Ethics (*Cercle Éthique des Affaires*),[3] a non-profit business network that includes most ethics and compliance officers developing programs in large French companies, noted in an interview: 'Companies in France did not come easily to ethics and today, great reserve remains in the way they approach the subject' (Besset 2002, pp. 17–18). We saw similar reactions during interviews we conducted with groups of American, French and other (primarily) European managers working for a large multinational manufacturing group with roots in France.[4] The French managers generally proved very hostile to American conceptions of business ethics. They questioned the company's legitimacy to act as an engine of ethics, whether in defining guide-lines or using surveillance and sanctions systems to ensure employee compliance. The French managers' reactions matched those of the French public at large when confronted with the role ethics plays in American political life – for instance, we note the French cannot comprehend why former president Bill Clinton's personal peccadilloes merited a judicial enquiry – nor do they tolerate the United States' general self-image as a crusader for good. We questioned the sources of these two countries' differences, given that in many ways they seem to share the same general values.

Ethics and social control: two opposing views

To understand the intensity of French reactions to American conceptions of business ethics, and more generally to the place of ethics in American society, we must look at the gap sepa-rating the two ethical traditions. That means returning to at least the time of the Reformation and its great rupture with tradition, a break that the secular movements influencing both societies have not subsequently erased.

The Reformation's impact on religious and social morality

A dual ethical heritage influenced European history. A biblical legacy – primarily New Testament – superimposed itself on a very different ancient Greek and Roman one (Manent 1994). One celebrates humility, the other greatness and magnanimity. One imposes the same duties on the powerful and the humble; the other radically differentiates the duties of various stations in life. In European societies before the Reformation, these two ethics coexisted, each having standards, supervisory bodies, rewards for obedience and sanctions for trans-gressions. Social ethics, sanctioned by public opinion and tied to the requisites of honor, existed alongside religious ethics that were carried by the Roman Catholic Church and tied to the requisites of virtue. Sometimes these requisites were radically opposed – for instance, in dueling or men's sexual morality. Strict adherence to standards of the Gospel was reserved for monks, who vowed to 'acquire perfection', while the Church largely put up with 'com-promises between the requisites of temporal morality and Christianity's original morality' (Troeltsch 1991, p. 61). Everyone was accountable for compliance with 'worldly' morality to the court of public opinion, and for compliance with Christian morality to a priest, who was often quite forgiving about the world's demands.

For Martin Luther, and even more for John Calvin, the Reformation represented a radical break with this amiable accommodation with the world. With the suppression of monks and monastic communities, the distinction vanished between those who vowed to rigorously follow Christian morality and those expected to accept a compromise between Christian and worldly moralities. Moreover, when confession was suppressed, the religious community assumed control of monitoring obedience to Christian morality. Troeltsch (1991) notes that Calvin's Protestant dogma

> imposed a militant development on Christian morality – each person monitored the other…Religious order covered a person's whole life, even strictly temporal affairs… The distinction between high and low Christian moralities disappeared.
>
> (pp. 15, 59, 60)

Within this context, Catholic countries saw political power torn between worldly and religious ethics, leaning toward one side or the other depending on the period and country; 'Catholic' monarchs could alternate with 'libertine' kings. Protestant countries largely instrumentalized political power, enforcing religious ethics in tandem with the community and in a far more coherent way than their Catholic counterparts.

Europe's political emancipation movement, influenced by the rejection of all authority not constituted by popular will, had different impacts on Catholic and Protestant societies (especially Calvinist ones). In Catholic societies, the movement stimulated public rejection of religious authority, as held by the Catholic Church apparatus; the Church had not only claimed to rule society but had legitimized the power of the throne. The Church's influence – and that of religion more generally – subsequently tended to be limited to the private sphere. By contrast, in Protestant societies where the religious community possessed more of religion's authority, the triumph of democratic ideas did not call this authority into question. Troeltsch (1991, p. 112) points out that all of the Protestant revolutions followed a different logic to that of the great French Revolution: they did not need to completely break with tradition or dethrone religion, since Protestant culture and the religious upheaval it provoked had already accomplished a fundamental revolution from the inside. Correspondingly, on the Catholic side, religious ethics tended to be a strictly private affair, while the public continued to elevate worldly morality and tended to see the state as safeguarding the law rather than ethics. During this time, on the Protestant side, the state and the community continued to work together to ensure obedience to a Christian ethic.

The Reformation's transformation of ethical constructs had great impact in the economic sphere. In the Catholic tradition, the faithful certainly did not think that the gospel inspired people to pursue the lure of profit or to defend material interests; they tolerated such behavior in 'ordinary' Christians as a compromise with the times. With the Reformation, such compromise became unacceptable; Protestant societies therefore subordinated economic behavior to a Christian ethic, severely condemning the enjoyment of wealth from that point forward. However, the same standard did not apply to acquisition of wealth; this was, perhaps, another form of unspoken compromise with the times. Work 'became a binding obligation for everyone, requiring them to put their abilities at the service of the whole of civil society' (Troeltsch 1991, p. 157). Moreover, in the wake of changes definitively analyzed by Max Weber (1905), business success became a sign of salvation for Calvinists, especially dissident Puritans:

> Ascetism looked upon the pursuit of wealth as an end in itself as highly reprehensible; but the attainment of it as a fruit of labour in a calling was a sign of God's blessing.
>
> (Weber 1905, ch. 5)

Over time, Calvinism strengthened the link between conduct worthy of the saved and business success: rectitude sustained that good reputation, which led to success in its turn.

When focusing on the religious background of these Protestant sects, we find in their literary documents – especially among those of the Quakers and Baptists – up to and throughout the seventeenth century, jubilation again and again over the fact that the sinful 'children of the world' distrust one another in business but that they have confidence in the religiously determined righteousness of the pious.

(Weber 1906)

American 'puritanism' and the community's moral monitoring

The Protestant conception of society flourished even more in the United States. Unlike Europe, early Americans in colonial New England had no need whatever to work around an existing order based on other principles. 'The states of New England lacked the old structures of European corporatism and [so] [...] political institutions sprang up out of religious ones' (Troeltsch 1991, p. 83). America's political institutions bore the influence of the Protestant sects' ethical constructs (Bellah et al. 1985, p. 245); the various sects were extremely concerned with their members' moral purity. 'A fairly reputable sect would only accept membership of one whose "conduct" made him appear morally *qualified* beyond doubt' (Weber 1906). The religious community governed members' conduct: 'the sect placed disciplinary power predominantly in the hands of laypersons. No spiritual authority could assume the community's shared responsibility before God' (Weber 1906). The regulation applied to each member appeared all the more necessary as it was believed that man was weak by nature – 'ambitious, vindictive and rapacious' as affirmed, for example, by the sixth *Federalist* paper in 1787 (Hamilton et al. 1996, p. 20), in need of society's guidance and regulation in order to progress towards goodness.

Of course, not all early Americans saw their reflection in Puritanism. It co-existed with a utilitarian individualism little concerned with religion; Benjamin Franklin was the utilitarians' most widely-heeded spokesman. These two currents of thought – Puritanism and utilitarianism – easily met on the issue of morality, perceived as a source of material success. Franklin counseled that when 'you are mindful of what you owe, it makes you appear a careful as well as an honest man, and that still increases your credit' (Franklin 1748, cited in Weber 1905, ch. 2). The doctrine of enlightened self-interest, where self-interest and morality are compatible, matched religion's moral requisites by reconciling morality with each person's right to defend his or her own interests. During his travels through the United States in 1831, Alexis de Tocqueville, struck by this doctrine's power, wrote:

I doubt whether men were more virtuous in aristocratic ages than in others, but they were incessantly talking of the beauties of virtue, and its utility was only studied in secret. But since the imagination takes less lofty flights, and every man's thoughts are centered in himself, moralists are alarmed by this idea of self-sacrifice and they no longer venture to present it to the human mind.

They therefore content themselves with inquiring whether the personal advantage of each member of the community does not consist in working for the good of all; and when they have hit upon some point on which private interest and public interest meet and amalgamate, they are eager to bring it into notice. Observations of this kind are gradually multiplied; what was only a single remark becomes a general principle, and it is held as a truth that man serves himself in serving his fellow creatures and that his private interest is to do good. [...] In the United States hardly anybody talks of the beauty of virtue, but they maintain that virtue is useful and prove it every day.

(Tocqueville 1835–40, part II, ch. VIII)

The value Americans give to morality is also supported by morality's links to political freedom. Tocqueville explains:

> In the moral world, everything is classed, coordinated, foreseen and predetermined. In the political world, everything is agitated, disputed and uncertain. One world features passive, albeit voluntary obedience: the other, independence scornful of experience and jealous of all authority. These two tendencies, so opposite in appearance, do not conflict; they advance together and seem to provide mutual support. Religion sees in civil liberty a noble exercise of men's faculties [...]. In religion, liberty sees a companion for its battles and triumphs, the cradle of its infancy, the divine source of its rights. Liberty considers religion its customs' safeguard – customs such as guaranteeing rights and pledging its own duration.
>
> (Tocqueville 1835–40, part I, ch. 2)

In a culture that evolved this way, in contrast to European Protestant countries, there is even less place for a worldly ethic to compete with a religious one. Even today, American moral obedience prominently involves the community, rather than depending solely on an individual's relationship with his or her conscience. Rather than being separate, the ethic that regulates private relationships, particularly familial ones, is the same ethic that regulates public promises. The contrast or congruence between public and private behavior appears as both an indicator of character and a predictor of likely conduct in public life. Unlike the French, Americans can scarcely conceive that that a person could lack virtue in his or her family life and still act honorably in public life. This explains Americans' interest in their politicians' private morals, an interest that sometimes shocks the French.

Since its founders' time, or even since Tocqueville wrote his observations about it, American society has been influenced by secularization, but the latter has its limits: each banknote affirms 'In God We Trust.' In 2001, under dramatic circumstances – the September 11 attacks – the American president, George W. Bush, did not hesitate to entrust the nation to God's hands (Bush 2001). Moreover, the Industrial Revolution and nineteenth- and twentieth-century urban growth have eroded the effectiveness of concrete moral governance systems within local communities. Although much of the American population escaped these monitoring systems (primarily in the economic sphere) as they moved to take factory jobs and find other work large urban areas (Daly 1998, p. 40), the enduring touchstone lingers of a small-town community overseeing its members' morality, inspiring nostalgia for the local social ties of bygone days (Bellah et al. 1985). Furthermore, for reformers who have moralized about the recurrent economic crises that have marked the American economy since the days of the 'robber barons',[5] this model still remains a source of inspiration today, giving form to their propositions. During the mid-twentieth-century manufacturing boom, though, Americans transposed the supervisory body monitoring its denizens to the company: designed as a community, it took the place of the local, small-town (and religious) community.

This view of the company as moral community continued to expand as long as faith in the utility of virtue endured. And that faith seemed quite affirmatory once Americans introduced social monitoring processes that could make virtue pay off. In the United States at the beginning of the twentieth century, Max Weber observed that membership in a club, sect or secular association – one that paid attention to its members' morality – was a critical pledge of an individual's creditworthiness and success in business (Weber 1905, pp. 261, 268). Even today, the notion that honesty in business is worthwhile for the long term remains a central tenet of American business ethics. In all, Americans still share a vision of a society united around moral values; an individual's adherence to them proves his or her credibility – and creditworthiness – leading to success in the world.

The private character of morality in French society

At the end of the Ancien Régime (the political and social system that existed in France before the 1789 Revolution), the prevailing ethical conceptions were very different from those current in the United States during the same period. Although France called itself 'the Church's eldest daughter' and its monarch was supposed to defend the Catholic religion, in practice a worldly ethic based on honor competed with the Christian one. Earlier in the eighteenth century, Montesquieu wrote:

> In monarchical and moderate states, the power is limited by its very spring, I mean by honor, which, like a monarch, reigns over the prince and his people. They will not allege to their sovereign the laws of religion; a courtier would be apprehensive of rendering himself ridiculous. But the laws of honor will be appealed to on all occasions.
>
> (Montesquieu 1914, part I, III, 10)

This honor ethic differs from the Christian ethic by its precepts, and especially by the impulses it calls forth. The honor ethic is linked to the notion of *grandeur* or greatness and disdain for all that is low or common. Contrary to the Christian ethic, which subjects the prince and the peasant to the same laws, and claims to unite the faithful in a shared indignation towards sinners, the honor ethic's edicts vary greatly depending on one's place in society: bourgeois honor is not the same as aristocratic honor, men's not the same as women's. Honor is 'the prejudice of every person and rank' (Montesquieu 1914, part I, III, 6).

The honor ethic invites each person to cultivate whatever separates him or her from the common, base, or low.

> The virtues we are here taught are less what we owe to others than to ourselves; they are not so much what draws us towards society, as what distinguishes us from our fellow-citizens.
>
> (Montesquieu 1914, part I, IV, 2)

This concern with greatness affects the practice of apparently shared virtues in other contexts. Thus:

> Truth, therefore, in conversation is here [in monarchies] a necessary point. But is it for the sake of truth? By no means. Truth is requisite only because a person habituated to veracity has an air of boldness and freedom. And indeed a man of this stamp seems to lay a stress only on the things themselves, not on the manner in which they are received. Hence it is that in proportion as this kind of frankness is commended, that of the common people is despised, which has nothing but truth and simplicity for its object.
>
> (Montesquieu 1914, part I, IV, 2).

Similarly, 'politeness [...] arises from a desire of distinguishing ourselves. It is pride that renders us polite; we are flattered with being taken notice of for behaviour that shows we are not of a mean condition' (Montesquieu 1914, part I, IV, 2).

Furthermore, a person may be both a man or woman of honor and a libertine. While the reign of honor did not prevent pious souls from clinging to a Christian ethic, it prompted discretion about this attachment (see for example Rousseau's portrait of Parisian women in his *Confessions*). A witness to the times explained: 'When we were well-behaved, it was for personal reasons and not out of pedantry or prudery' (Taine 1986, p. 107). Obedience to the religious ethic came from inner convictions, not from a religious community (identified with a body politic) that monitored its members' behavior. At the same time, the French did not find in honor and self-interest a counterpart to the American alliance of virtue and self-interest. They perceived honor, even bourgeois honor, as motivating people to sacrifice their vulgar material interests to something higher, allowing people to rise above their station in life. Hence, when cultivated for a reason, honor became nothing more than a sham, a surface appearance, something that demeaned rather than elevated. The most noble thing could not serve the most common without demeaning itself.

The French Revolution and its heirs sought radical innovations, but fell short of their goals. Article 6 of France's Declaration of the Rights of Man alludes to virtue, a virtue founded on reason, on love of the public good. This was not a Christian virtue, but like it and unlike honor, it aimed to be universal, equally involving all humanity beyond what distinguishes one person from another. For some leaders of the French Revolution – Robespierre, Saint-Just – this virtue, linked to the religion of humanity, lay at the heart of the French Republic (Furet 1988, pp. 151–52). Many efforts were made to ensure its place in society; philosophers were considered its priests. These efforts continued well into the nineteenth century, when Jules Ferry and other leaders of the Third Republic (1870–1940) wanted to turn schools into tools to spread virtue.

Doubtless this morality, founded on reason, was not radically different in its precepts from the religion-inspired morality influencing the United States at the time; however, it had nowhere near the same place in society. The militant secularists certainly intended their morality to apply to all French citizens, but in practice it often remained in competition with the society's religious morality; most citizens remained 'unconverted'. The militant secularists of the first French Republic gave up their battle against religious morality, and found themselves defending no more than a 'secularist morality', thenceforth relegated to the private sphere, like religious morality. And like religious morality, secular morality came not from the control exercised by a community of 'believers' – citizens – but from each citizen's conscience. The period when the sans-culottes (radical militants from the lower classes) had claimed such control now appeared as an epoch of tyranny. Secular morality certainly provided the basis for laws; in doing so, it exercised indirect social control through citizen's compliance with the law. Indeed, the Napoleonic Code of 1804 replaced previous customs and feudal laws. But this obedience was not monitored under the seal of morality, only legality: in France, 'moral order' has sharply negative connotations to this day.

During the Third Republic, the individual's relationship with society – still influenced by the honor ethic – strongly affected prevailing conceptions of duty in the nineteenth century, just as it does today. The bourgeoisie's triumph struck a heavy blow to the aristocratic ethos and view of an honorable mode of life; but this did not hold for honor's role in the conception of duty (Iribarne 1989). Today, ethics remain linked to the idea of greatness, the goal being to raise oneself up rather than to strive for the public good. Every political or professional body – doctors, lawyers, engineers, public administrators at all levels – sees itself as the principal judge of its members' compliance with its particular ethic; each remains averse to a common jurisdiction's involvement in what it considers its internal affairs. Thus, in contrast to practice in the United States, France's administrative tribunals and highest jurisdiction, the Conseil d'État (Council of State) play a considerable role in assessing administrative actions.

Many French, uneasy with the term 'ethics', prefer to talk about 'deontology', meaning professional ethics; they perceive legal obedience in different tones and terms from ethical obedience.[6] Traditionally, conceptions of the prince's honor strongly influenced the ethicality of a prince's actions (or those of any person in power). Thus, the French accept a form of duplicity if it is associated with grand designs and not base ones. Montesquieu declared that: 'Honor allows of cunning and craft, when joined with the notion of greatness of soul or importance of affairs; as, for instance, in politics, with finesses of which it is far from being offended' (Montesquieu 1914, part I, IV, 2).

This point of view finds ample illustration in former French president General de Gaulle's duplicitous actions in Algeria; he publicly maintained he would fight to keep it a French colony up to the day he granted the country its independence from France. Or former French president François Mitterrand: he published false bulletins about his robust health as he fought cancer in private during his term, justifying his lies as being for the good of the people.

In France, the attitude persists that those who devote themselves to the lowest pursuits (such as seeking wealth) remain ill-placed to judge the ethics of those who pursue higher ones (for example practicing a profession) and who maintain a strong sense of the inherent duties such pursuits entail.

Business ethics assessed by American and French views of social ethics

In this section we will specifically consider how different conceptions of ethics and their place in social life, as described above, help us understand the American approach to business ethics and the French reluctance to embrace it.

The American company as a moral and commercial community

Business ethics found fertile ground in the legacy of America's New England colonial society, where the pursuit of self-interest and obedience to strict principles were supposed to be 'naturally' related – where defense of common interests and unity through moral values 'naturally' combined as the foundation of community. A company simultaneously constitutes an economic unit and a moral community. As an economic unit, its right to defend its interests coincides with its duty – as a moral community – to supervise its members.

Once the observer grasps this point, Americans' intense focus on values – so shocking to the French – no longer surprises. If we look at American firms' ethical codes, or those of British firms strongly marked by an American influence, ethics and the pursuit of interests are tied on two levels: a good reputation, founded on great integrity, is a fundamental element of business success, and this success generates resources needed to do good. For instance, the American oil major Exxon Mobil Corporation claims on its website, under the heading 'International Anti-corruption Efforts', that 'At ExxonMobil, our Standards of Business Conduct require that all employees comply with all laws and uphold the highest business integrity', claiming that 'corporate policy requires strict observance of all laws and follows the course of highest integrity' and 'A well-founded reputation for scrupulous dealing is itself a priceless company asset' (ExxonMobil 2011b). The chief executive of the British energy company BP presented its business policies following BP's merger with rival Amoco, claiming from the start that 'A good business should be both competitively successful and a force for good.' Among his corporation's fundamental values, he declared that 'a belief in honest exchange and an awareness that a strong reputation is essential for business success' (BP 2011). An article in *Fortune* magazine claims that 'In tough times, it's all the more important to remember that ethics pay off in the end, and on the bottom line', before supporting this claim with a mass of data, including a comparison of share price trends for a 'list of major companies that paid a lot of attention to ethical standards' and the stock market values of these Dow Jones Industrial Index companies (Labich 1992).

We found this same view in statements made by American managers at Total whom we interviewed:

> I think that this code of conduct concept is what you want to promote [...]. You need to stress integrity and honesty [...] and if you make this part of cultural development then [...] those with whom you conduct external business will appreciate it [...]. Our ability to succeed in business often relies on our reputation...so I'm particularly sensitive to maintaining a good level of support in terms of requiring our people to meet the required standards.
>
> (Iribarne 2002)

In the interviewee's moral language and worldview, employees form a community whose members police the rectitude of both their own actions and those of their colleagues. Another American interviewee confirms this view:

> I don't know if I give much help but it's a collective effort. We are all part of the [firm's] integrity and honesty; you have to have both of them to be successful. If you don't have any of those standards, with a high standard of integrity – and hopefully we have grown up with that – then you are not going to be successful.
>
> (Iribarne 2002)

In American codes of conduct or business ethics, and the British ones they inspire, the word 'we' indiscriminately refers to the enterprise as such and to all of its employees, the central actors in any ethical engagement:

> Exxon Mobil Corporation is committed to being the world's premier petroleum and petrochemical company. To that end, we must continuously achieve superior financial and operating results while simultaneously adhering to the highest standards of business conduct.
>
> (ExxonMobil 2011b)

> BP wants to be recognised as a great company – competitively successful and a force for progress. We have a fundamental belief that we can make a difference in the world. We help the world meet its growing need for heat, light and mobility. We strive to do that by producing energy that is affordable, secure and doesn't damage the environment.
>
> At the core of BP is an unshakeable commitment to human progress. Our products and services are creating the freedom to move, to be warm, to be cool, to see and enjoy a better quality of life. We believe this freedom is inseparable from the responsibility to produce and consume our products in ways that respect both human rights and natural environments.
>
> (BP 2011)

In this view, Americans (and their British counterparts) emphasize an ethical approach shared by all company members – not a chain of responsibility that descends from top management, where each employee is concerned only with his or her own responsibilities and does not take on those of colleagues. Although this top-down chain applies in other aspects of American management, when it comes to ethics all employees are responsible for all they see; they cannot say 'That's none of my business.' This ethical tone provides a communitarian counterpoint to the contractual language that dominates elsewhere. The entire community within the company works to ensure legal compliance, which represents only part of the ethical approach – and not the main part; all employees care about fulfilling the company's legal responsibility. Under these conditions, everything that French employees would regard as 'tattling' or 'informing', American employees see as the normal exercise of their responsibility. An American manager explains:

> Could be [that] every employee is required to advise the company [...]. The concept is that if something is going on which is unethical, you have access, and the access is someone anonymous whom you can talk with...[...]. I think you have to have a procedure where employees can report unethical issues. I mean you know. It is just to put everything on the table.
>
> (Iribarne 2002)

The American manager frames this approach as helping managers to do their job correctly: 'Not every manager can be aware of unethical practices that are going on, and they should be given a fair opportunity to know...in a practical manner' (Iribarne 2002). A company may be seen as a commercial community founded to defend its interests; when all employees uphold ethical standards, that counts as an asset. It also serves the company's responsibility as a moral community charged with guiding its members on the path to the good. Therefore, it follows that Americans have two reasons to hold every employee accountable for rectitude and to impose sanctions if he or she strays from the right path.

Senior executives serve the company by defending ethics as a source of its reputation – as an asset – in line with their responsibility to shareholders; they also serve its moral mission in measure with the leadership they exercise in the community; they teach the gospel by setting an example (Peters and Waterman 1982). Since Americans do not perceive these two roles – defender of interests and preacher of morality – as conflicting in any way, their co-existence bothers no one, in contrast to how the French would respond.

French rejection of the American approach to business ethics

The historical factors that ground American companies' legitimate use of ethics to control and supervise employees do not exist in France, nor are the French ready to extend the same legitimacy to companies. This explains their reluctance to embrace American-style business ethics. The French do not share Americans' conviction that ethics and self-interest naturally go together well. The legitimacy of any company playing a leading role in ethics, as a corporate body represented by its management, seems especially dubious. French employees have difficulty seeing companies as more responsible for supervising ethics than they are themselves; they question the very notion. Isn't the company subject to its economic objectives, a kind of cold monster devoid of honor that situates itself clearly on the side of its own interests? Doesn't management, accountable for these interests, sometimes naturally put pressure on the company's members to act in unethical ways? Isn't it really up to the employees to claim an ethical point of view supported by an elevated vision of their job? 'Today, they [management] scare you but then say business must go on', claimed a French manager we interviewed (Iribarne 2002). In these conditions, the company appears out of place in claiming to play a role in ethics. Some French managers take a radical stance: 'The company's sphere and the ethics sphere remain two distinct areas; ethics are an individual's personal business. I do not see how a company can have an ethic', and 'Ethics are a person's value, not a company's' (Iribarne 2002).

There is, of course, a basis for ethical conduct in any French firm, but French employees see ethics stemming from free pursuit of individual notions of duty, rather than from the actions of a community that strictly controls its members, supervising and sanctioning them. This holds whether one speaks of a religious ethic that depends on personal conscience, or an honor ethic that requires that a person not stoop low to commit a dubious act, or even an honorable act performed under duress. The French see individuals, supported by their own convictions, as the carriers of ethical conduct. Our French interviewees gave a chorus of examples: 'Everyone talks about ethics. For me, ethics is the way each person perceives things and behaves as best he or she can.' 'I have my own conscience and it is sufficient.' 'The lack of a code didn't make us less ethical' (Iribarne 2002). This emphasis on a personal ethic leads employees to see external pressure, especially from management, as outside of the field of ethics. 'We fall into a deal made by management, the censor and the others if we make someone else responsible for our responsibilities. You have to make your own commitment to ethics' (Iribarne 2002).

While ethics are generally seen as one entity in the United States, linking honesty in management, benevolence in the community, and discipline in personal life, French distinctions between types of ethics prove much clearer, resulting in two different spheres. One sphere includes all that concerns the firm and managerial rectitude, even if it is left up to employee-members to commit themselves individually. Another sphere covers all that is 'private' life, where French employees truly cannot tolerate company meddling. A French manager explained, 'In the French system, we want to protect our personal life and we try to separate personal from professional life. [...] It's not the same for Anglo-Americans' (Iribarne 2002). For instance, the French remain highly critical of the way American companies try to 'indoctrinate' their employees in collective expressions of good feelings, going beyond purely managerial requirements. A French manager explains:

> Americans [...] contribute a lot to charitable organizations and non-profits – that's their involvement in local communities. In American companies' internal newsletters, we often see the CEO going off to wash cars to raise money for good causes. That is *very* American. They do it – it's not just pretty words, they actually do it. But for us [the French], that has no impact on us, the context isn't the same, the culture isn't the same – for us, that wouldn't work.
>
> (Iribarne 2002)

In French culture, it is necessary to distinguish between the firm and the individual. A French manager notes, 'Helping charitable organizations or contributing money *as a company*, okay, but having people get involved *personally*, no'[7] (Iribarne 2002). In the same way, a company cannot legitimately meddle in issues perceived as a matter of personal choice. Several of the managers we spoke with were critical of American practices, citing, for example, how American companies forbid staff to drink wine with lunch in the company cafeteria where security is not an issue (Iribarne 2002).

French workers see this American attitude – lumping what the French consider different ethical registers into a single ethos – as the expression of a 'moralizing' approach, one that almost becomes a 'catechism'; this reaction reflects a refusal to allow a religion-based morality to regulate what comes within public life. As one petrochemical manager put it, 'We must not fall into the out-of-control moralizing [of Anglo-American codes]; Exxon is famous for that; […] of course, behind the ethic there are general moral principles, but that is no reason to make it a catechism' (Iribarne 2002).

The French do not show off their ethics

The French find it difficult to accept that a company displays its values. They show a sort of modesty or reserve about the subject – even those who believe that a firm, just like an individual, may possess values. The French managers we interviewed demonstrated this reserve in their responses:

> In this company, we have very strong values that are not seen in the document [the draft business conduct code], but we don't talk about these values; they are implicit […] When it comes to values – needless to say – they come from one's upbringing, deep down.
>
> (Iribarne 2002)

The interviewee has a very clear idea of these implicit values, however:

> The company's strong, long-time values are not communicated. […] It's not about making a profit at all costs. Deep down, the company cares about developing employee careers, about the long term. The group takes pretty good care of the widows and orphans, so to speak.[8]
>
> (Iribarne 2002)

The French interviewees consider that if the company has an ethic, it is inappropriate to display it. They emphasized the breadth of this gap with American business culture.

> We don't see this [business ethics] code posted in the [CEO's] office, although the CEO of Exxon might do that; he may even be obliged to!
>
> (Iribarne 2002)

> We have already seen this way of showing off values in our contacts with the United States; we hesitated to make our own version of values [for a subsidiary], and in the French context, we didn't do it in the end.
>
> (Iribarne 2002)

A flaunting of ethical positions readily comes across as insincere. From the French perspective, the self-interested, highly 'unnatural' character of such displays invalidates what they stand for, prompting skepticism and irony. We see this clearly in the responses of various French managers: 'If the company really does this, it's great. But there is our very French reaction: we are never excited, never naïve, always a little critical, and skeptical. It's cultural.' The interviewees talk about the risk of hypocrisy run by a person or company in showing off their ethical intentions, if their actions are not irreproachable. 'You have to show it's not a gimmick; that it's not meant to hide something […]. [Otherwise] there will be laughter in the press and smirking in-house.' 'Outside the company, the need is very ambiguous. Media relations in France are difficult; everyone can turn against you' (Iribarne 2002).

The enterprise that proclaims its ethics may face suspicions that it wants to 'clear its name' for (possibly problematic) past actions, or 'to stop media accusations'. Internally, 'employees are caught between two attitudes: you must have rules, but at the same time it's an externally directed display to satisfy ethical [investment] funds, etc. There is the suspicion of covering over reality' (Iribarne 2002).

French interviewees demonstrate a strong desire to not be taken in, to neither fool themselves nor see the world in a childlike way. 'It is naïve to pretend we can reconcile all of the major ethical maxims with our businesses' requirements; we dream of making them compatible. This tends to weaken the impact of the message.' '"We reject corruption" […] – for a Latin temperament that is very naïve' (Iribarne 2002). In other words, it is not that the company should do nothing; it is good to seek a 'spirit' or 'culture', but also necessary for managers to look at things clearly and remain aware of the world's complexity.

> Emphasizing ethics is a good thing, but we should show we are not kidding ourselves, that we are not stonewalling, that we realize reality isn't so pretty, but that this is the spirit in which we mean to work. Communication must show that we consider people adults, that we want to have a culture […] The company has to communicate and show that it doesn't think people are children. Say that we know it's easy to say, but that the circumstances are very complicated sometimes.
>
> (Iribarne 2002)

The French reaction to sanctions

The French interviewees' reluctance to view their companies as drivers of ethical behavior includes a rejection of American means of motivating employees to uphold ethical standards; indeed, they reject all measures enforcing an ethical approach – even the word 'enforce- ment' is a loaded term. At best, they view the enterprise as capable of prompting employees' sense of their own duty. 'The company should make employees aware that there are laws, rules, an ethic, that people should adhere to of their own volition', one manager noted (Iribarne 2002). For the French employees, any action that acknowledges the company as a driver of ethical behavior appears debatable at best, or shocking at worst. The French employees find it especially hard to accept the American view that companies should imple- ment procedures that make every employee 'accountable' – an American notion – for breaching ethical standards, thereby prodding them into acting correctly. When it is a matter of legal compliance, French employees find it natural that the firm – responsible for follow- ing the law – looks, in turn, to its staff and asks them to answer for their actions, but ethics come under another jurisdiction. The French managers are eloquent on the subject:

> The Anglo-Americans are very careful about the way all that is going to be applied, careful of legalities. It must all be precisely defined in order to mean anything. They think of it almost in terms of a contract. There are other countries where people have very negative reactions to applying a code of business ethics too formally. At Exxon, they go much further; they have to sign a declaration each year. That's going too far.
>
> (Iribarne 2002)

In the French interviewees' view, each person – responsible for his or her own ethics – is best equipped to evaluate situations, taking account of their complexity; once again, this attitude leads them to oppose American notions:

> Our company asks the heads of its subsidiaries to consider where [in which country] they are located; that's the opposite of American companies who arrive with a doctrinal code, and little room to change it [...] Either you can choose the American way, or you can trust that employees' intelligence will lead them to act appropriately.
>
> (Iribarne 2002)

We also found a strong resistance to the idea of sanctions for ethical code violations; again, American methods are rejected by a French manager: 'In the United States, there are sanctions and in Europe, not a word about them. [...] Code and sanction must be separated' (Iribarne 2002). Even raising the subject of sanctions creates a high risk that employees will reject the entire approach, as one manager notes:

> Here [in France], if we suggest hypothetical sanctions, no one will accept it – it's not part of our cultural model. It would cause rejection; for me, it wouldn't work. Even if we are in an international company, we follow a very French approach. Writing a paragraph about sanctions would cause people to reject [the code and the whole approach]. They would say, 'We're going to be policed.'
>
> (Iribarne 2002)

The French interviewees find it normal to punish lawbreakers, but for them, ethics means something different to obeying the law:

> It's not at all part of our culture to talk about sanctions in writing; we say that we obey laws and regulations, that there are legal sanctions; we do not say that an employee who runs afoul of the law will be protected. Punishment will be given – there's no need to write it out.
>
> (Iribarne 2002)

French interviewees' negative attitude toward sanctions sometimes joins with their sharp critique of a (implicitly unethical) tendency of Anglo-American companies: throwing their responsibility back onto employees. 'At Mobil, the code served to cover the company – management's idea was, we don't want to know what you do, and if you get caught, you signed the code, you will be fired' (Iribarne 2002). These reactions to sanctions may sharply differ for individuals working in an environment defined by honor ethics versus religious ones. In the latter, enforcement helps the sinner make amends and get back on the path to goodness, while in the world of honor, the penalty proves a source of humiliation. Furthermore, sanctions imply monitoring to identify infractions. There again, American and French customs differ, as an American manager explains:

> In an American company, management requires blood tests on a regular basis to verify that employees are not taking drugs, etc. [...].This company [Total] is not going to listen to private conversations in employees' offices, or monitor emails. [...]. It would have the right to in the United States.
>
> (Iribarne 2002)

Furthermore, the idea of asking employees to alert management to colleagues' unethical behavior provokes radically different reactions in France compared to the United States. While Americans may perceive this as a civic duty, the French view such informing on colleagues as highly condemnable:

> I wondered if they were going to implement what the Anglo-Americans call 'whistle-blowing': when an employee notices that ethical standards are breached, he can call a kind of toll-free number to confidentially report it…Here, without talking about whistle-blowing, they say that any employee may ask a question, but they don't say how […]. How can we be sure that it has nothing to do with denunciation, with informing on colleagues? In the United States, there's a toll-free number to denounce people who don't follow ethical standards. That's informing on them…It's better not to have that – afterwards, it turns into something horrible.
>
> (Iribarne 2002)

Towards a French approach to business ethics

As in the preceding sections, the French perspective on the 'right' way to approach business ethics discussed below further demonstrates the cultural divide between two very different worldviews. The French managers' sharp criticism of American business-ethics practices – exceptionally sharp compared to the criticism we usually see in our international research on cultural encounters within companies – reflects the subject's sensitivity and the gap separating American and French attitudes. This point proves even more striking given that the French managers interviewed generally had spent considerable time working with American firms; they spoke from experience, not hearsay. They saw the typical American company attempting to create a moral community that keeps each of its members on the right track, linking its own prosperity to its members' reputation for integrity, and boasting about this reputation – a conception foreign to French culture. The latter prescribes that each employee be guided by the elevated idea he or she has of the duties of the job, rather than the somewhat petty sphere of self-interest or an excessive attachment to all that falls within it. French culture also asserts that the way employees (and all citizens) behave in public has no relation to their private virtues.

All of this raises some questions: Does this mean that managers of multinationals cannot seriously establish business ethics in France? Are business ethics destined to become mere public-relations exercises, targeted at ethical investment funds – funds whose selections may affect the company's share price – without having any real impact on the way the company operates? Or rather than applying American-style business ethics, should managers of companies in France create their own form of ethics, adapted to the cultural context? We have already found many signs of such adaptations in French companies, but they do not yet make these adaptations systematically. Although the French employees we interviewed appear little disposed to allow their company to dictate their view of right and wrong, or to slip into their private lives, they appear very sensitive to the idea of responsibility (which creates duties) tied to prominent positions and power. As they feel they hold such responsibilities commensurate with their place in the firm, they can easily extend this attitude to the corporate body. While they feel ill at ease talking about ethics, they do not mind talking about work-related responsibilities. Even if the two notions overlap in many ways, the second aligns better than the first with the French worldview of the public sphere.

Some French multinationals have developed ethical statements that prove particularly well-adapted to these cultural conceptions. For example, we may examine a document from the French water company, Suez Lyonnaise des Eaux, entitled 'The Group's Values'. It uses phrases such as the following:

> We make a commitment to our clients, shareholders and especially ourselves: Our place and our ambition to be a global leader [...] obligates us to not only be good professionals, but the best.
>
> (GDF Suez 2000)

In this wording, we see a perfect expression of the honor ethic, tied to the duties implied by the company's ranking, duties to others and – above all – to itself. This ethic finds an echo in the words of a Total (France) manager we interviewed:

> Companies the size of our new group [Total merged with Elf] [...] since they often have powers greater than those of certain countries, are not going to behave in a purely commercial way, like our competitors can allow themselves to [...] It is normal that we have rules that are a little above the rest [...] We must lead on this subject and not follow the others.
>
> (Iribarne 2002)

If the company wants to be worthy of its superior position, its 'size', 'power' and perceived greatness impose duties on it. These duties forbid the company from behaving 'in a purely commercial [not to say base] way', even if supposedly lesser competitors may do so, requiring the company – and by extension the employees – be 'above other companies'. We have gathered many statements from French interviewees along the same lines: 'When we expand somewhere new, we cannot content ourselves with using local labor laws, because we are [XYZ company]'. 'We have to remember the size of the company, our sense of responsibility.' 'We also have our gentlemen's ethic' (Iribarne 2002).

Furthermore, we find adaptations to the cultural context in the way French companies present employee duties. Where the English-language version of a French corporation's business code of conduct will say, 'Every employee is required to take the necessary measures', the French-language version says, 'Every collaborator takes necessary measures' (TotalElfFina 2000). The English version is not afraid to present the firm as requiring ethical conduct; by contrast, the French version avoids requiring anything – every employee appears to adopt such behavior on his or her own initiative.[9]

Under these conditions, what ethical role might companies play in France? We would argue that it is not negligible. The French generally expect a corporation to act in a 'socially responsible' way, commensurate with the place it occupies in society and well beyond simply complying with its legal obligations. In addition, a company may play a large part in each staff member's behavior, but this role does not reflect the American conception. To adapt to the French context, we suggest that a company focus less on monitoring and punishing than on helping employees develop their situational intelligence for use when ethical dilemmas arise. Employees often face such dilemmas at work, especially when the company plunges them into a situation in a foreign country where local practices prove very different from those that prevail in France. Just how far must expatriated employees adapt to the situation, whether in the name of realism or in rejection of cultural imperialism, and where must they refuse to compromise? We do not lack extreme cases. For instance, a European manager recounts conflicts over the correct approach to child labor in partner countries:

> Child labor? In Thailand, they use baby labor. Our shareholders would be offended to learn that we use such workers, even if Thais present it as a necessity for local residents. We have an obligation to uphold a larger ethical framework.
>
> (Iribarne 2002)

In these types of circumstance, although the company did not have the authority to dictate employee behavior, the company was welcome to help its employees think things through – individually and collectively – when they confronted difficult situations. And while these employees would also react adversely if the company required peers to inform on one another, they would respond with equivalent favor to wise advice.

From fighting corruption to showing respect for employees

The fight against corruption

The excuse of a 'cultural exception', often invoked to dispense with anti-corruption measures, proves increasingly unacceptable in international business circles and elsewhere. However, we see many questions about how anti-corruption efforts should accommodate cultural differences. The World Bank, fully aware of this issue, struggles to provide an adequate response; in one of a series of papers 'dedicated to summarizing good practice' (Berstein and Arvis 2002),[10] the Bank states that 'research does not support claims that American-style compliance systems encounter strong resistance in other cultures' (Berstein and Arvis 2002). However, the report immediately qualifies this finding:

> The challenge for companies is to formulate core principles and implement credible procedures adapted to local business cultures. In particular, for companies operating in industries with substantial local ownership (as is common in China), the need to adapt training, dissemination, and information systems to local customs is more than an intellectual exercise.
>
> (Berstein and Arvis 2002, p. 1)

The purity ethic and the loyalty ethic[11]

We find it useful to distinguish two types of ethical ideal. The first, which we will call a 'purity ethic', fosters individual 'goodness': one must be pure, dignified and compliant with a transcendent ideal, whether following a religious law, code of honor, or universal principles.[12] These ideals underpin an individual sense of duty; one's relationship with others provides the substance.[13] Correspondingly, each person has a duty to others – humanity in general, outsiders, even enemies. The pledge of a reward – from God, the gods, reason – turns duty's obligations into actions, even in the absence of external supervision.

By contrast, a second ideal – 'loyalty ethics' – promotes a person's loyalty to the groups he or she belongs to – family, clan, brotherhood, crony network, and so forth. A group member must prove his or her total willingness to give the group everything – time, possessions, and even one's life; however, any behavior is permissible vis-à-vis outsiders. If a group member fails in loyalty, he or she will suffer the group's vengeance rather than the outrage of a transcendent authority. The group will implement means of control and retaliation, including hidden measures that escape external observation.

We can characterize these ethics in various ways. The nature of one's duty contrasts purity (or virtuous) ethics to loyalty ethics; the scope of obligations opposes universalism to relativism; and the nature of supervisory bodies differs in the ethics of transcendence versus the ethics of immanence. In practice, these three dimensions are strongly linked. A universalist ethic – drawing on the transcendent ideals of purity ethics – entails obligations to others even when they have no retaliatory power over the individual; such an ethic can hardly function without a transcendent supervisory body. In many European cultures (more in Northern than Southern Europe), various forms of ethics grounded on principles are the norm. However, in some other parts of the world, purity ethics are not the norm. At one extreme, the loyalty ethic reigns without many challengers in most Sub-Saharan African cultures; it largely accounts for the feeling of strangeness that foreigners often experience in these societies. Outsiders find it disturbing to see tasks they perceive as strictly fulfilling professional duties interpreted in terms of personal relationships. South Americans also prize this ethic of loyalty to one's own, bound by close alliances, families and crony networks. However, their loyalty ethic coexists with a form of purity ethics, based on (mostly religious) principles; the latter attract most South Americans, even if purity ethics do not really govern their lives. Given their fondness for principles, most South Americans will not immediately suspect that a person striving to comply with a purity ethic might have a hidden agenda. Instead, that person will inspire genuine respect, even from people who do not follow the same teachings. Similarly, Moroccan society professes a religious tenet of respecting principles, even though this usually plays only a marginal role in business. Moroccans who make decisions based on their rectitude inspire respect, even from those who act in opposing ways (Iribarne 2007).

A moral condemnation of corruption carries the greatest weight in cultures whose prevailing ethic rests on principles. In such places, the value given to the general precepts of honesty anchors values that relate to company operations – rules for selecting staff and vendors, evaluating a subordinate's performance, punishing safety violations, and so forth. Within this type of principle-based ethics, employees find it sensible to refuse to compromise these precepts or rules on behalf of a special, binding relationship – a parent, friend or member of a mutual aid circle. This is the type of ethic where – in the name of professional duty – it makes sense for employees to refuse the temptation of payoffs that would otherwise let the employee assist relatives and fulfill a duty to support them.

These behaviors, undoubtedly laudable in a society where a purity ethic prevails, become much more questionable in a society where a loyalty ethic predominates (Banfield 1958). Where the latter prevails, acting in an 'honest' way, according to principle-based standards, may appear to mean that loyalty to the firm trumps that to family or friends. Moreover, since such a preference often seems scarcely credible to the 'betrayed', they readily suspect the 'betrayer' of having hidden motives, such as wanting to keep the firm's exploitable advantages for him or herself. Or the betrayed may suspect that the betrayer does not really have the power he or she claims, such as in hiring decisions. The betrayed may believe the betrayer is naturally 'mean'. In a society guided by a loyalty ethic, it would appear more in keeping with ethical conduct to accept various forms of 'corruption' than to refuse them. The person who 'betrays' his or her own circle risks severe penalties, ranging from ostracism to witchcraft.

How to fight corruption where the dominant cultural ethic is loyalty to one's own

Differences between an ethic based on principles and one based on loyalty to one's own circle should strongly affect the way firms organize their anti-corruption efforts. Where a purity ethic and respect for principles prevail, employees' honesty is self-motivated. Of course, management must find ways to monitor and enforce employee behavior to prevent ambiguities from arising along the practical boundary of illicit versus licit actions; such controls should also help prevent the less scrupulous from gradually leading others astray. We would argue that these means of enforcement should have a secondary role and must avoid becoming counter-productive, as could happen if they insult the most upright employees. Most of the benchmark management practices now used worldwide were designed for this cultural context. Firms count on the majority of their employees strongly internalizing a principle-based ethics.

However, in cultures where loyalty ethics prevail, managers should not expect employees to spontaneously comply with such principles. In extreme cases where the loyalty ethic enjoys an almost complete monopoly, local culture does not even treat corruption as such. Rather, the corruption's stigma comes from outside the local culture, or at least from the influence of an external point of view. When loyalty and purity ethics intermingle, the value employees give to respecting principles may prove strong enough to prompt them to talk about corruption, but not strong enough to provide a powerful barrier against it. Does this mean that societies where a loyalty ethic prevails are irremediably doomed to corruption? Does it mean that to fight corruption effectively, firms must change local culture – an indubitably utopian project? In reality, the situation is not so bleak.

In such societies, firms must protect employees working in positions where temptations exist, and must keep family and friend pressures at bay. These employees must be able to show their circle that they refuse demands not because they lack loyalty, but because they cannot do otherwise without getting into serious trouble. Such an approach prevails in Sub-Saharan Africa, for example in traditional savings institutions known as *tontines* (Henry et al. 1991). The *tontine* administrators severely punish any member who does not fulfill his or her savings obligations. This threat of sanctions allows the saver to justify saving money to family and friends when they demand immediate financial assistance. More generally, in loyalty-based cultures, a firm should set up strict, closely-monitored procedures to create boundaries for all employee work susceptible to corruption.

Employees will not perceive such strict controls the same way in a culture dominated by a loyalty ethic as in one dominated by a purity ethic. In cultures where the latter predominates, employees will perceive all verifications as evidence of mistrust. Such distrust proves particularly insulting to employees following an ethic of honor; it may prove more acceptable in cultures where a religiously-inspired ethic predominates, since employees will accept the notion that humans are naturally sinners and must be controlled. Managers' very different reactions to verifications in France compared to the United States illustrate this phenomenon, as noted above. On the other hand, when an ethic of loyalty to one's own prevails, no one takes offense at the force the group – or the firm – uses to check up on its members. Members accept such audits all the more positively, since members who succumb to their circle's solicitations do not necessarily do so wholeheartedly; they find it hard to refuse without credible reasons. In these situations, employees may find the firm's supervision quite positive, as it furnishes reasons to resist others' demands. This is also true where a loyalty ethic competes with a purity ethic, as in an Argentinian case we will examine. When systematic checks protect employees from their circles' demands, employees avoid many 'temptations' and 'internal conflicts', and consider the verifications 'helpful', an 'aid' and source of 'comfort'. In addition to stringent checks, a careful division of responsibility may also help protect employees from hard-to-resist pressures, by making it impossible for an individual to authorize favors for outside friends on his or her sole authority.[14]

When purity and loyalty ethics share an equal weight in a culture, managers should nudge them to run in the same direction rather than in conflict. The more the firm constitutes a strong group with intensely loyal members, the more employees' membership carries obligations that outweigh – or at least counterbalance – obligations to other groups. Furthermore, the more a firm shows solidarity with its employees' other groups, for example their families or local communities, the more employees will feel that their loyalties to the latter coincide with company loyalty.

At times, the great religiously-driven moral precepts constitute benchmarks for society, but apply to business very unevenly. A certain ethical wavering arises, combining clear principles with an uncertain application. In these situations, firms must provide a bridge between principles and practices. We will see how the Argentinian subsidiary of a French multinational succeeded in doing this.

An anti-corruption approach in Argentina

Argentina suffers from a fair amount of corruption, in politics and business alike. Some firms have effectively tackled corruption. By studying one successful Argentinian company's policies, we were able to see how its success rested on adapting its approach to the local cultural context.[15]

The company had three divisions; in the relatively recent past, two divisions had experienced pronounced levels of corruption. At first sight, the instruments that management used to address corruption and get back on the right track do not seem unusual. The human resources department made great efforts to hire upright people, dismissing corrupt employees and those who had insinuated themselves into situations of conflicting interests; these dismissals served as an example, particularly when managers were fired from important positions. The firm's main division established a set of tools: a 'contracts committee' to monitor purchasing decisions that exceeded a set value; a code of conduct that covered corruption and conflicts of interest at great length; and an 'ethical advisor' available to all employees to help resolve questions about interpreting values and ethical principles.

Yet closer inspection of these tools and their use reveals many traits that have nothing in common with US-style ethics enforcement tools. For instance, the ethical advisor occupies an awkward position. The advisor does not constitute some kind of ethical counterweight independent of the firm's upper management, but rather is a member of it. In one of the company's three divisions, the integration proves even stronger. A member of the board of directors notes, 'When we talk about these things, we take off our director hat and put on our ethical committee hat' (Iribarne 2007). In the US model, whistleblowers contact a department independent of the firm's upper management, and accusations are relayed to the board of directors anonymously; by contrast, the Argentinian whistleblower must identify him or herself to the firm's human resources director.

These differences made us wonder how the Argentinian firm adapted a so-called 'universal' approach to the specificities of Argentinian culture's ethical benchmarks. We found Argentinians torn between the two ethical ideals discussed above. On the one hand, a purity ethic founded on religion and honor contrasts what is good or evil, honest or dishonest. Simultaneously, a loyalty ethic marks Argentinian society's daily life; here a strong solidarity rules, for better or – sometimes – worse. Doubtless, the coexistence of a commitment to principles and a requirement of loyalty to one's own has a universal character. However, it proves particularly challenging in the Argentinian context. Unlike other societies, in Argentina we observed no shared view of the circumstances where one or the other of these two logics should prevail.

The business world notoriously lacks shared conceptions of the border between good and evil; very strict conceptions coexist with very lax ones, depending on the individual employee. These wavering benchmarks make it difficult to move from grand principles and strong ethical precepts at a very abstract – not to say philosophical – level to a set of rules effectively enforced by systems of social control, systems that draw the line between honesty and dishonesty in a variety of concrete situations. When management shows lax interpretations of high principles in a given milieu, employees have no interiorized conceptions of their own with which to resist that moral negligence. Frequently, employees' solidarity with groups of 'friends' takes precedence over principles; this leads to organized corruption within the firm, founded on a network of complicity. Meanwhile, many employees have doubts about what is 'good'. They are aware of many different views about what constitutes the practical line between good and evil, and readily believe they are on the right side. However, they also feel anxious about being unsure of the line, so they seek an external frame of reference that can remove their doubts and reassure them.

The company we examined tried to enlist the logic of group solidarity in its anti-corruption efforts; it also used a combination of enforcement and sanctions to fight corrupt networks. Instead of allowing an honesty principle and group membership to compete for employee adherence, the firm sought a situation where these two contradictory influences could move its employees in the same direction. The company tried to develop a kind of virtuous network within the organization, using traditional anti-corruption tools and adapting them to meet its objective.

In this situation, where the practical consequences of following grand principles remained particularly uncertain, the firm had to 'continually define the limits of…what is good… and bad', noted an Argentinian manager. Generally, promulgating a code of ethics will easily clarify such matters. However, in Argentina, finding an appropriate place for such a code proves no easy task. If the code simply declares principles without going into detail, it competes with what each employee learned early in life, leading the employee to reject or ignore it. Thus we saw that it was better for management to set precise limits in writing; in this way, lax interpretations of principles may be avoided. However, if a firm wants to close all loopholes, managers must set up tighter safeguards. The division of the firm that we observed put its Code of Conduct (*Principios de Ética*) at the center of anti-corruption efforts. (Each division had its own code.) The Code included a 'Declaration of Values and Ethical Principles (*Declaración de Valores y Principios Éticos*) that summarizes both in two small pages. Despite the Declaration's brevity, it expresses the firm's rejection of corruption in unusual detail:

> [The company] prohibits its employees from offering, requesting or accepting any kind of bonus, favor, gift, money, bribe or compensation (*incentivo, obsequio, dadivo, dinero, sobornno o recompensa*) that may be interpreted as a reward for acts related to his or her work for the firm.

> (Iribarne 2007)

The series of words used to describe the various forms corruption may take makes sense in such a context, spelling out corruption beyond euphemisms. However, such a radical vision does not easily enter everyday mores; an Argentinian manager notes, 'A desktop alarm clock can be a present – I do not think that it is an ethical lapse to accept a present of this kind from a supplier' (Iribarne 2007). In these conditions, a firm committing benchmarks to paper will not relieve employees' need to interpret the text, leaving them to struggle with doubts. That is where the 'ethical advisor' plays a crucial role. The executives and managers we interviewed had a very subjective view of ethics and often referred to their 'doubts', to points that were not 'clear', to situations that 'may be interpreted' as a conflict of interest, to what everyone 'believes', what 'seems' good or evil, what 'may not be' transparent, what is 'considered' bad, or 'frowned upon'. The ethical advisor helped employees who questioned good or bad actions find an answer to their concerns and regain their 'peace of mind'. The ethical advisor relied on a collegial structure of peers. The highly involved human resources director could have his own doubts; in such cases, the ethical advisor turned to these peers to set ethical benchmarks collectively. In addition, the parent company's international ethics committee constituted a 'defining' body that the local ethical advisor could consult, 'to resolve questions that may have seemed ambiguous to us', as one peer put it (Iribarne 2007). In this structure, employees remain unconcerned that their ethical advisor comes from management's ranks. The advisor is not a pure messenger of transcendent ethical principles imposed on the firm independently of its managers' views. Rather, he manifests the way the firm interprets such principles as a specific community united around its officers.

The firm took a creative approach to traditional ethical supervisory bodies; it wanted its employees to feel they were part of a group with pronounced, mutually trusting and supportive relations. Therefore, while the firm positioned its internal control mechanisms as sources of punishment, it deployed them just as much (if not more) as sources of assistance and support, protecting employees from external solicitations and internal temptations. Thus the 'contracts committee' was widely seen as a way to help – to 'give a hand' to employees who wanted to do the right thing. Employees seemed to perceive it as a source of 'comfort', especially when the best decision was not evident according to obvious criteria and could therefore come into question. In addition, employees were less tempted to deviate once they found support when they had trouble, rather than turning to a group of corrupt accomplices for help. In this way, each employee saw that loyalty to the firm was the best way to meet obligations to family and friends: if he or she attempted to act wrongly, it could result in dismissal and loss of the ability to help anyone. Furthermore, when the company showed that it cared about its employees' problems, it developed 'trusting' relationships that built 'team spirit' and fostered a sense of common interests that all employees had a stake in safeguarding, thus promoting employee honesty in the workplace.

While the firm made great progress in its anti-corruption efforts, its approach came to require further improvements. The issue facing management was how to transmit motivation from the top to rank-and-file employees. Such communication assumes that personal, trusting relations existed between these two poles – upper management and the lowliest worker – such as exists in a group of 'friends' who know each other well. This combination of authority and proximity is usually present in a family and in small, family-run businesses, without any special measures being needed. However, the situation is very different within a large multinational company, comprised of individuals who live thousands of kilometers away from one another, who cannot know each other personally.

This change in scale creates two types of obstacles that impede trusting relationships. Upper management and the rank-and-file live in two different worlds, whereas a group of friends usually shares social and/or geographical proximity. In Argentina as elsewhere, someone from a modest rank finds it difficult to address 'important' people of higher rank. Some employees found the firm's efforts insufficient. In addition, in a national or multinational firm with many divisions and companies spread out across a large country, managers must not underestimate communication difficulties that arise as soon as employees work far from headquarters in Buenos Aires. Managers at headquarters worry that distant employees might turn inward, breaching ethical standards without even knowing it. We have no doubt that managers would see more progress if they could set up a chain of relays to pass the ethical impulse from one group of employees to the next, from the top management to each division and department in the firm's most socially and geographically distant parts.

The great interest of this case lies in the complexity of the firm's cultural context. We see a commitment to the principle of honesty alongside a commitment – for better or worse – to groups of friends and crony networks. The tools the firm uses prove effective in both registers simultaneously. To the extent that the ethical advisor helps employees resolve questions of conscience, he enables a purity ethic to function well. At the same time, as human resources director and through the quality of relationships formed with employees, the ethical advisor is also a member of each employee's crony network and group of friends. Similarly, the supervisory bodies simultaneously find their place in both ethical registers. What seem to be oddities – compared with American-style anti-corruption policies – prove excellent adaptations to the local cultural context.

An intracompany ethical approach based on employee respect and dialogue

One aspect of an ethical approach to business depends on showing respect for employees internally. This type of respect finds meaning worldwide; openness to others and willingness to discuss issues generates mutual trust and cooperation everywhere. However, once again, cultural factors are liable to affect the embodiment of this approach to ethics. Very different conceptions of 'good cooperation' come into play, of what it means to work together, of the meaning of responsibility and respect for others. We had a special opportunity[16] to investigate this phenomenon by analyzing how two Asian subsidiaries, in Jordan and Malaysia, reacted to a French multinational's approach to company ethics.[17]

The effects of very different conceptions of coexistence

What we observed in Malaysia and Jordan confirmed that 'desirable' modes of coexistence vary considerably from one end of the Earth to the other. An outsider might imagine that these two Muslim countries would share many such concepts, but this proved not to be the case at all. In Jordan, we found an extreme form of honor that had no counterpart in Malaysia. In fact, as shown in Clifford Geertz's (1968) work in Indonesia and Morocco, Islam – like all belief systems widely diffused throughout the world – takes on forms largely marked by a variety of pre-Islamic contexts. Nonetheless, these two countries have non-European cultures in common; their shared traits illuminate the singularities of European culture in the largest sense, (including that of the United States and other countries with a largely European heritage). We found four points that merit special emphasis: the balance maintained between results versus processes, the role given to an instrumental conception of ethics and each person's place in society, the recognition of weaknesses, and the value given to discussion and debate.

Processes and results

In both Jordan and Malaysia, we observed that employees resisted a vision of the world where 'accountability is ultimately about delivering results' as Lafarge's *Principles of Action* (2012) put it in English.

European societies legitimatize notions such as commitment to results, performing one task to achieve a separate goal, asserting control of future events, or determining one's destiny. While religious texts occasionally affirm that individuals must not be driven by results, as in the biblical parable of the 'lilies of the field that neither toil or spin' (Holy Bible, Matthew 6:28), these texts also exhort readers to consider results enough to think ahead, unlike the 'foolish man who built his house on sand' (Matthew 7:24). Certainly, one European philosophical tradition (derived from the Stoics) professes that individuals must remain detached from the results of their actions; it postulates that it is somehow impure to do something for ulterior motives, even when doing good, as in a Kantian obedience to law. In contrast, another Christian tradition professes that 'the Sabbath was made for man, not man for the Sabbath' (Mark 2:27) and calls for judging 'each tree by its own fruit' (Luke 6:44). In this context, we may see the emphasis on results as arising from a grand vision of good, one that would eventually merge with the somewhat cynical utilitarianism that also runs through Western thought, as embodied by Benjamin Franklin. Today, in a business context, some followers of W. Edwards Deming (Deming 1982) – the apostle of quality – strongly denounce what they perceive as Western (particularly American) firms' excessive focus on results, one that prevents managers and workers from paying enough attention to process quality. Clearly, however, these adherents are preaching against the choir.

Conversely, Asian societies find that some detachment from an action's consequences seems inseparable from a grand vision of good. In a far more radical way, Asians see pretending to master the consequences of one's acts as a manifestation of human hubris, particularly in Hinduism and Buddhism. For instance, we can cite Krishna's words to Arjuna on the battlefield, extolling the virtue of doing his duty and remaining unconcerned with the consequences of his actions:

> One whose every undertaking has no motivation in material desires and sense gratification and who has incinerated all actions in the fire of pure knowledge – the spiritually intelligent describe him as educated. After giving up attachment to material results, always satisfied, indifferent to external phenomena, he – in spite of being active – does not do anything at all. Bereft of desire, controlled in mind and body, relinquishing all conceptions of proprietorship, that person never incurs sinful reactions, performing only those actions that maintain bodily sustenance. Satisfied with whatever comes by its own accord, tolerant of dualities, devoid of envy to others; while performing, he is equiposed, never affected in success or failure. For one who is unattached to material nature, who is liberated, whose heart is situated in transcendence, who performs all actions as sacrifice unto the Ultimate Personality, all reactions are dissolved.
>
> (*Bhagavad Gita*, ch. IV, verses 19–24)

These words are not singular: the sages of Zen Buddhism and Confucianism affirm the primacy of the right attitude over pursuit of results. In the contemporary world, it is not by chance that Japan proves a fertile ground for quality strategies that emphasize process over immediate results, stopping production lines when a process fails. Islam also affirms that the future is in God's hands and it would be sacrilegious for man to pretend to control it.

Of course, this does not mean that widely held stereotypes of 'the Oriental' as passive and detached hold true. In Asian societies as elsewhere, extremely entrepreneurial individuals seek paths to success. However, we would argue that in many cases, these entrepreneurs act individualistically, defending their personal interests, without a concern for the wider community, rather than promoting a communitarian ethic where a successful individual is one who serves the common good. Therefore, promoting these results-focused attitudes carries the risk of reinforcing these entrepreneurs' inherent individualism. By contrast, European cultures possess the singular trait of linking the primacy of results with modes of cooperation based on grand ideals, as seen in Max Weber's analysis of the modern entrepreneur (Weber 1905). The latter methodically seeks success without renouncing the demands of a great ideal, in line with Protestant asceticism.

The interviews we conducted with Lafarge managers in Jordan and employees from all levels in Malaysia confirmed their reluctance to elevate results over upright conduct. In Jordan, Lafarge alluded to this reluctance in the Arabic version of its *Principles of Action*; the *Principles*' managing editor emphasized results as a complement to upright actions: the Jordanian version proposes 'evaluating work by its results and not only by the efforts and good intentions', normally lauded in Muslim countries. Interviewees often cited the Prophet Mohammed, saying 'All actions are judged by motives, and each person will be rewarded according to their intention' (Abdulsalam 2006). In a section of the *Principles* centered on performance, the translation of the word 'performance' into Arabic – *adda* – emphasizes the way performance is accomplished over the results achieved. This was borne out in our interviews with Jordanian managers, who frequently shifted attention from results to effort. When asked 'What does it mean to evaluate work results and not the effort and good intentions alone?' they offered the following comments:

> When management sets objectives, it does not mean that we give only what we have. They ask me to achieve an objective, I have to achieve it, and I *have to make an effort* and really try to get it done. That will affect me and the firm in meeting its strategic objective.
>
> The performance culture is very beautiful, it sounds good…It is certain *that uniting around precise work principles*, and working in teams, feeling responsible – that is the performance culture for an employee.

Similarly, in Malaysia we found that employees paid attention to the way things were done, although with differences between ethnicities: the Chinese-origin employees seemed more focused on performance and competition than employees of Indian or Malaysian origin. That did not prevent all employees from invoking 'the right attitude' as soon as ethics entered the discussion.

> The criteria [sic][18] is not only your performance, your criteria is your behaviour.
>
> (Lafarge manager)

> We are working for the company full heartfully [sic]. The boss must look after our feelings and our welfare.
>
> (Lafarge worker)

> One thing I noticed, is that: things only get done if you have the people with the right attitude. That is important, basic thing is your attitude. Your attitude, your honesty,

integrity and sincerity, this is very important. I mean, though you are stupid, you have the right attitude, you can be […]. This is what I always believe.

(Lafarge manager)

At the same time, managers do not stress individual objectives:

I say *we* failed. I always say that, as a team we failed. This is our team; everybody must contribute to the success of the cooperation, not individual success. That philosophy I always expand…

(Lafarge manager)

An instrumental view of ethics

In American culture, a company, manager or any businessperson can state unabashedly that high ethical standards constitute an asset, an important part of his or her reputation and ability to make a profit. Ultimately, this instrumental view of ethics pushes the claim that only results matter. Outside the United States, most cultures perceive this as perfectly cynical, contributing, no doubt, to misunderstandings between Americans and the rest of the world. Thus, in the English version, the Lafarge *Principles* declare from the start: 'Our goal is to strengthen this leadership position by being the best, *through* our commitment to be the preferred supplier of our customers [and for employees, our local communities and shareholders]'.[19] In the Arabic version of the *Principles* as translated by local staff we find: 'Our objective is to be in [the] position of leader [in order] *to be* [come] our clients' preferred supplier'. In the English version, the objective is economic success ('strengthen this leadership position'), and the quality of relationships with suppliers, employees and others constitutes a means to achieve it ('through'). The Arabic version promotes the opposite. 'Being in' leadership position (using the verb 'to be') is presented as a means of serving relationships with the same stakeholders. In Malaysia, we did not have access to a localized version of the *Principles*, but we did find a commitment to a stand-alone ethical position – the 'right attitude' – in our interviews with employees, as cited earlier.

Recognizing weaknesses

In the English and French version of the *Principles*, we find many passages that glorify admissions of weakness: 'address repeated failures', 'learn from their…mistakes', 'to compensate for our weaknesses and shortcomings'. In many other cultures, such admissions prove highly problematic, as we found in Jordan and Malaysia.

In European cultures, and especially in the United States, admitting weakness and mistakes finds meaning in three different and probably interdependent images: the sinner who repents in front of his brothers and emerges stronger, the seeker who quests after an elusive truth, and the man committed to his own interests who learns from failure. These diverse images share the notion that recognizing weakness does not demean a person; rather, he or she finds meaning in a vision of grandeur achieved through bearing defeat without losing heart. Such images do not play the same role in many other cultures. In Jordan, Lafarge's Arabic *Principles* do not include the admissions of failure. Thus the passage 'They [managers]…help them [employees] to learn from their achievements and mistakes' is changed in the Arabic version to 'Regularly giving employees constructive comments about their performance'. Mistakes and the lessons employees might learn from them are no longer relevant because the Jordanian context makes it difficult to recognize weakness in a positive way. In a worldview where honor dominates, admissions of weakness are sooner perceived as demeaning.

Similarly, Lafarge launched an 'Honesty, Integrity and Sincerity' program in its Malaysia factories soon after their acquisition; among other things, the program emphasizes employees' moral obligation to report mistakes. 'Sincerity means that you must tell the truth, whatever you did wrong', explained a Malaysian interviewee. However, this has proven hard to put into practice because of face-saving issues, and because mistakes usually incur punishment, as a Malaysian manager noted:

> The problem here, especially with old-timers – I could feel our people do not say anything when there is a failure. Most people are afraid to share such things, those failures, because the team – it will not be rewarded…They only want to share a good performance; if they do not do very well, you see, they want to escape. [They think:] 'When people see my bad performance, I will be punished, I will not get a bonus or a raise.' They are always thinking; 'what kind of punishment am I going to get?'
>
> (Lafarge manager)

The value of discussion and debate

In the American and French versions of Lafarge's *Principles* we found several references to situations where people disagree and have divergent views and interests; these differences generate discussions or even conflicts that are regarded as normal aspects of working in an organization, and that should even be exploited, as the *Principles* (2012) state:

> Dealing with conflict is an integral and part of teamwork. Teamwork is not about reaching consensus on every issue. It is about each individual…seeking differences of opinion as a source of progress.
>
> We want to promote an environment where individuals and teams seek to constructively challenge and be challenged.
>
> Being a 'multi-local' organization [means]…involving Business Unit management teams in addressing the permanent conflicts that arise from operating globally in local businesses.
>
> Managing the tension between 'local' and 'global' is one of the key challenges of our Group and defines the way we are organized.
>
> They [divisions] have a key role in challenging the Business Units to achieve greater performance ambitions.

These versions of the *Principles* have plenty of references to unity, to sharing, to everything that brings employees together – 'share[d] experiences', 'common goals', 'dialogue'. We see a worldview where agreement always mixes with disagreement, and where the idea of perfect harmony evokes a totalitarian society that crushes differences under group pressure, rather than an image of authentic unity. The French and American versions resemble one another on this point, not because of universal references but rather because of a shared tradition. A belief in the merits of democratic debate draws on virtues preached in the medieval disputations (*disputationes*); it also shares a dual Greek and biblical heritage where unity does not exclude controversy, a common trait in European culture. However, when members of such a culture enter other contexts, they soon find views of unity that do not sit easily with celebrations of difference.

We saw this in Jordan. In the Arabic version of the *Principles*, the translators systematically eliminated all references to conflict situations, differences of opinion, and questioning by others, in contrast to everything that referred to unity – 'teamwork', 'sharing', 'helping one another'. The notion of 'dialogue' – which signifies differences and unity simultaneously – was used for relationships outside the firm, such as with local governments, but was eliminated for internal relationships.[20]

The Jordanian employees we interviewed welcomed the goal of creating a 'unified'[21] vision, with comments such as the following:

> The main idea I have about the LFT [Leader for Tomorrow] project is that there was a unified objective for factory workers and the firm's workers. I mean, the firm's workers had a single objective, one single vision in their working in the JFC [Jordanian subsidiary]. That is the most important idea I got out of the meeting, in addition to changing the firm's work culture for employees, I mean, to create a single culture.
>
> (Lafarge employee, Jordan)

We also found this strong reference to unity in Malaysia, where consensus – not debate – is valued. 'Confrontation is against Asian culture. People won't say things directly, even in a meeting. They will say things later, behind the screen', explained a Malaysian employee. In contrast to Jordan, we also saw that this unity should coalesce around a vision from above, in this case from Lafarge headquarters; the interviewees make this clear:

> I actually had a meeting; I noticed that we all have different objectives. The objectives were different, the cooperation was weak. So I only asked, 'What is our objective?' Our objective is not there, we all failed. Our best objective is Lafarge objective. So I just ask: 'What is THE objective, not AN objective.' So I say; this is very important. So, what are we going to do? We all must consensus, agree and adjust to each other, this is very important. Now I think, every time we share that belief, the Lafarge philosophy; [we have to ask ourselves] what is our objective?
>
> (Lafarge employee)

Openly challenging the established order is somewhat problematic:

> In the mindset of people, especially for Malay and Indian, we have to follow whatever has been set up, has been ruled by the person that you respect. Even in the family or in the group or in the company. This is why people think whatever has been directed by the top boss they will think you have to follow…We have to follow and we have to commit to whatever has been instructed.…We respect our king, our law, our company.
>
> (Lafarge employee)

Of course, some employees claim things should change; they talk about how hard that is:

> In our culture, when bosses ask us to do certain things we prefer straight away to say 'yes'. We don't like to say, 'no, we should do this way'. We will say 'yes' and we will do. I think we must say 'no' and explain why it is. We don't see that much until today.

People prefer to do what boss said. The thing is, we don't like to argue with boss, especially in a meeting.

(Lafarge employee)

How to localize principles that combine universal precepts with cultural specificities

We identified several factors that will help ensure workable connections between universal principles and local mores when adapting Lafarge's 'international' *Principles*. Each baseline (French and English) version of the *Principles* is a composite of several parts. Some evoke sufficiently general, more or less universal conceptions of modes of coexistence and cooperation; these notions can be directly translated into local languages from relatively abstract words such as 'share', 'respect' and 'dialogue'. Other parts of the *Principles* contain references to more particular, culturally-defined modes of operating. In this way, the company may adapt the *Principles* to local contexts, focusing on the universal and on specifics while staying close to notions that are meaningful locally, and by substantially modifying or leaving out the too-foreign elements. This would normally occur with the text's translation into the local language; indeed, such adaptations may work best when translators attempt a simple linguistic transposition, without much awareness that this presents a different conception of collective work. Subsidiaries may also adapt the *Principles* by promoting selected aspects as they are implemented, while embodying those aspects in a locally-meaningful way.

In most non-European societies, conceptions of cooperative work occur in a dominantly communitarian frame of reference; this does not mean, however, that such a framework actually guides everyday life. It does mean that local versions of the *Principles* may emphasize community, while obscuring everything related to commercial relationships and/or compliance with abstract ethical principles.

The Jordanian adaptation of the Lafarge *Principles* provides a good illustration of this; local personnel created this version without input from headquarters. We saw that the locals erased some aspects of the baseline English version, while preserving or even emphasizing others to ensure passage from one cultural context to another. For instance, the notion of 'leader' was perfectly transposable, even if the representation of a leader and the role he or she plays in society differs greatly between Jordan and the United States. In both countries, references to the firm's economic success also resonate. Internal operating modes were less easily transposed when they followed a customer–supplier relationship model with clear definitions of individual objectives and the employee in the role of supplier. On the other hand, the notion of teamwork translated easily, even though it its application was not the same. The Arabic version of the *Principles* reuses terms such as 'teamwork', 'sharing', 'support' and 'respect' while adding 'helping one another' and 'reciprocal recognition of everyone's contribution to shared work'.[22] In addition, the idea of the firm acting to help local communities was readily transposed, although the form of such help might also differ. In Lafarge's Arabic *Principles*, we found phrases such as 'initiatives for social and charitable works' and 'helping local communities when unforeseen events occur'; these phrases have no equivalent in the original English version, just as the Arabic version has no equivalent for 'acting as responsible members of our communities' or 'contributing to economic progress through healthy and vigorous competition'.

In Jordan and Malaysia, employees did not react to headquarters' version of the *Principles* by criticizing the parts that were unacceptable locally, as French employees do when responding to American-style codes of conduct; French reactions tend to be corrosive, as we have seen. In this respect France, rather than the United States, proves the exception. Elsewhere, especially outside of Europe, employees expect their managers to show the way, including on ethical points. For example, Malaysian employees responding to a survey made comments along these lines: 'Everyone should quickly embrace the Lafarge Culture; must move away from old style.'

In these situations, the employees' first reaction is not to analyze in detail what headquarters is trying to convey – as the French would – but rather look to the overall approach and pull out whatever seems familiar, giving meaning to the *Principles* by relating them to their own worldview.

We saw these types of reactions in both Jordan and in Malaysia. No one tried to highlight what was foreign in the English version of the *Principles*. Instead, they tried to assimilate the contents with precepts conveyed by their own culture. Sometimes they commented on a precept in the *Principles*, interpreting it within their worldview. For example, with regard to 'leading by example', employees we interviewed in Jordan used phrases such as: 'Leading by example – it is like an ideal mother and father who behave in an exemplary fashion with their children. For example, the Prophet is a great leader, he did everything right.' Another Jordanian manager added:

> [Managers] leading by example matters one-hundred percent. For me, leading by example, it is like when a son follows his father or mother, it is exactly the same thing. How can you be an ideal mother or father if you do not set an example; how do you want your son to follow you if you say one thing and do another? *Alkoudoua* means 'be an example'. It is like the Prophet when he set an example, he did everything right and afterwards people followed his example.
>
> (Lafarge manager)

Local reception of an international code may also entail a more general assimilation of its principles to local conceptions, as occurs for Lafarge in Malaysia. We found a column in a subsidiary's internal magazine dedicated to the 'Leader for Tomorrow' (LTF) program, written by its then-president, a Malaysian:

> As a member of the Lafarge Group, we have to implement LFT. This should not be difficult for us since we have the same aspiration in Malaysia as the Group has in the world, and LFT incorporates most of the principle and ethos that we already have.

We found the same attitude in our interviewees, one of whom stated 'LFT is mostly similar to what we had before so it is not difficult for us to apply' (Lafarge manager).

Expectations about ethical frameworks

An ethical framework will meet the best reception in cultures that differ from the one that shaped it not only because it allows for many interpretations that fit diverse local contexts, but because it may also have the potential to greatly enrich or improve the local situation, as much, more or less than it did in its original context.

In Jordan and Malaysia, we observed a phenomenon that we have seen in other places: small groups with special ties show common forms of good cooperation. Such forms prove insufficient for collectively running a larger firm that has country-wide operations; this leads to frustration. Employee expectations for the Leader for Tomorrow program arose in such a context. Thus a Jordanian manager summarized the situation in Lafarge's Jordanian subsidiary as follows, applying what we observed in Jordan to the entire Arab world:

> Teamwork is a problem in the Arab world, because teamwork is not done scientifi-
> cally – it is based on the type of relationship I might have with a colleague. If we get
> along, we will work together well. You will see that at Rachidiya [a factory] because
> people work together in the factory, they see each other in the afternoon, their families
> live next door – that is why some working teams succeed, but it is not based on scien-
> tific principles – the relationship governs teamwork. We work together because we are
> friends.

In contrast, the subsidiary's head office and its factories constitute two largely foreign worlds; cooperation between them remains very poor. Jordanian managers characterize their relationship in these terms:

> For them [the factory workers], the worker who tires himself out – who produces
> things – makes money for the firm. Whereas the fellow at headquarters sits around, is
> comfortable, and does not do anything – he does not give the firm as much as the worker
> gives him, and management has even more privileges than he does. Worker fatigue
> benefits executives in Amman – that is what most of the firm's employees think. That is
> why we do not see any of the firm's managers around – very rarely – or when they do
> come, they only come to this building and do not go into the factory. Maybe the work
> the upper managers do is great, grandiose, but the factory workers have no idea what
> those upper managers in Amman are doing. That frustrates employees.
>
> (Jordanian manager)

What we have here is not a lack of desire for better work cooperation, in a world where everyone would feel closer, governed by rules that everyone would follow – a world where subordinates' dedication would find echoes in their superiors' benevolence and guidance. But everyone recognizes that reality remains far from these aspirations. Compared to what we usually observe in the other fifty countries where we have conducted research, the gap between aspirations and reality appears much deeper. The Leader for Tomorrow program offers the hope of reducing this gap, by envisioning a well-ordered world where managers set the example and everyone joins to emulate it. 'We first hope that there will be a little more clarity, and second, some justice for employees. This is how we will get out of a vicious circle of exceptions, complications and conflicts', one manager offered. 'Leading by example is a kind of behavior. We need an environment where the boss can implement these ideas [the *Principles*]; over time, an employee can learn a lot from his manager' (Lafarge manager).

Certainly, the employees are not looking for the advent of Western-style modes of operat-ing collectively, favoring a characteristic Western autonomy; we doubt that anything in the *Principles* relevant to such modes of operating, such as insisting on individual performance evaluations and open debate, would influence practices very much. But employees would like to find a better mode of working together, a more efficient one.

We find the same type of situation in Malaysia; good cooperation commonly involves small groups whose members are very close-knit:

> Now [here in Kantan] we are in a team, in a family. We know each other for a long time…The people here have worked in the plant for at least 15 years or more. I am a junior with nine years. They…know each other, we go to their families.
>
> (Lafarge employee)

> [In Langkawi] they are very cooperative. The teamwork spirit is there. I think because of that…they all…you know….They are all local people there, they are all in one group.
>
> (Lafarge employee)

In contrast, while we do not find the same tensions we saw in Jordan, we see a sort of reciprocal indifference on a larger scale in Malaysia; an employee notes, 'Cooperation among departments is very much lacking. Each department takes care of [its] own interest'. Employees react favorably to the idea that the firm could foster relationships that involve closer proximity and especially more attention from superiors, as one explains:

> I found that it is good to get the Lafarge way, to help people progress…a different culture…from Blue Circle, from Malaysian…They are different…I mean the way of growing. The Lafarge way of coaching, I found that there is some good in it…very good…a coaching culture rather than the teaching culture. Yes, there is a difference between the Lafarge and before.
>
> (Lafarge employee)

Conclusion

Ethical questions illustrate the way the universal combines with the local in managerial affairs. If managers, business writers, consultants, and others use a sufficiently abstract vocabulary, referring to values such as honesty, respect, openness, dialogue, commitment and so forth, they can design an ethical framework with universal reach. In this respect, all people may be said to share the same values. Employees universally allude to the ideal of a well-run society; they appear to understand such an entity can exist only if everyone shares a sense of common good rather than automatically and selfishly taking advantage of situations. Other common notions include helping others and caring about their concerns.

The moralist may be satisfied with such findings, but the manager cannot be. We have seen in this chapter how management practitioners cannot rely solely on universal notions when moving from grand principles to practical ways of promoting ethical conduct. This is primarily because what seem to be normal means of prompting proper employee conduct in one culture – supervision, rewards and punishments – may provoke very different results in another culture. Employees may experience the same type of supervision very differently, depending on the context. A certain type of supervision may be offensive in a society attached to codes of honor, where individuals think they have to answer only to their own consciences. Alternately, employees may welcome the same type of supervision when it helps them escape from pressures exerted by their personal circle, external to the firm – 'friends' who will accuse an employee of disloyalty if he or she does not grant favors at the firm's expense. In each context, managers must recognize which forms of social pressure will appear legitimate, and choose accordingly which systems of control or encouragement to implement.

Notes

1 The word 'ethic' comes from the Greek *êthos* meaning the characteristic spirit of a culture, era, or community as seen in its beliefs. 'Customs' comes from Latin *consuetudin-, consuetudo*, from *consuescere* to accustom, from *com-+ suescere* to accustom; akin to *suus*, 'one's own'.
2 This section is largely based on Iribarne (2002).
3 M. du Besset is also president of the European Circle of Ethics Officers (*Cercle Européen des Déontologues*) a sub-unit of the Association for Business Ethics.
4 We assisted the management of the French 'super-major' oil and gas multinational, Total S.A., in thinking about an ethics approach that took account of the variety of cultures working within the corporation. We interviewed managers from various countries, mostly European (French, English, Belgian, Dutch, Swiss, Italian and Spanish) and a few Americans, collecting their reactions to an ethical code project prior to its finalization. Jean-Pierre Segal, Frédéric Lefebvre, Sylvie Chevrier, Alain Thomasset and Alain Henry helped conduct the interviews.
5 This term dates from the 1880s and 1890s, specifically the period before antitrust legislation in the US. The coinage was re-popularized during the Depression to connote unscrupulous industrialists who made fortunes in the 1920s.
6 For his part, Montesquieu affirmed honor's commandments even more strictly as legal sanctions are impossible: 'The third is that those things which honour forbids are more rigorously forbidden, when the laws do not concur in the prohibition' (Montesquieu 1914, part I, IV, 2).
7 This type of reaction is particularly French. For instance, when the global food products company, Danone, wanted to mobilize its personnel for a humanitarian cause to mark the year 2000, giving the equivalent of one hour of pay for each of its employees worldwide, and inviting its employees to do the same, response was especially poor in France. The head of Danone's initiative indicated,

> In France, this operation prompted more rejection than anywhere else since the company's legitimacy in initiating actions that usually come under an individual's personal choice is much less than in other societies where the company is seen as a guarantee of seriousness and transparency.
> (Giraud 2000)

8 The notion of taking care of 'widows and orphans' draws from the French chivalrous (originally, knightly) code of conduct, carried on to this day as an idiom in French and English alike.
9 We found the same difference in the English and French versions of the Lafarge *Principles of Action* (Iribarne 2012).
10 The paper was based on much investigative work reported in Arvis and Berstein (2002).
11 This section is largely based on Iribarne (2000).
12 For Kant, the 'dignity of a rational being' comes into play (Kant 1985).
13 For Aristotle, 'the good man will need people to do well by' (Aristotle 1999, p. 157).
14 See e.g. Kessy (1998) for a particularly instructive example.
15 This case study is presented more fully in Iribarne (2007); we interviewed twenty managers at the Argentinian subsidiary of a French multinational in December 2000 in Buenos Aires.
16 We analyzed the way the French cement company, Lafarge, designed and distributed its so-called *Principles of Action* (Core Principles) to its subsidiaries in a program known as 'LFT'. Jean-Pierre Segal and Héla Yousfi assisted in the analysis.
17 Since the present chapter was written, the author has conducted further research in China; see Iribarne (2012).
18 The interviews with Malaysian employees have been transcribed verbatim from the spoken vernacular, with errors found in 'Manglish', a combination of Malay and English.
19 The same passage in the French version of the Lafarge *Principles of Action* states: 'Our objective is to reinforce our position as world leader by being the best everywhere *and* by becoming our clients preferred supplier [and so on for other stakeholders]'. The 'through' in English expresses that the quality of relations with others is a means of attaining a leadership position; this contrasts with the 'and' in the French version that expresses a juxtaposition of two objectives. In France, employees do not consider it honorable to use relationships as a means of succeeding, finding it more honorable to think of success as something achieved as a bonus.
20 Even the notion of 'trust' was eliminated. This point deserved to be examined further; we imagine this word also signifies a mixture of difference and unity.
21 'Unified' is a literal translation from the Arabic; 'homogeneous' may also be used.

22 Within these teams, individual members appeared to expect less autonomy in vision but greater respect for personal stakes, compared to French or American counterparts. We observed similar situations in a Moroccan subsidiary of ST Microelectronics, where very strong moral unity joined with careful attention to each worker's own interests; moral unity was perceived as a condition for respecting these personal interests (Iribarne 2007).

Bibliography

Abdulsalam, M. (2006) 'The role of intention in the acceptability of religion worship by God'. Retrieved from www.islamreligion.com/articles/360/

Aristotle (1999) *Nicomachean Ethics*. Kitchener, ON: Batoche Books.

Arvis, J.-F. and Berstein, R. (2002) *Implementing Anticorruption Programs in the Private Sector: Lessons from East Asia*. Washington, DC: World Bank.

Banfield, E. C. (1958) *The Moral Basis of a Backward Society*. Glencoe, IL: The Free Press.

Bellah, R., Richard Madsen, William M. Sullivan, Ann Swidler and Steven M. Tipton (1985) *Habits of the Heart*. Berkeley: University of California Press.

Berstein, R. and J.-F. Arvis (2002) 'Implementing anticorruption programs in the private sector', *Prem Notes* (4)66: 1. World Bank, Washington, DC. Retrieved from http://www1.worldbank.org/prem/PREMNotes/premnote66.pdf

Besset (du), P. (2002) 'Entretien', *Institutions européennes et finance* 102, in *Problèmes Économiques*, 2778: 16–19.

Bhagavad-Gita Trust (1998) *Bhagavad Gita*. www.bhagavad-gita.org/

British Petroleum (BP) (2011) 'Code of conduct and values statement'. London: BP.com. Retrieved from www.bp.com/sectiongenericarticle.do? categoryId=9002630&contentId=7005204

Bush, G. W. (2001) September 20th, 2001, speech before a joint session of Congress. Retrieved from www.historyplace.com/speeches/gw-bush-9-11.htm

Daly, F. (1998) 'The ethics dynamic', *Business and Society Review* 102(1): 37–42.

Deming, W. E. (1982) *Out of the Crisis*. Cambridge, MA: MIT Center for Advanced Engineering Study.

ExxonMobil (2011a) 'Governance'. Irving, TX: ExxonMobil.com. Retrieved from www.exxonmobil.com/Corporate/ investor_governance_ethics.aspx

—— (2011b) 'Standards of business conduct'. Irving, TX: ExxonMobil.com. Retrieved from www.exxonmobil.com/Corporate/files/corporate/sbc.pdf

Franklin, B. (1905) 'Advice to a young tradesman, 1748'. In *The Writings of Benjamin Franklin*, ed. Albert H. Smyth, 10 vols. New York: Macmillan.

Furet, F. (1988) *La Révolution*, Paris, Hachette.

GDF Suez (2000) 'The group's values'. From author's notes. No longer on website; for current statements, see: www.gdfsuez.com/en/group/ethics-and-compliance/ethics-and-compliance/

Geertz, C. (1968) *Islam Observed: Religious Development in Morocco and Indonesia*. Chicago: University of Chicago Press.

Giraud, B. (2000) 'L'entreprise confrontée à sa responsabilité sociale'. École de Paris du Management, Séminaire Vies Collectives (Paris School of Management, Collective Lives Seminar), 20 January.

Hamilton, A., J. Madison and J. Jay (1996) *The Federalist or the New Constitution* (1787–88). London: Everyman.

Henry, A., G. H. Tchente and P. Guillerme-Dieumegarde (1991) *Tontines et banques au Cameroun. Les principes de la société des amis*. Paris: Karthala.

Herder, J. G. (2000) *Histoire et culture: une autre philosophie de l'histoire* (1774). Paris: Flammarion.

Iribarne, P. d' (1989) *La Logique de l'honneur*. Paris: Seuil.

—— (2000) 'Éthiques d'entreprise et mondialisation', in M. Canto-Sperber (ed.), *Dictionnaire d'éthique et de philosophie morale*, Paris: Presses Universitaires de France.

—— (2002) 'La légitimité de l'entreprise comme acteur éthique en France et aux États-Unis.' *Revue Française de Gestion* 28(140): 23–39.

—— (2007) 'Successful companies in the developing world: managing in synergy with cultures', Agence Française de Développement, Notes et Documents n° 36. Retrieved from www.afd.fr/webdav/site/afd/shared/PUBLICATIONS/RECHERCHE/Archives/Notes-et-documents/36-notes-documents-VA.pdf

—— (2012) *Managing Corporate Values in Diverse National Cultures: The Challenge of Differences*. Abingdon: Routledge.

Kant, E. (1985) *Foundations of the Metaphysics of Morals* [1785]. New York: Prentice Hall.

Kessy, Z. (1998) *Culture africaine et gestion de l'entreprise moderne*. Abidjan, Ivory Coast: CEDA.

Labich, K. (1992) 'The new crisis in business ethics', *Fortune*, 125(8), April 20: 167–76.

Lafarge (2012) *Principles of Action*. Retrieved from www.lafarge.com/wps/portal/1_2_3-Principes_d_action

Manent, P. (1994) *La Cité de l'homme*. Paris: Fayard.

Montesquieu, Baron de (1914) *The Spirit of Laws* [1747]. Translated by Thomas Nugent, revised by J. V. Prichard [1998]. London: G. Bell & Sons, Ltd. www.constitution.org/cm/sol.htm

Peters, T. and R. Waterman, Jr. (1982) *In Search of Excellence*. New York: Harper & Row.

Taine, H. (1986) *Les Origines de la France contemporaine* [1875]. Paris : Bouquins, Robert Laffont.

The Holy Bible, King James Version (1999) New York: American Bible Society. Retrieved from www.bartleby.com/108/

Tocqueville (de), A. (1835–40) *Democracy in America*. Retrieved from http://xroads.virginia.edu/ HYPER/DETOC/ch2_08.htm

TotalElfFina (2000) *Code of Business Conduct: Confidentiality and Insider Trading*. Retrieved from www.total.com/fr/groupe/presentation-du-groupe/principes-ethiques/code-conduite-900024.html.

Troeltsch, E. (1991) *Protestantisme et modernité* [1909, 1911, 1913]. Paris: Gallimard.

Weber, M. (1905) *The Protestant Ethic and the Spirit of Capitalism*. Trans. Talcott Parsons. London and Boston: Unwin Hyman [1930]. New edn with a new introduction by Anthony Giddens, London: Routledge [1992]. Transcribed by Andy Blunden [2005], http://marxists.org/reference/archive/weber/protestant-ethic/index.htm

—— (1906) 'The Protestant sects and the spirit of capitalism', *Gesammelte Aufsatze Zur Religionssoziologie*, 1, pp. 207–36. Trans. Moriyuki Abukuma [2000], retrieved from www.ne.jp/asahi/moriyuki/abukuma/weber/world/sect/sect_frame.html

Part III
Practices

7 Managing multicultural teams

Sylvie Chevrier

Translated from the French by
Suzan Nolan and Leila Whittemore

Introduction

As one of the major trends driving the transformation of businesses, globalization has forced companies to enlarge their scope of operations on an international scale. A growing number of organizations now operate well beyond the borders of their country of origin. In this widened context, firms set up networks of sub-contractors, partnerships and alliances to gain the resources they lack, allowing them to concentrate their time and money on developing what they do best. These reconfigurations change the profile of business teams and their ways of working. Because of globalization, business teams combining different national, professional and company origins are now the rule, homogeneous teams the exception. Cultural diversity demands adaptations on the part of these teams' members, particularly their managers. Managing multicultural teams therefore constitutes an important challenge for firms today.

This chapter offers a synthesis on the management and function of multicultural teams. In the first part, we show that such teams vary widely, and propose a typology for their main configurations. Indeed, no manager can pretend that all multicultural teams call for the same oversight, especially when many of their particularities do not reflect cultural issues. In the second section, we examine how cultural differences affect work in groups, and argue that managers need to go beyond their team members' viewpoints to understand the complexity of intercultural dynamics. In the third and final part, we will discuss how firms overcome cultural barriers and encourage team efficiency.

The diversity of multicultural teams

Multicultural teams cover a great variety of situations that call for more than one analytic approach. Cultural diversity grafts itself onto many other team characteristics; we will break these down in the next section, showing their palpable effects on a team's intercultural dynamics.

Characteristics of multicultural teams

Teams differ first by their objectives and tasks. Some international teams only have coordination tasks, i.e. ensuring coherence between actions taken locally; other international teams aim to produce a shared object, such as a new product design. The first case allows teams to combine different but convergent ways of approaching tasks; the second requires them to set up shared means of achieving goals. In other words, the nature of the task influences the degree of integration the team requires.

Multicultural teams also differ according to their participants' profiles. Some include multiple nationalities in varying proportions; others have equal representation of two nationalities, while still others may have a few foreign team members 'submerged' in a more or less homogeneous cultural group. A bicultural team is more likely to become polarized into groups with mutually critical perceptions than a heterogeneous group that mixes many different cultures. A team's composition also rests on its members' experience in different physical locations. Some team members, socialized in various places, acquire a vast experience in different ways of doing business, while others only discover different approaches at a later stage of life, having acquired their work and social experiences in a single country or even a single company (see Chapter 2). Managerial and employee awareness of cultural differences within their teams does not automatically ensure adaptation to intercultural work, but it does constitute a factor in its favor.

Teams also differentiate themselves through their ways of interacting; some work together face-to-face on a daily basis, while others meet only sporadically, or through virtual links, for example telephone or video conferences. The physical presence of team members helps them make mutual adaptations, whereas distance tends to increase misunderstandings. Some teams are stable and permanent, such as those forming a department in an international organization; others change according to temporary assignments that last only as long as a project. The longer team members are able to interact, the greater their opportunities to experiment and learn from each other.

Teams evolve in an institutional context marked by structural divides, selfish interests, and power plays that all influence their modes of working. Some teams belong to a single business unit in a single organization, while others comprise representatives from different subsidiaries or organizations that – as individual entities – may have divergent interests. When institutional divides overlap with cultural ones, confusion tends to arise about the cause of conflicts: organizational conflicts may be read as cultural ones and vice versa. Institutional conflicts generally have repercussions for intercultural relationships. A study of the European aeronautic multinational, EADS (Airbus parent European Aeronautic Defence and Space), clearly illustrated this dynamic. A crisis related to the low productivity of a factory in Hamburg, Germany delayed production of the A380 jetliner, raising the threat of cancelled orders and heavy job losses; this sparked sharp tensions between EADS' German and French partners (Behrens and Clouet 2009).

Table 7.1 summarizes team characteristics and their effects on the way teams work.

Typology of multicultural teams

Beyond the singularity of each team – arising from a particular combination of the variables just categorized – we can distinguish six major recurring configurations, as summarized in Table 7.2.

The strategic coordination team

The first configuration refers to a team coordinating strategy between different national business units. For example, at a regional headquarters, a team may comprise the directors of national subsidiaries in a given geographic region. In this case, intercultural collaboration means assuring a minimal coherence between the management of semi-autonomous entities. But since these directors remain committed to the same institutional objective, for example the company's regional leadership, they do not engage in close, daily collaboration.

Table 7.1 Characteristics' repercussions on team dynamics

	Team characteristics	Repercussions on team dynamics
Objective or task	Coordination versus shared production	Degree of integration required
Participants' profile	Number of cultures represented Intercultural experiences	Degree of the team's diversity, eventual polarization between cultures with the most members Awareness of differences
Ways of interacting	Face-to-face or at a distance Frequency	Degree of risk of misunderstanding and opportunities for mutual adaptations
Duration	Permanent or temporary	Opportunities for experimentation and learning from other team members
Institutional context	Homogeneity or heterogeneity of participants' contexts, e.g. organization, job, department	Degree of convergence around a mission Intercultural climate

Intercultural coordination allows entities in each country to follow their own paths to some degree; different local ways of doing business may coexist, and each entity enjoys a certain level of autonomy. Strategic coordination teams meet periodically; within these teams, representatives speak out for and defend the interests of their respective entities.

Managing mixed nationalities in a single business unit

The second configuration appears in team projects drawing employees from two different countries; such projects include those shared between organizations or those concerned with managing daily operations. Teams introduced during international mergers, alliances or joint ventures fall into this category. In such cases, management teams from both firms must agree on priorities and make decisions. Structural and national divides match exactly. Intercultural collaboration is simultaneously inter-organizational collaboration; management must agree on common working modes in place of traditional operations from different companies and countries. Salk (1996) analyzed a case where a Japanese company acquired a German one, showing how managers – often after some hitch appeared – gradually implemented work rules acceptable to both parties. Most current internationalization strategies tend to produce business units that mix national cultures, whether these arise by choice or obligation.

Interaction between headquarters and subsidiaries

Situated at the heart of the relationship between a head office and its subsidiaries, or more generally between a center and dispersed units, interface teams ensure information flows between the two entities. In one direction, they translate overall policy directives coming from the center for local application; in the other, they send local-entity data to headquarters. This interface work – collecting, formatting, translating and distributing information – often falls to employees in each entity who share a profession. For example, a subsidiary's head comptroller remains in constant contact with the head office's comptroller, charged with analyzing and consolidating the group's financial and management reports. The interface teams, sometimes reduced to only two people, generally work at a distance from one another

Table 7.2 Multicultural teams typology

	Participants	Objective	Institutional context	Mode(s) of interaction	Duration	Illustration
Strategic coordina-tion	Representatives of national entities	Ensure coherence of local actions	Each member defends his/her interests	Periodic group meetings	Permanent	European subsidiaries directors committee
Manage-ment of nationally mixed units	Two nationally balanced groups	Daily operations management	National divides map over operational divides	Daily coopera-tion and compro-mise to define a modus vivendi	Permanent	Management of an alliance or joint venture
Interaction between headquar-ters and subsidiar-ies	Managers in interfacing positions at HQ and subsidiaries	Communicate, format, translate information and directives between HQ and subsidiaries in both directions	Headquarters/subsidiary relationship: tension between control and autonomy	Interactions generally at a distance	Permanent	Subsidiary head of accounting interacting with HQ chief accounting officer
New product develop-ment projects	Team with multiple nationalities, entities and job descriptions	Design new products (or services) for international markets	Strong cost, timing and profitability constraints	Close daily interactions	Temporary	Projects to design and develop new services
Teams sharing the same profession	Multiple nationalities but a shared profession	Collaboration between professional experts	Profession's uniting effect	Generally alternates between face-to-face and distant meetings	Temporary	Research team
'Sub-merged' in a homo-geneous team	National team with rare exceptions	Variable depending on the nature of the team	Organization based in the local environment	Local way of working	Variable	A department with a few foreigners within a national entity

although they may periodically meet physically. Their joint mode of work reflects traditional headquarters–subsidiary tensions; the head office tries to enforce conformity with the group's standards, while the subsidiary tries to modify these standards to take local specifici-ties into account. As we suggested earlier, these challenges may tarnish mutual perceptions, with some team members quick to highlight the others' lack of discipline or rigidity. While these reciprocal criticisms may first emerge in a headquarters–subsidiary context, they may soon graft onto misunderstandings arising from differences in political culture: team members do not necessarily share the same vision or definition of 'accountability'.

New product development project teams

A fourth configuration features teams that develop and launch new products. When a firm decides to introduce a product into international markets – an increasingly frequent occurrence – it puts together a new team with two components: a marketing team made up of representatives from the firm's target market(s), and a product development team of design specialists drawn from various departments. Team members usually come from the same company or its subsidiaries. They work upstream on the product's conception, design and development, and downstream for its production, sales and after-sales service. They must achieve their common goal under sharply limited time and cost constraints. Generally, a strong management team heads up these very heterogeneous teams (in terms of nationality and job description); team leaders take responsibility for results, which are subject to precise evaluations. Such teams work under high pressure, given the economic stakes involved; they experience multiple tensions that may or may not take on divisions along cultural lines. We followed the work of such a team in the telecommunications sector (Chevrier 2000). It mobilized engineers and technicians from several development centers located in France, Germany, Italy and Belgium to design a cellular radio-telephone network with an Australian pilot client. Team members struggled to build a shared approach to tasks, as each defended his or her solution rather than make compromises; these solutions reflected individual specialty and national legal, technical and cultural requirements, but did not always fit with other team members' constraints.

Teams sharing the same profession

A fifth configuration features teams composed of workers from different geographic origins who share the same profession, for example international research and development teams, auditing teams, etc. Their task and team are more or less integrated depending on the team's purpose and their entity's goal, and team members may come from one or several organizations. The higher the degree of integration required by the project – for example, designing a new vehicle where each component (lights, dashboard, drivetrain) must articulate with the overall layout and exterior design – the more the team must interface and communicate effectively. From the beginning, intercultural collaboration takes the form of either an integrated project, or of pursuing relatively independent additional work on a common topic. Examples might include a large company's internal team with precise research objectives, or a team from a multi-company consortium seeking external research financing, but not necessarily driven by the same scientific aims or long-term commercial goals.

So far we have focused on multicultural team configurations that feature executive-level team members, all representing the cutting edge in globalizing firms. However, as Tarrius (2006) suggests, globalization also occurs from the bottom up. Firms may create multicultural teams of immigrant workers, such as those we studied in an industrial cleaning company (Chevrier 2005); the firm maintained the Paris metro system with workers from Algeria, France, Mali, Mauritania, Morocco, Senegal, Tunisia and other nations. This study suggested that a common profession with its own jargon, techniques, methodologies, etc., does not tend to promote unity in teams of low-skilled workers.

'Submerged' in a homogeneous team

Our final multicultural team configuration describes an essentially national team that nevertheless includes one or two 'foreigners'. Such cases differ from those where headquarters sends an executive to act as managing director in one of their subsidiaries abroad; in those situations, the 'foreign' director occupies a special position of power in the team he or she joins and will act to disseminate the head office's practices. In the case we examine here, the foreigner occupies a job at the same level as other team members, and he or she is entirely submerged in the local company's culture. Most often, the foreigner is there for personal reasons rather than at the company's behest. For example, intercultural marriages generally result in one spouse's 'submersion' in the other's country.

The repercussions of cultural differences on teams

In the preceding typology, we implicitly associated teams' international dimension with their multicultural character. However, international companies are not the only ones that must manage intercultural differences. Managers know this well; they are often quick to blame some of their problems with teams on different professional and/or company cultures. In this section, we articulate various aspects of cultural diversity to complete our overview of multicultural teams. We will then look at how this diversity, whether recognized or ignored, affects the way teams work together.

Intercultural dimensions

In companies and teams, cultural diversity essentially takes three forms: company culture, professional culture and national or political culture.

Company culture

Since the 1980s, a vast body of sociological and managerial literature has shown that organizations produce their own rules, standards and values. For example, Bonarelli (1994) describes an organizational culture marked by much informal communication and quick decision-making, based on a few clear principles known to all employees. He compares that to a more formalized culture where decision-making requires several experts' reports, formal communications and meetings between multiple levels of management. To the degree that all personnel share these elements, they create organizational cohesiveness, improving communication, interaction and overall staff cooperation. However, when workers from different organizations form a team, as occurs in a merger or an acquisition, they no longer have shared rules, values or norms; team members experience genuine culture shocks that raise questions about their habitual modes of operating. Differences in company cultures constitute a first level of intercultural encounters. The 2000 merger of two petroleum companies, TotalFina and Elf, supplies an example. As they integrated their teams into common professional divisions, the firms' different organizational cultures came to the fore; Elf's was still strongly marked by its recent history as a state-owned company. Its workforce was highly unionized compared to Total's, and its decision-making process was far more bureaucratic than Total's relatively proactive process (Personal interview with Total employee, September 2000).

Professional culture

Differences in culture between professions constitute another level of intercultural encounters, with two further modifying factors: industry sector and job. People working in the same industry share some expertise and worldviews, such as their conception of the work environment. In a French telecommunications services group, we observed that different approaches to the market strongly affected cooperation between workers in fixed-line, mobile-phone and Internet services; for example, the Internet team's culture of fast reaction to rapid technological changes clashed with the more formalized fixed-line culture (Chevrier and Segal 2011).

Professional cultures also distinguish themselves at the level of job description. Different priorities and relationships to objects, techniques, clients, people and time may create recurrent conflicts between 'salespeople' and 'producers' or 'human resources directors' and 'bean counters'. Indeed, learning a job includes learning its technical and methodological aspects, and also includes a socialization that conveys the profession's particular values and ideas. For example, Midler (1993) studied an automobile-related project team and showed that representatives from different jobs had different concerns, rationales and approaches to problems and work languages. 'Job doctrines' – the source of competing visions for the object under design – prevented mutual understanding; joint work threatened to devolve into 'a confrontation between monologues, lasting until the project's deadline cuts it off' (Midler 1993, p. 125).

Political cultures

Intercultural issues also arise when carriers of different political cultures meet. Over the course of their history, nations develop particular ways of governing people. Legitimate means of exercising authority and agreeing upon action vary palpably from one place to another (Iribarne et al. 1998). When we speak of legitimate forms of government in a given context, we do not mean that all of the observable practices in a place strictly follow these legitimate forms. We mean that people socialized in a given context share the notion of an ideal type, and judge actions accordingly. In other words, political culture constitutes a frame for interpreting management practices in an organizational and/or collaborative context. Employees draw on their political culture to assess whether or not a manager treats them well, inspects them fairly, and makes demands that are legitimate in form and substance. As Jean-Pierre Dupuis reminds us, every culture is characterized by its means of combining dignity and hierarchy. Following Iribarne et al. (1998), we intentionally use the term 'political' rather than 'national' culture. The latter carves out old-fashioned nation-state zones, useful for distinguishing political cultures that are homogeneous enough to give meaning to the 'national'. However, a national definition of uniformity is not always appropriate: the case of Quebec shows how regional or provincial zones may prove more useful when designating political cultures on a national scale.

A political culture rests on a society's shared, foundational myths that precisely map good manners for coexistence. It is also based on an institutional consensus – around education and justice in particular – that conveys specific views of social ties. In multicultural teams, these different political conceptions cause misunderstandings and mutually negative perceptions that we will revisit later.

Articulation between levels of culture

We note that various intercultural issues overlap. A team resulting from a merger of two firms from different countries may compound differences in company, professional and political cultures, following the national or regional origins of its members. We also note that each of these levels may interact with the others. For example, political cultures influence company cultures in each country. This does not mean that all firms in a given country have the same type of culture, but rather that any given company's culture will prove compatible with the national political culture. By the same token, a company culture cannot unite its employees unless the latter can view its rules, principles and standards positively, in accordance with their political culture(s). Similarly, company culture is liable to influence professional culture; conceptions and practices associated with the same job title may differ from one organization to another. For instance, the merger of two large French banks, BNP and Paribas, revealed their divergent ideas on banking as a profession. BNP valued its public service aspect and retail bank, while Paribas valued its merchant bank status. At the employee level, these company cultures translated into stereotypes; the retail bankers called the investment bankers 'mercenaries' while the latter called the retail bankers 'shopkeepers' (Personal interview with BNP Paribas employee, June 2000).

Apparent and hidden cultural differences

In a multicultural team, members quickly become aware of differences in behavior, ways of conducting business, and approaches to tasks. The next section outlines the major differences cited in the literature that appear particularly relevant to management.

Observable behaviors

Among these visibly different behaviors, modes of communicating take top billing, as noted by Hall (1959). In our own research (Chevrier 2000), we have noted how some team members will take additional 'turns' at speaking, sometimes by interrupting others who scrupulously await their turn. Some do not hesitate to oppose another's expressed point of view, while still others never contradict anyone. Some speak in a lively fashion and allow their enthusiasm and passion to carry them away, while others remain unmoved and express themselves calmly. Members of international teams note that some participants establish a sealed border between their private and professional lives, while others happily pour out details of their personal life at work. Many will begin a conversation by discussing aspects of their personal lives before addressing professional issues.

These readily-seen surface differences inspire reactions from team members and managers that range from one extreme to another – from annoyance with behavior judged as inappropriate to an appreciation of the 'exotic'. Some members of international teams take offense at never being allowed to finish speaking without someone brutally cutting into their enthusiasm; others judge colleagues as cold when their phone calls plunge straight into the subject at hand, omitting even ritualistic inquiries after the call's recipient. Similarly, some expatriates like the rigor of equally-distributed chances to speak and a strictly-followed agenda, and say they must re-adapt when they return to a national context where colleagues often interrupt them. Between these two extremes, most participants in international teams tolerate differences and adapt to the others' attitudes. While these differences in communicative practices provoke some friction at worst and curiosity at best (if not outright amusement), they hardly pose insurmountable problems to working together.

Differences in cultural conceptions

Behind these surface differences emerge others concerned with various conceptions of legitimate governance. Clashes between cultural conceptions are not always identified as such; even when they are, they raise other, more serious difficulties for an international team. Team members may exert themselves as needed to avoid interrupting, to wait their turn or to vigorously defend their opinion, in order to get along in a group. However, they will find it much harder to renounce basic beliefs about reaching agreement, or to calmly accept the dictates of a boss whose behavior they perceive does not respect their personal dignity. This is the level where international teams' principal difficulties arise.

We base our argument here on Iribarne's study (1989) of cultural shocks in a Franco–Swedish project team. The team, charged with designing a new product, comprised engineers from both countries; it faced differences in opinion around appropriate technical choices, and even on the process for making these choices. On the French side, team members measured the quality of a decision by how well it followed a technical rationale. In their view, the solution chosen should be optimized, based on criteria hashed out by the firm's experts. In the debate, each team member fiercely defended his or her position with scientific arguments, their vehemence simply a sign of their conviction. When these experts could not agree, they expected their boss – sitting above the fray – to make the final decision, guaranteeing a global rationality that transcended their local ones. If, with additional study, a solution had emerged that would better satisfy the technical criteria, the French team would substitute that solution for the previous one, objectively judged inferior.

On the Swedish side, the quality of a decision was measured by the consensus it created. During technical discussions, team members would list arguments not in order to firmly defend their positions, but to see what concessions might be needed to reach an agreement. Long discussions would gradually lead to a compromise solution; once participants had agreed to it, it would figure as a sacred agreement, closed to further questioning.

Our comparison of these two ideal types of decision-making processes sheds light on the Franco–Swedish team's many misunderstandings. Each group of engineers took a contrasting approach to their meeting; the French, having refined their arguments, used them to convince their interlocutors, while the Swedish politely listened to everyone's opinion as they sought a compromise. Quickly, the Swedes made concessions without getting anything back from the French, who were not playing by the same implicit rules. This imbalance frustrated the Swedish engineers, while the French felt they were winning through solid arguments. Their mutual incomprehension peaked when some French managers reversed one of the engineering team's decisions in a meeting, convinced they had found a better technical solution. The Swedish team members felt betrayed by this questioning of a joint decision obtained after long negotiations. The French team members found the Swedes' reaction narrow-minded or even stupid for refusing a solution that had undeniable technical advantages in their (French) eyes.

These divergent conceptions of decision-making reflect different conceptions of hierarchical relations. On the French side, the boss would not necessarily attend the arguments, but would participate in technical choices to ensure the rationality of the entire project. The boss enjoyed the role of arbiter and had the power to make decisions. On the Swedish side, the boss had essentially no technical role; his or her job was to encourage consensus, to allocate speaking turns, to listen, and to direct the team towards compromise. He or she could not imagine reversing a team decision. The Swedish boss had a functional role, but did not visibly stand out from his or her colleagues through any particular status or privilege.

These divergent conceptions of decision quality and decision-making process also grew into misunderstandings and mutual negative perceptions. For example, the Swedes perceived the French bosses as autocrats who imposed their points of view on their subordinates, without comprehending that French colleagues who accepted such decisions did not lose their autonomy of thought or their critical perspective. Similarly, since the Swedish bosses did not get involved in technical matters, the French engineers did not understand their contribution. In the eyes of the French engineers, the Swedish bosses' actions as managers, peacekeepers and molders of consensus added no value to the teams; these roles were simply invisible to the French. This example shows how differences in cultural conceptions can damage a team's efficiency and its members' mutual perceptions. From an operational point of view, it shows how difficult it is for a team to make a choice when its members do not share views on reaching agreement. It underscores how cooperation itself may suffer through mutual misjudgments – as when some resent a decision imposed from above rather than one collectively discussed, or else view their colleagues as incompetent because they do not engage in the expected arguments over technical solutions.

Cultural differences in an organizational context

As we saw in the first section, a multicultural team works in an organizational context; a manager cannot simply 'manage' its intercultural dimension without regard for its other characteristics. Generally, the manager must determine how much a team's cultural divides reflect or amplify other divides, particularly power-sharing disparities and divergent interests. In a nationally-mixed management team, for example, cultural and organizational boundaries coincide, while in a homogeneous team with a few 'submerged' foreigners, cultural differences do not necessarily follow the lines of other divides. When cultural, organizational, structural and political divides follow the same lines, negative intercultural perceptions tend to prolong conflicts.

We studied a case where a manufacturing group charged several subsidiaries with jointly designing a new product; the French and German subsidiaries – previously two different companies, recently acquired by the manufacturer – each had their own proven development methodology and software. For the project, design team participants had to adopt a common methodology; choosing an existing one would have hampered the other team, since changing methods would require costly investments for software and user training. This problem of conflicting interests was prolonged by the French and German teams' mutually negative judgments. Moreover, they moved the dispute from the domain of conflicting interests to the domain of cultural differences. A French designer declared, 'The Germans are not very flexible, or autonomous – they cling to their pecking order, to what they have done in the past'. (Chevrier 2000) This judgment presents the Germans' resistance to the French methodology – possibly a defense of well-understood interests – as the result of a supposed cultural rigidity. Such stereotyping – disqualifying the 'other' as rigid, limited and dependent – tends to mask more fundamental conflicts.

More generally, competitive situations may lead participants to manipulate cultural identities to serve their own interests. Sherif et al. (1961) show that conflict between two groups activates individual feelings of identification with one's own group; it also triggers further prejudices, discriminatory attitudes and hostility towards other group. In other words, group members reason that if they cannot achieve a meeting of the minds, it is not because satisfying their own interests can only occur at the others' expense; rather, they judge the others incapable of acting properly due to their intrinsic cultural characteristics.

In other situations, individuals use 'auto-stereotypes' or self-stereotyping to cloak conflicts of interest and power. When an American group, Service Corporation International, took control of the French services firm OGF-PFG, the French employees invoked the cultural and institutional character of 'French-style public service' to signal that the foreign jurisdiction stopped at the border; in this way, they hoped to conserve greater decision-making autonomy (Margerie 1995). The French employees defended their strategic interests under the cover of preserving inalienable cultural specificities; claiming a cultural identity seemed more legitimate than retaining prerogatives that no one wanted to give up.

When cultural divides join other differences, the groups involved sometimes instrumentalize culture and use it to mask self-interested ploys. This does not mean that real cultural differences may not also be at work in their interactions, making collaboration difficult, as we saw earlier. Real collisions between culturally-determined views are doubtless at play behind the cultural alibi, without being recognized as such (Chevrier 2009).

At the same time, managers tend to underestimate the complex repercussions of cultural differences on teamwork. Team members see obvious differences, the ones that do not preclude collaboration, and attribute culturally-driven misunderstandings to other problems, such as personality or incompetency; this prompts them to minimize the consequences of perceived differences. Furthermore, when team members explicitly stigmatize or invoke culture, this may only further mask legitimate conflicts of interest; this tends to discredit culture's role in intercultural collaboration problems. However, as the Franco–Swedish case discussed above has shown, manageable cultural differences remain at the origin of team dysfunctions (Box 7.1)

How to manage multicultural teams?

Diversity management in multicultural teams must reconcile the ethical requirement to respect differences with the obligation to achieve economic efficiency. Managers can accommodate cultural differences in four ways; we will present them in order, explaining the effects of each on cooperative climate and team efficiency, as well as limits and problems left unresolved.

Relying on spontaneous tolerance and ability to adapt

Until recent times, international team management paid no special attention to cultural issues; the manager left his or her teams alone to struggle with their diversity. We can suggest theoretical and practical reasons for this strategy. In part, management theories posit themselves as implicitly or explicitly universal, fed by economic theories founded on rational self-interest, a behavior presumed to transcend cultural particularities. Many managers willingly embrace this approach, following Jack Welch, the former president of General Electric and initiator of many international acquisitions. He claimed he never worried about cultures, counting on good stock options plans to bring employees together (Barre 2000).

Convergence theories postulate forces that incline industrial societies toward cultural homogenization (see e.g. McLuhan, 1964); they tend to overlook the residual variables of cultures that face extinction. In management practice, these theories generally translate into standardization and its corollary, the spread of 'best practices' from one firm to the next. This persistent belief in a single, ahistorical and acultural 'best strategy' encourages managers to ignore cultural issues – even though contingency theories debunked such beliefs in the 1950s (see e.g. Hickson and McMillan 1981). Comparative management studies emphasize the need to adapt management methods to firms' cultural contexts (Hofstede 1980; Iribarne et al. 1998), but they do not supply formulae for intercultural team adaptations.

This absence of cultural differences management produces a more or less peaceful coexistence of heterogeneous interpretations and practices – in work methods, exercise

Box 7.1 Multicultural teams: between creativity and conflict?

Multicultural teams are often perceived as highly creative yet combative, assembling divergent views that may create opportunities as well as a climate of conflict. Nancy Adler (1987) was one of the first to formalize the advantages and disadvantages of multicultural teams, citing increased capacity for innovation on one side and a lack of cohesion due to mistrust, misunderstandings and stress on the other. She argues that management of these differences determines the outcome: a productive and creative dynamic or paralysis from the failure of joint decision-making. We would further argue that multicultural teams work best at producing new ideas in the upstream project stages, rather than downstream when managers must guide teams to solutions and implementation. In terms of efficiency, recent research shows that working in multicultural teams may lead to a gradual convergence and mutual, effective adjustments. Team members borrow what they perceive as the best task approaches to achieve goals collectively, and innovate in the process, at least in their working modes (Piron and Lucas 1998). Intercultural work may also spiral into misunderstandings and conflicts, as when some team members perceive others' goodwill gestures as hostile (Yousfi 2006). Mutual understanding does not automatically increase with the frequency of interactions. Rather, explicit clarifications of cultural differences will increase understanding, giving meaning to members' perceptions and legitimizing observed behavior.

However, even though members of multicultural teams say they learn a great deal, and appreciate the personal and professional enrichment of working with colleagues from other cultures, few find that the effectiveness of such teams surpasses that of more homogeneous ones. For example, Anglo–American members usually criticize multicultural teams' slowness and the lengthy discussions needed to reach agreement. Focused on action and results, they find the cost of convergence very high. French members often deplore solutions based on compromise rather than on optimization and coherence. Furthermore, team members uncomfortable with speaking a second language – who have trouble communicating or presenting their views with finesse – often perceive team debates and arguments as less than optimal (Welch et al. 2005). Practitioners and scholars generally recognize that the intercultural dimension supports learning and innovation, but employees may not succeed in sharing expertise efficiently – or at all, particularly in early stages of collaboration – unless managers take steps to facilitate effective communication. Moreover, research has not established the degree to which intercultural contact promotes innovative outcomes. However, as we noted earlier, this dimension must not be isolated from other factors that influence team dynamics. A multicultural project team may prove more innovative than a national team because the former taps more competencies. Companies often set up multicultural teams to achieve synergies between different business units, or to enlarge the talent recruiting pool; this promotes innovations not directly linked to the intercultural dimension.

of authority, communication behaviors, and so forth. In international teams with a low need for internal integration, participants work around their differences even as these cause small frustrations. However, in cases where firms strongly press for integration and need more uniform modes of operating, production imperatives and scheduling deadlines require a common methodology, one form of organization, a single technical solution – and consequently, require teams to achieve compromises. Whether or not the firm demands integration, the lack of institutional cultural management means relying on staff openness and self-restraint, tolerance of different approaches and behaviors, and acceptance of concessions that allow the team to function. Concretely, openness means that team members sometimes give up familiar ways of operating to adopt new ones. Tolerance implies that participants will accept behaviors they would otherwise tend to reject spontaneously. In the Franco–German case cited above, German workers confided that they couldn't accept other Germans coming to meetings unprepared, but they tolerated the French who did it; even when irritated, they held back from saying anything to avoid provoking a conflict (Chevrier 2000).

In this 'rely on the individual' approach to intercultural management, the team's work quality depends on its members' personal qualities – openness, restraint, patience. This minimalist approach becomes an active strategy when international team managers reject intercultural management as such – for instance, in the name of equal treatment, that is, 'I do not want to treat employees differently' – and explicitly call on their colleagues to show flexibility and adaptability. Team members appear willing to show these qualities because they either minimize or emphasize cultural differences. Those who 'minimize' will stress team unity and the modest nature of the necessary adaptations. Those who 'emphasize' will express an appreciation for the exotic that, as we saw earlier, systematically leads them to value other cultures; they see their efforts at openness as a fair trade for enriching their lives through contact with other cultures.

In a homogeneous team that owes its intercultural character to the presence of one or a few 'submerged' foreigners, collaboration mostly rests on the latter's unilateral adaptation; they are clearly the ones expected to change their ways. For other team members, daily operations management takes place in a self-contained world rarely modified by the foreigner's presence. At most, the foreigner may casually explain how operations differ in his or her native culture. Other team members see this as interesting 'folklore', but do not change their behavior toward the foreigner.

Generally speaking, the minority individual must adapt to the team's dominant culture, but linguistic adaptation may prove an exception. Sometimes, teams will accommodate a single member who does not speak the local language by having the whole team speak English (assuming that it is not the local language and can serve as the lingua franca). In these cases, however, the foreigner can only access formal communications; even if English allows functional work communication, informal conversations take place in the local language, which remains a powerful factor in the foreigner's exclusion.

An individual's goodwill towards team members from other cultures provides only the backdrop for effective adjustments; the relative malleability of the individual's behavior makes these adjustments possible. Individual worldviews and references will guide actions, but will not unequivocally determine behavior in a given situation; an interpretive frame is not a complete repertoire of possible conduct. Faced with the same situation and using the same interpretive lens, individuals may act very differently. Some may even behave in ways deemed 'deviant' by other members of their cultural community, despite knowing the consequences. Jacques Demorgon (1996) calls this malleability in relation to a cultural frame 'oscillation'. The oscillation we observe in intercultural situations – and even in uniform cultural groups – allows individuals to adapt to others, learn from them, or even acculturate to perceived differences.

Whether as a default approach or a strategy voluntarily adopted for equity's sake, this sole reliance on team members' goodwill, without managerial or institutional guidance, may limit team efficiency, personal satisfaction and cooperative climate. The last, in particular, reflects the cosmopolitan ideology of tolerance that infuses these teams, one that insists on 'intercultural courtesy', a form of political correctness that inhibits public expressions of prejudice. Team members cannot acknowledge the difficulties they experience working together, because this amounts to a confession of professional incompetence or a lack of openness. This leads to teamwork marked by tensions and conflicts that remain latent because they find no legitimate expression.

As for team efficiency, we observe that individuals do not always change willingly; when team members can only rely on others' goodwill, they often fail to find solutions to disagreements If they do not comprehend a problem's source, team members cannot easily move toward a common solution. Moreover, not all intercultural problems boil down to a few superficial misunderstandings; when one worldview legitimizes actions that appears improper according to another, a head-on cultural collision ensues. Mere tolerance can no longer overcome the ethnocentric reflex to condemn what is different. Furthermore, as Philippe Pierre shows, multiple international job transfers and experiences do not necessarily increase an individual's ability to adapt to otherness.

The experience of working in an international team may teeter between satisfaction and frustration; the more or less depends on the individual. The personal enrichment of discovering otherness comes at the price of constant questions – of one's business conduct, modes of operating and reference points. The frustrations team members accrue through self-censorship slip out during breaks or in side conversations between nationals, where individuals can blow off steam and express more raw, negative judgments about others. These moments between national team members (or other small, like-minded groups) help dissipate the stress of the constant self-control they exercise to avoid unfortunate outbursts in public; they also relieve the tensions that arise from their efforts to adapt and change working styles. We re-emphasize here that efficiency pressures oblige teams to accept compromises, ones that some members will see as regrettably below standard. Finally, participants may believe that the adaptation process requires extra negotiation time and results in less efficiency, since managers will accept inferior solutions (Chevrier 2000).

Encouraging adaptation by developing conviviality

In practice, mutual adaptation between individuals results from an iterative process of trial and error. By working together, team members learn to know what their partners will positively welcome, what they will reluctantly accept, and what they will find intolerable. But participants may not necessarily grasp the sources of their team members' consent or refusal. The compromises that team members establish over time shape an adaptation that does not distinguish between differences due to personality or national, regional, ethnic, sexual, company or professional culture, each of which has some eventual impact on composite team members (Sackmann et al. 1999).

Intercultural team managers may also promote adaptation through conviviality. Organizing social events outside of work hours allows participants to establish friendly and helpful relationships. An engineer working for a European consortium that regularly organized team dinners confided to us that years of working together encouraged 'get[ting] to know people. Relationships are relaxed; we know each other very well, some are even friends. We don't hesitate to pick up the phone to call each other.' Another team member added, 'We behave formally at work, but we are relaxed in meetings. Relations between co-workers are informal, friendly; everyone talks with one another, even with people not in the same working group. We mix together often' (Chevrier 2000, p. 34). Team leaders take on the challenge of transforming intercultural work into interpersonal encounters – far more effective than didactic presentations about an abstract, foreign world. The warm relationships and friendly ties that participants establish help dissipate their initial mistrust, making teamwork easier. This management strategy gradually introduces routines and work behaviors for intercultural team members.

One limit of this iterative approach lies in the time required: participants need to get to know each other well enough to make effective compromises. However, research on group dynamics shows that all teams need time to become effective (Gersick 1988). More fundamentally, a conviviality strategy and a trial-and-error process run up against the fragility of interpersonal adaptations. First of all, team members do not automatically make efforts to understand and mutually adapt. On the contrary, they may have confrontations that reinforce negative stereotypes, particularly if they profoundly disagree about the joint project. Good relationships between individuals may not suffice when they must mesh their different readings of a situation, or untie the ultimate crux of a conflict. Furthermore, a change of interlocutors – which happens frequently in teams working on long-term projects – or a change in circumstances may nullify the modus vivendi so patiently established. Continuously changing work situations limit the effects of local interpersonal understandings and agreements.

Capitalizing on common transnational cultures

When international team leaders view success as something more than an outgrowth of personal qualities and goodwill, they may propose institutional strategies to manage differences. In the absence of a common political culture, the manager relies on other transnational cultures to unify their teams. Some managers aim for a company culture that homogenizes practices and irons out differences. Others draw on team members' technical values, forged in their academic and professional lives through work with technologies, materials, concepts and objects; these include values such as speed, accuracy, creativity, reliability, etc. Teams working with their specific 'substrate' – computer engineers with algorithms, doctors with patients, drivers with trucks – frame their own ways of working, partially compensating for the lack of shared references.

In highly technical projects, such as product research and development, a shared professional culture tends to facilitate teamwork. More precisely, professional culture catalyzes team exchanges by enhancing communication, notably via a subject and a means of expression. Team members belonging to the same profession share some basic interests, knowledge and expertise, as well as a technical language. In one team we studied, computer specialists discussed highly specialized, cross-boundary concerns via English-language references and a common technical jargon. One engineer explained, 'The details of the technology are very complicated and each person masters his little piece of it. But in the big picture, we all do software engineering applied to telecoms. In this domain, people have a shared language; we understand each other and know common techniques.' An engineer from another team added,

> The most important thing is someone's educational background. If one guy has an engineering degree from a university in Lille [France] and the other guy got one from a university in Stuttgart, they will be closer than a French philosopher and a French technician.

> (Chevrier 2000, pp. 80, 84)

Here, intercultural coordination occurs through the standardization of professional qualifications (Mintzberg 1979). Grappling with technical objects on a daily basis fuels the development of professional skills; it also builds specific ideas and views, structuring the mental space of a profession. Eventually, such shared professional culture tends to transcend national borders; one project leader points to 'tightly-knit teams working on project objectives that allow them to ignore [each other's] cultures' (Chevrier 2000).

But does a focus on solid technical results prevent misunderstandings linked to different political cultures? While professional culture plays an undeniable role, we urge managers to recognize its limits. In the first place, this intercultural management strategy has its own problems; not all international teams belong to the same professional culture, even when the shared work object has a strong technical component. Most new product development projects draw co-workers from different professions – in fact, that is one of their main purposes. The common nucleus then narrows to a sector of activity with great internal heterogeneity. As an engineer engaged in a research project explains, 'We can tell if someone comes from software or telecoms engineering by what he does, by his interests. Some are still interested in [programming] languages, others in actual services' (Chevrier 2000, p. 84). As for technical vocabulary, meanings may vary significantly between specialties. The workers we interviewed noted that the terms 'configuration' or 'services' provoked misunderstandings between IT technicians and telecom specialists (Chevrier 2000, p. 84).

Even when team members share a common profession, intercultural misunderstandings remain, as international teams of astronauts have seen. While a shared profession and common technical culture may suffice during short missions, they cannot prevent incomprehension during longer ones. As we saw in the first section, professional and political cultures do not form separate systems of meaning. We have shown elsewhere (Chevrier 1998) that notions of quality for a highly technical product, for example a power sub-station, are closely linked to notions about working relationships. In other words, political cultures influence professional cultures insofar as the work, however technical, involves social interactions. Furthermore, identities associated with various professions, for example social status and belonging, do not necessarily cross borders. Lasserre (1989), Grelon (1998) and Sorge (1998) show this in studies about engineers: the French identify themselves with their school of origin and the elite, Germans with their company, and Americans with their job.

Where they lack a professional culture to draw upon, international team managers may look to a unifying company culture to overcome national differences. Two situations tend to arise in such cases. The international project team – like any other internal project team – may benefit from a well-defined company ethos. Or, as often occurs with mergers, acquisitions, and long-term intercompany projects, the team may acquire a new organizational culture – one built specifically for it or, sometimes, within it. Each situation has its own implications for management strategy.

When managers create a new team within a pre-existing, strong company culture, cooperation does not work through individually arranged agreements, but rather through team convergence around shared institutional norms. At a first level, the company culture facilitates teamwork through prescribed rituals to ensure that team members will feel secure and comfortable. This ritualization of contact between strangers neutralizes (at least partially) the potential for aggressive behavior in any cultural confrontation. At a second level, the company culture provides a work structure as well as shared methods; these improve team effectiveness, and promote integration via a repertoire of procedures and prescriptions for various business situations. In other words, company culture works through a kind of standardization of procedures, to use Mintzberg's (1979) coordination mechanisms typology. Thus the biggest international consulting firms distribute methodology manuals to all of their employees, describing how to conduct a mission from initial client contact to the end of the contract. The uniform institutional practices help each consultant work effectively in any team in the company, regardless of location.

When an international team includes employees from different organizations, developing a common culture poses real challenges, especially in a merger. As Sainsaulieu (1977) shows, the firm is the seat of cultural production; working relationships formed therein shape collective views. Leaders of teams with members drawn from different firms try to create a unified culture by homogenizing decision-making and personnel evaluation as well as by spreading shared values, for example commercial, technical and financial priorities. Ideally, a charismatic leader will bind his or her team members and link the team through highly symbolic events, such as a kick-off meeting at the project's beginning or a party celebrating a key milestone.

Even though managers play an essential role in creating company culture, they are not the masters of the game. Some scholars (Labounoux 1987; Aktouf 1988; Le Goff 1992) insist that company culture is a product of daily work relationships; the values and the company culture that managers proclaim should not be confused with the culture that arises from the ground up. Managers' attempts to manipulate company culture for their own purposes run up against resistance; for example, employees may create counter-cultures. Company culture is not a simple management tool easily deployed within an intercultural strategy. Not all team members will perceive their leaders' vaunted values as legitimate, depending on their individual worldviews and references.

Similarly, managerial methods may transfer successfully from their original contexts once workers align or 'read' them within their local worldviews (Iribarne and Henry 2007); or the team may brutally or – more often – insidiously reject the methods, which remain in force officially, but defunct in practice. Practices cannot be exported at will; their diffusion depends on reinterpretation within cultural systems of meaning. Furthermore, 'charismatic' leadership, widely perceived as a key to unification, does not appear to cross all borders. The workings of leadership are not universal and even the notion of 'charisma' finds no equivalent in all cultures (Bjerke 1999; Javidan and House 2002).

Even when a strong transnational company culture exists, it does not efface national cultures. A shared sense of belonging to a company does not signify that all personnel share the same ideas and views. Employees' shared dedication to the firm may follow very different rationales; it may spring from a win–win economic logic or a merger of identities. Sainsaulieu (1977) suggests that even though the firm is an autonomous site of cultural production, cultural currents beyond its purview flow through it, such as national or class cultures. The famous survey Geert Hofstede (1980) conducted in IBM offices worldwide provides the clearest demonstration that national cultures do not dissolve in the culture of a multinational corporation.

Managing diversity through company culture resolves problems due to surface differences – for example by setting common standards for speaking turns, work hours or meeting preparation. However, it has three major pitfalls. First, when managers try to integrate techniques and work methods without understanding local mentalities, they expose themselves to cultural rejection or a veiled resistance behind a facade of obedience (Kostova and Zaheer 1999). If, on the other hand, managers take real care to respect differences, they face a difficult choice. The unified transnational company culture they promote may rest on a very low common denominator, compatible with all employees' references; this considerably reduces the potential modes of work-sharing, leading to a denial rather than exploitation of usefully diverse viewpoints. Or the company culture may be conceived as a reflection of its members' diversity; it then becomes 'polycentric' or unifying in the Merkensian sense (1999).

This allows local differences to coexist within business units, but does nothing to resolve conflicts that emerge in cross-functional international teams.

Building intercultural synergies

The final strategy for managing cultural differences – drawing on intercultural synergies – rests on three hypotheses. The first is that – contrary to the assumptions of the strategies above – a manager must comprehend his or her team members' universes of meaning to define sustainable, collective and universally accepted ways of working. This comprehension does not come from general intercultural training sessions; these often help legitimize and reinforce stereotypes, which managers apply to intercultural decoding with little finesse. Instead, this comprehension draws on concrete situations and participant experience. The second hypothesis is that it is possible to create working synergies between several cultures. Culture-specific systems of meaning may legitimize a variety of previously unknown, innovative practices; intractable, head-on oppositions between such systems account for only a small share of workers' cultural conflicts. The third hypothesis is that cultural mediators can assist participants in making these compromises and in creating new intercultural solutions. Simple contact between cultures will not, in itself, promote mutual understanding and a shared search for creative solutions. On the contrary, repeated contacts between diverse team members tend to polarize them and inflate reciprocal negative stereotypes, particularly in situations where self-interest and power plays divide the cultural groups involved. Managers can avoid this by having a third party help intercultural teams through their adaptation process. Concretely, this synergies strategy rests on the three-step process described below, applied in successive meetings with all team members.

The first step uses specialists in intercultural mediation or other external multicultural parties. The mediators ask participants to think about misunderstandings and critical incidents that they have experienced in the course of the team's working life. Each participant then describes the situation(s), the team members involved, and his or her reactions to the problem(s). At this stage, the mediators aim for a climate of trust and security that allows participants to raise genuinely troubling problems; the mediators must do this without relying on superficial, polite questions that would preserve the diplomatic courtesy that is de rigueur in international settings. While the mediators allow participants to express negative accusations, they must also help each speaker focus on specific situations the group can analyze. And they must not empower the accusations to the point that they feed stereotypes, or imaginary 'us versus them' conflicts. In practice, many firms and mediators prefer not to call these sessions 'intercultural seminars' to avoid stigmatizing cultural differences; rather, they present this work as team-building or under another rubric that allows managers to address differences without appearing to do so.

In the second step, the mediators classify the inventory of reported problems, paying attention to the recurrence of key words and relationship structures (for example, those who take the initiative and/or the responsibility for decisions, and those who prefer to consult others). This work provides all participants an opportunity to clarify or further detail the incidents they have raised. When the mediators have finished the classification, they take up the most significant incidents with the participants, comparing their views about each situation. One part of this work is self-reflective, allowing each participant to gain full awareness of his or her own worldview and references. The other part helps participants step back from their own interpretive frame; they put their first impressions and judgments aside to delve into their team members' views. The mediators' cultural knowledge aids participants in this arduous decoding process. Once participants grasp each other's universes of meaning and interpretive frameworks, they can see actions as legitimate that previously seemed shocking or surprising; they can also clarify misunderstandings that result from crossed interpretive wires.

In the third step, the mediators reinvest new participant knowledge – that of managers and employees alike – into practical solutions, helping them adapt to intercultural differences; these joint solutions address specific professional situations. In other words, participants devise practices that everyone finds legitimate, even if this legitimacy rests on different criteria in each system of meaning. Sometimes solutions are relatively easy to establish. Managers of a German–Japanese joint venture, for example, set a maximum of two preparatory meetings for all decisions. This was a compromise between the Japanese preference for several meetings, seen as necessary for shared decision-making and monitoring, and the German preference for a single one; the Germans saw meetings as places to make decisions, and were frustrated when multiple sessions did not produce them (Salk 1996). Sometimes, synergistic solutions require more intercultural creativity on the team leader's part; this assumes that managers and teams have enough 'wiggle room' within their organizations to invent their own way of working. Finding practical solutions requires three steps: the participants define possible solutions in a session attended by all; they try out the solutions in real situations; then they share their experiences in another plenary session, refining the solutions or – if need be – more deeply modifying and retesting various solutions.

The intercultural synergies strategy has the advantage of not betting exclusively on a cognitive analysis of different worldviews; it also considers the team's technical and practical circumstances and the situation's emotional dimensions. Suitable behavior does not spontaneously arise on either side through mutual knowledge of cultural references. Adequate changes in attitudes and behaviors only occur through this back-and-forth between necessary action, self-reflective distance, and the feelings that actions provoke.

Such an approach requires a large commitment on the team's part to achieve the strategy's objectives, and this may limit its effectiveness. More fundamentally, given its reliance on a relativistic view of meaning systems, this mutual-learning strategy may not accord with all participants' views.

Conclusion

Multicultural teams encompass specific contexts, work requirements, and team composition; they operate in different ways and demand suitable management approaches. Managers must therefore ask specific questions to determine the best approach for a given team: how much integration does the team need? What cultures – professional, company, political – does the team include? Does the team assemble multiple cultures or only two? Which cultures do team members share? What divergent issues map themselves onto cultural differences? Who is explicitly or implicitly responsible for adapting to other(s)? How do team members feel about the cultural conceptions at work in the team?

In the first part of this chapter, we addressed the dimensions that managers must consider, and summarized the most common multicultural team configurations. In the second part, we examined how cultural differences affect these teams by mapping the main cultures at work in organizations – company, professional and political. We showed that the interplay between cultures is complex because their levels interweave, and because some cultures – particularly political cultures – prove hard to grasp fully. Political cultures play a front-stage role in the problems that multicultural teams experience; managers and other participants too often ignore these political issues, preferring to look for directly observable phenomena. In the last section, we presented approaches to legitimate and effective management of cultural diversity. Where a team's need to integrate cultures is low, a manager may count on members' spontaneous ability to adapt to differences, or even encourage these adaptations through social events that unify teams. When the need to integrate is high, and the team brings together two nationalities, the manager will achieve better results by helping his or her team build a cooperative strategy – a modus vivendi – at the intersection of the two cultures. We have postulated throughout that multicultural team management rests on this necessary adaptation to diversity; this implies that managers must find a range of approaches, adapting each time to team specificities. Further experimentation will be needed – new approaches to intercultural management, adaptations to different team configurations – given the immature state of current practices.

References

Adler, N. *International Dimensions of Organizational Behavior*. Boston: Kent Publishing Company, 1987.
Aktouf, O. 'La communauté de vision au sein de l'entreprise: exemples et contre-exemples', in G. L. Symons (ed.), *La Culture des organizations*, Quebec: Institut Québécois de Recherche sur la Culture, pp. 71–98, 1988.
Barre, N. 'General Electric boucle avec la prise de contrôle de Honeywell la plus grosse acquisition industrielle de l'histoire'. *Les Échos*, 24 October 2000.
Behrens, K. and Clouet, L. M. 'EADS: une normalisation européenne entre intérêts nationaux et mondialisation'. *Visions Franco-Allemandes*, 14. Paris: IFRI, 2009.
Bjerke, B. *Business Culture and Leadership: National Management Style in the Global Economy*. Cheltenham, UK: Edward Elgar, 1999.
Bonarelli, P. *La réflexion est-elle rentable?* Paris: L'Harmattan, 1994.
Chevrier, S. 'Le solide contre l'ingénieux: malentendus dans la gestion de projets franco-suisses', in P. d'Iribarne, A. Henry, J.-P. Segal, S. Chevrier and T. Globokar (eds), *Cultures et mondialisation, gérer par-delà les frontières*, Paris: Seuil, pp. 137–51, 1998.
—— *Le management des équipes interculturelles*. Paris: Presses Universitaires de France, 2000.
—— 'Cultural interbreeding among migrant workers'. Egos Colloquium, Freie Universitat Berlin, July 2005.
—— 'Is national culture still relevant in a global context? The case of Switzerland'. *International Journal of Cross-Cultural Management*, 9(2), 169–84, 2009.
Chevrier, S. and Segal, J-P. 'The coordination of multicultural teams in multinational companies: actors searching for guidelines'. *Revue Française de Gestion*, 37(212), 145–56, 2011.
Demorgon, J. *Complexité des cultures et de l'interculturel*. Paris: Anthropos, Economica, 1996.
Gersick, C. J. G. 'Time and transition in work teams: toward a new model of group development'. *The Academy of Management Journal*, 31(1), 9–41, 1988.
Grelon, A. 'Le poids de l'histoire: l'héritage de l'ingénieur contemporain', in C. Lanciano, M. Maurice, J.-J. Silvestre and H. Nohara (eds), *Les acteurs de l'innovation et l'entreprise: France, Europe, Japon*, Paris: L'Harmattan, pp. 201–16, 1998.
Hall, E. *The Silent Language*. New York: Doubleday, 1959.
Hickson, D. J. and McMillan, C. J. *Organisation and Nation: The Aston Program IV*. Surrey, UK: Gower, 1981.
Hofstede, G. *Culture's Consequences: International Differences in Work-Related Values*. Beverly Hills: Sage, 1980.
Iribarne, P. (d'). *La logique de l'honneur*. Paris: Seuil, 1989.
Iribarne, P. (d') and Henry, A. *Successful Companies in the Developing World*. Paris: AFD, 2007.

Iribarne, P. (d'), Henry, A., Segal, J.-P., Chevrier, S. and Globokar, T. (eds) *Cultures et mondialisation, gérer par-delà les frontières*. Paris: Seuil 1998.

Javidan, M. and House, R. J. 'Leadership and cultures around the world: findings from Globe'. *Journal of World Business*, 37(1), 1–2, 2002.

Kostova, T. and Zaheer, S. 'Organisational legitimacy under conditions of complexity: the case of the multinational enterprise'. *Academy of Management Review*, 24(1), 64–81, 1999.

Labounoux, G. 'Socialité organisationnelle', in Collectif Sciences Humaines Paris IX–Dauphine, *Organisation et Management en Question(s)*, Paris: L'Harmattan, pp. 64–79, 1987.

Lasserre, H. *Le pouvoir de l'ingénieur*. Paris: L'Harmattan, 1989.

Le Goff, J.-P. *Le mythe de l'entreprise: critique de l'idéologie managériale*. Paris: La Découverte, 1992.

Margerie, P. (de). 'Les pompes funèbres entre le rituel et la gestion, séminaires crises et mutations'. Ecole de Paris du Management, Seminar, 23 juin 1995.

McLuhan, M. *Understanding Media: The Extension of Man*. New York: McGraw-Hill, 1964.

Merkens, H. 'Management ethnocentrique, polycentrique, eurocentrique et géocentrique', in J. Demorgon and E.-M. Lipiansky (eds), *Guide de l'interculturel en formation*, Paris: Retz, ch. 17.1, pp. 261–64, 1999.

Midler, C. *L'auto qui n'existait pas*. Paris: Interéditions, 1993.

Mintzberg, H. *The Structuring of Organizations: A Synthesis of the Research*. Upper Saddle River, NJ: Prentice Hall, 1979.

Piron, P. and Lucas, O. *La conception en alliance intégrée. Le cas de l'alliance européenne des missiles tactiques*. 'Ressources Technologiques et Innovation' Seminar, Ecole de Paris du Management, 21 October 1998.

Sackmann, S. A., Phillips, M. E. and Goodman, R. A. 'The complex culture of international project teams', in R. Goodman (ed.), *Modern Organizations and Emerging Conundrums: Exploring the Post-industrial Sub-culture of the Third Millennium*, San Francisco: Lexington Books, pp. 23–33, 1999.

Sainsaulieu, R. *L'identité au travail*. Paris: FNSP, 1977.

Salk, J. 'De la créativité interculturelle: un exemple germano-japonais'. *Les Annales de l'École de Paris du Management*, III, pp. 337–45, 1996.

Sherif, M., Harvey, O. J., White, B. J., Hood, W. R. and Sherif, C. W. *Intergroup Conflict and Cooperation: The Robbers Cave Experiment*. Norman: University of Oklahoma Book Exchange, 1961.

Sorge, A. 'La construction sociale de l'innovation et des innovateurs en Allemagne et en Grande-Bretagne', in C. Lanciano, M. Maurice, J.-J. Silvestre and H. Nohara (eds), *Les Acteurs de l'innovation et l'entreprise: France, Europe, Japon*, Paris: L'Harmattan, pp. 125–44, 1998.

Tarrius, A. *La mondialisation par le bas*. Paris: Balland, 2006.

Welch, D. E., Welch, L. S. and Piekkari, R. 'Speaking in tongues: the importance of language in international management processes'. *International Studies of Management and Organisations*, 35(1), 10–27, 2005.

Yousfi, H. 'Le contrat dans une coopération internationale: de la rencontre des intérêts à la rencontre des cultures'. Doctoral thesis, University of Paris X–Nanterre, 2006.

8 Managing multiculturalism in the workplace[1]

Eduardo Davel and Djahanchah Philip Ghadiri[2]

Introduction

As organizations increasingly operate on an international level, they are predictably faced with culturally diverse employees. The overlapping of globalization with continual migration and an increasingly international mass culture reveals intensified intercultural relations, both on local and international levels. It is no longer necessary to travel long distances in order to experience culture shock. One can experience culture shock while sharing a meal with friends, attending university, or even while interacting with colleagues. In this sense, it seems that cultural limits are becoming blurred and evolving within smaller, local daily spheres. Furthermore, organizations have seldom been as culturally diverse as they are today and the phenomenon continues to expand.

The increased complexity of the cultural mix within organizations is an invitation to reflect on the employees' multicultural characteristics and the resulting cross-cultural interactions. In this chapter, the terms multicultural and cross-cultural will be used without taking a stand in the debates surrounding these two notions or theoretical fields. The idea of multiculturalism commonly refers to the coexistence of several distinct cultural communities. However, we use this idea of multiculturalism on the assumption that there is no clear-cut distinction between cultural groups (often referred to as 'communities' or 'minorities') and that they influence and communicate with each other, as well as evolve in time and space. We therefore conceive boundaries between cultures as being less stable and more porous, permeable, and changing than the conservative approach to multiculturalism would suggest. In other words, multiculturalism is considered a phenomenon that evolves based on social interactions. Within the context of multiculturalism, interactions between communities that have been defined as culturally distinct are closely watched in the area of cultural diversity management. In fact, these cultural interactions are considered to be important sources of tension and misunderstandings, as well as enrichment and mutual learning.

In order to analyse the cross-cultural aspect of managing multiculturalism in the workplace, we referred to the field of diversity management. This field does not take only the cultural aspect into account, but also considers age, sex, disabilities, religion, physical appearance, sexual orientation, regional roots, and more. In this chapter, we will focus on diversity in terms of ethnocultural background.

Also, it should be kept in mind that the management of multiculturalism in the workplace does not constitute a clearly defined set of practices. Rather, it is characterized by a large range of different practices. This variety arises partly from the influence of the different contexts in which they are implemented (legal, historical or political), the various views of diversity that are favoured in different institutions, the propensity of each of these organizations to make it a strategic issue or not, more or less in agreement with the multiple levels of management. Ultimately, cultural diversity management extends beyond institutionalized programmes and includes a set of reflexive practices that must be directly linked to the singularities and evolution of the context and of the cross-cultural situations at which they are directed. Therefore, we will not promote a ready-made solution. This being said, we will attempt to isolate transverse issues inherent to cultural diversity management and to define ways of addressing them in a learning context.

The present chapter will be organized as follows. First, we will define the challenges of cultural diversity management, allowing us to understand the practices in a larger, more complex and multidimensional context. We will then introduce four potential perspectives and strategies of cultural diversity management. In the following section, one of these perspectives, learning, is discussed. We will analyse the various intercultural conflicts as a preferred means of learning as well as the tools for understanding and managing these conflicts. In the last section, we will focus on training practices as a formal aspect of cross-cultural learning. We will examine the key principles underlying a training initiative as well as the aspects that facilitate the training operability and the various available teaching tools.

Managing cultural diversity: challenges

Cultural diversity management derives from a fairly recent theoretical field, which is very popular among organization consultants and practitioners. Like any new subject area, cultural diversity management is faced with many challenges. Three of its major challenges are: (a) the biases in the discourse on diversity, (b) the dilemma of cultural diversity, and (c) the political issues related to cultural diversity management.

Biases in the discourse on diversity

The managerial trend of diversity management usually portrays diversity as a positive phenomenon with considerable economic impacts. This discourse is usually upheld by management practitioners and consultants, and it puts forward how diversity can benefit business development. For Prasad and Mills (1997), this discourse derives from a certain naivety that turns away from the conflicts and breakdowns that are an inherent part of a diverse and changing work environment.

Therefore, diversity management is often perceived as an organization-changing programme ingrained in its strategy for the improvement of organizational efficiency. For instance, Cox (1993) proposed a model (Figure 8.1) in which he set forth various factors and aspects of diversity and organizational efficiency. This model allows the contemplation of different types of factors (individual, organizational, collective) at the root of the multicultural climate in an organization. It also allows the contemplation of the influence of this climate on organizational efficiency and on how people relate to their work. Furthermore, Kossek et al. (2006) analysed the various effects of diversity, whether organizational, individual, or related to groups.

Positive discourses support the idea of diversity being an invaluable option for businesses due to its impact on competitive efficiency and capacity. For example, a common argument is that managing diversity can facilitate recruiting and keeping the best talents available in a social-demographic context in which skilled labour tends to be scarce. Diversity can also stimulate and improve marketing efforts inasmuch as consumers from ethnic groups prefer organizations that value cultural diversity management; they identify with the employees

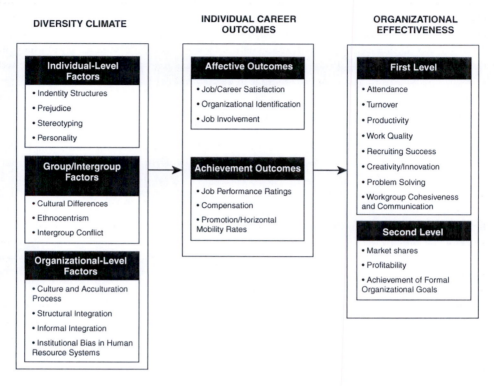

Figure 8.1 Cultural diversity management models
Source: Adapted from Cox (1993, p. 7)

and their way of doing things. Moreover, ethnic networks are encouraged within national and international markets, making it possible to discover new types of ethnic networks and take advantage of their potential in order to achieve more efficient business transactions.

Another argument relating diversity to organizational efficiency is about teamwork and problem solving. Multicultural teams are perceived as capable of tackling problems in creative and innovative ways because they brings various points of view to the table, grasping different aspects of a problem. For this reason, it is assumed that organizations that value innovation are more comfortable with multiculturalism (Kanter, 1983). In fact, taking the views of an organization's minorities into account is perceived as a method to find alternatives in problem solving and conflict resolution.

Conversely, in the spirit of celebrating diversity, a lack of diversity management is perceived as leading to eventual stereotypes, prejudice and misunderstandings, at the root of many issues (negative effects on the staff's mood, communication difficulties, atmosphere of anxiety, decision making obstacles, etc.). Consequently, diversity management is often perceived as a way to raise motivation and involvement at work, which translates into a positive impact on the organization's efficiency.

That being said, even if consultants, researchers and managers favour an exclusively positive view of cultural diversity and its management, employee perception and experience can still be significantly different from each other. Thus, diversity management can be faced with resistance within organizations (Dick and Cassell, 2002). Also, according to Bond and

Pyle (1998) cultural diversity management within an organization can have unexpected effects, either positive or negative. According to these authors, any attempt to address diversity must include an understanding of: (a) the interaction between the various meanings that diversity has for different individuals (for example, threat vs. opportunity); (b) the organization's capacity to support the change (both formally and informally); and (c) the options and limitations established by the political and legal framework.

One of the reasons why various drastically opposed visions about cultural diversity coexist and why managing it involves so much tension is the fact that it faces an important dilemma and that it is at the heart of crucial political issues.

The dilemma of cultural diversity

The dilemma at the centre of cultural diversity management corresponds with an important debate in most rich countries with sustained immigration: the integration policies for immigrants (Prasad et al., 2006). If on the one hand, assimilation, which involves suppressing cultural variations, can lead to a grudge within cultural minorities, and to non-realistic expectations from the majorities, cultural pluralism, on the other hand, which has its roots in multiculturalism, assumes that the dominant culture will accept, value and respect cultural differences rather than absorb them, and can lead to tensions in cultural spaces.

For example, Bond and Pyle (1998) note that diversity management can sometimes be silenced by other management initiatives that focus on team or organizational culture. Such initiatives may suggest in certain instances that the culture of a team or an organization take precedence over ethnocultural variations. In other words, cultural diversity management hesitates between imposing a 'forced identity' and 'ghettoization', which may only result in creating differences and conflicts.

Political issues related to cultural diversity management

Tensions surrounding cultural diversity management are also generated by the political issues addressed. This is the reason why many researchers call for more attention to be given to power struggles in diversity management (see, for example, Linnehan and Konrad, 1999; Foldy, 2002; Prasad et al., 2006; Ozbilgin and Tatli, 2008).

Zanoni and Janssens (2004) and Kozakaï (2007) suggest a concept of diversity as a social construct, a notion constructed historically and collectively through language. In other words, diversity is a historically dependent way of describing a population in terms of differentiating categories. Distinct cultures, born from this segmentation of a population into categories, do not represent cultural essences that would distinguish them in absolute terms. Rather, they are the result of a social process of categorization and identification which creates, reproduces or maintains relationships of power. In this sense, cultural diversity is politically tinged, having a number of impacts on social categories identified as culturally distinct. In other words, the way in which diversity is understood within a given population will lead to different ways of dealing with individuals perceived as members of these categories.

Beyond the social construct of diversity within a given population, one must also regard the concept of diversity itself as a social construct. One will perceive diversity itself in different ways, depending on context and situation (Klarsfeld, 2012; Chanlat et al., 2013). Thus, various discourses about diversity coexist (Zanoni and Janssens, 2004). This is why cultural diversity management depends mostly on the conception of diversity. Certain discourses about diversity build cultural differences in terms of essence (Zanoni and Janssens, 2004), coherent and distinct rather than complex and contradictory social constructs that change with interactions. Such a discourse could lead to dangerous short cuts by identifying individuals with the so-called essential attributes of their cultural background.

For instance, the emergence, meaning and importance of the Arabic–Muslim cultural category are mostly the result of a media and social construction process which were intensified after 9/11. An individual who is tagged as an Arab will be treated according to the traits that are believed to be part of the essence of the Arabic–Muslim cultural group, regardless of the uniqueness and singularity of the individual's background. However, many people who are treated according to this category will not identify themselves with it. They may consider themselves as secular, non-practising, Christian, non-Arab (for example, Berbers) or even as a part of the host society's cultural category. Moreover, even among those who do identify themselves as Arabic–Muslim, some will not recognize themselves in the image that people will have of them. In a post-9/11 Islamophobic context, this can have dramatic consequences of which we are already aware.

Conversely, other discourses on cultural diversity tend to view it as a social construct (Kozakaï, 2007) or as discursive resources mobilized with the idea of pursuing certain objectives (Barinaga, 2007; Ailon-Souday and Kunda, 2003). Furthermore, as previously shown, certain discourses will construct diversity as a blessing and others as a nuisance. These variations lead to very distinct means of managing cultural diversity which have different impacts on target populations. Ultimately, cultural diversity as a social construct allows for certain cultural diversity management practices and power relationships between culturally defined groups (Zanoni and Janssens, 2004).

Also, diversity management always takes place in context. The context is characterized by asymmetrical power relationships rooted in history. Although it should sometimes successfully reduce inequalities between different components of an organization (Linnehan and Konrad, 1999; Foldy, 2002), diversity management has been criticized for being nothing but a front, involving no actual or consequential changes (Foldy, 2002) and thus perpetuating inequalities in power relationships (Linnehan and Konrad, 1999; Foldy, 2002; Zanoni and Janssens, 2004). This becomes ever more important in today's context in which immigration is on the rise in rich countries and involves significant amounts of tension, discriminatory practices and inequalities of status and power (Prasad et al., 2006; Ozbilgin and Tatli, 2008; Klarsfeld, 2012; Chanlat et al., 2013). Researchers such as Linnehan and Konrad (1999) are putting forward a concept of diversity at work, addressing the problems of straightforward discrimination and oppression of certain social categories and cultural minorities.

Others, however, caution against the reification and legitimization of social categories on which inequalities of power and discriminatory practices are based (Thomas and Davies, 2005). Diversity management can indeed become a device reproducing social categories on which discrimination is based. In other words, focusing on cultural differences can lead to confirming and justifying the necessity to discriminate and exclude (Webb, 1997; Cockburn, 1991; Kirton and Greene, 2005). The dominant group tends to consider those that differ from the dominant norm as inferior, therefore justifying disqualification or the unequal use of those labelled as different. Thus, to bring up one's difference may ruin efforts to treat everyone equally (Liff, 1996). Therefore, individuals perceived as different, in a diversity management context, risk being ghettoized and seeing their differences turned against them by the organization (Kirton and Greene, 2005).

Certain researchers, inspired by critical and post-colonialist theories, see a source of resistance in the discourse about diversity, allowing those who experience differences to gain power within organizations. Others, on the contrary, see a way to depoliticize the matter of exclusion and exploitation of certain cultural categories and to sabotage the potential resistance that they represent for global capitalism (Prasad, 2006; Jones and Stablein, 2006; Mir et al., 2006; Banerjee and Linstead, 2001). Along the same lines, some challenge the legitimacy of diversity management, arguing that it is an attempt to distract employees from issues considered more urgent, such as material inequalities (Michaels, 2007).

Perspectives of cultural diversity management

Cultural diversity management does not follow one specific protocol. As we saw earlier, conceptions about diversity at work can vary drastically in terms of ontology (e.g. social construct vs. essence), value judgements (diversity as a positive vs. negative phenomenon), and the meanings attributed to equality and difference. For example, Zanoni and Janssens (2005) studied four organizations in the service sector, and they observed that the perception of diversity in each of the organizations determined the approach and the management strategy chosen.

Four perspectives stand out among others: (a) the resistance perspective, (b) the discrimination-and-fairness perspective, (c) the access and legitimacy perspective, and (d) the integration-and-learning perspective. These three perspectives were originally identified by Thomas and Ely (1996) and Ely and Thomas (2001), whereas Dass and Parker (1999) completed the picture by adding the resistance perspective. Furthermore, these authors identified diversity management strategies linked to each perspective. Each strategy introduces different problematics and concerns, as shown in Table 8.1. Note that these authors consider ethnocultural differences as being just another aspect of diversity.

The reactive strategy in diversity management derives from a perspective of diversity inspired by a spirit of resistance (Dass and Parker, 1999). This perspective refers to a way of conceiving diversity (in terms of nationality, skin colour or gender) as a threat to the establishment (ethnocentric white males). Perceiving diversity as a threat, managers favour a reactive strategy aiming at countering diversity, maintaining homogeneity and preserving traditional methods. This type of strategy often leads to the exclusion, manipulation and contempt of those who are not considered as equals (Dass and Parker, 1999).

According to Dass and Parker (1999), it is not surprising to meet managers and leaders who still favour these types of strategies today. In other words, there are still legions of racist and xenophobic reactions, sometimes inherent to diversity management, in work environments.

Table 8.1 Strategies of diversity management

Strategy	Diversity perspectives	Problematic	Desired outcome
Reactive	Resistance	Differences as threats	Protect the status quo and reinforce homogeneity
Defensive	Discrimination and equity	Differences as problems	Level the playing field for members of protected groups
Accommodation	Access and legitimacy	Differences as an opportunity	Access to employees and consumers
Proactive	Learning process	Differences offer learning opportunities	Individual and organizational learning for long-term effects

The defensive strategy and the discrimination-and-fairness perspective

The defensive strategy views diversity as an organizational problem that needs to be resolved. This strategy is part of a philosophy of diversity that emerged from the ideas of discrimination and fairness. In order to ensure the fairness of a certain situation and to counter discrimination in the work environment, management takes on the tasks of defending rights, negotiating, balancing and appeasing in the case of intercultural tensions. Employees are thus led to consider others as equals. For example, management will ensure that differences do not play into performance evaluations.

The discrimination-and-fairness perspective is characterized by the moral imperative to ensure social justice and fair treatment for all members of society. Management practices inspired by this perspective are focused on ensuring equal opportunities during recruiting, selecting and promoting, as well as on suppressing prejudicial attitudes and eliminating discrimination. This perspective considers that prejudice has systematically and historically excluded members of certain groups from certain types of employment. Equal access and fair treatment based on the law are both used to change this historical discrimination. It is a perspective rooted in legal decisions, more specifically in affirmative action policies and legislation concerning equal opportunities in employment.

An approach of this sort can lead to tensions within organizations. Members of the dominant cultural group can sometimes perceive this type of programme as a source of injustice. For instance, hiring a minimum quota of people from an ethnocultural group can cause defensive reactions if less qualified people end up being hired in the process.

Accommodation strategy and the discrimination-and-fairness perspective

Some organizations value diversity because they perceive it as a source of opportunity or an investment. In such a case, the accommodation strategy is favoured. An accommodation strategy is not based on legal constraints or on social grounds. It is more of a choice based on an interpretation of demographic changes and their impact on business. In other words, it is rooted in an understanding that consumers and employment markets are becoming increasingly culturally diverse. Consequently, hiring and maintaining multicultural employees becomes a way of gaining legitimacy with these markets and groups. Diversity is thus perceived as a means of connecting the business with the market; a vital investment for the business' commercial success.

Since diversity is linked to growth, an accommodation strategy-oriented management team promotes considerable levels of heterogeneity and inclusion within the organization. Leaders who favour such a strategy and understand diversity from this perspective will strive to create an organizational climate that will provide a channel through which differences can be expressed.

On the one hand, accommodation strategies favour culturally diverse employees in hopes of gaining access to the markets and its key components. On the other hand, they do not incorporate cultural skills developed by employees within the organization's core activities. This attribute can be associated with the proactive strategy and the integration-and-learning perspective.

The proactive strategy and the integration-and-learning perspective

The integration-and-learning perspective is intended for the inclusion of diversity in the organization's evolution. In other words, the ideas, skills and experiences that employees accumulate as members of a specific cultural group are potential resources that a group can use to rethink its main duties and to redefine markets, products, strategies and business practices (Ely and Thomas, 2001). Thus, it is a perspective that relates diversity to work procedures and to the way people do business and experience their work on a daily basis. Management practices therefore play a proactive role in making diversity a resource for continuous integration and learning, and for adaptive change.

The integration-and-learning perspective focuses on the appreciation of differences and similarities, and on the fact that they should lead to integration and learning in the long term. Similarities and differences are in fact viewed as two aspects of cultural diversity that cannot be dissociated from one another. For instance, if the emphasis is only put on differences, the members of a group could be led to believe that their only purpose is to offer knowledge associated with their group (Thomas and Ely, 1996), belittling their technical or general skills (Lorbiecki, 2001).

One of the strong points of the integration-and-learning perspective is that it sheds light on the need to take both diversified staff and diversified work into account when cultural diversity is identified as the core of organizational processes. In this perspective, learning is viewed as a key aspect, leading Lorbiecki (2001) to stress the need to study diversity management from theories about learning within organizations. In this chapter, we will highlight such a perspective by focusing on learning from intercultural conflicts and on the role of training in an intercultural learning effort.

Intercultural learning based on conflicts

According to the integration-and-learning perspective, the clashing of different points of view surrounding the interpretation of (and necessary actions involved in) daily work situations is a powerful learning mechanism in itself. The clash between the ways of understanding what is 'reality' and what should or must be done can lead to many misunderstandings and cultural conflicts. Intercultural conflicts emerge from clashes between values, norms and beliefs, occurring in various ways: different goals, competing for resources, assimilation vs. preservation of cultural identity (Cox, 1993). Moreover, Camilleri (1999) highlights the fact that conflicts of interest (related to work competition and social insecurity) are not necessarily cultural, although culture is used as an excuse.

In other words, intercultural conflicts are the result of a perceived or actual incompatibility between the values, norms, processes or objectives of at least two different culturally defined groups, in terms of identity, relationships and procedures (Ting-Toomey, 1999). This type of conflict involves: (a) intercultural perceptions (more or less ethnocentric and stereotyped); (b) spoken or non-spoken interactions that fuel or resolve conflicts (related to culture); (c) a certain relationship of interdependence between parties; (d) both mutual and individual goals; and (e) protecting the image of one's group (Ting-Toomey, 1999).

From an integration and learning perspective, it is necessary in a multicultural organization to take on disputes and conflicts with a positive outlook and not to attempt to avoid them. Considering disputes between people of different ethnocultural backgrounds can translate into fruitful intercultural learning opportunities. While it is tempting to regard such conflicts as issues to be avoided at all costs, others see them as an opportunity, if not a learning resource, for those involved and for the entire organization (De Dreu and Van de Vliert, 1997; Friedman and Berthoin Antal, 2005; Thomas and Ely, 1996). Thus, it appears that in addressing diversity and the cultural differences it carries with it, we have gone from ethnocentric discrimination to an equally ethnocentric denial of differences, to a celebration of differences, leading to this new learning perspective (Lorbiecki, 2001).

Dialogue and intercultural learning

Dialogue is a favourable way of dealing with intercultural conflicts constructively, creating a learning opportunity. More specifically, it is favourable to approach dialogue from a learning perspective (learning from our differences), as opposed to an ethnocentric perspective (rejecting differences by exploring them in a polarized manner, or denying their existence by suppressing them or putting them between brackets) or an adaptation perspective (encouraging and asserting differences). The ethnocentric perspective is based on the establishment of certain cultural practices as the only valid ones (Adler, 2000; Ting-Toomey, 1999). This leads to an atmosphere of distrust and impedes any attempt at establishing a constructive dialogue during an intercultural conflict (Ting-Toomey, 1999).

The adaptation perspective, in turn, implies recognizing and asserting differences, and adapting to them by having enough knowledge about the other culture to be able to change one's frame of reference and behaviour in order to adjust to its norms (Friedman and Berthoin Antal, 2005). The weak points of this perspective are that (a) it perceives national culture as a unitary system that influences its members in a deterministic and therefore predictable way; (b) it assumes that people are easily capable of intentionally changing from one cultural frame of reference to another; and (c) it prevents the learning of other ways of dealing with situations (Friedman and Berthoin Antal, 2005).

The integration-and-learning perspective would be the most favourable to support a multicultural organization and the management of multicultural issues. As a matter of fact, we support the idea that the more people differ from one another, the more they have to teach and learn from each other (Barnlund, 1998). However, it is important to highlight one of the possible pitfalls of this perspective, namely, its essentialist tendency. This approach suggests that working practices and methods will automatically differ depending on one's native culture (Lorbiecki, 2001). While it may be tempting to rely on cultural generalizations to understand the other, one must not forget that individuals are very often more complex than what may be inferred from their cultural background(s). It will therefore be our responsibility to prepare ourselves to deal with intercultural conflicts as unique and complex situations, involving human beings who are just as unique and complex (ourselves included) (Friedman and Berthoin Antal, 2005).

Another limitation of the integration-and-learning perspective concerns its sociopolitical biases (Lorbiecki, 2001). On the one hand, diversity management in a learning perspective is often based on managerial goals and can therefore be considered a manipulation and control device. On the other hand, this approach must open itself through memory (Bhabha, 1994), beyond pragmatic and instrumental differences that come into play in intercultural conflicts in the workplace, to the political and historical disputes that give them meaning and the emotions that they produce (Fineman, 1997). So diversity management may live up to the expectations it has generated. Therefore, intercultural conflicts could truly be considered learning opportunities, not only to work better, but to live better as a group.

While cultural conflicts can be rooted in history and politics, as we saw in Chapter 1, many intercultural conflicts in the world of organizations are caused by cultural misunderstandings. If these misunderstandings persist and are poorly managed or negotiated, conflicts may become polarized and more complex due to poor communication, faulty attributions or the ethnocentrism of either party (Ting-Toomey, 1999). There are therefore less learning opportunities.

Conflict management as a cultural issue

Dialogue, which favours intercultural learning, must also take into account the cultural differences related to conflict management. It is indeed crucial to take the time to explore the conflict management methods that are considered inherent to each culture: how one perceives the conflict, whether one is involved or not, and how one understands the goals to be achieved, may vary substantially from culture to culture (Ting-Toomey, 1999). In other words, the differences often revolve around goals related to content, identities, relationships and procedures in situations of conflict (Wilmot and Hocker, 1998). Issues about content seem external to the individuals involved, but they are often related to relationship, identity or maintaining face (Goffman, 1973, 1974; see Chapters 1 and 3), which concerns the type of relationship we want (more or less informal, or more or less close) and the image we have of ourselves and of the other. Finally, procedural matters affect the different styles and procedures followed when managing a conflict (Ting-Toomey, 1999).

Certain cultural characteristics are often considered relevant when it comes to understanding how approaches to intercultural conflicts may differ from one person to the next. Inspired by Hofstede (1980), Ting-Toomey (1999) suggests the following aspects: the degree of individualism versus collectivism, distance from power, self-conception and the type of communication used. The distinction between individualism and collectivism is a major theoretical aspect of cultural variability favoured in most disciplines to explain cultural differences in terms of relationships (Gudykunst and Ting-Toomey, 1988; Hofstede, 1980, Hui and Triandis, 1986; Triandis, 1988). Individualism is the tendency in a given culture to promote individual identities and rights at the expense of collective identities and obligations towards the group. Conversely, collectivism will focus on the collective identities and problems (Ting-Toomey, 1999; Ting-Toomey et al., 1991). For example, individualists tend to have a more direct style and a more linear management process focused on problem solving, whereas the collectivist approach favours an indirect style and holistic procedures aimed at maintaining a harmonious process (Ting-Toomey, 1999).

With regard to distance from power, it influences expectations about how one should be treated and how one should treat others (Ting-Toomey, 1999). In the world of organizations, this translates into a leader–follower relationship, more or less egalitarian and informal versus authoritarian and formal. Ting-Toomey and Oetzel (2001) focused on intercultural conflicts between the leaders and their followers, and proposed a model that identifies four predominant approaches to conflict favoured by managers when dealing with their subordinates: the impartial approach, the status achievement approach, the benevolent approach and the communal approach. Impartial and benevolent approaches are likely the most prevalent worldwide (Hofstede, 1991).

In the *impartial approach* (closer to power, an individualistic tendency), managers tend to feel independent and to have the same status as their employees. Freedom and equality are core values in this approach. Conflict resolution is more direct, open and objective, relying on impartial rules when possible. Managers tend to seek a compromise that will satisfy everyone (Ting-Toomey and Oetzel, 2001).

In the *status achievement approach* (farther from power, an individualistic tendency), managers want to achieve a high status in a context where everyone has a chance to reach it. They tend to see themselves as independent and different from others in terms of status. The core values are freedom and obtained inequality. These managers tend to expect their subordinates to comply with their decisions. In the event of a conflict, they seek to resolve it in favour of their own goals, even if it is detrimental to their employees' objectives, by adopting a more dominant and controlling style. Employees tend to perceive this behaviour as an abuse of power (Ting-Toomey and Oetzel, 2001).

In the *benevolent approach* (far from power, a collectivist trend), managers tend to see themselves as interdependent, with different status than the others. The two core values are inequality and obligation to others. Managers tend to concentrate on interpersonal relation-ships and maintaining harmony within their group by favouring its members in a conflict. This approach has a sense of family to it. Communication surrounding conflicts is more subtle and indirect, with a concern for protecting the protagonists' faces.

In the *communal approach* (closer to power, a collectivist trend), the least popular approach, managers tend to see themselves as interdependent, with the same status as the others. The core values are equality and proximity to others. In situations of conflict resolu-tion, they are more inclined to collectively find solutions that maintain relationships and deal with core issues. In this approach, one can even dispense of the manager and any attempt at resolving a conflict through domination or force is considered ineffective. In this approach, the focus is on collaborative dialogue.

Another aspect of the analysis of cultural differences in conflict management is self-conception in relation to one's culture. Individuals within the same culture will have a different relation to it, seeing themselves as being more independent, autonomous, and unin-volved or, on the contrary, as interdependent, fitting into their group and being linked by obligations and a quest for harmony within the group (Ting-Toomey, 1999). For example, if I meet someone with a Chinese background, it may well be that this person has an under-standing of himself that separates him from his home culture and leads him to act in a way that differs from what I had imagined his culture's demands to be.

The last aspect is high– or low-context communication (Hall, 1979). In other words, the communication of meaning and intentions of the parties involved in the conflict may be more or less explicit or dependent on the context (Chua and Gudykunst, 1987; Ting-Toomey, 1999). In some cultures, there is a tendency to communicate through explicit verbal mes-sages, increasing the ability to construct a clear and convincing message. In cultures charac-terized by high-context communication, one will come to further rely on the context (e.g. social positions) and nonverbal aspects (silence, tone of voice, pauses) of messages, playing more readily on subtlety, ambiguity and interpretative skills.

Using these dimensions to analyse the cultural variations in conflict management also lends itself to criticism (Adler, 1983; Bond, 1987; Boyacigiller and Adler, 1991; Lachman, Nedd and Hinnings, 1994; McSweeney, 2002, Redding, 1994; Roberts and Boyacigiller, 1984; Soin and Scheytt, 2006; Tayeb, 2001; Triandis, 1995, Trompenaars and Hampden-Turner, 1997; Williamson, 2002). For example, D'Iribarne (2004) noted that this approach does not reflect the heterogeneity of attitudes found within a certain culture, according to circumstances. It is once again about being careful and not having preconceived ideas about the other in intercultural situations. If these dimensions can help us think about how we and others manage conflicts, they should not in any way keep us from understanding the cultural uniqueness and complexity of each intercultural conflict. For instance, the Chinese are not all collectivists. Success in managing an intercultural conflict will depend largely on each party's openness and ability to listen to the peculiarities of the situation rather than on cultural knowledge that would lead to a simplistic categorization of the other according to apparent cultural background.

Intercultural conflict management skills

Several skills can be of use for the efficient management of intercultural conflicts in the workplace. The first comes from the *capacity to create a constructive environment*. Gudykunst (2004) suggests various courses of action in order to manage cultural conflicts in a constructive (versus destructive) manner, that is to say in a way that would allow all parties concerned to get along and achieve a better relationship. According to this author, it is a matter of developing an environment that is favourable to conflict management. In order to do this, it is necessary to define the conflict as being either a mutual problem that everyone would benefit from resolving, or a learning experience. Such a setting involves being descriptive rather than evaluating and judging others, and requires that all present parties treat one another as equals and express their ideas openly and honestly, with spontaneity and empathy. This also requires acknowledging that our point of view is not necessarily the best. Of course, this is not always easy to do within the organizational framework and it relies greatly on the managerial desire to institute a genuine constructive dialogue.

The ideas of both parties must be valued and listened to seriously and respectfully. Active listening and establishing perceptions are essential to effective communication, emphasizing and explaining the differences and similarities between the two parties. Premises and points of view must therefore be expressed in a manner that avoids disagreements being perceived as rejections. Gudykunst (2004) insists on the necessity of always being unconditionally constructive, regardless of the attitude adopted by the other party. This approach is based on the following premise: if we manage to change our attitude towards the other party and adopt a constructive mindset, then the other person will change progressively as well (Fisher and Brown, 1988).

Gudykunst (2004) emphasizes the importance of focusing on communication. He suggests adapting the method of communication to the approach of the interlocutor (for example, a collectivist would adapt to an individualist, and vice versa) in particular. If the process is constructive, it should lead to constructive results, that is to say that a sense of understanding should be present, that we feel we have influenced and have been influenced by the other party, that we are satisfied with the decisions and that we support the solution chosen, that we feel accepted, and that our ability to manage future conflicts is increased (Johnson and Johanson, 1982).

Another intercultural conflict management skill concerns *the validation of the identity and face-keeping*. Cultural conflicts are often based on one or both parties trying to maintain their identity. Rothman (1997) suggests that a majority of the most complex conflicts involve the parties' identities. Even in conflicts that are less focused on identity, Ting-Toomey and Oetzel (2001) underline the importance of being sensitive to the image that the other creates of himself, of using inclusive rather than polarizing vocabulary, and of avoiding depending on dominant interpretations of a topic by being open to other possible interpretations. It is also necessary to work on the face-keeping of both parties involved (Ting-Toomey, 1988; Ting-Toomey et al., 1991). One individual's face-keeping must not be at the expense of humiliating the other party. That being said, face-keeping varies from one culture to another. Therein lies the importance of acquiring certain cultural knowledge concerning the other party.

According to Ting-Toomey and Oetzel (2001), apart from general knowledge about cultural differences, the information acquired concerning the other person, on a historical, political, religious or other level, will greatly influence the outcome of the intercultural conflict's management. Such knowledge will be far from sufficient, however, without examining our own cultural biases and approaches to conflict. Thus, knowing oneself is essential to effective conflict management, which brings us to another major skill: reflexivity.

Reflexive attention and *lateral learning* constitute two major aptitudes in intercultural conflict management. For Ting-Toomey and Oetzel (2001), in order to be an attentive intercultural conflict interpreter, one must focus on one's personal premises, ways of thinking, and emotions, as well as those of the other person. It requires being attentive when listening, observing and comprehending. It also involves demonstrating an attentive reflexivity about one's own culture and the personal assumptions that come into play during conflicts. It is also important to focus on the unusual behaviours and cultural differences one can be exposed to in such situations, without judging others. Furthermore, a certain mental flexibility is required to adapt one's view and interpretation of the conflict's evolution. Finally, one must be open to the possibility of creating new categories in order to understand foreign behaviour. Lateral learning will be possible once all of these conditions have been satisfied.

With regard to reflexivity, Rothman (1997) suggests adopting what he calls *analytical empathy*, which is different from emotional empathy (feeling the same way as the other person). Analytical empathy is adopting the other individual's point of view in order to understand how he or she sees and experiences the situation, allowing for new ways of understanding the conflict to come to light. For example, in the case of a conflict between a Palestinian and an Israeli who are both employed in the same North American organization, the Israeli could try to put himself in the Palestinian's place (and vice versa), adopting his point of view in order to try to understand how he experiences the conflict and thereby view it differently himself.

According to Kikoski and Kikoski (1996), *reflexive communication* allows one to go beyond cultural knowledge of the other in order to open oneself to a more personal knowledge of the other and of their differences. Reflexive communication allows the co-construction of a new mutual reality based on the different meanings that each party gives to the same situation. In order to facilitate this type of communication, one must adopt three positions: that of the non-expert (who does not know what to think yet), that of curiosity (one who voices opinions tentatively and does not impose a definitive point of view) and that of collaboration (to bring out and build a common meaning). Only then will a *collaborative dialogue* as defined by Ting-Toomey and Oetzel (2001) be achieved, where all those present collaborate on the conflict's resolution in such a way as to satisfy both parties.

In the spirit of collaborative dialogue, Friedman and Berthoin Antal (2006) state that *negotiating reality* or *critical interactive reflection* is a crucial intercultural competency and is the most important ability in terms of common learning. For these authors, it is the best alternative to a simple adaptation of cultural variability that they deem impersonal (Friedman and Berthoin Antal, 2005, 2006). Three assumptions underline the concept of negotiating reality: (a) all parties deserve the same respect; (b) all parties, as cultural beings, are different because they have different cultural repertoires and in their ways of seeing and doing things; and (c) neither party's repertoire should dominate over the other's or should be seen as being superior.

Each cultural repertoire emerges from a specific context. New contexts, all the more so for complex cultural contexts, put into question the pertinence of existing repertoires. It is then a question of making them explicit and testing them in a new context, as well as making the attributions made about the reasoning and behaviour of others explicit and testing them. Negotiating reality allows one to learn in new contexts, notably those presenting a certain cultural complexity. Successfully negotiating reality involves expressing thoughts and desires; exploring and questioning one's own reasoning as well as others'. This requires deferring judgement, doubting and tolerating a certain degree of uncertainty until a new understanding is achieved. In certain tense situations where one may feel threatened, it can be difficult to embrace such an approach.

According to Friedman and Berthoin Antal (2005, 2006), the negotiation of reality is a privileged way to discover whether a conflict is based on identity through reasoning and exploring underlying emotions (Rothman, 1997). In fact, if a conflict is based on identity, Rothman (1997) suggests a conflict resolution model named 'ARIA'. There are four steps to follow: (a) antagonism (where differences emerge and animosity is analysed); (b) resonance (where common needs and motivations are articulated); (c) invention (where cooperative solutions are generated); and (d) action (where agendas are jointly set). The third step, invention, involves appealing to the imagination. In certain approaches such as the appreciative inquiry approach (Gergen et al., 2004), the conflict must be viewed as a new world to co-create rather than as a problem to be solved.

On the other hand, it cannot always be resolved as an intercultural conflict. It is often a matter of conflicts based on identity or on power that have become moral conflicts (Littlejohn, 1995). These moral conflicts are considered as being based on identity because they are founded on assumptions and values that participate in the definition of the self or of the other party. They imply questions of power inasmuch as a change in position could be considered losing face. Ting-Toomey (1999) suggests giving each individual the opportunity to express himself and to be listened to in order to create a common understanding. This is referred to as a *transcendent discourse*.

In the case of moral conflicts involving opposing visions of what should be, Gergen et al. (2004) suggest *transformational dialogue* in order to create new meanings that would allow for reconciliation, if not coexistence. In this light, self-narration (Gergen et al., 2004) demonstrates its powerful effects because it calls for a different commitment from listeners. Through sharing the life experiences that have led to the adoption of a particular point of view, the conflict is shifted from an incompatible abstraction to a more human plane where one can understand the other more easily. Self-narration calls for indulgence and appeasement rather than confrontation, and for avoiding the simplistic categorization and demonization of the other person. Thus, transformational dialogue and transcendent discourse lead to a better understanding of others and to respectful coexistence despite any disagreements that may occur.

One of the most crucial skills is being able listen to particularities, to details of the specific complex situation and of the complex individuals involved in the intercultural conflict. Ting-Toomey and Oetzel (2001) call this interaction adaptability. This skill corresponds to the 'phronesis', or *prudence* that Aristotle (1976) presented as being a form of practical intelligence that directs actions by sticking to the field's specificities. As a matter of fact, it allows one to choose which actions to take according to what is good for humans in new situations – situations where there are no pre-established rules for deciding what behaviour is appropriate (Castoriadis, 1996). For Castoriadis (1996, p. 212), phronesis is the power to pass judgements when there are no objective rules allowing judgements to be made.

Finally, knowledge that is gained from intercultural conflicts and the development of the necessary skills for their management can also be supported by a planned and structured training logic.

Intercultural learning based on training

Intercultural learning can be based on a formal training approach. In this section, the key concepts, the operationalization factors of the organizational context and the different methods of intercultural training will be discussed. The goal of intercultural training is to support the development of the necessary skills for learning about cultural diversity. It is a process that brings those concerned from a relative state of cultural ignorance to a state of awareness of the cultural diversity in the organization and the challenges associated with it (for example, in terms of mutual learning potential).

Very often and in most studies, intercultural training is considered a way to develop practical capacities, knowledge and attitudes required for those who work internationally. In this case, the kind of training and the educational methods used vary depending on the purpose of the tasks, on the length of trip, on the organizational strategy, and of the mandate's specifications, among others (Bennet et al., 2000; Brewster and Pickard, 1994; Harrison, 1994; Mendenhall and Oddou, 1986). The presence of several cultures in one organization will be emphasized over expatriation.

The key principles of intercultural training

Before establishing an intercultural training programme, it is important to examine certain key concepts. In this section, five essential principles will be examined: (a) interdisciplinarity, (b) embodiment, (c) non-essentialism, (d) decentration, and (e) progress by stages.

The first concept is derived from the *interdisciplinary character* of intercultural training. In order to define the different dimensions involved, knowledge from various disciplines must be used, such as anthropology, psychology, sociology, history, and politics. Demorgon (1999) states that intercultural exchanges require information from the sciences of communication, history and psychosociology in order to be fully understood. This does not necessarily mean that training must initiate a wide variety of disciplines. Rather, it implies a certain interdisciplinarity. However, initiation to the several social sciences and to an inter-disciplinary outlook on interpersonal relations in an intercultural context remains the best way to prepare someone to manage an intercultural situation with an open mind, curiosity, reflexivity, and a desire to learn.

The second concept, *embodiment*, involves taking into consideration the fact that cultur-ally adapted attitudes and behaviours are not developed in a purely cognitive manner. Bennett and Castiglioni (2004) discuss the body's role in learning about another culture and the importance of be able to 'feel' the culture in order to develop intercultural skills.

A third key concept consists of *avoiding essentialism*. A widely-accepted idea is that intercultural learning relies mostly on the description and comparison of traits that are par-ticular to other cultures. This idea implies the development of a 'chameleon' attitude, or an attitude of cultural adaptation, to facilitate cooperation through a unidirectional adaptation effort to learn to put oneself in the shoes of another and share his ways of being. This would be to make the other person feel at ease and familiar in the rapport (Demorgon, 1999). Nevertheless, the training must surpass a situation of essentialist description of cultural entities or of groups in the favour of understanding cultural dynamics (Abdallah-Pretceille, 1999). The essentialist tendency described above re-emerges here. The efforts to understand people and their behaviour through their cultures often converge to the stereotypes maintained in one's own cultural group, or shroud the singularity of those involved. Moreover, it is impor-tant to be vigilant and to avoid 'culturalizing' problems (Hampden-Turner and Trompenaars, 2004): every disagreement between members of different cultural groups does not necessarily originate from cultural differences.

The fourth concept is *decentration*. Decentration consists of getting a better understanding of one's frame of reference by momentarily distancing yourself from the situation. It is a matter of reflecting on yourself, realizing that you yourself have cultural baggage (for exam-ple, national, ethnic, professional, religious) that has been acquired and learnt, and that sup-ports your thoughts and behaviour. Intercultural interaction favours decentration because it allows representations of our value system, our preconceptions and our prejudice to emerge. If a person living inside a culture experiences it subconsciously in an internalized manner rather than as something external (Devereux, 1980), the other person, being different, becomes an essential element that allows the emergence of one's frame of reference. What is shocking about this other person, what seems the most disconcerting, will therefore act as a mirror reflecting one's own identity. Contrasting values, norms and views allow for the identification of obstacles to communication, so the other person's culture is important in revealing your own (Cohen-Émerique, 1995).

In addition, since every intercultural exchange involves at least two cultural entities, differences are established in both senses. It is therefore a bidirectional interaction that puts cultural differences into perspective, demonstrates the processes that affect the perception of the other party, and identifies new paths that lead to collaboration and harmony.

Moreover, defining one's own culture helps avoid building a hierarchy. Cultural relativism, the respectability of cultures, and the bidirectional aspect of the interaction create an intercultural situation that is interdependent, where establishing one culture's superiority over the others is not a priority (Camilleri, 1999). Rather, what is emphasized is the exchange itself. Nonetheless, becoming aware of and understanding the other party does not necessarily involve accepting his values or his behaviours. Instead, it is a question of recognizing one's identity, which will allow for a better knowledge of oneself, educating oneself about cultural relativism and examining one's values compared to those of the other party. Although the legitimization of the other's culture is an important condition for decentration, it is important to avoid giving it more or less importance than any other. Sure enough, intercultural dynamics involve an explicit or implicit consent to the principle of the exchange, of respectability, of bidirectionality, and of the transformations that are caused by the interaction (Camilleri, 1999).

Therefore, decentration is an important notion for achieving communication, understanding, and tolerance in a situation involving cultural diversity (Cohen-Émerique, 2000).

The fifth concept relies upon the idea of *progress by stages*; that is to say developing intercultural skills through a learning process that progresses in stages. In other words, as individuals experience differences and develop intercultural sensibility, their perception of intercultural aspects becomes more and more subtle and their competencies in cultural exchanges become more and more refined (Bennett and Bennett, 2004). Consequently, intercultural learning must be perceived as a process rather than as a unique experience.

Cox and Beale (1997) and Connerley and Pedersen (2005) suggest three steps in the intercultural learning process: sensitivity (awareness), comprehension (knowledge), and action (skills). Sensitivity is a stage where one becomes aware of the effects of cultural diversity on people's work and on the organization's effectiveness. It consists of a gradual transition from an ethnocentric to an ethnorelative position (Barmeyer, 2007). Intercultural sensitivity can be learned, but it cannot be taught. However, education can create conditions that are favourable to this kind of learning (Connerley and Pedersen, 2005). This stage of sensitivity can be divided into smaller steps (Figure 8.2), as is proposed by Bennett and Bennett (2004).

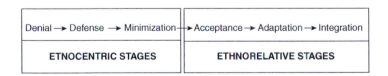

Figure 8.2 Steps to experiencing differences when developing intercultural sensitivity
Source: Bennett and Bennett (2004, p. 153).

In the first three steps, we find ourselves with an ethnocentric conception of intercultural issues, which translates into various ways of avoiding cultural differences. The first step, denial, consists of denying the other culture and considering your own culture as the reference standard and the only 'real' culture. The next step, defence, is less strong than denial in that we consider ours not as the 'real' culture, but as the 'right one', the only good point of reference. The third step of the ethnocentric conception is minimization, which considers our culture to be a universal one and cultural differences to be negligible variations of this universal standard. The second group of steps in the Bennett and Bennett (2004) model concerns cultural relativism. These steps explain a more or less marked effort to recognize and contextualize cultural differences. The fourth step is acceptance, which indicates the recognition of cultural complexities and the impossibility of hierarchizing cultures. The fifth step refers to the ability to modify our knowledge of another culture and to adapt to it. The sixth step, the most thorough on the scale of intercultural sensitization, concerns the capacity to integrate, conceive and adopt different cultural points of view.

Following the sensitization step, Cox and Beale (1997) anticipate the comprehension step (see the knowledge step suggested by Connerley and Pedersen, 2005). Of course, sensitization and comprehension are not entirely separate steps, but we can consider that, once we have developed a certain sensibility to intercultural aspects, we are capable of concentrating on acquiring specific knowledge and a greater understanding of how and why abilities related to diversity management are important for improving individual and collective development as well as organizational efficiency.

Opening up to others and understanding the various phenomena related to cultural diversity can lead to a change in attitude as well as to taking action. Once an individual has been sensitized and understands the issues stemming from intercultural relations, she is then capable of altering her attitude and behaviour (Cox and Beale, 1997). This step includes developing abilities on an intercultural level (Connerley and Pedersen, 2005) and is considered the action step by Cox and Beale (1997).

Following this principle, according to which intercultural learning is a process composed of steps, allows the adjustment of learning methods and the situation of individuals, groups or organizations according to their specific needs. For example, training aimed at people who are in an ethnocentric stage cannot be developed in the same way as training aimed at a person with a certain level of openness to other cultures. Of course, the training content or pedagogical method followed can simultaneously involve different learning steps, but the risk of failure is greater if the content and objectives are not harmonized with their various needs (Cox, 2001).

Intercultural training operations

According to research conducted by Rynes and Rosen (1995) among 700 organizations, only one third of cultural diversity training was viewed as having had a lasting effect. The success of intercultural training, besides the key principles mentioned here above, depends on taking into account and harmonizing certain aspects or parameters such as objectives, the type of context, the format, logistics, the type of participant, the amount of time available, and the skill level of the person in charge of the training (Cox, 2001). Table 8.2 suggests a correspondence between different types of objectives, pedagogical methods and learning evaluation methods.

It is important to prepare participants for the context and intercultural training objectives. Risks of failure are elevated if the participants' expectations greatly differ from the objectives and if the training objectives are not well understood from the very beginning. Participants

Table 8.2 Desired objectives for intercultural training, methods and evaluations

Desired objectives	Training methods and activities	Evaluation
Knowledge: Developing an understanding	Reading, songs, talks, brainstorms, television, radio, audio, video, computer content, programmed instructions, debates, interviews, fieldwork, stage	Written exams, oral exams, application through other training activities
Abilities: Developing a know-how	Demonstration and training followed by practice with retroaction to correct errors, role play, various games, training, case studies, simulations	Observation at work, in practice or during role play, observation with the help of a list, case study with a discussion, product development (developing a training method, newspaper, media materials, play)
Attitudes: Developing new values and perspectives	Discussions, role play, role model, value clarification activities, films and videos, case studies, critical incidents, debates, self-analysis, simulation, fieldwork	Indirectly, by behaviour observation (interpersonal relations, approaching subjects and problems)

must also be prepared to share their perceptions and experiences so as to favour the learning process. Through prior preparations, we can also think of lectures and discussions with colleagues about topics related to cultural diversity (Cox, 2001).

Once the objectives and main training themes have been established, it is important to reflect on the content's definition. Training should be adaptable to each organization's specific problematics, to a certain degree. In other words, the main themes and issues directly affecting the company should be understood in relation with the objectives set. The content does not have to target certain specific identity groups in order to demonstrate the impact of differences within relations. It can, however, address a specific type of professional category, as shown in Table 8.3 on the curriculum of managers looking to develop their abilities in cultural diversity management.

Also, operationalizing intercultural training must take both time and the type of pedagogical method adopted into consideration. In terms of time, failures in training are often linked to allotting insufficient amounts of time to meeting objectives and responding to situations that occur during training (Cox, 2001). According to Cox (2001), more training time has to be dedicated to the sensitization step, while avoiding concentrating the objectives related to the three learning steps (sensitization, comprehension and action) into one training session. The training programme must follow a gradual progression according to the skill levels required for each step of the learning process.

Another aspect that determines how much time should be allocated to a training session stems from the type of learning desired, either emotional or cognitive. As demonstrated by Cox (2001), during a training session, the educator can encourage people to tell their stories about the moment they were deeply affected by the behaviour of a member of a different ethnocultural group. Members of the group can be emotionally affected by these moving testimonials. However, the amount of time allotted to the training session may not suffice if it doesn't allow the development of a relationship of trust within the group. Therefore poor time management can lead to failures in intercultural training.

Another important variable in operationalizing intercultural training stems from the type of participant, the size of the group, the variety of types of employment, its cultural mix and

Table 8.3 Sample curriculum for managers

Meaning and importance of diversity	Define the main terms. Link diversity to the organization's diversity.
Diversity and organizational culture	Understand the standards that support diversity as well as those that weaken it. Perform the diagnosis of the organization. Grasp examples of cultural differences. Understand means of acculturation and their involvement in diversity. Understand the cultural distance and issues related to the search for a certain cultural conformity.
Prejudice, stereotypes, intergroup conflicts and positive discrimination	Define the main terms. Understand the displays of behaviour stemming from stereotypes and prejudice. Identify the concerns and characteristics of positive discrimination.
The effect on recruitment, promotion and performance evaluation	List the ways that management processes are influenced by factors related to socio-cultural identity. Understand measures for minimizing negative effects.
Institutionalization of abilities related to diversity	Develop tools for individuals and organizations. Define the next steps to be taken in order to improve intercultural knowledge and its development.

the mixed levels of hierarchy. According to Cox (2001), for certain methods such as talks, the group can be relatively large (more than twenty people). However, many situations demand that the group size be reduced in order to reach established learning objectives. Also, during the intercultural sensitization step, the diversity of types of employment and levels of hierarchy can be represented in the composition of the group of individuals taking part in the training session. If it is generally preferable to favour variety within these groups, in other situations the group's composition will be determined according to planned themes and objectives.

In ideal circumstances, the training participants can be chosen randomly. However, it is sometimes necessary to take samples based on ethnocultural groups. This favours exchanges in a mixed cultural environment.

Moreover, intercultural training requires abilities for managing situations that are at times emotionally charged (caused by situations of prejudice and discrimination), fiery controversies (for example, equal access programmes) or personal situations (for example, issues involving spirituality). The person giving the training must also show ability and empathy in order to maintain a good climate when controversies arise (Cox, 2001). He or she must maintain a climate of trust and safety, allowing individuals to partake in sharing significant intercultural experiences.

Among the aspects that favour the implementation of a lasting and efficient training process, teaching people within the organization to become trainers is assuredly one of the most important. Efforts to make training a strategic action in managing multicultural employees stem from the ability to create a small group of people who have developed expertise in the intercultural area. These people form a critical group which ensures the continuity and permanence of the problematic of cultural diversity in the workplace.

Intercultural training methods

Pedagogical methods for intercultural training should be selected in accordance with key principles and the aspects of operationalizing previously discussed. In this section, we briefly present various types of methods as well as styles and training tools. Let us first specify that the tools, styles and training methods are cultural products; they are not neutral, universal instruments. In other words, they are not the cultural result of a simple pedagogical aim, but rather the fruit of a system of values and beliefs. Therefore, although certain training techniques and methods can presuppose and assert open-mindedness, participants can judge this requirement inappropriate according to their cultural frame of interpretation (Kordes, 1999).

Each training style can be culturally perceived through its underlying strategies and ideologies. For example, this can manifest itself in the relations between majority and minority, nationals and migrants, and natives and foreigners that are evoked in each type of training. As shown in Table 8.4, Kordes (1999) maintains that experimental practices represent a group of training styles that have been further adapted to the intercultural problematic. In fact, this problematic is always more conflictual than the interactive techniques and informative didactics assume it to be. However, experimental practices are not free of monocultural and ethnocentric influences.

It can generally be assumed that intercultural training requires an active and interactive pedagogy focused on the learner, favouring decentralization and interdependence within the group. However, several methods and tools are available, each with its own set of advantages and disadvantages. For example, discussions among small groups, diversified according to cultural origins, allow people to experience different and more personalized points of view, while the presentations are more adapted to transferring knowledge and tools.

Fowler and Blohm (2004) discuss the relevance of several types of intercultural training methods, such as talks, lectures, computers, films, case studies, critical incidents, role playing, simulations, cultural contrast, intercultural analysis, intercultural dialogue, immersion, intercultural pairing, mentoring, visualization, the arts, sensitization and cultural assimilation. Paige (2004), in turn, suggests and discusses the relevance of several intercultural training tools.

Conclusions

At the beginning of this chapter, we presented the main challenges related to cultural diversity management. We then set out four management strategies related to four perspectives of cultural diversity. Among these perspectives we concentrated on learning, examining informal and emerging practices (intercultural conflicts as a source of learning) as well as formal and planned practices (intercultural training). A manager in charge of multicultural employees must find ways to link these two logics to the organization's daily activities

The commitment of senior management and leaders remains a pivotal aspect when it comes to managing a multicultural staff, whether with an emerging and/or planned logic. Leaders contribute to managing cultural diversity by promoting a vision, means of management, personal commitment to new practices, an enabling work organization, an efficient communication strategy and an integration of diversity within the organizational strategy (Cox, 2001; Ozbilgin and Tatli, 2008; Klarsfeld, 2012). In other words, leaders exert their influence on the management of cultural diversity as they give a meaning to diversity in connection with the organization's strategy, as they begin to share their vision of the problematic in a clear manner, as they incessantly communicate and behave consequently.

Table 8.4 Intercultural training styles

Aspects	Styles		
	Informative educational methods	*Interactive techniques*	*Experimental practices*
Situation	Relationship between teacher and learner	Relationship between facilitator and participants	Educational contestation between various leaders and facilitators
Objectives	Attentively perceive the other's culture in order to adapt to his or her standards, values and codes. Learn about cultural differences and train to interpret comparatively through the other's cultural perspective.	Discover your own culture attentively Develop a more refined cultural and ethnic sensitivity. Improve the effectiveness of intercultural collaboration.	Test the connections between culturally different groups or individuals.
Means of learning	Pre-structured information	Pre-structured interactivity	Open experience
Means	Exposition or discussion about relatively stabilized cultural knowledge (teaching). Presenting episodes and choices of various behaviour (exercises).	Activities (for example, role play) that provide retroaction on roles, standards or decisions (training). Exposing learners to an unfamiliar intercultural field (simulation).	Experiences of direct interaction with groups from other cultures (communication) in a meeting which forces the reinvention of rules of conduct and of organization (confrontation).
Exemplary techniques	File on a culture, newsflashes and critical incidents	Role playing about cultural contrasts, field training and triad model	Intercultural communication workshop, intercultural meetings and scenario exploration
Type of problematic	Typical interpretation and interaction problems between two different cultures	Cultural shock related to uncertainty, anxiety and stress between individuals from different cultures	Experiencing strangeness as a result of the relativization of social standards and of challenging preconceptions and habitual behaviour
Latent function	Understanding the host culture from the point of view of the dominant culture.	Readjusting to the pluralization and differentiation of cultural behaviours.	Becoming aware of individual cultural and geopolitical subconscious states. Movement of research and experime ntation in shaping intercultural meetings

Astonishingly, Cox (2001) notes that few leaders succeed at demonstrating a vision, the behaviour, or even the efforts necessary to ensure fruitful and lasting diversity management. In his opinion, it is one of the main reasons why cultural diversity management fails.

In fact, the success of lasting diversity management rests on the work of several leaders at different levels of management within the organization, and on the work of union leaders for unionized organizations. They all stimulate cooperation, helping manage conflicts on a daily basis and building coalitions. The head of personnel management can play a significant role in facilitating the sensitization to diversity, although he or she must avoid centralizing the responsibility for results. In the case of a planned and structured management process, it is desirable to include diversity management within a larger context of strategy, general policy and action plan promoted by the organization; and even before considering the modification of functional personnel management practices (for example, recruitment, selection, training). When it is ensured that the leaders are committed, the process of managing multicultural employees can project the development of a policy as well as the conception and implementation of an action plan. This process brings about a continual change, making cultural diversity a relevant aspect of the organizational culture and of the personnel management practices, such as recruitment, selection, employment integration, career progression, performance evaluation and training. More concretely, this translates into efforts to acknowledge acquired knowledge and employees' skills. It also translates into measures for managing racist behaviour and communication obstacles in the workplace as well as the use of institutional help, favouring professional integration and recruitment.

Still following planned logic for diversity management, when one mentions developing a policy and action plan, it is often a question of establishing a preliminary diagnosis, evaluating and collecting information, and giving a sense of responsibility to the various actors, aligning the management system, implementing retroactive and follow-up activities, evaluating results, and so on. However, it is the training and learning processes that represent the central element in any effort to make organizational changes. Formal and informal intercultural learning experiences solidify themselves in precious moments, helping the progression of multicultural personnel management within an organization. The importance of emerging management practices must not be underestimated, especially those revolving around learning from daily intercultural conflicts in the workplace.

Ultimately, if many people become emotionally invested in the management of cultural diversity, it presents significant challenges. We are still far from reaching the utopia of a multicultural organization. Cox (2001) defines it as an organization in which people with different ethnocultural backgrounds can develop and mobilize all of their work potential in order to accomplish both organizational and personal goals. This organization (a) integrates people from different cultural horizons within different functional levels and different levels of the hierarchy; (b) values pluralism, not just assimilation during the integration process for new arrivals; (c) includes people from different cultural horizons within informal networks; and (d) reduces the amount of interpersonal conflicts based on differences of identity, stereotypes, prejudice or ethnocentricity.

In conclusion, we would like to insist on a central idea concerning managing multicultural employees: our conceptions of cultural diversity are social constructions located locally and historically, significantly impacting the way that employees will experience it. Therein stems the importance for managers to reflect about the conceptions that lead them to manage cultural diversity one way rather than another.

Notes

1 We would like to thank HEC Montréal (La direction de la recherche) and Télé-université (University of Quebec) for their financial support in the translation of this chapter.
2 Special thanks to Natasha Normand for her help with bibliographic research, as well as Jean-Pierre Dupuis, Jean-François Chanlat and Ginette Dumont for their suggestions and comments. This chapter was made possible by an equal collaboration between the authors, who are presented in alphabetical order.

References

Abdallah-Pretceille, M., La formation des enseignants face au défi de la pluralité culturelle et de l'altérité, in: J. Demorgon and E. M. Lipiansky (eds), *Guide de l'interculturel en formation*, Paris, Éditions Retz, 1999.

Adler, N. J., A typology of management studies involving culture, *Journal of International Business Studies*, vol. 14, no. 3, pp. 29–47, 1983.

—— Domestic multiculturalism: cross-cultural management in the public sector, in: G. R. Weaver (ed.), *Culture, Communication and Conflict: Readings in Intercultural Relations*, Boston, Pearson Publishing, 2000.

Ailon-Souday, G. and G. Kunda, The local selves of global workers: the social construction of national identity in the face of organizational globalization, *Organization Studies*, vol. 24, no. 7, pp. 1073–96, 2003.

Aristotle, *The Nicomachean Ethics,* Harmondsworth, Penguin, 1976.

Banerjee, S. B. and S. Linstead, Globalization, multiculturalism and other fictions: colonialism for the new millennium? *Organization*, vol. 8, no. 4, pp. 683–722, 2001.

Barinaga, E., 'Cultural diversity' at work: 'national culture' as a discourse organizing an international project group, *Human Relations*, vol. 60, no. 2, pp. 315–40, 2007.

Barmeyer, C., *Management interculturel et styles d'apprentissage: étudiants et dirigeants en France, en Allemagne et au Québec*, Quebec, PUL, 2007.

Barnlund, D., Communication in a global village, in: M. J. Bennett (ed.), *Basic Concepts of Intercultural Communication: Selected Readings*, Yarmouth, ME: Intercultural Press, 31–51, 1998.

Bennet, R., A. Aston and T. Colquhoun, Cross-cultural training: a critical step in ensuring the success of international assignments, *Human Resource Management*, vol. 39, no. 2–3, pp. 239–50, 2000.

Bennett, J. M. and M. J. Bennett, Developing intercultural sensitivity: an integrative approach to global and domestic diversity, in: D. Landis, J. Bennett and M. J. Bennett (eds), *Handbook of Intercultural Training*, Thousand Oaks, CA, Sage Publications, 2004.

Bennett, J. M. and I. Castiglioni, Embodied ethnocentrism and the feeling of culture: a key to training for intercultural competence, in: D. Landis, J. Bennett and M. J. Bennett (eds), *Handbook of Intercultural Training*, Thousand Oaks, CA, Sage Publications, 2004.

Bhabha, H. K., *The Location of Culture,* London, Routledge, 1994.

Bond, M. A. and T. L. Pyle, Diversity dilemmas at work, *Journal of Management Inquiry*, vol. 7, no. 3, pp. 252–69, 1998.

Bond, M. H., Chinese culture connection: Chinese values and the search for culture-free dimensions of culture, *Journal of Cross-Cultural Psychology*, vol. 18, pp. 143–64, 1987.

Boyacigiller, N. and N. J. Adler, The parochial dinosaur: organizational science in a global context, *Academy of Management Review*, vol. 16, pp. 262–90, 1991.

Brewster, C. and J. Pickard, Evaluating expatriate training, *International Studies of Management and Organization*, vol. 24, no. 3, pp. 18–35, 1994.

Camilleri, C., Principes d'une pédagogie interculturelle, in: J. Demorgon and E. M. Lipiansky (eds), *Guide de l'interculturel en formation*, Paris, Éditions Retz, 1999.

Castoriadis, C., *La montée de l'insignifiance: les carrefours du labyrinthe IV*, Paris, Gallimard, 1996.

Chanlat, J.-F., S. Dameron, J.-P. Dupuis, M. de Freitas and M. Ozbilgin, *Management et diversité: lignes de tension et perspectives*, Introduction, Numéro spécial, Management et diversité, Management international, Printemps, 2013.

Chua, E. G. and W. B. Gudykunst, Conflict resolution styles in low- and high-context cultures, *Communication Research Reports*, vol. 4, no. 1, pp. 32–37, 1987.

Cockburn, C., *In the way of women*, London, Macmillan, 1991.

Cohen-Émerique, M., Le choc culturel: méthode de formation et outil de recherche, *Antipodes*, vol. 130, pp. 5–23, 1995.

—— L'approche interculturelle auprès des migrants, in: G. Legault (ed.), *L'intervention interculturelle*, Montreal, Gaetan Morin Éditeur, 2000.

Connerley, M. L. and P. B. Pedersen, *Leadership in a diverse multicultural environment: developing awareness, knowledge, and skills*, Thousand Oaks, CA, Sage Publications, 2005.

Cox, T., *Creating the Multicultural Organization*, San Francisco, Jossey-Bass, 2001.

——, *Cultural Diversity in Organizations: Theory, Research and Practice*, San Francisco, Berrett-Koehler Publishers, 1993.

Cox, T. and R. L. Beale, *Developing Competency to Manage Diversity: Readings, Cases and Activities*, San Francisco, Berrett-Koehler Publishers, 1997.

Dass, P. and B. Parker, Strategies for managing human resource diversity: from resistance to learning, *Academy of Management Executive*, vol. 13, no. 2, pp. 68–80, 1999.

De Dreu, C. K. W. and E. Van de Vliert, *Using Conflict in Organizations*, London, Sage Publications, 1997.

De Long, D. W., *Lost Knowledge: Confronting the Threat of an Aging Workforce*, Oxford, Oxford University Press, 2004.

Demorgon, J., L'économie et l'entreprise, in: J. Demorgon and E. M. Lipiansky (eds), *Guide de l'interculturel en formation*, Paris, Éditions Retz, 1999.

Devereux, G., *De l'angoisse à la méthode dans les sciences du comportement*, Paris, Flammarion, 1980.

Dick, P. and C. Cassell, Barriers to managing diversity in a UK constabulary: the role of discourse, *Journal of Management Studies*, vol. 39, no. 7, pp. 953–76, 2002.

D'Iribarne, P., Face à la complexité des cultures, le management interculturel exige une approche ethnologique, *Management international*, vol. 8, no. 3, pp. 11–20, 2004.

Ely, R. J. and D. A. Thomas, Cultural diversity at work: the effects of diversity perspectives on work group processes and outcomes, *Administrative Science Quarterly*, vol. 46, no. 2, pp. 229–73, 2001.

Fineman, S., Emotion and management learning, *Management Learning*, vol. 28, no. 1, pp. 13–25, 1997.

Fisher, R. and S. Brown, *Getting Together: Building Relationships as We Negotiate*, New York, Houghton Mifflin, 1988.

Foldy, E. G., Managing diversity: identity and power in organizations, in: I. Aaltio and A. J. Mills (eds), *Gender, Identity and the Culture of Organizations*, London, Routledge, 2002.

Fowler, S. M. and J. M. Blohm, An analysis of methods for intercultural training, in: D. Landis, J. Bennett and M. J. Bennett (eds), *Handbook of Intercultural Training*, Thousand Oaks, CA, Sage Publications, 2004.

Friedman, V. J. and A. Berthoin Antal, Negotiating reality: a theory of action approach to intercultural competence, *Management Learning*, vol. 36, no. 1, pp. 69–86, 2005.

—— Interactive critical reflection as intercultural competence, in: D. Boud, P. Cressey and P. Docherty (eds), *Productive Reflection at Work*, London, Routledge, 2006.

Gergen, K. J., M. M. Gergen and F. J. Barrett, Dialogue: life and death of the organization, in: D. Grant, C. Hardy, C. Oswick and L. L Putnam. (eds), *The Sage Handbook of Organizational Discourse*, London, Sage, pp. 39–59, 2004.

GIB, J., Defensive communication, *Journal of Communication*, vol. 11, pp. 141–48, 1961.

Goffman, E., *La mise en scène de la vie quotidienne*, Paris, Éditions de Minuit, 1973.

—— *Les rites d'interaction*, Paris, Éditions de Minuit, 1974.

Gudykunst, W. B., *Bridging Differences*, London, Sage Publications, 2004.

Gudykunst, W. B. and S. Ting-Toomey, *Culture and Interpersonal Communication*, Newbury Park, CA, Sage, 1988.

Hall, E., *Au-delà de la culture*, Paris, Seuil, 1979.

Hampden-Turner, C. and F. Trompenaars, *Au-delà du choc des cultures: dépasser les oppositions pour mieux travailler ensemble*, Paris, Éditions d'Organisation, 2004.

Harrison, J. K., Developing successful expatriate managers: a framework for the structural design and strategic alignment of cross-cultural training programs, *Human Resources Planning*, vol. 17, no. 3, pp. 17–35, 1994.

Hofstede, G., *Culture's Consequences: International Differences in Work-Related Values*, Beverly Hills, CA, Sage, 1980.

—— *Culture and Organizations: Software of the Mind*, London, MacGraw-Hill, 1991.

Hui, C. and H. Triandis, Individualism-collecitivsm: a study of cross-cultural researchers, *Journal of Cross-Cultural Psychology*, vol. 17, pp. 225–48, 1986.

Johnson, D. and F. Johanson, *Joining Together*, Englewood Cliffs, NJ, Prentice Hall, 1982.

Jones, D. and R. Stablein, Diversity as resistance and recuperation: critical theory, post-structuralist perspectives and workplace diversity, in: P. Prasad, J. K. Pringle and A. M. Konrad (eds), *Handbook of Workplace Diversity*, London, Sage Publications, 2006.

Kanter, R., *The Change Masters*, New York, Simon & Schuster, 1983.

Kikoski, J. F. and C. K. Kikoski, *Reflexive Communication in the Culturally Diverse Workplace*, London, Qorum Books, 1996.

Kirton, G. and A.-M. Greene, *The Dynamics of Managing Diversity: A Critical Approach*, London, Elsevier, 2005.

Klarsfeld, A., *International Handbook on Diversity Management at Work: Country Perspectives on Diversity and Equal Treatment*. London: Edward Elgar Publishing Ltd., 2012.

Knowles, M., *The Modern Practice of Adult Education*, Chicago, Associated Press, 1970.

Kohls, L. R., *Training Know-how for Cross-cultural and Diversity Trainers*, Duncanville, TX, Adult Learning Systems, 1995.

Kordes, H., L'évolution des méthodes de formation: des didactiques aux pratiques expérimentales, in: J. Demorgon and E. M. Lipiansky (eds), *Guide de l'interculturel en formation*, Paris, Éditions Retz, 1999.

Kossek, E. E., S. A. Lobel and J. Brown, Human resource strategies to manage workforce diversity: examining 'the business case', in: P. Prasad, J. K. Pringle and A. M. Konrad (eds), *Handbook of Workplace Diversity*, London, Sage Publications, 2006.

Kozakaï, T., *L'étranger, l'identité: essai sur l'intégration culturelle*, Paris, Payot, 2007.

Lachman, R., A. Nedd and B. Hinnings, Analyzing cross-national management and organizations: a theoretical framework, *Management Science*, vol. 40, pp. 40–55, 1994.

Liff, S., Two routes to managing diversity: individual differences or social group characteristics, *Employee Relations*, vol. 19, no. 1, pp. 11–26, 1996.

Linnehan, F. and A. M. Konrad, Diluting diversity: implications for intergroup inequality in organizations, *Journal of Management Inquiry*, vol. 8, no. 4, pp. 399–414, 1999.

Littlejohn, S. W., Moral conflict in organizations, in: A. M. Nicotera (ed.), *Conflict and Organizations: Communicative Processes*, Albany, State University of New York Press, pp. 101–25, 1995.

Lorbiecki, A., Changing views on diversity management: the rise of the learning perspective and the need to recognize social and political contradictions, *Management Learning*, vol. 32, no. 3, pp. 345–61, 2001.

McSweeney, B., Hofstede's model of national culture differences and their consequences: a triumph of faith: a failure of analysis, *Human Relations*, vol. 55, pp. 89–118, 2002.

Mendenhall, M. and G. Oddou, Acculturation profiles of expatriate managers: implications for cross-cultural training programs, *Columbia Journal of World Business*, vol. 21, no. 4, pp. 73–80, 1986.

Michaels, W. B., *The Trouble with Diversity: How We Learned to Love Identity and Ignore Inequality*, New York, Owl, 2007.

Mir, R., A. Mir and D. J. Wong, Diversity: the cultural logic of global capital? in: P. Prasad, J. K. Pringle and A. M. Konrad (eds), *Handbook of Workplace Diversity*, London, Sage Publications, 2006.

Ozbilgin, M. and A. Tatli, *Global Diversity Management: An Evidence-Based Approach*, London, Palgrave Macmillan, 2008.

Paige, R. M., Instrumentation in intercultural training, in: D. Landis, J. Bennett and M. J. Bennett (eds), *Handbook of Intercultural Training*, Thousand Oaks, CA, Sage Publications, 2004.

Prasad, A., The jewel in the crown: postcolonial theory and workplace diversity, in: P. Prasad, J. K. Pringle and A. M. Konrad (eds), *Handbook of Workplace Diversity*, London, Sage Publications, 2006.

Prasad, P. and A. J. Mills, From showcase to shadow: understanding the dilemmas of managing workplace diversity, in: P. Prasad, A. J. Mills, M. Elmes and A. Prasad (eds), *Managing the Organizational Melting Pot: Dilemmas of Workplace Diversity*, Thousand Oaks, CA, Sage Publications, 1997.

Prasad, P., J. K. Pringle and A. M. Konrad, Examining the contours of workplace diversity: concepts, contexts and challenges, in: P. Prasad, J. K. Pringle and A. M. Konrad (eds), *Handbook of Workplace Diversity*, London, Sage Publications, 2006.

Redding, S. G., Comparative management theory: jungle, zoo or fossil bed? *Organization Studies*, vol. 15, pp. 323–59, 1994.

Roberts, K. J. and N. Boyacigiller, Cross-national organizational research: the grasp of the blind man, in: B. M. Staw and L. L. Cummings (eds), *Research in Organizational Behavior 6*, Stamford, CT, JAI, 1984.

Rothman, J., *Resolving Identity-Based Conflict in Nations, Organizations and Communities*, San Francisco, Jossey-Bass, 1997.

Rynes, S. and B. Rosen, A field survey of factors affecting the adoption and perceived success of diversity training, *Personnel Psychology*, vol. 48, pp. 247–70, 1995.

Soin, K. and T. Scheytt, Making the case for narrative methods in cross-cultural organizational research, *Organizational Research Methods*, vol. 9, no. 1, pp. 55–77, 2006.

Tayeb, M., Conducting research across cultures: overcoming drawbacks and obstacles, *International Journal of Cross-Cultural Management*, vol. 1, pp. 91–108, 2001.

Thomas, D. A. and R. J. Ely, Making differences matter: a new paradigm for managing diversity, *Harvard Business Review*, vol. 74, no. 5, pp. 79–90, 1996.

Thomas, R. and A. Davies, Theorizing the Micro-politics of Resistance: New Public Management and Managerial Identities in the UK Public Services, *Organization Studies*, vol. 26, no. 5, pp. 683–706.

Ting-Toomey, S., Intercultural conflict styles: a face-negotiation theory, in: Y. Y. Kim and W. B. Gudykunst (eds), *Theories in Intercultural Communication*, London, Sage Publications, 1988.

—— *Communicating Across Cultures*, New York, Guilford Press, 1999.

Ting-Toomey, S., G. Gao, P. Truhisky, Z. Yang, H. S. Kim, S. L. Un and T. Nishida, Culture, face maintenance, and styles of handling interpersonal conflict: a study in five cultures, *The International Journal of Conflict Management*, vol. 2, no. 4, pp. 275–96, 1991.

Ting-Toomey, S. and J. G. Oetzel, *Managing Intercultural Conflict Effectively*, London, Sage Publications, 2001.

Triandis, H., Collectivism vs. individualism: a reconceptualization of a basic concept in cross-cultural psychology, in: G. Verma and C. Bagley (eds), *Cross-Cultural Studies of Personality, Attitudes and Cognition*, London, Macmillan, 60–95, 1988.

—— *Individualism and Collectivism*, Boulder, CO, Westview, 1995.

Trompenaars, F. and C. Hampden-Turner, *Riding the Waves of Culture: Understanding Cultural Diversity in Business*, London, Nicholas Brealey, 1997.

Webb, J., The politics of equal opportunity, *Gender, Work and Organization*, vol. 4, no. 3, pp. 159–67, 1997.

Williamson, D., Forward from a critique of Hofstede's model of national culture, *Human Relations*, vol. 55, pp. 1373–95, 2002.

Wilmot, W. and J. Hocker, *Interpersonal Conflict*, Boston, McGraw-Hill, 1998.

Zanoni, P. and M. Janssens, Deconstructing difference: the rhetoric of human resource managers' diversity discourse, *Organization Studies*, vol. 25, no. 1, pp. 55–74, 2004.

9   Managing international alliances

Fabien Blanchot

Translated from the French by
Suzan Nolan and Leila Whittemore

Introduction

Every year, companies form thousands of alliances (Kang and Sakai 2000; Cools and Roos 2005). During the first two years of the twenty-first century, more than 20,000 alliances were formed worldwide, compared with 15,000 mergers or acquisitions, according to a study by Harbison et al. (2000). However, between 1993 and 2008, more mergers and acquisitions occurred than alliances, and the difference in number appears to have widened since the mid-1990s, according to Thomson Financial data (Cools and Roos 2005). This apparent contradiction in the quantitative data is unsurprising, in part because strategic alliances remain less visible, and therefore probably underestimated, compared with more visible mergers and acquisitions. Also, the definition of 'alliance' varies between studies; for example, some only look at international alliances – more numerous than national ones, according to available censuses. If national alliances are included with international ones, their share compared to that of international mergers and acquisitions increases to more than 50 percent in some years (Kang and Sakai 2000).

Surveys about alliances' place in business strategies tend to make similar findings, suggesting the increasing importance of alliances. According to a study conducted by CFO Research Services (2004), finance directors increasingly consider alliances 'essential' and 'very important' for their companies. That finding echoes an observation by Harbison et al. (2000) that alliances contribute a growing share of revenue to the largest American and European companies. For example, the pharmaceuticals company, Merck, acknowledges that 38 percent of its gross income results from alliances; it believes the company's survival depends on successful partnerships (*Le Monde* 2005).

Without doubt, alliances provide companies with an essential strategic tool and constitute a lever to increase competitiveness, helping improve one or more components of the Cost–Quality–Dependability–Flexibility–Speed performance objectives matrix (Slack et al. 2009). They may also serve as a growth lever, substituting for or complementing organic or external growth. Organizations increasingly understand this and create new job functions dedicated to managing alliances. At the same time, the 'alliance manager' profession takes shape, as specific skills are required to search for and select partners, negotiate and design partnering agreements, and to steer relationships (Blanchot 2006b, 2006c).

What are alliances?[1] Many definitions exist, none better than the other since words have no substance. The definition to use is simply the one that corresponds to the phenomenon that we want to study first. In this chapter, we examine relationships between organizations that have three special characteristics. First, relations are established between entities that are and that remain legally independent. The partnering entities may be of any type: public or private sector, publicly traded or privately held, multinational, small or medium-size, and they may be competitors, operating at different levels of the same industry, or in a related one, or they may belong to different competitive fields. Second, the partnering entities create the relationships jointly. As Bernard Gazier (1993) explains:

> There is cooperation and cooperation. A well-understood interest leads participants in a project to collaborate and jointly pursue an objective defined by some of their colleagues. But it is another matter to jointly establish the nature of the work and the terms of collaboration, which is genuine cooperation.
>
> (p. 97)

Explicit, reciprocal and long-term commitments to do certain things define the third characteristic of alliances. These commitments may cover a wide range of possible contributions that depend on the alliance's goal. In some cases, the partners decide to carry out their joint operations through a shared subsidiary company, also known as a joint venture. This definition coincides with that used in the research about alliances referenced in this chapter. It excludes mergers and acquisitions in their strictest sense from the scope of study, i.e. when one company takes legal control of another, or when companies merge by absorbing one another or by creating a new company that replaces them. We will further focus on international alliances – for the most part, deals done between partners from different countries, or between two companies from the same country doing business in a foreign country, such as when Coca-Cola and McDonald's help each other expand internationally. The country-of-origin of international deal partners is, in part at least, a matter of choice. We choose to consider an alliance as 'international' when either the partners or the project has at least one cross-border aspect. This broad definition is consistent with this volume's purpose: examining management in an intercultural context. Whether working with a partner from one's own or a different country while serving similar customers in a foreign country, different organizational cultures and national cultures intermingle.

These cultural differences are often considered an obstacle to an alliance's success. In a survey conducted by CFO Research Services (2004), more than one in five respondents cite 'culture clash' as an important factor in an alliance's failure. What does this really mean? Do cultural differences hinder the success of alliances? How do such differences influence an alliance's success or failure? We will seek to answer these questions before looking at managing cultural differences in international alliances.

Cultural differences and an alliance's degree of success

Much research seeks to understand what lies behind the success or failure of alliances, especially since their failure rate remains high (Blanchot and Guillouzo 2011). But when can we say an alliance is a success or a failure? Such a question has no unequivocal answer because not only do gauges of 'success' differ, but success is rarely absolute and usually occurs in degrees. Some management scholars consider an alliance successful when each partner achieves their strategic objectives. Others link an alliance's success to its profitability, or to the fact that all of the partners achieve their initial strategic goals and/or are satisfied with the relationship. In reality, such black or white approaches to assessing success or failure are very reductive since they consist of binary reasoning, and lead to treating situations in a black-or-white manner – situations that often deserve a more nuanced interpretation. Such approaches prove even more problematic and questionable when they rely on a single indicator, since every indicator has limits and different indicators may give very different results. Therefore, we argue that it is worthwhile to use a combination of up to four different types of indicators to gauge an alliance's degree of success. These may include (1) four alliance 'performance' indicators, each of which may be based on past, future, static or dynamic objectives; (2) an alliance 'dynamic' indicator, measuring an alliance's stability or extent of change; (3) an alliance 'outcome' indicator that shows if an alliance is ongoing or has been dissolved; and (4) an alliance 'longevity' indicator showing how long an alliance lasts (see Figure 9.1).

Any one or all four performance indicators may be used to gauge an alliance's performance. First, an assessment may look at the alliance's past, present and future effects on the partners. This means measuring or estimating the real or potential[2] effects of the alliance on the partnering companies' financial performance, for example via financial results, market share or stock market valuations, and/or on their organizational performance, such as their innovations in organization, process and/or production or their acquisition of skills.

Second, attention may be focused on the alliance's purpose[3] and results – the achievements of the alliance's specific business/project, its activities or its transactions. For example, if an alliance is used to expand abroad, one could evaluate whether or not the objectives the partners set for a given date or period were met, and/or evaluate the economic results of the ensuing joint operation.

The third way to measure an alliance's performance may be to gauge the partners' relationship quality, its 'climate', that is, the way the participants feel about, evaluate or

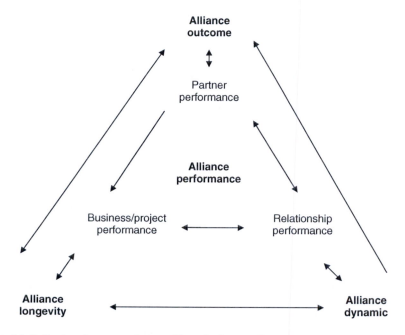

Figure 9.1 Indicators for measuring an alliance's degree of success
    Note: These relationships are not mechanical and vary between alliances; double-arrows show that causality runs in both directions.
    Source: Blanchot (2006a).

anticipate their relations within the alliance, and how they judge their partners. Using this gauge means characterizing the relationship via observable behaviors, such as the frequency and intensity of conflicts or the ability to make joint decisions. It may also mean measuring participants' feelings about organizational justice[4] and their partner's loyalty, their efforts to adapt and their forbearance, along with assessing their balance of power and mutual trust levels.

The fourth way to gauge alliance performance may use 'composite indicators' that cover several elements from any of the preceding three alliance performance indicators. Schematically, these elements would fall somewhere inside the smaller 'performance triangle' in Figure 9.1. For example, when participants are asked to indicate their overall satisfaction level with their alliance's performance – a gauge of relationship performance (the third measure above) – their reply would be situated in the alliance performance triangle to the lower right of Figure 9.1. Similarly, when we gauge the degree of achievement of the partners' objectives – the results (the second measure above), whether shared or private, initial or emerging – the answer would be situated closer to the double arrow in Figure 9.1 – 'partner performance–business/project performance'.

These alliance performance indicators are interdependent. For example, a poor relationship may harm the alliance's business/project performance, which may affect the partners' performance. Similarly, if internal or external factors cause an alliance to worsen a partner's performance, the alliance's business/project performance and the relationship performance may change. The relation between performance indicators is not mechanical, because the alliance's performance may depend on antecedents other than its own business activities.

Alliance performance also interacts with an alliance's dynamic, longevity and outcome; these constitute other indicators for gauging the degree of an alliance's success. Nevertheless, it is dangerous for management scholars and other observers to gauge failure or success using only these indicators, because doing so may induce errors in their interpretations. Regarding 'outcome' for example, some companies end alliances because the deal's initial purpose was achieved, not because they feel their alliance was a failure.

We have clarified notions about gauging an alliance's success, failure, degree of success, performance, dynamic, longevity and outcome; now we will examine the effect of cultural differences.

Contradictory results

Among the factors likely to influence an alliance's degree of success, we note the stakeholders' profiles, especially the partners' nationalities, and the resulting cultural distance. This cultural distance reflects the diversity between companies. The literature about strategic alliances distinguishes between two types of diversity (Parkhe 1991): Type I comprises differences in partners' capacities and resources, and Type II comprises differences in culture and processes or operational norms (Type II). The hypothesis generally made states that Type II diversity represents a factor for failure and a challenge to developing successful relationships (Parkhe 1991; Cartwright and Cooper 1993; Sirmon and Lane 2004). But in fact, not all empirical studies validate this hypothesis; in the studies cited (see Table 9.1); twenty-one tests confirmed the hypothesis, i.e. that cultural differences had a significant negative influence, but eight tests showed the opposite result, i.e. that cultural differences had a significant positive effect on an alliance's degree of success; twenty-five studies found the factor non-significant.[5]

Table 9.1 Primary research results from assessing national cultural differences on an alliance's degree of success

Research author(s)	National cultural differences indicator	Degree of success indicator	Observed effect
Harrigan (1988)	Partners of different nationalities	Performance as assessed by respondents	−
		Alliance longevity	+
Kogut (1988)	Partners of different nationalities	Joint venture mortality rate	−
Meschi and Roger (1994)	National cultural distance perceived by respondents	Employees' engagement and organizational climate	−
Hu andChen (1996)	Chinese company's partner's nationality	Business/project performance	+/−/ns ***
Park and Russo (1996)	Differences in nationality between partners	Joint venture longevity	ns
Barkema et al. (1997)	Cultural differences between incoming company and host country	Joint venture longevity	−
	Uncertainty avoidance (distance between incoming company's home country and host country)	Joint venture longevity	−
	Power distance (distance between incoming company's home country and host country)	Joint venture longevity	ns
	Masculinity (distance between incoming company's home country and host country)	Joint venture longevity	ns
	Individualism (distance between incoming company's home country and host country)	Joint venture longevity	−/ns
	Cultural distance[a] between incoming company and host developing country	Joint venture longevity	−
	Cultural distance between incoming company and host developed country	Joint venture longevity	ns
	Difference between incoming company's cultural group affiliation and the group affiliation of the host developed country (Ronen and Shenkar typology)	Joint venture longevity	−
Barkema and Vermeulen (1997)	Cultural distance[b] between incoming company and host country	Joint venture longevity	−/ns **
	Individualism (distance between incoming company's home country and host country)	Joint venture longevity	ns
	Uncertainty avoidance (distance between incoming company's home country and host country)	Joint venture longevity	−
	Masculinity (distance between incoming company's home country and host country)	Joint venture longevity	−
	Power distance (distance between incoming company's home country and host country)	Joint venture longevity	ns
	Long-term orientation (distance between incoming company's home country and host country)	Joint venture longevity	−
Mjoen and Tallman (1997)	Cultural distance as assessed by respondents (several elements)	Performance as assessed by respondents	

Research author(s)	National cultural differences indicator	Degree of success indicator	Observed effect
Park and Ungson (1997)	Cultural distance[a] between partners	Joint venture longevity	+/ns *
Makino and Beamish (1998)	Difference in partners' nationalities	Joint venture survival	−
Fey and Beamish (2001)	Cultural distance[a] between partners	Satisfaction with joint venture's performance	ns
Hennart and Zeng (2002)	Difference in partners' nationalities	Joint venture longevity	−
Luo (2002)	National cultural distance perceived by respondents	Sales/assets	ns
		Net profit/total investment	ns
		Interpersonal trust	−
		Interorganizational trust	−
Pothukuchi et al. (2002)	Cultural distance[a] between partners	Joint venture efficiency	+/ns *
		Joint venture competitiveness	+/ns *
		Relationship satisfaction	ns
	Individualism (distance between partners)	Joint venture efficiency	+
	Uncertainty avoidance (distance between partners)	Joint venture efficiency	ns
	Masculinity (distance between partners)	Joint venture efficiency	+
	Power distance (distance between partners)	Joint venture efficiency	ns
	Individualism (distance between partners)	Joint venture competitiveness	ns
	Uncertainty avoidance (distance between partners)	Joint venture competitiveness	ns
	Masculinity (distance between partners)	Joint venture competitiveness	ns
	Power distance (distance between partners)	Joint venture competitiveness	ns
	Individualism (distance between partners)	Relationship satisfaction	−
	Uncertainty avoidance (distance between partners)	Relationship satisfaction	−
	Masculinity (distance between partners)	Relationship satisfaction	−
	Power distance (distance between partners)	Relationship satisfaction	−/ns *
Lu (2006)	Cultural distance as assessed by respondents	Overall satisfaction	−/ns ****

a Cultural distance calculation based on an aggregated index developed by Kogut and Singh using Hofstede's data.
b Cultural distance calculation based on an aggregated index developed by Kogut and Singh combined with an Euclidian index developed by the author, using Hofstede's data.
* Result varies depending on the model's control variables.
** Result varies depending on whether cultural distance is calculated based on four dimensions or Hofstede's five dimensions. However, significance is little or unaffected by the observation period (periods tested between 1966 and 1994) or by the type of index used to measure cultural distance.
*** Result varies depending on whether the Chinese company's partner is from Hong Kong, Japan, America, Europe, or of another nationality.
**** Result varies depending on whether the managers surveyed and employed in China-based joint ventures are Japanese or Taiwanese.
s = Significant with a probability of error less than or equal to 5%

Reasons cultural influences sometimes prove negative

In organizational studies, the term 'cultural diversity' means that two groups may have different ways of thinking, acting and reacting, because they do not necessarily share the same references, norms, beliefs, values or systems for interpreting reality. For example, one group may perceive conflict as healthy, useful, natural and inevitable, while another perceives it as a destructive force that must be avoided (Parkhe 1991, p. 585). Cultural diversity may combine with linguistic differences and a habit of submitting (or not) to various institutions. Such diversity sometimes hampers an alliance's performance, dynamics or duration by perturbing interactions and relationships between groups. It may prevent partners from fully exploiting their complementary strengths – their company's resources, capacities, and ability to adapt to change. It may also reduce each individual's ability to adapt to and work cooperatively with the other, for at least three reasons.

First, cultural differences create misunderstandings. Not sharing the same interpretive systems, norms, beliefs or values leads to differences in how problems are assessed, perceived or approached (Iribarne et al. 2002; Kumar and Andersen 2000). Such differences may result in many managerial conflicts (Park and Ungson 1997, pp. 282–83) and in time-consuming, endless discussions that prevent fast and relevant decision-making (Yan and Zeng 1999, p. 400). Misunderstandings may also lead to an erroneous interpretation of the other partner's strategic intentions (Sirmon and Lane 2004), and constitute an obstacle to trust-building (Inkpen and Currall 1998; Faulkner and Rond 2000; Luo 2002).

Second, differences in language and communication styles – verbal and non-verbal – may lead to blunders and frustrations that harm the quality of a relationship (Emerson 2001; Chevrier 1996). They may also impoverish communication and render mutual learning more difficult, reinforcing misunderstandings and even increasing mistrust. A lack of trust and understanding may make dissatisfied partners reduce their participation in an alliance (Inkpen and Birkenshaw 1994), and make it impossible to renegotiate an alliance's terms as the business environment changes. These are some of the factors that cause the alliance's economic results to deteriorate, and eventually lead to its dissolution (Doz 1996; Arino and de la Torre 1998; Lane et al. 2001; Luo 2002).

Furthermore, linguistic and cultural differences may create factions or clans; they may serve as a source of distinct social identities that reinforce differentiation (Salk and Brannen 2000), promote negative feelings (Salk and Shenkar 2001), and elicit resistance strategies (Van Marrewijk 2004). Social identity theory suggests that individuals identify with social groups which may vary according to circumstances. Therefore, participants in a common project may identify with their same group, or with two clans distinguished by nationality, for instance. When all of a project's participants identify with the same group, communication improves, as does the speed and quality of decision-making and collaboration on implementation. If all participants do not all identify with the same group, conflict is likely (Li et al. 2002).

Third, cultural differences may also generate incompatibilities. In particular, mechanisms to resolve conflicts and promote cooperation, commitment and trust may vary between cultures; such mechanisms defy easy transposition from one culture to another (Parkhe 1991; Pothukuchi et al. 2002; Luo 2002). This may make it harder to spark cooperation and resolve conflicts. For example, it may be difficult to establish a trusting relationship between two individuals if one comes from a 'universalistic' culture and the other a 'particularistic' one (Trompenaars 1994; Child and Faulkner 1998, p. 235). For the 'universalist', general rules take precedence over the needs and claims of friends and other relationships, while the 'particularist' sees everything in terms of personal relationships. Universalists may believe their particularist partner unworthy of trust because the latter will always favor his or her friends when choosing between complying with rules versus honoring personal relationships. In the same way, a particularist may find their universalist partner unworthy of trust because the latter will elevate impersonal rules over personal relationships. In addition, when general principles for relationships remain unshared – the components of the social contract[6] – partners may frequently feel norms are violated. This negative assessment provokes a desire to end the relationship (Fréchet 2002; Monin 2002).

In contrast, the sociological and organizational literature often associates positive effects with shared similarities between people who must cooperate (Parkhe 1991). Similarity would be a factor for attraction – needs and objectives are shared – and thus of positive attitudes leading to positive results. In the same way, similar status and values serve as the basis for social relations, and would constitute a mechanism for social interaction and trust building.

Reasons cultural influences sometimes prove positive

If cultural differences sometimes have a positive influence on the success of an alliance, it is because they may generate advantages, as some managers strongly believe. For example, Carlos Ghosn, who was head of the Japanese automobile company Nissan and an architect of the alliance between Nissan and the French automobile company Renault – an alliance he now leads – declared on 29 May 2002 at the Maison de la Culture du Japon in Paris:

> Differences are a source of enrichment [...] One of the interests of the alliance between Renault and Nissan is to demonstrate that through actions [...] I am convinced that accepting differences and making them work together – breaking down the walls that separate us – is an extremely important factor in cultural and economic enrichment.
>
> (Ghosn 2002)

The literature on alliances does not often discuss the reasons why cultural diversity may create value in a cooperative venture between companies. We can nonetheless imagine at least five potential advantages. First, different approaches and systems of signification may stimulate innovation (Doz et al. 2004). Innovation proceeds not only from individual creativity, but also from 'confrontations with variety, with encounters between organizations and people who have different views, objectives and/or knowledge' (Romelaer 2002, p. 75). Along the same lines, some scholars suggest that only companies with different cultures have much to gain from one another in terms of sharing knowledge; the perceived differences constitute opportunities to improve their own processes (Faulkner and Rond 2000).

A second significant advantage may be found by partnering with a company located in the country targeted for expansion (Makino and Beamish 1998, p. 810), thus procuring the capacities needed to succeed. Capacities generally refer to what companies can do with their resources and organizational knowledge – a body of information, know-how and ways of thinking. This organizational knowledge is built into routines that constitute the company's 'recipes' or its know-how and organizational principles (Nelson and Winter 1982; Langlois and Robertson 1995, p. 16). These routines combine personal, organizational and technological knowledge in inextricable ways. They result from the company's specific history. They are complex and not very visible, and hard to teach or codify; it is difficult to reduce them to rules and relationships that are easily communicated and formalized. Hence they are, at best, imperfectly transferable outside of the company and not easily imitated (Kogut and Zander 1993). That is the reason companies differ in their capacities, and why their differences have lasting effects on their relative performance (Kogut and Zander 1992, p. 387).

Required capacities are the ones a company needs to expand internationally; they may differ from those the company already has. Such may be the case when the company enters an unfamiliar – because of technological or market reasons – domain; it may also be the case when a company works in a new cultural environment where ways of interacting with employees, suppliers and clients differ significantly. In particular, when the socio-cultural distance is large, the foreigners' customs and communication codes may render the company's management techniques and procedures less suitable. The missing know-how might be organizational, or specific to a market. Market knowledge may include a component that is built into the local context, making its acquisition difficult for a company that is not indigenous or that doesn't have long, local operating experience (Madhok 1997; Morosini et al. 1998). Since such knowledge is difficult to imitate and takes a long time to learn, partnering with a company that already has it, and at the same time has a different culture, lends strength to the company entering the market. Furthermore, the greater the cultural distance between the home country and the host country, the higher the potential for mutual value creation (Morosini et al. 1998), since the utility of the local partner's contribution logically increases according to the size of the gap between routines the incoming company has and the ones it needs.

A third advantage may spring from flagrant differences that encourage tolerance, respect and a strong effort to mutually adapt. Observable differences, such as when Americans, Northern Europeans and Southern Europeans work with Asians, have the advantage of creating a 'spontaneous sensitivity', an acute awareness of challenges which may motivate people to make bigger efforts; it may also lead to intensified communication and bolster cooperation (Sirmon and Lane 2004). In agreements where partners share the same nationality and/or speak the same language, such as French, English or Spanish companies in French-, English- or Spanish-speaking countries – cultural differences may be less obvious and not receive as much attention, even though their effects remain substantial (Sirmon and Lane 2004).

A fourth significant advantage may come from one company's built-in yet hidden ability to address more different social and cultural situations than can its 'foreign' partner; this reduces the competitive risk that the incoming partner can internalize the same competencies (Hamel 1991). The inability to see and copy a partner's competencies promotes a sustainable interdependence and an alliance's longevity.

The fifth advantage we can postulate rests on cultural combinations that may combat 'cultural bias' or resolve some typical problems in alliances. For example, a former Renault employee in charge of product development, design and engineering at Nissan in 2002, describes how cultural bias can be overcome:

> The Japanese do not like ambiguity at all, and have a hard time controlling it [...] they do not like to deal with it. Faced with ambiguity, they have two attitudes: either they reject it, meaning they go back over the details, looking for data that is practically impossible to find, or they delegate the ambiguity to someone else. In the Renault-Nissan alliance, a good deal of the management of ambiguity and uncertainty was delegated to foreigners, at least at first.
>
> (Pierre Loing, in Blanchot and Katika 2002, p. 30)

Similarly, when Indians, for example, work with companies from more 'masculine' societies, i.e. those that attach greater importance to economic success, the Indians may feel a kind of admiration and think that the joint venture's success is related to the importance their partner gives to economic success (Pothukuchi et al. 2002). The ambiguity of the joint-venture managers' perceived roles serves as an example of a typical problem for alliances. A big difference in the way that partners 'control uncertainty'[7] may stimulate communication and, by doing so, help enlighten a manager with respect to his missions and room for maneuver (Shenkar and Zeira 1992).

To a certain degree, cultural differences resemble a Janus head: one side contains hidden potential for value creation, and the other side contains sources of friction that may prevent the transformation of potential into real value. For Shenkar (2001, pp. 523–24), cultural differences may play a distinct role depending on where one places them strategically or operationally; they may be a source of synergies or an obstacle to exploiting partners' competencies.

Reasons cultural influences sometimes have varied effects

It remains necessary to explain why the effect of national cultural differences on alliance performance and outcome (survival) varies from study to study. For Shenkar (2001), the discrepancy in research results may proceed from questionable conceptual postulates and methodologies regarding 'cultural distance' (see Table 9.2). We also suggest that the discrepancies may be due to endogenous causes that are related to cultural distance-performance models and measurements. Or they may be exogenous, related to third-party variables.

Table 9.2 Questionable postulates about 'cultural distance'

Dimension	Postulate	Counter-argument
Construct	1. Symmetry of cultural distance	It is not self-evident that a Dutch company investing in China experiences the same cultural distance as a Chinese company investing in Holland.
	2. Constancy of cultural distance	The cultural distance between two countries may vary over time (while the research used to estimate distances is old).
	3. Linearity of the effect of cultural distance	The relation between cultural distance-performance may be curvilinear.
	4. Distance determined only by culture	Institutional and economic variables may also contribute to the distance.
	5. Cultural distance as a synonym for discord	Some cultural differences have a negligible impact on some activities and complementarities. For example, if sustainable cooperation requires paying attention to both performance (masculine values) and human relationships (feminine values), masculine and feminine cultures may very well complete one another.
Construct measurement (Kogut and Singh index)	6. Cultural homogeneity between companies from the same home country	Interactions between national and organizational cultures may occur.
	7. Cultural homogeneity within a country	Some studies suggest that intra-country diversity may be important.
	8. Equivalency of all cultural differences	Various works, including Hofstede's, suggest that some differences are less problematic than others for cooperative ventures.

Endogenous causes

We observe at least four endogenous causes for the variety of relations seen between national cultural differences and an alliance's success. First, the variety of results may be a product of a true relation between cultural differences and successful alliances, one that is not as simple as models often show. In the first place, cultural differences do not necessarily mean incompatibility, discord, friction or a lack of 'fit'[8] (cf. Table 9.2, Questionable Postulate 5, above). For example, some research (see e.g. Lin and Germain 1998) suggests that there may be a feeling of 'cultural fit' from an organizational point of view despite a national cultural difference. Next, it may be that – beyond cultural distance – the nature of the cultural differences is decisive (cf. Table 9.2, Questionable Postulate 8). Finally, if cultural distance has an effect, it may be that this effect is not linear (cf. Table 9.2, Questionable Postulate 3). Under these conditions, it is understandable that results vary depending on the composition of the sample studied.

In the second place, the variations in results may stem from the fact that the cultural distance estimated in studies does not always match the real distance, because of the non-validity of Questionable Postulate 2 in Table 9.2, the stability of cultural distance, or because distance estimates are based on invalid research, as in the work of Hofstede. Barkema and Vermeulen (1997) assess how much cultural distance varies in its effects on joint venture outcomes depending on whether the sample studies date from 1966–80, 1980–94, 1966–73, 1973–80, 1980–87, or 1987–94. We can consider this assessment a test of the constancy of cultural differences over time hypothesis; the results obtained do not rule the hypothesis out.

In the third place, the variety of results may stem from cultural difference being estimated differently depending on the study, i.e. a simple national or regional group difference, a calculation of 'overall' cultural distance, or a calculation using dimensions. In fact, differences in nationality or cultural group do not tell us anything about cultural distance. The differences in the partners' national context – differences in institutions, industry structure, laws and regulatory mechanisms – are sometimes thought capable of preventing efficient cooperative efforts because the companies haven't had the same opportunity to establish alliances according to their nationality in the past (Parkhe 1991), or because the companies may work in unsettling circumstances. For example, working in China, with a Chinese partner, may be unsettling for an American because of the huge differences in laws and business ethics (Parkhe 2001). Partners' nationality differences also constitute an indicator of belonging to different cultural environments, but do not allow the cultural distance to be predetermined.

In the fourth and final place, the results may vary because the indicator used to gauge an alliance's success differs from one study to the next. Harrigan's (1988) research, and that of Pothukuchi et al. (2002), is telling: the effect of a difference of partners' nationality varies depending on whether success is measured in terms of partners' mutual satisfaction with the alliance or in terms of its longevity. This suggests that a cultural difference may increase the risk of dissatisfaction and reduce the risk of breaking off the partnership, perhaps because it is harder, when working in a foreign country, to separate from a partner or change one. More generally, while variety within a group may incite conflict and dissatisfaction – a deterioration of relationship quality – it may also simultaneously improve the performance of the alliance's business/project – the synergies – or that of the partners. In particular, conflict may be a source of innovation. In this regard, we find it interesting that no research seems to exist on the relationship between cultural differences and innovation. Yet, such research would be a means to verify the virtues of this type of variety.

Exogenous causes

The varying results of studies looking at the link between national cultural differences and alliances' success may also be attributed to: (a) cultural difference is not the only variable influencing partners' aptitude for cooperating and adapting, and (b) the control variables used in the models explaining the degree of success vary from study to study. For example, studies done by Harrigan (1988) and Kogut (1988) do not simultaneously verify for the incidence of other variables, such that the rule of *ceteris paribus* is not followed. Since all other factors may not be the same, the results obtained in these two studies may simply come from the sample's composition.

When Park and Ungson (1997) found that Japanese–American joint ventures lasted significantly longer than ones between American companies, it may have been due to factors other than cultural differences, factors not controlled for. Hennart and Zeng (2002) sought to verify this by studying the role of cultural differences in joint ventures set up in the United States. They distinguish those set up between American and Japanese firms from those set up only between Japanese firms (in America). Furthermore, their research aims to verify the effects of other factors that increase the risk of misunderstandings and conflicts capable of threatening an alliance's survival. Such factors include the extent of the identity of the partners' industrial culture, convergence of partners' objectives, and balance in the partners' sharing of the joint venture's property rights; the presence of more than two partners; the joint venture's origin, i.e. created *ex nihilo* or by one of the partners buying shares in the other's subsidiary, or by the Japanese partners belonging to the same *keiretsu*; and by the size of each partner and changes in the alliance's business environment in terms of growth, competitive rivalry and dollar–yen parity. By checking these factors, the authors found that Japanese–American joint ventures set up in the United States lasted significantly less long than those set up between Japanese firms in the U.S.

This result suggests that when a firm sets up in a foreign country and needs a partner familiar with the local context, it should choose a firm that shares its nationality and that has operated in the host country for a long time. Such a conclusion should, however, be tempered for at least three reasons. First, these results only compare Japanese–American joint ventures to wholly Japanese ones. If we acknowledge the importance the Japanese give to reputation, conciliation, trust, and norms that encourage reciprocity, we can understand why Japanese firms succeed better when they work together than when they work with American firms, as the latter are reputed to be more sensitive to norms that encourage short term gains and opportunism (Park and Ungson 1997). We see no evidence that alliances between American firms in Japan are preferable to Japanese–American ones. Second, as we mentioned above, an alliance's longevity is not necessarily a synonym for its degree of success.

Third, Hennart and Zeng (2002) do not use an exhaustive set of variables. In particular, the authors neglect the role of differences in an organization's culture and climate. These differences may also create problems, have repercussions on an alliance's performance, and/or determine the direction and intensity of the influence of national cultural differences (Sirmon and Lane 2004; Parkhe 1991; Harrigan 1988; Meschi 1997). Differences in organizational culture and organizational climate become superimposed over differences in national cultural, amplifying or damping them. There are many definitions of organizational culture and climate;[9] all refer to an organization's values, beliefs, norms and managerial practices. National culture does not determine organizational culture; the latter varies between firms that develop in a given country, and organizations from different countries may resemble one another. Harrigan (1988, p. 67) notes that 'several observers have indicated that General Motors' values were closer to those of its partner, Toyota, than they were to Ford Motor Company's'. If this observation is true, we can imagine that international alliances could be less problematic than national ones. In part, the partners' values and managerial approaches may be closer in an international alliance than between partners of the same nationality. In addition, the fact that differences in organizational cultures are less obvious to and neglected by participants in national alliances may result in less tolerance and more conflicts. That would explain Saxton's (1997) observation of a negative relationship between respondents' perceptions of 'organizational fit'[10] and the alliance's performance.[11] This perception of organizational closeness may neglect real differences, resulting in misunderstandings. The result showing international alliances as less problematic than national ones may also derive from the virtues found in organizational cultural differences, just as national cultural differences sometimes have positive effects, as noted earlier.

However, that does not preclude organizational cultural differences from also generating problems. Differences in organizational culture, such as no or few shared values, standards or managerial practices, have repercussions on partners' mutual trust, commitment and information exchange (Sarkar et al. 2001). Differences increase the risk of conflicts (Fréchet 2002) and may detract from partners' satisfaction with their relationship (Pothukuchi et al. 2002). These differences may also affect project performance (Sarkar et al. 2001), the ability of each partner to attain its objectives (Sarkar et al. 2001) and/or the overall performance of the alliance (Fey and Beamish 2001). Moreover, when alliance partners have different organizational routines and relationships to time, such as for making decisions or resolving problems, shared learning between them is likely to be blocked (Doz 1996; Lane and Lubatkin 1998). Learning about the alliance's business and cultural environments, about each others' skills, real objectives and ways of working together, constitutes a key element in the ability to improve how an alliance functions as it proceeds (Doz 1996).

What goes for organizational cultures is equally valid for professional cultures (Sirmon and Lane 2004). Alliances that require cooperation between individuals coming from different professional cultures are likely to be disappointing. The main reason lies in the fact that the participants lack common databases that would allow them to interact efficiently. Employees and managers have to invest time and energy developing shared routines whose efficiency is not a sure bet. Furthermore, constructing shared systems takes time and may disrupt the ability to achieve other goals. In addition, individuals from different professional cultures may have very distinct approaches to problems that may be hard to reconcile if the employees suffer from the 'not invented here' syndrome.[12] Similarly, unity of professional culture constitutes a kind of cement that may counterbalance – but not erase – problems related to national cultural differences (Chevrier 1996).

Many other factors determine an alliance's degree of success; they reflect the stakeholders' profiles, and the alliance's context, initial terms and steering (Blanchot 2006a). These factors may also interact with cultural differences. For example, the type of alliance may influence the effect of cultural differences (Pothukuchi et al. 2002; Sirmon and Lane 2004; Cartwright and Cooper 1993). In particular, the role of cultural differences is likely to be larger in alliances where success depends on many, high-quality interactions between partners, i.e. in alliances based on complementarities, known as 'links', more than in alliances based on scale. That means the contribution of national cultural differences to an alliance's degree of success may prove weak, even though it is greater than a subsidiary's contribution (Barkema and Vermeulen 1997, note 8). For example, in the work of Pothukuchi et al. (2002), the variance due to cultural differences oscillates between 1 percent and 2 percent depending on the model tested – a barely significant effect.[13] This weak statistical relationship does not necessarily signify a systematic absence of effects and a negligible role for cultural differences. In part, it may hide large disparities from one alliance to the other, and may reflect the existence of real intercultural management efforts. Surprisingly, none of the research we found measures the effects of various management methods on cultural differences.

Managing cultural differences in alliances

The dominant but limited conception of cultural-differences management consists of trying to control their negative effects, or reducing them when they pertain to organizational differences. We will argue here for a broader conception of intercultural management that includes these efforts but goes beyond them. Our conception rests on the idea that being able to control negative effects is never guaranteed, no matter what systems are deployed. For example, managers and employees in a cooperative venture are never safe from misunderstandings that arise from cultural differences, even if they have experience with their partner's culture or are sensitive to it. In such conditions, one objective may be to prevent cultural differences' negative effects from combining with other centrifugal forces that are more easily controlled, and compensating with centripetal forces that make cooperation desirable or even necessary. We propose a conception of cultural-differences management as the management of centrifugal and centripetal forces that act on a coalition or a group of actors whom we want to cooperate with one another, working together as best possible (Figure 9.2).

Following this perspective, managing cultural differences in alliances can consist of two types of action: actions that aim to weaken or to control factors that break up the coalition, and those aiming to strengthen it in such a way that the coalition resists any remaining break-up factors. After we have presented the possible control levers that managers may use to act on the effects of cultural differences, we will try to show the levers at work in the intercultural management of the Renault–Nissan alliance.

Multiple control levers

The control levers for weakening centrifugal forces or for strengthening centripetal ones vary depending on the alliance's maturity. Before an alliance deal is completed, the companies involved can act on their choice of partner(s). During initial negotiations with a chosen partner, it is possible to act on the terms of the agreement and the profile of people working in the cooperative effort. And once an agreement is completed, it is sometimes possible to change the participants' profiles and the objective attributes of the alliance; this assumes that the managers are aware of the immediate stakes, at the very least.

In reality, all the control levers do not need to be applied systematically. In part, their deployment depends on the consequences of an alliance's failure. If a breakdown poses no significant problem because a partner is easily replaced, for example, one or the other partner may find it economically defendable to minimize the investment of time or money to manage cultural differences. However, if the stakes are high, the partners may consider it prudent to combine and use several control levers. It also depends on a partner's degree of intervention in the alliance; if a partner's participation is primarily financial, or if the goal is essentially to learn about a firm – the other partner – presumed to be a model, the intercultural issues and associated management needs are likely to be reduced.

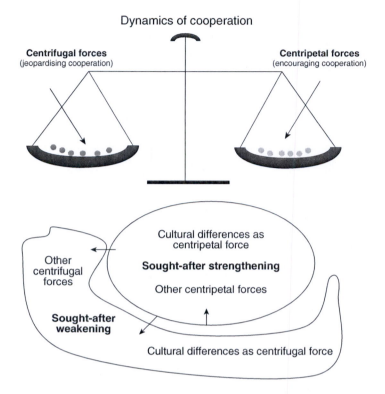

Figure 9.2 Managing cultural differences in alliances as the management of centrifugal and centripetal forces
Source: Author.

To control or reduce cultural differences

The company that initiates an alliance may first act on the partner's profile. When entering a foreign country, the initiating company can sometimes choose a domestic firm in a related industry that has target country experience, rather than choosing a foreign partner. To ensure cultural compatibility with a potential partner, a firm may conduct – or have a consultant conduct – a 'cultural audit' of the potential partner company; this involves attempting to understand the potential partner's organizational culture by highlighting its salient traits (Thevenet 2003; Delavallée 2002). A comparison of two firms' cultures that shows their main differences may serve as a basis for judging 'cultural fit', or the potential partners' ability to combine their differences and define a strategy for cultural integration, if needed (Meschi 1997). Furthermore, this approach can help sensitize individuals to cultural differences, whether or not it discerns the potential partners' 'true' cultures. This approach also highlights the need to get along with the differences and the interest of learning from them – new ways of thinking and acting, or the ways some of one partner's practices could help improve the other's processes, and so forth. Consultants recommend this approach to potential partner selection.[14]

Another way of selecting a culturally compatible partner consists of choosing a firm where a successful history of working together already exists (Cauley de la Sierra 1995, ch. 2).[15] In most cases, this shared experience is associated with both an initial satisfaction between partners and an alliance's success (Saxton 1997; Park and Ungson 1997; Zollo et al. 2002). That may be because the time spent working together allowed the partners to learn how to manage their cultural differences (Meschi 1997). It may also be attributable to past experiences that allowed trust to develop through shared learning (Inkpen and Currall 1998; Gulati 1995), encouraging cooperative behavior and developing standards for reciprocity (Kogut 1989). Such experiences also allow the partners to better manage coordination, since they know each other's strengths and weaknesses. In addition, experiences built up between the partners may help maintain their relationship (Ring and Van de Ven 1994) for economic reasons – investments made for the relationship – and also psychological and social ones, for example employment contracts, social networks, and so forth. The shared experiences may also facilitate the relationship's evolution towards more effectiveness and efficiency (Reuer et al. 2002).

A firm may also use a human resources management approach to select partners. The selection of the individuals who will serve as the alliance's interface, particularly the alliance managers, may constitute a control lever. Many practitioners believe that alliance managers should have a particular profile to ensure an alliance's success (Blanchot 2006b, 2006c). They should know how to build trust and mutual respect, influence and facilitate joint decisions, be open, good listeners, diplomatic, autonomous and fair. Their expertise or experience should give them legitimacy. They should be able to exploit diversity's richness, and be visionary, creative, innovative, entrepreneurial, conciliating, clarifying, pragmatic and motivating. They should also be experienced managers, have completed an advanced degree, and shown talent when they have been at the controls in conflicting roles – such as managing divergent expectations between an individual's work and his or her behavior – and in ambiguous roles that lack clear expectations.

Even though this desired profile accounts for a small share of the alliance's business/ project's performance (Parker et al.1996), it appears that choosing an alliance manager with intercultural skills and an ability to understand and adapt to intercultural situations proves important for an international alliance's relationship quality (Huang et al. 2003). Selecting individuals who have had several successful international experiences in other alliances, or who have a multicultural profile through their education, may be a judicious precaution (Child and Faulkner 1998, pp. 240, 253). Choosing people who can speak the partner's language is also desirable for facilitating communication. When two companies form a joint subsidiary, management may find it worthwhile to hire external people rather than transferring or expatriating one or the other partner's internal employees, to help avoid employees' identification with the head offices rather than with the subsidiary. External hiring also helps avoid mixing two groups of employees impregnated with their original company's organizational culture, and consequently facilitates employees' adhesion to any new culture that the joint subsidiary may try to create.

However, the profile of interacting partners and employees is only one important aspect, among others. Their roles, and especially that given to alliance managers, also matter (Blanchot 2006b, 2006c). Raising awareness about a partner's cultural particularities and environment may also constitute a control lever in any attempt to mitigate cultural differences' negative effects. All the same, intercultural training does not guarantee success (Cerdin and Peretti 2000). Its impact depends on course content, duration, when classes are given, and whether or not courses include foreign language training (Eschbach et al. 2001). In particular, training classes primarily centered on differences run the risk of reinforcing stereotypes likely to accentuate 'us versus them' attitudes, paralyzing action and preventing the joint construction of common rules. Instead, it is better to promote a more positive view of differences, as Carlos Ghosn suggests:

> Imagine a French executive arriving in Japan. He might say to himself, 'My, they are very slow to make any decisions!' There he criticizes the difference. He could also say, 'Their execution is perfect. We could learn something.' Here he capitalizes on the difference. It is the same thing for the Japanese executive. He goes to France and says, 'They talk a lot but don't do much.' Or he could find a conceptual richness, where he can learn strategic thinking and decision-making. The entire art is in looking at the positive side and asking yourself, 'What can I learn from Japan, or from France?' One of our key concepts is to look at the bottle as being half full rather than half empty!
>
> (Ghosn 2002, p. 9)

Furthermore, as we acknowledge that culture does not determine a person's preferences and that his or her (always) superficial knowledge of another culture makes it difficult to predetermine what the other person will find acceptable or not, we do not want to suggest there is a list of interdictions that everyone should know in advance. Faced with uncertainties that arise – especially in multicultural situations – we believe experimentation should be encouraged through the joint building and evaluation of rules. In this regard, we note the potentially useful role of 'relationship climate surveys' to understand the complex dynamics of international alliances. Although not a control lever *per se*, such surveys may be a useful tool. The business literature on alliances does not highlight this approach, even though the companies use it in real life, as in the Renault–Nissan case. Relationship climate surveys ask the workforce about participants' feelings and thoughts about an alliance, its partners and its practices. Notably, the surveys measure the tensions and divisions between groups, dissatisfaction with practices, and dominant behaviors.

We also note the importance of retaining the same people to interact with partners (Ring and Van de Ven 1994); their constancy helps develop personal relationships that gradually supplant role-based relationships, facilitating conflict resolution. Similarly, alliance managers and coordinators who think they are 'in transit' will have reduced levels of commitment to and identification with the alliance (Salk 1997a, 1997b), making conflict resolution harder. Furthermore, shared learning between alliance partners depends on this constancy.

Another lever to control the effects of cultural differences is found in the organization of relationships between alliance partners or between the joint subsidiary and its corporate parents. In the first instance, the range of the interface may be called into play. If it is truly difficult to work with a partner given the difference in operational approaches, sometimes it is possible to divide up tasks rather than share them. Naturally, that assumes a clear definition of each partner's share of tasks, a reduction of interdependences, and a full explanation of coordination mechanisms (Doz 1996). This way of proceeding may reinforce the force of stereotypes because it creates multiple, separated sites *de facto* (Salk 1997a, 1997b). But that is not necessarily a problem since the need for cooperation is reduced.

Reorganizing joint working teams may also help; team structure influences the way alliance participants feel about their cultural differences. When cultural frontiers coincide with an organization's structural divides – hierarchical relations and the division of work – there is a risk of many negative effects. Sub-groups may grow polarized; negative stereotypes and caricatures may tint thoughts about the other; ethnocentric, disdainful and critical attitudes may appear; open or germinating conflicts may spoil interpersonal relations, tensions may rise in communications and the relationship climate and efforts toward intercultural adaptation may evaporate or run in only one direction (Chevrier 1996).

These risks suggest that when managers constitute shared teams, cumulating differences between cultural sub-groups should be avoided. All the same, the principle of sharing jobs based on a strict criterion of equality between partners, rather than on competency, maintains divisions between cultural groups and encourages tensions and conflicts (Salk 1997a, 1997b). The work done on social identification in alliances (Salk and Shenkar 2001) allows us to see that this principle leads to the persistent domination of national identities, rather than promoting identification with a common organization.

A final lever that may be used to control relationships in an alliance plays with the degree of autonomy allowed to the joint venture (or other cooperative entity) so that it has sufficient freedom to define an internal mode of operations in harmony with the cultural universes present in it (Chevrier 2003, p. 10). The right dose of autonomy also allows the venture to build its own identity.

Beyond organizing relationships with a partner firm, the managers of a to-be-allied international company may act on the equilibrium of relationships they intend to establish. They may try to respect identities present: each group of employees may identify with a country, a culture, a history or a language, for instance. Or the managers may encourage a dominant identity, although a domination strategy will likely lead to cultural resistance (Van Marrewijk 2004; Child and Faulkner 1998). A domination strategy consists of trying to take power over a coalition at the outset, notably by imposing a language and/or management methods, systems and key personnel. It is also characterized by a tendency to ignore a partner's cultural particularities and impose one's own culture. Such an approach is called 'ethnocentric' (see especially Perlmutter [1969]).

Cultural resistance consists of mobilizing counter-forces. In the case of an international alliance where the imposing partner comes from another country and aims to enter a developing country, the 'junior', local partner may mobilize its employees, and also journalists and the political class, by raising their awareness of the threat constituted by the incoming partner on the host country's national interests, cultural legacy and traditions. The junior partner may even exaggerate cultural differences or insist on the incoming partner's 'neo-colonialist' behavior, focusing on colonial histories between countries, when applicable. That is what telecommunications companies in Saint Martin and Curacao in the Dutch Antilles did when the Dutch telecommunications company KPN tried to dominate them (Van Marrewijk 2004); their actions caused a planned alliance to fail. The Dutch firm digested this experience and acted differently when it later decided to ally with an Indonesian partner. The larger Dutch firm then adopted a more 'polycentric' strategy that consisted of acknowledging and respecting the cultural specificity of its partner and its partner's environment. Furthermore, the relationship was built far more gradually and with all of the stakeholders in the project, including local journalists and the Indonesian government. To learn about cultural differences and avoid creating a feeling of domination when a partner is smaller, the larger partner will find it helpful to begin cooperating through small projects, allowing personal relations and the trust needed for a larger commitment to develop on both sides. In particular, when entering a developing country, alliance planners and managers must recognize that the process may be long and that the return on investment is rarely rapid (Lane and Beamish 1990).

Time may also serve as a control lever. Inasmuch as perceptions of cultural distance tend to attenuate over time, it would be incorrect to believe that a difficult multicultural situation must certainly lead to breaking off a relation (Meschi 1997). There is no reason to conclude that intercultural problems will automatically resolve themselves with time, either. An initial effort to become familiar with the partner's culture, coupled with experimentation and learning, may help discover mutually acceptable ways of interacting. This is an incremental and time-intensive process. Following this perspective, some management scholars suggest taking a gradual approach, consisting of joint information, training and discussion sessions that involve participants from both partner companies so they can develop a mutual understanding before having to really work together (Doz 1988, p. 49).

We believe it may also be helpful to curb possible ruptures in the relationship by obligating the partners to find areas of agreement. That is one of the tactics Reuters and Dow Jones used in 1999, when they created their joint subsidiary, Factiva, specializing in economic news for businesses (Crovitz 2004). The two firms were long-time competitors and their approaches were anchored in different national cultures, Reuters in London and Dow Jones in New York City. The two companies decided to create obstacles to exiting the partnership to increase the chances their alliance would succeed. They made it so that the price of withdrawing from the alliance was dissuasive for both sides. That is a way to signal mutual commitment and the need to seek and find ways to accommodate one another, given the alliance's durability. It is also a way for companies to give themselves the time they need to build mutually acceptable principles together, creating a culture for the shared subsidiary.

Alliance planners and managers can also act on the way information is treated, managing communications to reduce the uncertainty or ambiguity that may result from cultural differences. Uncertainty reflects an inability to estimate the probability of future events, to foresee the consequences of a decision, or the difficulty of establishing causal relationships between certain phenomena. Uncertainty may be considered to result from a lack of information, so encouraging information exchange is vital for reducing partners' uncertainty. Simple media, such as written reports, may be sufficient; the information exchanged must be precise, relevant and credible (Mohr and Spekman 1994; Parkhe 1991).

Ambiguity refers to equivocal situations that may be interpreted in multiple ways. It does not arise from a lack of information, but from the fact that decision makers interpret and understand information differently because of their different frames of reference. Multicultural situations often prove ambiguous since they run up against two or more different systems of meaning. To reduce ambiguity, managers must facilitate intersubjective exchanges that may help build a common system of meaning. Facilitative, high-touch media must be used, such as face-to-face meetings and two-way discussion groups, allowing the exchange of verbal and non-verbal signals, feedback and emotional sharing that helps shared meanings emerge. The richness of these media must be fully exploited, saturating the participants, such as when a group meeting allows free discussion. In contrast, there is no saturation when there is only one meeting, or when only the manager presents his or her viewpoints without other interaction, discussion or two-way communication. Sharing experiences may be considered particularly useful. As Nonaka and Takeuchi (1997) emphasize:

> Without some form of shared experience, it is extremely difficult for one person to project themselves into another person's thought processes. Just transferring information will generally provide little meaning if the information is abstracted from the emotions associated with it and from the specific contexts where shared experiences are cemented.
>
> (p. 84)

To fortify cooperation

If we admit that some aspects of cultural differences and their effects are implacable, we have to accept that they may constitute a never-ending source of tensions between participants in a cooperative venture. They form a kind of permanent weight on the side of 'centrifugal forces' on a scale counterbalanced by centripetal forces.[16] There are two ways to tip the scale toward centripetal forces: reduce other centrifugal forces or bolster centripetal ones. These two ways of managing competing forces constitute another component of managing cultural differences in alliances – the 'great, missing thing' from the literature that may, in fact, be decisive. In effect, managers must try to bolster relationship quality and develop the potential for value creation for alliance stakeholders. Without presuming to be exhaustive, we can suggest several possible control levers.

One of the first levers in the process of building an alliance is to undertake a discussion about the objectives to aim for and the strategy to implement in order to achieve them (Beamish and Delios 1997). That is one way to evaluate the strategic compatibility between partners[17] (Parkhe 1991), to assess the threat of divergent ambitions, to verify that partners' interests and objectives are shared or compatible (Parkhe 1991; Doz and Hamel 1998; Luo 2002). If managers sidestep this discussion on ends and means, the risk of conflict and failure increases. Obviously, we do not mean that objectives and means should not change over time, as circumstances change. As the work of Doz (1996) suggests, not only is it important to reduce information asymmetry and ambiguity about partners' expectations, but also that these expectations be flexible and realistic rather than ambitious and optimistic.

Managers may also play with partners' financial (and other) contributions and commitments, and with the range or scope of the alliance. The size of contributions and credibility of commitments constitute investment wagers on the alliance and factors that develop trust (Bleeke and Ernst 1992; Gulati et al. 1994). Commitments are credible when they can hurt the firm that made them if it breaks off the cooperative venture. They may take the form of setting up a long-term contract with a third party that only makes sense within the context of the venture, or engaging a firm's reputation by extensively advertising the alliance, or dissolving a division that performs tasks that have been assigned to a partner. The size of the commitments and the scope of cooperation may also increase an alliance's potential for value creation, facilitating mutual adaptations after the fact, because of the stakes invested in the alliance (Reuer et al. 2002). Furthermore, the complementarities and exclusivity of each partner's contribution increases their interdependency and exit costs if they leave the relationship; this helps motivate cooperation. The level of interdependence refers to the degree each partner needs the other to achieve its objectives. The higher the degree, the more the partners will have an interest in prolonging the alliance (Puthod 1996) and in engaging in the relationship. In addition, the higher the mutual dependence, the more senior managers fear conflict since it may lead to a break-up, and the more alliance managers seek to avoid or manage it (Das and Teng 2003, p. 293; Fréchet 2002). The initial level of interdependence depends on the resources allocated to the alliance; these, in turn, depend on the firms' capacities and their willingness to commit to the alliance.

When seeking a partner, a firm has an interest in not looking only at the resources and capacities a potential partner may bring to it; it must also verify that its own resources and capacities are sought by the potential partner. Furthermore, when looking for a sustainable interdependence, a firm must verify that the contributions it will make will be useful to the partner for as long as the firm will need that partner. Dynamically, the level of interdependence is a function of interorganizational learning: if a firm absorbs the competencies of its partner that justified the cooperative venture, its dependency may disappear. This means that the partners may have an interest in protecting some of the knowledge the alliance is founded on, if they want to sustain it.

In the same way, it is possible to play with remuneration. In an alliance, the partners are often sensitive to equity as a standard of distributive justice (Lucas and Piron 1998; Blanchot and Romelaer 2002; Monin 2002). Equity exists when there is equality in the relationship between each partner's contribution and remuneration. In reality, equity may refer to a subjective perception as much as an objective reality, given that it is difficult to assess all of everyone's contributions and remunerations. For example, it is not easy to estimate the gains made by each partner from interorganizational learning. The alliance manager's challenge is to regularly sound out everyone's feelings about the equity of the arrangement. The manager can try to act on these feelings by adjusting communications to reduce information asymmetries and, if necessary, by redefining the contributions and remuneration of all or some of the partners. It is possible to influence individuals' motivation to cooperate by linking part of their remuneration and career path to their ability to overcome the difficulties they experience in the relationship.

To bolster relationship quality, it is also possible to act on the way decisions are made. Alliance participants have a stronger sense of commitment when they feel that decisions that affect them are fair and legitimate (Monin 2002; Johnson et al. 2002). In addition, a shared feeling of procedural justice influences profitability, an effect that is more marked the greater the cultural distance (Luo 2005). Theory suggests eight principles must be respected to develop a feeling of procedural justice (Folger and Cropanzano 1998):

1. Uniformity principle: apply the same rules to everyone; for example, when managing conflicts.
2. Exactitude principle: verify that information used in making decisions is exact, for example, give the alliance's managerial team the feeling that decisions made about their project are founded on a good understanding of the situation.
3. Neutrality principle: ensure the neutrality of the people making decisions.
4. Representation principle: take the interests of everyone into consideration when making a decision; this assumes everyone's view is solicited.
5. Appeal principle: make it possible to correct errors; for example, allow participants to challenge and refute decision makers' viewpoints.
6. Ethical principle: respect the group's ethics standards.
7. Clarity principle: provide information and explanations for decisions.
8. Respect principle: treat others in a polite and respectful manner.

These principles also apply when conflicts emerge; research on conflict resolution mechanisms used in alliances confirms their importance. Partners' satisfaction increases when they use joint problem-solving techniques (Mohr and Spekman 1994; Lin and Germain 1998) and when they favor compromise (Lu 2006). Problem-solving techniques consist of openly discussing problems, worries, priorities, and ideas and seeking solutions that will satisfy each partner's expectations. Compromise consists of adopting a solution that meets each partner's position halfway. Two other imaginable approaches appear unsatisfactory or even destructive: domination founded on power, which may be an expert's power, for instance; and arbitration by a public or private mediator.

Seeking intercultural management in the Renault–Nissan alliance[18]

An alliance between Renault and Nissan was set up officially on 27 March 1999, after 9 months of secret negotiations. It was an ambitious operation from the start, since it meant forming a binational group that would rank fifth in the world for automobile market share as soon as it was created. The alliance took the form of a comprehensive cooperative venture, with Renault taking a 36.8 percent stake in Nissan Motors' capital. Comprehensive coopera-tion meant that the partners intended to work together at every stage of their respective value chains. In particular, the two firms aimed to save $3.6 billon between 2000 and 2002, shav-ing $1.755 billion from purchasing costs, and to gain a 17 percent joint market share in Europe by 2005, and more than 10 percent of the global automobile market by 2010. Managers agreed to the alliance as Nissan was trying to emerge from a crisis that started in 1993. Nissan had been profitable in only one year since then, and had a high level of debt estimated at €18–€25 billion depending on what was counted. It also had a worldwide market share that had declined from 6.6 percent in 1991 to 4.9 percent in 1998, and an oper-ating margin of only 1.4 percent in 1999. At the beginning of the alliance, Nissan's stock market value was €9 billion, compared with Renault's €8.4 billion. The French automobile group had an operating margin of 5.9 percent in 1999, an 11 percent market share in Europe, and a 4.3 percent market share worldwide.

Overall positive results despite significant cultural differences

Seven years later in 2007, we assessed the coming together of Renault and Nissan using the main indicators that gauge the degree of an alliance's success (see Figure 9.1). We found several results and changes that suggested that the alliance's business/project performance was rather satisfactory. Purchasing synergies created savings of $1.9 billion, higher than forecast. Joint purchases rose from 30 percent in 2001 to 70 percent in 2005, indicating more success in cooperative purchasing. The alliance's successive financial statements also cited many joint actions; however, their financial impacts were little mentioned in shareholder reports. The multiplicity of these cooperative endeavors suggests the large size of expected potential synergies, even as the scarcity of information about how these synergies translate financially led us to believe the results were not always as high as hoped.

The alliance's effects on the partners seem positive overall. After joining forces with Nissan, Renault's stock market valuation tripled to €25.6 million on 16 May 2006, and Nissan's rose five-fold, to €45.7 billion on 15 May 2006. These performances were remark-able compared with the dynamics of the main stock indexes and their competitors' valuation trends. For example, at the beginning of 2006, DaimlerChrysler had a stock market value of about half of what it was in March 1999. In terms of market share, Renault–Nissan's perfor-mance since 1999 showed more contrasts. Nissan's worldwide share increased by nearly 1 percentage point (based on 2005 data) while Renault's fell by 0.2. In Europe, the two manufacturers did not achieve their joint objective of 17 percent, as they had only 13 percent of the market in 2005.

We also note the many beneficial skills transfers between the two partners. For example, Renault was able to reduce development time for the Logan model by 21 months by using Nissan's know-how. Similarly, Nissan benefitted from the financial and managerial efforts Renault made to ensure Nissan's turnaround: Renault invested about €5 billion in Nissan and mobilized a team of its best managers to help the company; doubtless, this was detrimental to Renault in the short term in terms of lost opportunity costs for investing in its own range of vehicles. Nissan's turnaround was spectacular: it returned to profitability in 2000, achieved a more than 8 percent operating margin from 2002 to 2006, and had zero debt in 2005. Expectations about the potential for further value creation appeared strong, judging by the alliance's strategic vision as announced on its fifth anniversary.

The partners aimed to be recognized by their clients as one of the top three automobile groups in the world on several counts: the quality and attractiveness of their products and services in each region of the world and in each segment of their product range; in terms of key technologies, with each partner a leader in precise domains of excellence; and to constantly achieve operational results though a high margin and sustained growth, putting the alliance among the top three global automobile companies.

There was almost no public information available about the quality of the partners' relationship, but we found some revealing indicators. On 17 June 2004, the partners launched their fourth survey of employees' perceptions of the alliance; the first took place in January 2000, the second in December 2000, and the third in November 2002. These surveys (a type of relationship climate survey discussed earlier in this chapter) collected the opinions of 8,000 randomly selected employees – 4,000 from Renault and 4,000 from Nissan. The 2004 questionnaire had thirty-six questions grouped by topic: information, perception, support, the alliance today, threats to the alliance, its future, and its strategic vision. According to an internal memo from Renault (2003) about the results of the third survey, more than 80 percent of the two companies' employees supported the alliance, a more than 15 percentage point increase over the first survey. Other findings included:

- The fear of losing one's job or identity in each company declined.
- More than 80 percent of employees expressed their confidence in the alliance's success. For Renault's employees, success was tied to Nissan's contribution to quality control. For Nissan's employees, success was tied to the open vision and cooperation promoted by Renault and the geographic complementarity of the two firms.
- Nearly 90 percent were in favor of maintaining the identity of each brand and nearly 70 percent wanted management autonomy.
- Confidence in a shared future showed 56 percent for Nissan employees, up 13 percentage points over the previous survey, and 88 percent for Renault employees.
- Employees felt they were well informed about the alliance, an increase at Nissan of more than 30 percentage points over the 2000 survey.
- Employees felt their knowledge of both firms was growing.
- Employees mentioned a need for more clear and detailed information about the alliance's projects.

The fact that the survey results were not communicated in detail either internally or externally – the data were reserved for the alliance steering committee members – may signal that some tensions existed. The contacts that we were able to establish with several Renault executives allowed us to confirm this hypothesis: tensions had always existed and persisted between employees of Renault and Nissan. However, these tensions did not prevent cooperation in many domains and the achievement of remarkable results. This suggests that as of 2007, the firms had succeeded in overcoming the biggest difficulties that could have resulted from their cultural differences, both organizational and national.

The alliance survived and experienced a positive dynamic in the sense that the cooperative aspects were reinforced over time rather than fading. Several 2007 indicators point to this fact:

- The number of cooperative groups increased from 12 to 19.
- Purchases allocated to the joint purchasing group that was set up in 2001 increased from 30 percent of annual purchases to more than 70 percent.
- Capital stakes and investments increased: Renault's stake in Nissan rose to 44.3 percent and Nissan acquired 1 percent of Renault's non-voting shares.
- The alliance's governance structure solidified: the initial management structure was replaced by a new joint entity where decisions could no longer be blocked legally.

All alliances do not follow such a favorable trajectory. In comparison, we can cite the DaimlerChrysler–Mitsubishi alliance, as it resembles Renault–Nissan in many ways. Set up in 2000, it united a European automobile company, DaimlerChrysler, and a Japanese one, Mitsubishi. At the time, Mitsubishi was having financial difficulties and was over-indebted. In July 2002, DaimlerChrysler acquired 34 percent of Mitsubishi's capital; the cooperative venture was meant to be global. DaimlerChrysler had to help with Mitsubishi's turnaround. Although the DaimlerChrysler–Mitsubishi alliance had some similarities to Renault–Nissan in its initial terms, it did not follow the same trajectory. In fact, DaimlerChrysler announced the sale of its stake in Mitsubishi in November 2005, signaling the failure of Mitsubishi's and the end of the two companies' global cooperative venture.

When we take the preceding observations into consideration, we gauge the Renault–Nissan alliance closer to 'success' than to 'failure' on a scale of success, and this despite significant cultural differences. Besides their language differences, the Japanese and the French tend to differ in the ways they conceive of and establish relationships between individuals, between the individual and the group, in their relationship to nature, and in their ways of communicating. Without trying to distinguish what springs from national versus organizational culture, a high-level Renault manager expatriated to work at Nissan observed that:

> Looking at the past two years, the thing that was the most surprising was Nissan's organization – this giant company – that differed fundamentally from Renault's. It had to do as much with cultural differences as with differences between the two firms, with their two very different histories. At Nissan, it is clear that management has a very big and respected role [...]. Nissan's upper management, like Renault's, determines the main directions, clearly. But, at an intermediate level, the manager's role is more that of *nemawashi* – that means 'a role attained by consensus based on grand general principles'. In France, we are less accustomed to this role: a department head sets or copies over the main directions without fundamental discussion. In Japan, the middle manager acts more as a catalyst than as someone who sets a direction.
>
> (Pierre Loing, in Blanchot and Kalika 2002, p. 32)

From the time an alliance is announced, these cultural differences constitute a source of concern and are even sometimes perceived as an insurmountable obstacle. The credit rating agency, Moody's, underscored the difficulties related to the two groups' cultural differences (Blanchot and Kalika, 2002). Giovanni Agnelli, when chief executive of the Italian car company, Fiat, declared:

> 'Renault taking on Nissan? They are very brave [...] it is true that they complement each other in everything [...] except here' (tapping his index finger on his head).
>
> (Gallard 1999)

In a similar vein, Jacques Calvert, former chief executive of the French automobile company PSA (Peugeot) observed:

> I would never get involved in such a project because of the drawbacks, the financial risk, the juxtaposition of two product ranges that are more competitive than complementary, and especially because of the enormous difficulty to make teams work together who are light-years apart culturally – all that overwhelms the advantages in my mind.
>
> (Ghosn and Riès 2003, p. 184)

How is it that these cultural differences, deemed 'colossal' even by Carlos Ghosn (2002), did not lead to the alliance's failure?

A comprehensive explanation

At first sight, we believe the Renault–Nissan alliance constitutes a good intercultural management textbook case, since it is a large scale cooperative venture that produced significant results despite significant cultural differences. So we wanted to describe the alliance's intercultural management in this chapter, to characterize it. But if we limited ourselves to what participants in the cooperative venture had to say, we would not gain much insight. For example, when we asked the Nissan manager responsible for long-term new product development whether cultural differences were actively 'managed' in the alliance, he replied:

> Not as such. However, clearly the group sent to Japan had received training about Japan at the beginning, about the Japanese, about working in Japan … In the same way, you should know that at Nissan, we started some training sessions for the Japanese employees, at least for those who would work with French employees on a daily basis, about France, and about how French people think […]. At one time, the goal was to have joint sessions. It was very enriching for the French, I think, to see the Japanese employees' image of them a year later. I think that the opposite was also true – what is clear, is that the sessions helped even out cultural differences.
>
> (Pierre Loing, in Blanchot and Kalika 2002, video extract)

We can provide a plausible explanation for this response. One contributing factor is that managers do not necessarily have a precise idea of what 'cultural-differences management' covers. Another is that they may consequently think that 'real' cultural-differences management should reduce, erase or modify differences. In these circumstances, raising awareness about cultural differences would only be a 'lite' version of cultural-differences management. Even when we review comments about the alliance made by Louis Schweitzer, former chairman and CEO of Renault, or Carlos Ghosn, we find little or no direct reference to intercultural management. However, if we look at the way the alliance was designed and steered (cf. Blanchot and Kalika 2002, 2006), we very quickly see that the alliance was built around an especially rich management of cultural differences. Management mobilized a good number of control levers to reduce or compensate for cultural differences (Table 9.3).[19]

Nissan was not a partner of Renault's before the alliance (Lever 2 in Table 9.3). The two company's coming together resulted from the alignment of Nissan's needs – it was seeking a partner to help it get out of its financial difficulties – and Renault's ambitions – it wanted to be a leading global brand, not just a European one (see in particular Emerson 2001). Louis Schweitzer, Renault's chief executive in 1999, initiated the cooperative venture.

Table 9.3 Main control levers used in the Renault–Nissan alliance for intercultural management

Orientation	Control lever	Applied? (yes/no)
To control and reduce cultural differences	1. Choosing a partner serving a related industry	No
	2. Choosing a partner with whom work experience has already been shared	No
	3. Choosing interfacing employees with multicultural backgrounds	Yes
	4. Recruiting personnel from outside partner firms	No
	5. Raising awareness about cultural differences	Yes
	6. Surveying the workforce relationship climate	Yes
	7. Maintaining constancy in interacting personnel	?
	8. Reducing the scope of the interface	Yes
	9. Structuring cooperative teams without increasing the number of divides	Yes
	10. Giving the cooperative venture teams autonomy	?
	11. Using a equilibrium strategy rather than one of domination	Yes
	12. Raising exit barriers	Yes
	13. Reducing uncertainty through abundant information	?
	14. Reducing ambiguity by using 'rich' mediums	?
To bolster cooperation by compensating for unavoidable tensions related to cultural differences	15. Discussion of goals, objectives and strategies	Yes
	16. Size and credibility of commitment(s)	Yes
	17. Vast range of cooperative area/Size of stakes	Yes
	18. Complementarity and exclusivity of partners' contributions	Yes/?a
	19. Fairness of partners' remuneration	Yes/?b
	20. Individual reasons to cooperate	?
	21. Process aiming to develop a feeling of procedural justice	Yes

Notes: a = 'Yes/?' here means we do not have sufficient data to answer yes or no with certitude whether contributions are exclusive

b = 'Yes/?' here means that the managers' discourse affirms the adoption of a distributive justice principle but that we do not have enough information to verify if their employees actually share the feeling that remuneration is fair.

According to what he has said, the idea was to create a binational group founded on respect and mutual understanding, and maintaining the two companies' identities (Levers 5 and 11). Ghosn and Riès (2003) further explained:

> The alliance's success was grounded on the fact that we took care to always control all of the tendencies that could destroy value, on both sides. When Nissan was near death, the risk of seeing these tendencies win out was mostly situated on the Renault side. But the French company's management was smart enough to resist the temptation to make a power play. This attitude deserves to be emphasized even more as it is rather exceptional in the 'cold, cruel' business world. Louis Schweitzer's behavior was diametrically opposed to that of Jürgen Schrempp, DaimlerChrysler's CEO.
>
> (p. x)

This avoidance of domination (Lever 11) and awareness of cultural differences (Lever 5) are notably the fruit of Renault's failed attempt to ally with the Swedish automobile company,

Volvo, in the 1990s. Schweitzer even suggested this as he talked about the results of Renault–Nissan alliance 5 years after its creation:

> While the merger with Volvo made sense on paper, and we thought it was a done deal, the Volvo people were delighted when it went on the rocks. We did not see their rejection coming. We had a system that was good in theory, but in practice ignored this psychological dimension. With Nissan, we fundamentally did exactly the opposite by setting up something that was hard theoretically but proved do-able.
>
> (*Le Monde*, March 30, 2004)[20]

In fact, Renault's stake in Nissan's capital should not be considered an indicator of Renault's domination in the alliance. The managers knew how to separate the 'shareholder report' from the 'partnership report'.[21] Rather this financial participation constituted a credible commitment (Lever 16), vital at the start of the relationship; it represented almost €5 billion invested when a return was far from ensured, as doubts surrounded Nissan's ability to survive. Five billion euros was proof of a strong commitment.

The partnership's strategic vision was discussed during the negotiation phase (Lever 15), following an assessment of potential synergies conducted by several working groups. The stakes were high for both potential partners (Lever 17). For Nissan, it was possibly its last chance, its final attempt to turn itself around. For Renault, it was a unique opportunity to expand and realize its ambition. A strong will to overcome obstacles, including cultural ones, emerged. The principle of a vast scope of cooperation (Lever 17) was retained, given the importance of the partners' complementarity (Lever 18). In general, Renault was strong where Nissan was weak, and vice versa, for example market penetration, quality, design, automation and purchasing. While each partner's contribution was complemented by the other's, nothing indicates they were exclusive; other partners could have made the same contributions. Be that as it may, the multiplication of shared operations – rationalizing purchasing, developing shared platforms, installing common IT systems – rapidly constituted barriers to ending the relationship (Lever 12).

To raise employees' awareness about cultural differences (Lever 5), training programs were put in place on both sides, and several hundred people participated in them. In addition to a conference on French and Japanese culture, a special session, 'Working with Japanese/French partners', was offered. This seminar helped key participants in the alliance from both companies understand their respective cultures and ways of working, focusing on three major areas: communications, project management and resolving conflicts while maintaining a 'positive partnership'. We also found 'team-working seminars', aimed at alliance entities as well as jointly used organizations, for example suppliers, consultancies, and so on. These seminars aimed to improve the efficiency of teamwork, strengthen personal ties and mutual trust, construct an identity for the teams, and enable the sharing of common objectives. From the seminars' launch in 2003 until 2007, twenty-one teams set up team-working seminars, involving more than 360 participants. In addition, English lessons – the alliance's working language – were encouraged and the legitimate use of translators was allowed, if necessary to ensure perfect mutual comprehension.

The alliance also composed a code of conduct; it aimed to promote the new group's shared values, confidentiality, and shared working rules on a daily basis. Notably, the code stipulated that 'the alliance will be fair and balanced' (Levers 11 and 19). Furthermore, certain attitudes and behaviors were encouraged, promoting respect for cultural differences (Levers 5 and 11) and procedural justice (Lever 21):

- Shared design of and respect for common work rules (uniformity principle).[22]
- Transparency in personal exchanges, as well as sincerity and reliability of shared information (exactitude principle).
- Adoption of solutions and decisions understood and accepted by all parties (representation and clarity principles).
- Joint problem resolution (representation principle).
- Deep, regular and loyal communication that respects each other's history (ethics and respect principles).
- Care taken to be understood (clarity principle).
- Attention to cultural differences, recognition and combining the strengths and styles of both cultures.
- Respect for each person's culture and origins (respect principle).
- Active listening and trying to understand before judging.

The setting up of cross-company teams[23] was based on dual criteria: parity and competency (Lever 9). Each group was composed of an equal number of people from Renault and from Nissan. All the same, management was not conjoint except for the group thought to be the most strategic; among management groups, the strategy group was unique because it systematically had a deputy from both companies present. The choice of a single upper-management leader rather than using co-directors for the majority of project groups is understandable in terms of efficiency and effectiveness imperatives; joint decisions for operational activities would be too costly and slow (Lever 8). Competency informed the selection of the single Renault or Nissan employee to lead a group. Here competency meant organizational skills more than individual skills. In fact, it appeared that about half the groups were directed by Renault employees and half by Nissan's. The parity and competency principles paid respect to the identities in place; they did not create divides that would indicate domination by Renault. Furthermore, working groups were constituted of people who belonged to a related industry and exercised the same profession, such as engineering or purchasing (Lever 9).

Compared with the cooperative venture's range, the interface between the two companies was rather limited (Lever 8). From the beginning of the alliance until 2007, discussions and communications involved only 462 people, including those in shared organizations (suppliers, consultants, etc.). These 462 were not the only ones involved in the alliance's operations. One hundred or so others worked in other alliance entities: cross-company working groups, coordination offices, alliance steering committees. But in total, employees involved in the alliance represented a very small proportion of the nearly 30,000 people employed by the two companies.

Along with Louis Schweitzer, the best known alliance manager is Carlos Ghosn, an archetype of the 'multicultural' manager (Lever 3). He has international experience and defines himself as the product of several cultures, born in Brazil to Lebanese parents and educated in France. He also has international work experience, having worked in France, Brazil and the United States before setting up in Japan. In Ghosn's opinion, his multicultural experiences provided a trump card when it came to steering the alliance (Emerson 2001). Ultimately, the partners knew how to make the initial terms of the alliance evolve as their mutual learning increased and circumstances changed. It was a wager on the sustainability of alliances (see Blanchot 2006a). In particular, they decided to use relationship-climate surveys (Lever 6); these may be interpreted as indicator for the alliance's management dashboard, and particularly as a tool to manage cultural differences.

Conclusion

Available research does not fully validate the received wisdom that cultural differences have a negative effect on alliances' success. They may certainly contribute to the deterioration of relationship quality or to a break up, but such outcomes are not mechanical. Cultural distance may even have positive effects. At least one of many explanations proves interesting for management practitioners: part of the variation seen in the effects of cultural differences may be attributed to the manager's 'visible hand'. The absence of determinism is reassuring, but may also cause anxiety, giving a manager a responsibility that determinism could have spared him or her. An alliance manager may fear being blacklisted the moment a misunderstanding or conflict emerges in the alliance he or she steers, but that would overestimate his or her power.[24] As with any manager, the alliance manager can influence, but only rarely determine outcomes.

To affect outcomes, the alliance manager has several control levers at his or her disposal. Some allow the manager to act on cultural differences, such as the choice of partner. Others, such as awareness exercises, can help attenuate the negative effects of differences, or can reveal their virtues. The alliance manager can also use levers to bolster cooperation and make the negative consequences of cultural differences less threatening, even if they cannot be changed in any way. That illustrates our 'enlarged' conception of intercultural management, which rests on two realistic postulates. First, the undesirable effects of cultural differences may never be completely controlled. Second, the more fragile a coalition, the more cultural difference effects may contribute to its breaking up. Therefore, one of the missions of intercultural management should be to bolster cooperation. Two complementary approaches are possible. The first consists of 'ring-fencing' the cooperative venture from other sources of tension, and the second consists of increasing the cooperative venture's attractiveness. In other words, the manager can reduce the centrifugal forces and strengthen the centripetal ones, beyond the cultural differences. In some ways, disequilibrium toward the centripetal side ensures the alliance's equilibrium.

We have shown how this 'enriched' intercultural management worked in the Renault–Nissan alliance; it helps explain how 'colossal' cultural differences did not prevent this unconventional alliance from succeeding. It gained strength from its hybrid character: as in a merger or acquisition, all of the two companies' potential synergies were explored, but as in an alliance, each partner's identity was preserved and their interests balanced.

Notes

1 For more detail, see Blanchot (2007).
2 Sometimes managers speak of potential value creation.
3 Purpose in the sense of the point or subject of the alliance.
4 Organizational justice in terms of both distributive justice and procedural justice.
5 A result that is significant for one model and non-significant for another using the same sample is counted twice. This can occur when several models composed of different variables are tested within the same study.
6 This social contract acts like a psychological contract that reflects what an individual sees as the contract tying his or her company to another one, adding to or substituting for a legal contract, creating its own, specific expectations.
7 See Hofstede's work.
8 Fit in the sense of compatibility and harmony.
9 Fey and Beamish (2001) explain the difference between the two concepts.
10 Organizational fit refers here to the perceived closeness of information systems, structure, human relations and culture. 'Fit' signifies harmony or at least compatibility.

11 Other research also finds a negative relationship. For example, Cartwright and Cooper (1989) observed a negative link between apparent similarities of organizational culture and success. Lane and Lubatkin (1998) found that some forms of managerial similarity, i.e. centralization and formalization, harmed interorganizational learning. Sarkar and his colleagues (2001) found the 'level of congruence between partners' technical capacities, organizational procedures and managerial aptitudes' had a negative effect on the partners' level of achievement for their own strategic and learning objectives.

12 The 'not invented here' syndrome refers to the tendency of some groups to ignore, reject or not seek 'outside' ideas, even if it means they must reinvent the wheel.

13 In the same study, the distance between organizational culture accounted for 1 percent to 19 percent of the variance, an entirely significant effect from a statistical point of view.

14 See e.g. Harbison and Pekar (1997), Cools and Roos (2005) and Ertel et al. (2001).

15 More generally, we suggest retaining only partners who fulfill the '3Cs': Compatibility, Capacity and Commitment.

16 In following this line of thinking, we are quite close to the work of Lawrence and Lorsch (1967); they suggested that integration mechanisms should compensate for differentiations within an organization.

17 The partners may have hidden agendas, of course. But the problems will be even larger if the partners have no shared objective (Luo 2002).

18 This section is based on data from the Renault–Nissan cases 1 and 2 developed by Blanchot and Kalika (2002, 2006). They are available from the CCMP (Centrale de Cas et de Medias Pédagogiques) and the Paris Chamber of Commerce.

19 In the explanation that follows the table, we cite the relevant lever number in parentheses.

20 For a complementary analysis of intercultural problems associated with the Renault–Volvo merger, see chapter 4 in Iribarne et al. (2002).

21 The question of whether Renault–Nissan is an alliance or acquisition is treated elsewhere; see e.g. Blanchot and Kalika (2002). In fact, it is halfway between an alliance and either an acquisition or a separate company.

22 The principles noted in parentheses come from the theory of procedural justice; we find they could be related to the attitudes and behaviors promoted by the alliance's charter.

23 Cross-company teams may be abbreviated CCT, also used to abbreviate cross-cultural training (see e.g. Parkhe 1991, p. 585).

24 The gravity of the situation may also be misunderstood: as long as misunderstandings and conflict do not become commonplace they can be a source of creativity.

References

Arino, A., and J. de la Torre, 'Learning from Failure: Toward an Evolutionary Model of Collaborative Ventures', *Organization Science*, 9 (3): 306–25, 1998.

Barkema, H. G., O. Shenkar, F. Vermeulen and J. H. J. Bell, 'Working abroad, Working with Others: How Firms Learn to Operate International Joint Ventures', *Academy of Management Journal*, 40 (2): 426–42, 1997.

Barkema, H. G. and F. Vermeulen, 'What Differences in the Cultural Backgrounds of Partners are Detrimental for International Joint Ventures?' *Journal of International Business Studies*, 28 (4): 845–64, 1997.

Beamish, P. W. and A. Delios, 'Improving Joint Venture Performance through Congruent Measures of Success. Cooperatives Strategies', in P. W. Beamish and J. P. Killing (eds), *European Perspectives*, San Francisco, CA: New Lexington Press, 1997.

Blanchot, F., 'L'alliance comme levier et lieu du changement', in O. Meier (ed.), *Gestion du changement*, Collection Gestion Supérieure, Paris: Dunod, 2007.

—— 'Alliances et performances. Un essai de synthèse', Cahier de recherche CREPA-DRM, Paris., 2006a.

—— 'Qu'est-ce qu'un manager d'alliances?', Cahier de recherche CREPA-DRM, Paris, 2006b.

—— 'Le manager d'alliance(s): un bâtisseur et un pilote', in M. Barabel and O. Meier (eds.), *Manageor: les meilleures pratiques du management*, Paris: Dunod, pp. 263–77, 2006c.

Blanchot, F. and R. Guillouzo, 'La rupture des alliances stratégiques: une grille d'analyse', *Management International*, 15 (2): 95–107, 2011.

Blanchot, F. and M. Kalika, 'L'alliance Renault–Nissan: de 1999 à 2006', Cas Multimédia, CCMP, 2006.

—— 'L'alliance Renault–Nissan', Cas Multimédia, CCMP, 2002.

Blanchot, F. and P. Romelaer, *Le partage des tâches et des coûts dans le cadre d'une activité conjointe*, Research report Dauphine/CREPA, Paris, for GDF, 2002.

Bleeke, J. and D. Ernst, 'Réussir une alliance transfrontalière', *Harvard-L'Expansion*, 66–77, 1992.

Cartwright, S. and C. L. Cooper, 'The Role of Culture Compatibility in Successful Organizational Marriage', *Academy of Management Executive*, 7 (2): 57–70, 1993.

—— 'Predicting Success in Joint Venture Organisations in Information Technology', *Journal of General Management*, 15 (1): 39–52, 1989.

Cauley de la Sierra, M., *Managing Global Alliances. Key Steps for Successful Collaboration*, Wokingham and New York: Addison-Wesley, 1995.

Cerdin, J.-L. and J.-M. Peretti, 'Les déterminants de l'adaptation des cadres expatrié', *Revue Française de Gestion*, 129, 58–66, 2000.

CFO Research Services. 'The CFO'S Perspective on Alliances', CFO Publishing Corp, 2004. www.cfoenterprises.com/research.shtml (retrieved 14 March 2007).

Chevrier, S., *Le management interculturel*, Paris: Presses Universitaires de France, 2003.

—— 'Le management des projets interculturels. Entre le rêve du melting pot et le cauchemar de la tour de Babel', *Gérer et Comprendre*, 45, 1996.

Child, J. and D. Faulkner, *Strategies of Cooperation. Managing Alliances, Networks, and Joint Ventures*, Oxford: Oxford University Press, 1998.

Cools, K. and A. Roos, *The Role of Alliance in Corporate Strategy*, BCG Report, Boston: The Boston Consulting Group, 2005.

Crovitz, G., 'Crafting a JV Prenup', *Harvard Business Review*, 82 (11): 30–30, 2004.

Das, T. K. and B.-S. Teng, 'Partner Analysis and Alliance Performance', *Scandinavian Journal of Management*, 19: 279–308, 2003.

Delavallée, E., *La culture d'entreprise pour manager autrement*, Paris: Éditions d'Organisation, 2002.

Doz, Y. L., 'The Evolution of Cooperation in Strategic Alliances: Initial Conditions or Learning Processes?', *Strategic Management Journal*, 17: 55–83, 1996.

—— 'Technology Partnerships between Larger and Smaller Firms: Some Critical Issues', *International Studies of Management*, 17 (4): 31–57, 1988.

Doz, Y. and G. Hamel, *L'avantage des alliances. Logiques de création de valeur*, Translation of *The Art of Creating Value through Partnering* [1998], Paris: Dunod, 2000.

Doz, Y., J. Santos and P. Williamson, 'Diversity: the Key to Innovation Advantage', *European Business Forum*, (17): 25–27, 2004.

Emerson, V., 'An Interview with Carlos Ghosn, President of Nissan Motors, Ltd. and Industry Leader of the Year (Automotive News, 2000)', *Journal of World Business*, 36 (1): 3–10, 2001.

Ertel, D., J. Weiss and L. J. Visioni, 'Managing Alliance Relationships. Ten Key Corporate Capabilities', Boston: Vantage Partners, 2001.

Eschbach, D. M., G. E. Parker and P. A. Stoerberl, 'American Repatriate Employees' Retrospective Assessments of the Effects of Cross-Cultural Training on their Adaptation to International Assignments', *Journal of Human Resource Management*, 12 (2): 270–87, 2001.

Faulkner, D. O. and M. D. Rond, *Perspectives on Cooperative Strategy*, Oxford: Oxford University Press, 2000.

Fey, C. F. and P. W. Beamish, 'Organizational Climate Similarity and Performance: International Joint Ventures in Russia', *Organization Studies*, 22 (5): 853–82, 2001.

Folger, R. and R. Cropanzano, *Organizational Justice and Human Resource Management*, London, Sage Publications, 1998.

Fréchet, M., *Les conflits dans les partenariats d'innovation. Gestion*, Toulouse: Université de Sciences Sociales, 2002.

Gallard, P. 'Nissan: mais que viens donc faire Renault dans cette galére?', *L'Expansion*, 593, 18 March 1999. www.lexpansion.com/art/134.0.124340.0.html (retrieved 14 March 2007)

Gazier, B., *Les stratégies des ressources humaines*, Paris: La Découverte, 1993.

Ghosn, C. (2002) 'Intercultural Management', Speech on 29 May at the Maison de la Culture du Japon. www.cefj.org/fr/archives/CR/Ghosn.pdf, 9. Paris: MCJP (retrieved 14 March 2007).

Ghosn, C. and P. Riès, *Citoyen du monde*, Paris: Éditions Fasquelle, 2003.

Gulati, R., 'Does Familiarity Breed Trust? The Implications of Repeated Ties for Contractual Choice in Alliances', *Academy of Management Journal*, 38 (1): 95–112, 1995.

Gulati, R., T. Khanna and N. Nohria, 'Unilateral Commitments and the Importance of Process in Alliances', *Sloan Management Review*, Spring: 61–69, 1994.

Hamel, G., 'Competition for Competence and Inter-Partner Learning within International Strategic Alliances', *Strategic Management Journal*, vol. 12: 83–104, 1991.

Harbison, J. and P. Pekar, *Cross-Border Alliances in the Age of Collaboration*, New York: Booz-Allen & Hamilton, 1997.

Harbison, J., P. Pekar, D. Moloney and A. Viscio, *The Alliance Enterprise: Breakout Strategy for the New Millennium*, New York: Booz-Allen & Hamilton. www.boozallen.com/home/publications/ Inc., 2000 (retrieved 14 March 2007).

Harrigan, K. R., 'Strategic Alliances and Partner Asymmetries', *Management International Review* (Special Issue): 53–72, 1988.

Hennart, J.-F. and M. Zeng, 'Cross-Cultural Differences and Joint Venture Longevity', *Journal of International Business Studies*, 33 (4): 699–716, 2002.

Hu, M. Y. and H. Chen, 'An Empirical Analysis of Factors Explaining Foreign Joint Venture Performance in China', *Journal of Business Research*, 35 (2): 165–73, 1996.

Huang, Y., C. Rayner and L. Zhuang, 'Does Intercultural Competence Matter in Intercultural Business Relationship Development?', *International Journal of Logistics: Research and Applications*, 6 (4): 277–88, 2003.

Inkpen, A. C. and J. Birkenshaw, 'International Joint Ventures and Performance: An Interorganizational Perspective', *International Business Review*, 3 (3): 201–17, 1994.

Inkpen, A. C. and S. C. Currall, 'The Nature, Antecedents, and Consequences of Joint Venture Trust', *Journal of International Management*, 4 (1): 1–20, 1998.

Iribarne, P. d', A. Henry, J.-P. Segal, S. Chevrier and T. Globokar, *Cultures et mondialisation. Gérer par-delà les frontières*, Paris: Seuil, 2002.

Johnson, J. P., M. A. Korsgaard and H. J. Sapienza, 'Perceived Fairness, Decision Control, and Commitment in International Joint Venture Management Teams', *Strategic Management Journal*, 23 (12): 1141–1160, 2002.

Kang, N.-H. and K. Sakai, 'International Strategic Alliances: Their Role in Industrial Globalisation', *STI Working Paper* 2000/5, Paris: OECD, 2000.

Kogut, B., 'The Stability of Joint Ventures: Reciprocity and Competitive Rivalry', *The Journal of Industrial Economics*, 38 (2): 183–98, 1989.

—— 'Joint Ventures: Theoretical and Empirical Perspectives', *Sloan Management Review*, 9: 319–32, 1988.

Kogut, B. and U. Zander, 'Knowledge of the Firm and the Evolutionary Theory of the Multinational Corporation', *Journal of International Business Studies*, 625–45, 1993.

—— 'Knowledge of the Firm, Combinative Capabilities and the Replication of Technology', *Organization science*, 3 (3): 383–97, 1992.

Kumar, R. and P. H. Andersen, 'Inter Firm Diversity and the Management of Meaning in International Strategic Alliances', *International Business Review*, 9: 237–52, 2000.

Lane, H. W. and P. W. Beamish, 'Cross-Cultural Cooperative Behavior in Joint Ventures in LDCs', *Management International Review*, 30 (Special Issue): 87–102, 1990.

Lane, P. J. and M. Lubatkin, 'Relative Absorptive Capacity and Interorganizational Learning', *Strategic Management Journal*, 19: 461–77, 1998.

Lane, P. J., J. E. Salk and M. A. Lyles, 'Absorptive Capacity, Learning, and Performance in International Joint Ventures', *Strategic Management Journal*, 22 (12): 1139–61, 2001.

Langlois, R. N. and P. R. Robertson, *Firms, Markets and Economic Change. A Dynamic Theory of Business Institutions*, London: Routledge, 1995.

Lawrence, P. R. and J. W. Lorsch, *Organization and Environnment*, Cambridge, MA: Harvard University Press, 1967. French translation: *Adapter les structures de l'entreprise*, Paris: Éditions d'Organisation, 1967.

Le Monde, 6–7 November 2005.

Le Monde, 30 March 2004.

Li, J., K. Xin and M. Pillutla, 'Multi-Cultural Leadership Teams and Organizational Identification in International Joint Ventures', *Journal of Human Resource Management*, 13 (2): 320–37, 2002.

Lin, X. and R. Germain, 'Sustaining Satisfactory Joint Venture Relationships: the Role of Conflict Resolution Strategy', *Journal of International Business Studies*, 29 (1): 179–96, 1998.

Lu, L.-T., 'Conflict Resolution Strategy between Foreign and Local Partners in Joint Ventures in China', *Journal of the American Academy of Business*, 8 (1): 236–40, 2006.

Lucas, O. and P. Piron, 'La conception en alliance intégrée. Le cas de l'alliance européenne des missiles tactiques', *Annales de l'Ecole de Paris*, vol.V, 1998.

Luo, Y., 'How Important are Shared Perceptions of Procedural Justice in Cooperative Alliances?', *Academy of Management Journal*, 48 (4): 695–708, 2005.

—— 'Building Trust in Cross-Cultural Collaborations: Toward a Contingency Perspective', *Journal of Management*, 28 (5): 669–94, 2002.

Madhok, A., 'Cost, Value and Foreign Entry Mode: The Transaction and the Firm', *Strategic Management Journal*, 18: 39–61, 1997.

Makino, S. and P. W. Beamish, 'Performance and Survival of Joint Ventures with Non-Conventional Ownership Structures', *Journal of International Business Studies*, 29 (4): 797–818, 1998.

Meschi, P.-X., 'Longevity and Cultural Differences of International Joint Ventures: Toward Time-Based Cultural Management', *Human Relations*, 50 (2): 211–27, 1997.

Meschi, P.-X. and A. Roger, 'Cultural Context and Social Effectiveness in International Joint Ventures', *Management International Review*, 34 (3): 197–215, 1994.

Mjoen, H. and S. Tallman, 'Control and Performance in International Joint Ventures', *Organization Science*, 8 (3): 257–74, 1997.

Mohr, J. and R. Spekman, 'Characteristics of Partnership Success: Partnership Attributes, Communication Behavior, and Conflict Resolution Techniques', *Strategic Management Journal*, 15: 135–52, 1994.

Monin, P., 'Vers une théorie évolutionniste réaliste des alliances stratégiques', *Revue Française de Gestion*, (139): 49–71, 2002.

Morosini, P., S. Shane and H. Singh, 'National Culture Distance and Cross-Border Acquisition Performance', *Journal of International Business Studies*, 29 (1): 137–158, 1998.

Nelson, R. and S. Winter, *An Evolutionary Theory of Economic Change*, Cambridge, MA: Belknap Press of Harvard University, 1982.

Nonaka, I. and H. Takeuchi, *La connaissance créatrice. La dynamique de l'entreprise apprenante*, Brussels: De Boeck University Press, 1997.

Park, S. H. and M. V. Russo, 'When Competition Eclipses Cooperation: An Event History Analysis of Joint Venture Failure', *Management Science*, 42 (6): 875–90, 1996.

Park, S. H. and G. R. Ungson, 'The Effect of National Culture, Organizational Complementary and Economic Motivation on Joint Venture Dissolution', *Academy of Management Journal*, 40 (2): 279–307, 1997.

Parker, B., Y. Zeira and T. Hatem, 'International Joint Venture Managers: Factors Affecting Personal Success and Organizational Performance', *Journal of International Management*, 2 (1): 1–29, 1996.

Parkhe, A., 'Interfirm Diversity in Global Alliances', *Business Horizons*, 44 (6): 2–4, 2001.

—— 'Interfirm Diversity, Organizational Learning, and Longevity in Global Strategic Alliances', *Journal of International Business Studies*, 579–601, 1991.

Perlmutter, H. V., 'The Tortuous Evolution of the Multinational Corporation', *Columbia Journal of World Business*, 14 (1): 9–18, 1969.

Pothukuchi, V., F. Damanpour, J. Choi, C. C. Chen and S. H. Park, 'National and Organizational Culture Differences and International Joint Venture Performance', *Journal of International Business Studies*, 33: 243–65, 2002.

Puthod, D., 'Alliances de PME: un diagnostic', *Revue Française de Gestion*, no. 110 (September): 30–45, 1996.

Reuer, J. J., M. Zollo and H. Singh, 'Post-Formation Dynamics in Strategic Alliances', *Strategic Management Journal*, 23 (2): 135–51, 2002.

Ring, P. S. and A. H. Van de Ven, 'Developmental Processes of Cooperative Interorganizational Relationships', *Academy of Management Review*, 19 (1): 90–118, 1994.

Romelaer, P., *Innovation and Management Constraints*, Working Paper 77, CREPA, University of Paris IX, 2002.

Salk, J., 'Partners and Other Stangers. Cultural Boundaries and Cross-Cultural Encounters in International Joint Venture Teams', *International Studies of Management and Organization*, 26 (4): 48–72, 1997a.

—— 'Gérer une joint venture internationale', *Décisions Marketing*, (10): 7–14, 1997b.

Salk, J. E. and M. Y. Brannen, 'National Culture, Networks, and Individual Influence in a Multinational Management Team', *Academy of Management Journal*, 43 (2): 191–202, 2000.

Salk, J. E. and O. Shenkar, 'Social Identities in an International Joint Venture: An Exploratory Case Study', *Organization Science*, 12 (2): 161–78, 2001.

Sarkar, M., R. Echambadi, S. T. Cavusgil and P. S. Aulakh, 'The Influence of Complementary, Compatibility, and Relationship Capital on Alliance Performance', *Journal of the Academy of Marketing Science*, 29 (4): 358–73, 2001.

Saxton, T., 'The Effects of Partner and Relationship Characteristics on Alliance Outcomes', *Academy of Management Journal*, 40 (2): 443–61, 1997.

Shenkar, O., 'Cultural Distance Revisited: Towards a More Rigorous Conceptualization and Measurement of Cultural Differences', *Journal of International Business Studies*, 32 (3): 519–35, 2001.

Shenkar, O. and Y. Zeira, 'Role Conflict and Role Ambiguity of Chief Executive Officers in International Joint Ventures', *Journal of International Business Studies*, 23 (1): 55–75, 1992.

Sirmon, D. G. and P. J. Lane, 'A Model of Cultural Differences and International Alliance Performance', *Journal of International Business Studies*, 35: 306–19, 2004.

Slack, N., Chambers, S. and Johnston, R. 2009. *Operations Management* (6th edn) London: Financial Times/Prentice Hall.

Thevenet, M., *La culture d'entreprise*, Paris: Presses Universitaires de France, 2003.

Trompenaars, F., *L'entreprise multiculturelle*, Paris: Maxima, 1994.

Van Marrewijk, A., 'The Management of Strategic Alliances: Cultural Resistance. Comparing the Cases of Dutch Telecom Operator in the Netherlands Antilles and Indonesia', *Culture and Organization*, 10 (4): 303–14, 2004.

Yan, A. and M. Zeng, 'International Joint Venture Instability: A Critique of Previous Research, a Reconceptualization, and Directions for Future Research', *Journal of International Business Studies*, 30 (2): 397–414, 1999.

Zollo, M., J. J. Reuer and H. Singh, 'Interorganizational Routines and Performance in Strategic Alliances', *Organization Science*, 13 (6): 701–13, 2002.

Index